Better Homes and Gardens®
ANNUAL
Recipes
2008

**SKILLET PEACHES
À LA MODE**
page 181

Meredith Books
Des Moines, Iowa

TUNA NOODLE CASSEROLE
page 103

We like to think that every recipe we publish is a "keeper"—a dish you'll love today and tomorrow. That's why year after year we produce our handsome recipe annuals. They let you keep 12 months' worth of *Better Homes and Gardens*® recipes in one handy spot.

Looking through the food pages of 2008, this year especially seems to be all about keepers—the very best recipes for every occasion. Flip to February, for example, and you'll find a cache of keepsake cakes, recipes to turn to again and again for life's happiest gatherings. Head to September and you'll find a collection of great American pies. These favorites from our readers will, we hope, become favorites of yours for many years to come.

And who couldn't use a few more keepers for everyday cooking, those go-to recipes you can call on for busy weeknights. In May we brought new flavors to the crowd-pleasing casseroles with which you grew up. Chicken and rice, tuna and noodles, ham and potatoes—we've updated the classics Mom relied on to satisfy this generation of families.

In April we asked well-known pros—food stylists, cookbook authors, chefs, and professional recipe developers—to give us quick, all-new ways with chicken, one of the most weeknight-friendly choices around. The results were braised, grilled, sauteed . . . and awesome.

And talk about keepers! February's issue gathered the cream-of-the-crop prizewinners in the "Your Best Recipes" contest. These recipes partner with winners in our ever-popular Prize Tested Recipes® contest, and together the two contests bring you the very best tried-and-true recipes from readers all over the country.

At *Better Homes and Gardens*® magazine, all kinds of cooks contribute all kinds of recipes. Whether sent in from a home cook, developed by one of our magazine's food editors, or contributed by a well-known chef or cookbook author, every single recipe has one thing in common: Each has been tested and perfected by the pros in our Better Homes and Gardens® Test Kitchen. You can be sure that every recipe will work well and taste great the first time you make it and every time after. And that's what makes all our recipes "keepers."

From our kitchen to yours—enjoy!

Gayle Butler

GAYLE BUTLER, EDITOR IN CHIEF
Better Homes and Gardens® magazine

Better Homes and Gardens.
ANNUAL
Recipes
2008

Test Kitchen

Our seal assures you that every recipe in *Better Homes and Gardens® Annual Recipes 2008* has been tested in the Better Homes and Gardens® Test Kitchen. This means that each recipe is practical and reliable, and meets our high standards of taste appeal. We guarantee your satisfaction with this book for as long as you own it.

All of us at Meredith® Books are dedicated to providing you with information and ideas to enhance your home. We welcome your comments and suggestions. Write to us at: Meredith Books Editorial Department, 1716 Locust St., Des Moines, IA 50309-3023. *Bettr Homes and Gardens Annual Recipes 2008* is available by mail. To order editions from past years, call 800/627-5490.

Editor: Jan E. Miller
Assistant Art Director: Catherine Brett
Contributing Editor: Stephen J. Exel
Contributing Writer: Winifred Moranville
Editorial Assistant: Sheri Cord
Book Production Manager: Mark Weaver
Contributing Proofreaders: Susan J. Kling, Terri Fredrickson, Gretchen R. Kauffman
Contributing Indexer: Elizabeth Parson
Test Kitchen Director: Lynn Blanchard
Test Kitchen Culinary Specialists: Marilyn Cornelius, Juliana Hale, Maryellyn Krantz, Jill Moberly, Colleen Weeden, Lori Wilson
Test Kitchen Nutrition Specialists: Elizabeth Burt, R.D., L.D.; Laura Marzen, R.D., L.D.

Meredith. Books
Editorial Director: John Riha
Deputy Editor: Jennifer Darling
Managing Editor: Kathleen Armentrout
Brand Manager: Janell Pittman
Assistant Brand Manager: Jane Merten
Group Editor: Jan E. Miller
Copy Chief: Doug Kouma
Senior Copy Editors: Kevin Cox, Jennifer Speer Ramundt, Elizabeth Keest Sedrel
Assistant Copy Editor: Metta Cederdahl

Executive Director, Sales: Ken Zagor
Director, Operations: George A. Susral
Director, Production: Douglas M. Johnston
Business Director: Janice Croat

Vice President and General Manager, SIP: Jeff Myers

Better Homes and Gardens. Magazine
Editor in Chief: Gayle Goodson Butler
Deputy Editor, Food and Entertaining: Nancy Wall Hopkins
Senior Editor: Richard Swearinger
Associate Editor: Erin Simpson
Editorial Assistant: Renee Irey

Meredith Publishing Group
President: Jack Griffin
Executive Vice President: Doug Olson
Vice President, Manufacturing: Bruce Heston
Vice President, Consumer Marketing: David Ball
Consumer Product Associate Marketing Director: Steve Swanson
Consumer Product Marketing Manager: Wendy Merical
Business Manager: Darren Tollefson

Meredith Corporation
Chairman of the Board: William T. Kerr
President and Chief Executive Officer: Steve Lacy

In Memoriam: E.T. Meredith III (1933–2003)

SALMON POTATO CAKES
page 41

**BACON AND EGG
SALAD SANDWICHES**
page 175

Just what is the difference between grass-fed and grain-fed beef? Can I make that gorgeous Red Velvet Cake in a fluted tube pan? And how do I get those appetizing grill marks in perfect diamond shapes across a steak? Will someone please give me some new ideas for chicken—creative, flavor-charged ways to serve this quick-cooking meat on a busy weeknight?

No matter how seasoned you are in the kitchen, chances are you have these questions now and then. Page after page of this book offers the answers and inspiration you seek to put great meals on your table. You'll find hundreds of recipes, tips, solutions, and ideas for making your cooking better, easier, more healthful, and more creative.

LOOK FOR:

- Our Monthly Feature: Each chapter kicks off with seasonally inspired recipes. Easy-to-fix winter soups and stews that are filled with flavor. Easter dinner that's bright and beautiful, just like spring. Summer steaks that sizzle in all-new ways. When baking season officially reopens in autumn, you'll love our great American pies—favorites shared by our readers. And as the holidays approach, we have you covered with recipes and ideas brimming with great taste and good cheer.
- What's Cooking: Here we offer a closer look at a seasonal technique, cooking style, or recipe category—ways to help your cooking become better, fresher, and easier throughout the year. In April we zero in on risotto, telling you everything you need to know to about this classic dish. May brings a cache of beautiful cookies and bars. Looking for great sides to round out grilled entrées? Take a look at "What's Cooking" in June. October features convenient slow cooker showstoppers.
- Everyday Easy: Sure, cooking for gatherings and special occasions is a joy, but we also know your daily dilemma is "what's for dinner tonight?" Each month brings an answer for each weeknight—offering fresh and simple recipes meant to be filling, fast, easy on the budget, and easy on you.
- Build a Better: From cheeseburgers to guacamole, we'll show you clever see-and-do secrets for making something you love even better.
- Good and Healthy: Supernutritious salads, healthful sandwiches, lightened-up dips and snacks—here are doable ideas and up-to-date information to bring good nutrition to your daily routine.
- Prize Tested Recipes®: Starting on page 272, you'll find the entire year's winners in our monthly recipe contest, along with Honor Roll recipes—those that didn't make it into the magazine, but were too delectable to omit from this book.
- Recipe Icons: Many recipes are marked with icons that tell you if they're Fast (under 30 minutes), Kid Friendly, or Low Fat (for the nutrition guidelines, see page 335).
- Ingredient Substitution Guide: In a pickle because you're out of capers? Use chopped green olives instead! Here you'll find realistic substitutions for foods you forgot to pick up at the store.

2008 CONTENTS

**CRISPY CHOPPED
CHICKEN SALAD**

**GRAPE AND
ROSEMARY FOCACCIA**

**SKILLET VEGETABLES ON
CHEESE TOAST**

ROSEMARY APPLE PIE

**THANKSGIVING
PUMPKIN PIES**

SPINACH PEA RISOTTO

CHICKEN WITH ASPARAGUS AND PEAS
page 177

RED VELVET CAKE
page 35

JANUARY

THIS MONTH SPAN THE GLOBE WITH MEALTIME ADVENTURES. STOPS ALONG THE WAY INCLUDE A TENNESSEE NEW YEAR'S FEAST, A COLLECTION OF CLASSIC AMERICAN SOUPS AND STEWS, AN ENGLISH TEATIME TREAT, AND AN ASIAN-INSPIRED QUICK-FIX SUPPER.

BUFFALO CHICKEN SOUP page 14

By the Bowlful

SAGE CHICKEN DUMPLING SOUP page 15

SMOKED TURKEY PANINI page 21

MEDITERRANEAN VEGGIE DIP page 23

by the bowlful

COME WINTER EVERYTHING'S BETTER IN A BOWL.
FILLED WITH FLAVOR AND EASY TO FIX, THESE ONE-POT
WONDERS PUT A SPIN ON CLASSIC SOUPS AND STEWS.

BY RICHARD SWEARINGER
PHOTOS **ANDY LYONS**
PROP STYLING **KAREN JOHNSON** AND **SUE MITCHELL**
FOOD STYLING **SUSAN BROWN DRAUDT**

SAGE CHICKEN DUMPLING SOUP

Who doesn't have a soft spot for this favorite? Turned into a thick chicken soup with olives and mushrooms, it's a bit more modern than grandma's. Savory stovetop biscuits keep it classic.

page 15

TRIPLE-TOMATO SOUP

This chunky version of a time-honored comfort food satisfies in taste and convenience. It combines pantry-ready tomatoes—canned, dried, and paste—with onions, celery, and parsley. For tradition, serve it with a grilled cheese sandwich.

page 15

WHITE CHILI
page 16

Variety is the spice of these mighty-meal bowls. Think modern ingredients, good-for-you additions, new techniques, and fun serving ideas.

SOUTHWESTERN NOODLE BOWL
page 16

SKILLET BEEF STEW
page 16

GOOD GREENS SOUP
page 17

WINTER WOODS CHILI
page 17

Whether sit-down dinner or curl-up-on-the-sofa supper, steaming bowls of soup are fuss-free nourishment. Clockwise from top left: **White Chili** is a tender mix of pork and white beans with mangoes and lime. **Skillet Beef Stew** is down-home goodness—beef and vegetables over mashed potatoes. Loaded with nutrients, **Good Greens Soup** is health in a bowl. **Winter Woods Chili** with bacon and beef warms you right up—however much chili powder you add. **Southwestern Noodle Bowl** is a nest of pasta with flank steak, sweet peppers, and salsa.

BUFFALO CHICKEN SOUP

PREP 30 min. **COOK** 15 min.

INGREDIENTS

2		Tbsp. butter
½		cup coarsely chopped celery
½		cup chopped onion
2		14-oz. cans reduced-sodium chicken broth
1½		cups milk
1		tsp. bottled hot pepper sauce
1½		cups shredded mozzarella cheese (6 oz.)
1¼		cups crumbled blue cheese (5 oz.)
½		cup shredded Parmesan cheese (2 oz.)
⅓		cup all-purpose flour
1		2¼- to 2½-lb. deli-roasted chicken, skinned, boned, and coarsely shredded
		Bottled hot pepper sauce (optional)

PREPARATION

1. In 4-quart Dutch oven melt butter over medium heat. Add celery and onion; cook and stir until onion is tender. Stir in broth, milk, and the 1 teaspoon hot pepper sauce.

2. In bowl toss together mozzarella, *1 cup* of the blue cheese, Parmesan, and flour. Add gradually to soup, stirring after each addition just until melted. Stir in *three-fourths* of the shredded chicken; heat through. Top with remaining chicken, blue cheese, and hot sauce. **Makes 6 servings.**

EACH SERVING *490 cal, 28 g fat (15 g sat. fat), 144 mg chol, 1,134 mg sodium, 12 g carbo, 1 g fiber, 45 g pro. Daily Values: 15% vit. A, 3% vit. C, 47% calcium, 10% iron.*

BUFFALO CHICKEN SOUP

SAGE CHICKEN DUMPLING SOUP

Recipe pictured on page 10.

PREP 30 min. **COOK** 18 min.

INGREDIENTS

2	cups sliced fresh mushrooms
1	cup chopped onion
1	Tbsp. olive oil
¼	cup all-purpose flour
6	cups reduced-sodium chicken broth
1	2- to 2½-lb. deli-roasted chicken, skinned, boned, and cut in chunks
2	cups frozen peas
½	cup pitted kalamata olives, halved
1	Tbsp. lemon juice
1	tsp. ground sage
1	recipe Buttermilk Dumplings
	Thinly sliced green onion (optional)
1	recipe Fried Sage Leaves (optional)

PREPARATION

1. In 4-quart Dutch oven cook mushrooms and onions in hot oil over medium heat 6 to 8 minutes or until liquid has evaporated. Stir in flour until combined. Add broth all at once; cook and stir until thickened and bubbly. Stir in chicken, peas, olives, lemon juice, and sage. Return to boiling.

2. Prepare Buttermilk Dumplings dough. Drop dough, ⅓ cup at a time, onto boiling soup. Simmer, covered, 10 minutes or until toothpick inserted near centers comes out clean. To serve sprinkle with green onion and Fried Sage Leaves. **Makes 8 servings.**

Buttermilk Dumplings Combine 2 cups *all-purpose flour*, ½ teaspoon *baking powder*, ¼ teaspoon *baking soda*, and ¼ teaspoon *salt*. Stir in ¼ cup sliced *green onion* and 1 tablespoon snipped *Italian (flat-leaf) parsley*. Add 1 cup *buttermilk* and 2 tablespoons *olive oil*; stir until moistened.

Fried Sage Leaves Heat ¼ cup *olive oil* over medium heat. Add 8 *sage sprigs*, 2 at a time; cook until crisp, 30 to 60 seconds; drain.

EACH SERVING *367 cal, 12 g fat (2 g sat. fat), 56 mg chol, 776 mg sodium, 37 g carbo, 4 g fiber, 25 g pro. Daily Values: 5% vit. A, 13% vit. C, 6% calcium, 16% iron.*

LOW FAT

TRIPLE-TOMATO SOUP

PREP 20 min. **COOK** 45 min.

INGREDIENTS

1	large onion, sliced
1	Tbsp. butter or olive oil
1	28-oz. can whole tomatoes, undrained
¾	cup dried tomatoes (not oil packed)
½	of 6-oz. can no-salt-added tomato paste
1	14-oz. can reduced-sodium chicken broth or vegetable broth
½	cup sliced celery (1 stalk)
2	Tbsp. snipped Italian (flat-leaf) parsley or parsley
2	to 3 tsp. lime juice or lemon juice
	Fresh Italian (flat-leaf) parsley
	Dairy sour cream (optional)

PREPARATION

1. In 4-quart Dutch oven cook onion in hot butter, covered, over medium-low heat for 10 minutes or until tender. Add undrained whole tomatoes, *½ cup* of the dried tomatoes, tomato paste, broth, celery, and parsley. Bring to boiling; reduce heat. Simmer, covered, 20 minutes; cool. Meanwhile, in microwave-safe bowl cover remaining dried tomatoes with water. Microcook on high (100% power) 1 minute. Cool. Drain and snip into pieces; set aside.

2. In blender blend half the tomato mixture at a time until smooth. Return to saucepan; add lime juice; heat through. Top with snipped dried tomatoes, parsley, and sour cream, if desired.

Makes 4 side-dish servings.

EACH SERVING *128 cal, 4 g fat (2 g sat. fat), 8 mg chol, 786 mg sodium, 22 g carbo, 5 g fiber, 6 g pro. Daily Values: 19% vit. A, 56% vit. C, 10% calcium, 21% iron.*

TRIPLE-TOMATO SOUP

LOW FAT

SOUTHWESTERN NOODLE BOWL

START TO FINISH 30 min.

INGREDIENTS

1½ lb. beef flank steak or beef top round steak,
     cut in bite-size strips
1   tsp. ground cumin
¼   tsp. salt
⅛   tsp. ground black pepper
2   Tbsp. cooking oil
2   cloves garlic, minced
2   14-oz. cans lower-sodium beef broth
1   14-oz. can reduced-sodium chicken broth
6   oz. dried angel hair pasta
2   medium red or yellow sweet peppers, seeded and chopped
6   green onions, trimmed, cut in 1-inch bias slices
½   cup refrigerated hot-style salsa
¼   cup snipped fresh oregano
     Refrigerated salsa
     Purchased pepper seasoning blend (optional)

PREPARATION

1. Season meat with cumin, salt, and black pepper; set aside. Heat
1 tablespoon of the oil in 12-inch skillet or wok over medium-high
heat; add garlic, stir-fry 15 seconds. Add half the beef at a time; stir-
fry 2 to 3 minutes or until done; set aside. Remove and repeat with
remaining oil and beef. Return beef to skillet; add broth;
bring to boiling.
2. Add pasta, sweet peppers, and onions to skillet. Cook, uncovered,
2 to 3 minutes, until pasta is tender. Stir in the ½ cup salsa and
oregano; heat through. Ladle into bowls; twirl pasta into nests. Top
with salsa and pepper seasoning blend. **Makes 8 servings.**

EACH SERVING *260 cal, 9 g fat (2 g sat. fat), 28 mg chol, 616 mg sodium,*
21 g carbo, 2 g fiber, 24 g pro. Daily Values: 23% vit. A, 70% vit. C, 6% calcium,
14% iron.

WHITE CHILI

Recipe pictured on page 12.

PREP 25 min. **COOK** 1 hr.

INGREDIENTS

2   Tbsp. cooking oil
3   lb. pork shoulder roast, fat trimmed, cut in 1- to 1½-inch cubes
2   medium onions, peeled and chopped
4   cloves garlic, minced
3   19-oz. cans cannellini beans, rinsed and drained
2   14-oz. cans reduced-sodium chicken broth
⅓   cup lime juice
1   tsp. ground chipotle chile pepper
½   to 1 tsp. ground white pepper
¼   tsp. ground nutmeg
2   mangoes

PREPARATION

1. In 4-quart Dutch oven heat oil over medium heat. Brown *half* the pork
at a time; remove and set aside. Add onions and garlic; cook until onions
are tender. Return pork to Dutch oven; add beans, broth, lime juice, chile
pepper, white pepper, and nutmeg. Bring to boiling; reduce heat.
Simmer, covered, 1 hour or until pork is tender.
2. Peel and seed mangoes; halve. Coarsely chop 3 halves; slice
remaining half. Stir chopped mango into chili. Heat through. Top with
sliced mangoes. **Makes 8 servings.**

EACH SERVING *428 cal, 17 g fat (5 g sat. fat), 60 mg chol, 820 mg sodium,*
45 g carbo, 11 g fiber, 29 g pro. Daily Values: 8% vit. A, 34% vit. C, 13% calcium,
22% iron.

KID FRIENDLY

SKILLET BEEF STEW

PREP 25 min. **COOK** 55 min.

INGREDIENTS

2   Tbsp. cooking oil
2   lb. beef stew meat, cut in 1-inch cubes
2   tsp. dried thyme or oregano, crushed
6   medium carrots, peeled and quartered
4   stalks celery, cut in 2-inch lengths
2   medium onions, cut in ½-inch slices
6   cups lower-sodium beef broth
⅓   cup all-purpose flour
1   recipe Potato Mashers

PREPARATION

1. In 12-inch skillet brown beef in hot oil over medium-high heat
with thyme and ¼ teaspoon each *salt* and *ground black pepper*.
Remove from heat; set aside. Add carrots, celery, and onions to
skillet; cook and stir 5 minutes. Return beef to skillet. In bowl whisk
together broth and flour; add to skillet. Bring to boiling; reduce heat.
Simmer, covered, 45 minutes. Uncover; simmer 10 minutes or until
meat is tender. Serve with Potato Mashers. **Makes 8 servings.**
Potato Mashers In microwave-safe bowl, microcook 8 *Yukon gold*
potatoes (2¾ lb.), half at a time, on high (100% power) 8 minutes,
covering bowl with vented microwave-safe plastic wrap. Mash
potatoes with 1 cup *milk*, ½ teaspoon *salt*, and ½ teaspoon *ground*
black pepper.

EACH SERVING *380 cal, 10 g fat (3 g sat. fat), 64 mg chol, 739 mg sodium,*
40 g carbo, 6 g fiber, 31 g pro. Daily Values: 157% vit. A, 59% vit. C, 10% calcium,
23% iron.

SOUTHWESTERN
NOODLE BOWL

GOOD GREENS SOUP

SKILLET BEEF STEW

WINTER WOODS CHILI

GOOD GREENS SOUP

START TO FINISH 35 min.

INGREDIENTS

2	leeks, trimmed, halved, and sliced
2	stalks celery, chopped
2	cloves garlic, minced
1	Tbsp. olive oil
3	14-oz. cans reduced-sodium chicken broth
1	14.5-oz. can diced tomatoes with basil, garlic, and oregano
4	cups coarsely shredded kale
2	medium zucchini, halved and sliced
1	5-oz. pkg. baby spinach
½	cup snipped fresh Italian (flat-leaf) parsley or basil
2	Tbsp. red wine vinegar

PREPARATION

1. In 5-quart Dutch oven cook leek, celery, and garlic in oil over medium heat for 10 minutes or until beginning to brown. Stir in broth, undrained tomatoes, kale, zucchini, ¼ teaspoon each *salt* and *ground black pepper*. Bring to boiling; reduce heat. Simmer, covered, 5 minutes, stirring once. Reserve a few spinach leaves; stir in remaining spinach, parsley, and vinegar. Top with reserved spinach leaves. **Makes 8 side-dish servings.**

EACH SERVING *90 cal, 2 g fat (0 g sat. fat), 737 mg sodium, 14 g carbo, 2 g fiber, 5 g pro. Daily Values: 153% vit. A, 101% vit. C, 12% calcium, 14% iron.*

WINTER WOODS CHILI

PREP 30 min. **COOK** 2 hr.

INGREDIENTS

4	slices bacon
3	lb. beef stew meat
1	large onion, sliced ½ inch thick
4	cloves garlic, minced
2	28-oz. cans whole tomatoes
1	15.5-oz can navy beans, rinsed and drained
1	15.5-oz. can red beans, rinsed and drained
2	to 3 Tbsp. chili powder
2	Tbsp. red wine vinegar
	Shredded cheddar cheese
	Snipped fresh oregano
	Cooked bacon, crumbled

PREPARATION

1. In 4- to 6-quart Dutch oven cook bacon and beef, *half* at a time, over medium heat until beef is browned. Drain fat. Return meat to pan. Reduce heat; add onion and *half* of the garlic. Cook and stir until onion is tender.

2. Add undrained tomatoes, beans, and *1 tablespoon* of the chili powder. Bring to boiling; reduce heat. Simmer, covered, for 1 hour, stirring occasionally. Stir in remaining garlic, chili powder, and vinegar. Cook, covered, 1 hour. Add *water* to reach desired consistency. Season to taste. Top servings with cheese, oregano, and crumbled bacon. **Makes 6 servings.**

EACH SERVING *546 cal, 23 g fat (9 g sat. fat), 107 mg chol, 1,222 mg sodium, 31 g carbo, 8 g fiber, 54 g pro. Daily Values: 19% vit. A, 37% vit. C, 25% calcium, 41% iron.*

READY
IN 20
MINUTES!

Dinnertime Express

Things to do, places to go? Stay on track with quick-to-fix meals.

BY **PEG SMITH** RECIPES **MARYELLYN KRANTZ** PHOTOS **ANDY LYONS** FOOD STYLING **JILL LUST**

CHICKEN WITH CORNMEAL DUMPLINGS

START TO FINISH 20 min.

INGREDIENTS

- ½ cup all-purpose flour
- ½ tsp. ground sage
- 12 oz. skinless, boneless chicken breast halves
- 2 Tbsp. cooking oil
- 2 cups frozen mixed vegetables
- 1 14-oz. can reduced-sodium chicken broth
- ½ cup milk
- 1 11.5-oz. pkg. refrigerated corn bread twists
- ½ cup shredded Mexican cheese blend

PREPARATION

1. Preheat oven to 450°F. In resealable bag combine flour, sage, and ¼ teaspoon each *salt* and *ground black pepper.* Cut chicken in bite-size pieces. Add to bag; coat.
2. In skillet over medium-high heat stir and brown chicken in hot oil for 2 minutes. In colander run cold water over vegetables. Add vegetables along with broth and milk to chicken. Bring to boiling; stir. Divide chicken-vegetable mixture among four small baking dishes. Separate corn bread strips; place four strips over chicken-vegetable mixture in each dish. Sprinkle with cheese. Bake 9 to 10 minutes. **Makes 4 servings.**

 EACH SERVING *612 cal, 25 g fat (7 g sat. fat), 64 mg chol, 1,259 mg sodium, 60 g carbo, 3 g fiber, 34 g pro. Daily Values: 78% vit. A, 14% vit. C, 17% calcium, 20% iron.*

ANCHO GRILLED SALMON

START TO FINISH 20 min.

INGREDIENTS

- 2 medium sweet potatoes
- 1 Tbsp. sugar
- 1 tsp. salt
- 1 tsp. ground cumin
- 1 tsp. ground ancho chile pepper or chili powder
  Olive oil cooking spray
- 4 5- to 6-oz. skinless salmon fillets
- 2 Tbsp. chopped fresh cilantro or fresh cilantro sprigs

PREPARATION

1. Preheat broiler. Scrub potatoes. Halve lengthwise; cut in ¼-inch slices. Place on greased rack of unheated broiler pan. In bowl combine sugar, salt, cumin, and chile pepper. Coat potatoes with cooking spray; sprinkle both sides with half the spice mixture. Broil 4 inches from heat 10 minutes or until tender; turn once midway through cooking.
2. Meanwhile, rinse salmon; pat dry. Sprinkle with remaining spice mixture. In skillet cook fish in 1 tablespoon hot *olive oil* over medium heat 8 to 12 minutes or until fish flakes when tested with fork; turn once midway through cooking. Add cilantro. **Makes 4 servings.**

EACH SERVING *363 cal, 19 g fat (4 g sat. fat), 84 mg chol, 710 mg sodium, 17 g carbo, 2 g fiber, 29 g pro. Daily Values: 193% vit. A, 17% vit. C, 5% calcium, 6% iron.*

ANCHO GRILLED SALMON

FAST!

SPICY BEEF-NOODLE BOWL

START TO FINISH 20 min.

INGREDIENTS

1	lb. boneless beef sirloin steak, cut in thin strips
1	Tbsp. cooking oil
2	14-oz. cans reduced-sodium beef broth
⅓	cup bottled peanut sauce
1½	cups medium egg noodles (3 oz.)
2	cups broccoli florets
¼	cup bias-sliced green onion (optional)

PREPARATION

1. In Dutch oven brown beef strips in hot oil over medium-high heat. Add beef broth and peanut sauce; bring to boiling.
2. Stir in noodles; reduce heat. Simmer, uncovered, 4 minutes, stirring occasionally to separate noodles. Add broccoli; return to boiling. Reduce heat. Simmer, uncovered, for 3 to 4 minutes more or just until noodles are tender, stirring occasionally.
3. Divide beef and noodle mixture among four bowls. Sprinkle with green onions. **Makes 4 servings.**

EACH SERVING *316 cal, 12 g fat (3 g sat. fat), 60 mg chol, 762 mg sodium, 18 g carbo, 2 g fiber, 31 g pro. Daily Values: 6% vit. A, 68% vit. C, 5% calcium, 15% iron.*

GARLICKY PEPPERS AND SHRIMP

SPICY BEEF-NOODLE BOWL

FAST!

GARLICKY PEPPERS AND SHRIMP

START TO FINISH 20 min.

INGREDIENTS

1	9-oz. pkg. refrigerated spinach fettuccine
4	Tbsp. extra virgin olive oil
3	small red, green, yellow, or orange sweet peppers, seeded and cut in strips
2	medium onions, cut in thin wedges
4	cloves garlic, thinly sliced
1	lb. peeled and deveined medium shrimp
⅛	tsp. cayenne pepper

PREPARATION

1. Cook pasta according to package directions; drain and return to pan. Toss with *2 tablespoons* of the olive oil. Keep warm.
2. Meanwhile, in skillet heat the remaining 2 tablespoons olive oil over medium-high heat. Stir in peppers, onions, and garlic; stir-fry 4 to 6 minutes or until crisp-tender. Add shrimp and cayenne pepper. Cook 2 to 3 minutes more or until shrimp are opaque, stirring occasionally. Serve over pasta. **Makes 4 servings.**

EACH SERVING *477 cal, 18 g fat (3 g sat. fat), 229 mg chol, 256 mg sodium, 45 g carbo, 4 g fiber, 33 g pro. Daily Values: 46% vit. A, 140% vit. C, 13% calcium, 29% iron.*

FAST!

SMOKED TURKEY PANINI

START TO FINISH 20 min.

INGREDIENTS
- ⅓ cup broken walnuts (optional)
- 8 ½-inch slices country Italian bread
- ½ cup refrigerated classic bruschetta topper
- 2 Tbsp. mayonnaise
- 12 oz. sliced cooked peppered turkey breast
- 1 cup large spinach leaves
   Olive oil

PREPARATION

1. Preheat large skillet over medium heat. Add walnuts; cook and stir 2 minutes to toast. Remove from skillet; set aside.

2. To assemble sandwiches, spread 4 bread slices with bruschetta topper and 4 slices with mayonnaise. On bruschetta slices layer walnuts, turkey, and spinach; top with mayo slices. Lightly brush sandwiches with olive oil.

3. Place sandwiches in hot skillet; weight with additional skillet (add food cans for more weight). Grill 2 minutes; turn. Replace weight; cook 2 minutes more or until golden and hot. **Makes 4 servings.**

EACH SERVING *448 cal, 23 g fat (4 g sat. fat), 43 mg chol, 1,522 mg sodium, 35 g carbo, 2 g fiber, 26 g pro. Daily Values: 18% vit. A, 4% vit. C, 9% calcium, 13% iron.*

SMOKED TURKEY PANINI

Dips and Nibbles

With calories subtracted and flavor added, these easy-to-serve snacks are healthful choices at the party table.

MEDITERRANEAN
VEGGIE DIP

BY **RICHARD SWEARINGER**
PHOTOS **ANDY LYONS**
FOOD STYLING **JILL LUST**
RECIPES **LAURA MARZEN**

MEDITERRANEAN VEGGIE DIP

START TO FINISH 15 min.

INGREDIENTS

1	recipe Yogurt Cheese
¼	cup chopped bottled roasted red sweet peppers
¼	cup crumbled reduced-fat feta cheese
2	Tbsp. thinly sliced green onion
2	Tbsp. chopped pitted kalamata or black olives
2	Tbsp. snipped fresh Italian (flat-leaf) parsley
2	tsp. snipped fresh oregano or ½ tsp. dried oregano, crushed
	Dippers: toasted pita bread, whole grain crackers, carrot sticks, broccoli florets, cucumber spears, or sweet pepper strips

PREPARATION

1. In a small bowl combine Yogurt Cheese, sweet peppers, feta cheese, green onion, olives, parsley, and oregano. Cover; chill up to 24 hours. Stir before serving. Serve with dippers.
Makes 12 (2-tablespoon) servings.

Yogurt Cheese Suspend a sieve or colander over a bowl. Line sieve with three layers of 100-percent-cotton-cheesecloth or paper coffee filter. Spoon in one 16-ounce carton *plain low-fat yogurt*. Refrigerate, covered with plastic wrap, at least 24 hours. Remove; drain and discard liquid. Refrigerate Yogurt Cheese, covered, up to 1 week. **Makes about 1 cup.**

EACH SERVING (2 TBSP. DIP) *33 cal, 1 g fat (1 g sat. fat), 3 mg chol, 82 mg sodium, 3 g carbo, 0 g fiber, 3 g pro. Daily Values: 2% vit. A, 17% vit. C, 8% calcium, 1% iron.*

FRUIT AND NUT CHOCOLATE STICKS

START TO FINISH 15 min.

INGREDIENTS

1	3.5-oz. pkg. individually wrapped 60-calorie rich dark chocolate sticks (9 sticks)
4½	tsp. creamy peanut butter
3	Tbsp. snipped dried cranberries or golden raisins
3	Tbsp. chopped nuts, such as peanuts, toasted pecans, macadamia nuts, or toasted hazelnuts

PREPARATION

1. Holding each chocolate stick with a paper towel, spread about ½ teaspoon peanut butter on half or more of the stick. Roll coated stick in dried fruit and nuts. **Makes 9 servings.**

EACH SERVING *101 cal, 6 g fat (2 g sat. fat), 0 mg chol, 37 mg sodium, 10 g carbo, 0 g fiber, 2 g pro. Daily Values: 1% iron.*

FRUIT AND NUT CHOCOLATE STICKS

Dishing Up Good Luck

RECIPES BY **NANCY HOPKINS**
PHOTOS **ANDY LYONS**
FOOD STYLING **JILL LUST**

Food Editor Nancy Wall Hopkins starts every New Year with a delicious bang—and this year she shares her special menu with you. This simple meal is a tribute to her Tennessee past. "For tradition's sake, the meal has to include black-eyed peas, greens, and cabbage. It brings luck, wealth, and health if you eat some of each. Prep these recipes in just over an hour and let them simmer while you watch the games."

LOW FAT

BRAISED GREENS

"For a head start, blanch and refrigerate the greens up to 24 hours before serving," Nancy says.

START TO FINISH 45 min.

INGREDIENTS

5	lb. assorted greens: collard, kale, mustard, beet, and turnip
2	Tbsp. olive oil
1	cup finely chopped fully cooked country ham or ham
6	cloves minced garlic
1	medium fresh jalapeño pepper, seeded and finely chopped (See Note, page 101)
1/3	cup chicken broth
1	Tbsp. packed brown sugar
1/4	tsp. coarsely ground black pepper
	Balsamic or cider vinegar (optional)

PREPARATION

1. Remove stems and thick ribs from greens. In large saucepan of *boiling water* immerse greens, one-fourth at a time, for 30 seconds. Remove greens with tongs to colander. Rinse under cold running water; cool. Coarsely chop.

2. In 4-quart Dutch oven heat oil over medium-high heat. Add ham, garlic, and jalapeño; cook and stir 1 minute. Add broth and brown sugar; stir to dissolve sugar. Add greens and black pepper; cook and stir until heated through. Serve immediately; sprinkle with vinegar. **Makes 10 (3/4-cup) servings.**

EACH SERVING *86 cal, 4 g fat (1 g sat. fat), 6 mg chol, 290 mg sodium, 9 g carbo, 5 g fiber, 6 g pro. Daily Values: 164% vit. A, 44% vit. C, 18% calcium, 2% iron.*

LOW FAT

GOOD-FOR-YOU CABBAGE

Nancy says, "I make my cabbage with a spin on redeye gravy, made with coffee and molasses."

PREP 20 min.   **COOK** 30 min.

INGREDIENTS

2	small heads cabbage (1 1/2 to 2 lb. each)
4	slices thick-cut smoked bacon
1 1/2	tsp. whole mustard seeds
1	tsp. caraway seeds
1/2	tsp. cumin seeds
1/2	tsp. fennel seeds
1	tsp. sea salt or 3/4 tsp. salt
1/2	tsp. cracked black pepper
1	cup brewed strong coffee
3	Tbsp. molasses

PREPARATION

1. Rinse cabbage; remove outer leaves. Cut in eight wedges; set aside.

2. In large skillet with tight-fitting lid cook bacon over medium heat. Reserving 3 tablespoons drippings in skillet, transfer bacon to paper towels; drain, crumble, and set aside. To drippings add mustard, caraway, cumin, and fennel seeds; salt; and pepper. Cook and stir 1 minute. Add half the cabbage wedges at a time; cook, searing edges, 3 to 5 minutes. Place all cabbage wedges in skillet, overlapping slightly.

3. For gravy, stir together coffee and molasses; pour over cabbage. (Gravy does not blend.) Heat to boiling. Reduce heat; simmer, covered, 30 to 35 minutes. Transfer cabbage to platter; sprinkle with bacon. Pass gravy. **Makes 8 side-dish servings.**

EACH SERVING *78 cal, 5 g fat (1 g sat. fat), 6 mg chol, 196 mg sodium, 8 g carbo, 2 g fiber, 3 g pro. Daily Values: 2% vit. A, 52% vit. C, 5% calcium, 4% iron.*

BRAISED GREENS

GOOD-FOR-YOU CABBAGE

CRUSTY CORN BREAD

Nancy says, "This corn bread mixes regular cornmeal and stone-ground cornmeal—it's uniquely tender and firm at the same time."

PREP 20 min. **BAKE** 25 min. **OVEN** 425°F

INGREDIENTS

4	Tbsp. butter
1	cup yellow cornmeal
½	cup stone-ground cornmeal
2	tsp. baking powder
1	tsp. salt
½	tsp. cracked black pepper
1	8-oz. carton dairy sour cream
¾	cup buttermilk or sour milk (see Note, page 35)
2	eggs, beaten
1	cup finely shredded cheddar cheese

PREPARATION

1. Preheat oven to 425°F. Place butter in 2-quart square baking dish; melt in hot oven 5 to 6 minutes, rotating and tilting dish to coat bottom and sides; set aside.
2. In large bowl combine both cornmeals, baking powder, salt, and pepper. In medium bowl stir sour cream and buttermilk into beaten eggs. Pour sour cream mixture into cornmeal mixture. Stir cornmeal batter until well combined and glossy. Pour excess melted butter from baking dish into batter; stir to blend. Stir in cheddar cheese.
3. Pour cornmeal mixture into prepared pan. Bake 25 to 28 minutes or until corn bread is golden and begins to pull away from dish. Serve warm. **Makes 8 servings.**

EACH SERVING *281 cal, 19 g fat (11 g sat. fat), 97 mg chol, 529 mg sodium, 20 g carbo, 2 g fiber, 9 g pro. Daily Values: 13% vit. A, 2% vit. C, 19% calcium, 7% iron.*

CRUSTY CORN BREAD

LOW FAT

BLACK-EYED PEAS

"I love to stir the black-eyed pea pot with different ingredients. This year, I added a bit of heat with crushed red pepper," says Nancy.

PREP 20 min. **STAND** 1 hr. **COOK** 1 hr. 15 min.

INGREDIENTS

2	16-oz. pkg. dried black-eyed peas
12	cups water
6	cups chicken broth
6	cups water
4	cooked smoked pork hocks (about 2 lb. total)
3	stalks celery, sliced (1½ cups)
1	large onion, chopped (1 cup)
1	large green sweet pepper, seeded and chopped (1 cup)
5	cloves fresh garlic, halved
2	Tbsp. dried oregano, crushed
1	tsp. crushed red pepper
½	tsp. sea salt or salt
5	cups cooked white or brown rice
3	Tbsp. snipped fresh oregano leaves
	Bottled hot pepper sauce

PREPARATION

1. Rinse peas well; remove blemished peas. In 8- to 10-quart stockpot combine peas and 12 cups water. Bring to boiling; reduce heat. Simmer, uncovered, 2 minutes. Remove from heat. Cover; let stand 1 hour. Drain and rinse beans.
2. Return peas to stockpot; add broth and 6 cups water. Bring to boiling; reduce heat. Simmer, covered, 45 minutes.
3. Meanwhile, in large skillet brown pork on all sides 4 to 5 minutes to release juices. Add celery, onion, sweet pepper, garlic, oregano, red pepper, and salt. Cook and stir 5 to 7 minutes or just until vegetables are tender.
4. Using tongs, carefully place pork hocks beneath simmering peas; add celery mixture to peas. Cook, covered, 30 minutes or until peas are tender, stirring occasionally. Remove hocks to cutting board; cool slightly. Cut meat from bones; discard bones. Chop meat and return to pea mixture. Stir together rice and fresh oregano. Serve pea mixture over rice mixture. Pass hot pepper sauce. **Makes 10 (1¾-cup) servings.**

EACH SERVING *489 cal, 6 g fat (2 g sat. fat), 21 mg chol, 1,031 mg sodium, 80 g carbo, 11 g fiber, 30 g pro. Daily Values: 5% vit. A, 23% vit. C, 12% calcium, 43% iron.*

BLACK-EYED PEAS

Sweet Treat

CELEBRATE *with*
Pam Anderson

While visiting my daughter in England, I came to appreciate teatime. Now, working, shopping, or traveling, I make time for tea and a sweet.

APRICOT-PISTACHIO OAT BARS

PREP 20 min. **BAKE** 30 min.
OVEN 325°F

INGREDIENTS

	Nonstick cooking spray
½	cup all-purpose flour
½	cup regular or quick-cooking rolled oats
⅓	cup packed brown sugar
¼	cup butter, melted
¾	cup sweetened condensed milk
1	pinch saffron threads or ½ tsp. ground cardamom (optional)
1	cup flaked coconut
1	cup shelled dry-roasted pistachio nuts
1	cup chopped dates
1	cup dried apricots, snipped

PREPARATION

1. Preheat oven to 325°F. Line an 8×8×2-inch baking pan with foil, extending foil over pan edges. Lightly coat foil with nonstick cooking spray; set aside.
2. In medium bowl combine flour, oats, and brown sugar. Stir in butter until mixture clings together. Press ¾ cup oats mixture into bottom of pan.
3. For filling, in small saucepan over low heat bring condensed milk and, if desired, saffron or cardamom to boiling. In bowl combine coconut, nuts, dates, and apricots; add condensed milk mixture. Stir to combine. Pour coconut mixture over oats layer, using a spatula to spread evenly. Sprinkle remaining oats mixture over filling.
4. Bake 30 minutes or until lightly golden. Cool on rack 5 minutes. Lift from pan by foil edges; cool completely. Cut in rectangles. **Makes 16 bars.**

EACH BAR *247 cal, 10 g fat (5 g sat. fat), 13 mg chol, 63 mg sodium, 37 g carbo, 3 g fiber, 4 g pro. Daily Values: 22% vit. A, 2% vit. C, 6% calcium, 7% iron.*

Cheesecake

America's favorite dessert takes a bow with toppers that steal the show.

BY **PEG SMITH**
PHOTO **ANDY LYONS**
PRODUCED BY **JILL LUST**

BHG BASICS

Slice cheesecake with a long thin-blade knife. Before each cut, dip the knife in a container of hot water, then dry it on a towel.

1. THE BERRIES Blackberries, raspberries, honey, sage leaves

2. CARAMEL APPLE Crisp apple slices, warm caramel

3. ZESTY BLUES Lemon curd, blueberries, lemon zest

4. SWEET GINGER Port-poached pears, candied ginger

5. PEPPERMINT TWIST White chocolate sauce, crushed peppermint candies, fresh mint

6. TART & SWEET Orange marmalade, mandarin orange segments, cranberry relish

7. NIGHTCAP Irish cream, gingersnaps, hazelnuts

8. SUGAR PLUM DELIGHT Sliced sugared plums

9. SUNDAE Hot fudge, mixed nuts

10. TROPICAL Dried apricots, toffee, toasted coconut

FEBRUARY

IN FEBRUARY THERE'S A WHOLE LOTTA LOVE—TWELVE SUMPTUOUS CAKES TO SAY "I LOVE YOU" ALL THROUGH THE YEAR, A ROMANTIC CHOCOLATE FONDUE, AND 20-MINUTE RECIPES THAT ENCOURAGE EATING IN. AND WE LOVE *YOU* TOO! THIS MONTH FEATURES THE WINNERS OF THE *YOUR BEST RECIPES* CONTEST.

Piece of Cake

DATE-AND-SPICE CAKE
page 37

PINEAPPLE CHICKEN
page 44

NEW WORLD CHILI
page 47

piece of cake

The ideal cake is beautiful and a pleasure to make.

Here are 12 keepsake cakes that taste as good as

they look—you'll bake them again and again.

BY **MIKE BUTLER**
PHOTOS **CON POULOS**
PRODUCED BY **NANCY WALL HOPKINS**
FOOD STYLING **SUSAN SUGARMAN**
PROP STYLIST **PAMELA DUNCAN SILVER**
RECIPES **MARYELLYN KRANTZ**

Chocolate-Sour Cream Cake with Fudgy Frosting

Opposite: Sturdy, dense, and loaded with chocolate, this is the cake you dream about with a glass of milk.

page 35

Buttermilk White Cake with Coconut

This page: This delicate, supertender cake will remind you of a gentle snowfall. It's especially beautiful for christenings and weddings.

page 35

Red Velvet Cake

A little cocoa and red food coloring turn the classic white cake into a red-hot dessert enveloped in buttercream.

page 35

Buttery Yellow Citrus Cake

Tart lemon, lime, and orange tango with pure sweetness. It's light and elegant for any memory-making occasion.

page 37

Date-and-Spice Cake

Aromatic cinnamon, allspice, nutmeg, and cloves are sensory delights when you're yearning for cool-season comfort foods.

page 37

Chocolate-Espresso Chiffon Cake

For a coffeehouse moment, dollop slices of this airy treat with espresso cream.

page 37

Caramel-Frosted Hummingbird Cake

Sweet potatoes, bananas, and pineapple provide moistness and "just one more slice" flavor.

page 38

Pecan-Laced German Chocolate Cake

For special occasions, this dessert features many favorites—pecans, coconut, and a hint of coffee.

page 38

CHOCOLATE-SOUR CREAM CAKE

With fudgy frosting holding this hefty cake together, it's ideal for potlucks and tailgates. Recipe pictured on page 32.

PREP 45 min. **BAKE** 25 min. **OVEN** 350°F

INGREDIENTS
2   eggs
1½   cups all-purpose flour
⅓   cup unsweetened cocoa powder
1   tsp. baking powder
½   tsp. baking soda
½   tsp. salt
½   cup shortening
1¼   cups sugar
1   tsp. vanilla
3   oz. bittersweet chocolate, melted and cooled
1   8-oz. carton dairy sour cream
1   cup milk
1   recipe Fudgy Frosting

PREPARATION
1. Let eggs stand at room temperature 30 minutes. Preheat oven to 350°F. Grease and flour two 9-inch round cake pans; set aside.
2. In small bowl combine flour, cocoa powder, baking powder, baking soda, and salt. In large bowl beat shortening and sugar on medium speed until combined. Beat in eggs and vanilla until combined. Beat in melted chocolate and sour cream. Alternately add flour mixture and milk; beat on low after each addition just until combined. Spread batter in prepared pans.
3. Bake 25 minutes or until tops spring back when lightly touched. Cool on wire racks 10 minutes. Remove from pans; cool.
4. Prepare Fudgy Frosting. Place one layer, flat side, down on plate. Spread top with 1 cup frosting. Stack second layer, flat side down. Spread with remaining frosting.
Makes 16 servings.
Fudgy Frosting In large pan over low heat melt and stir one 12-oz. pkg. *semisweet chocolate pieces* and ½ cup *butter*. Cool 10 minutes. Stir in 8-oz. carton *sour cream*. Stir in 4½ cups (1 lb.) sifted *powdered sugar*; stir until smooth.

EACH SERVING *555 cal, 27 g fat (14 g sat. fat), 56 mg chol, 201 mg sodium, 77 g carbo, 2 g fiber, 4 g pro. Daily Values: 8% vit. A, 9% calcium, 11% iron.*

KID FRIENDLY

BUTTERMILK WHITE CAKE WITH COCONUT

"This is simply the best cake," says food editor Nancy Hopkins, of this moist, tender cake enveloped in fluffy frosting and coconut. Recipe pictured on page 33.

PREP 1 hr. 15 min. **BAKE** 25 min.
COOL 10 min. **OVEN** 350°F

INGREDIENTS
4   egg whites
2   cups all-purpose flour
1½   cups sugar
2   tsp. baking powder
½   tsp. salt
¼   tsp. baking soda
1   cup buttermilk or sour milk*
½   cup shortening
2   tsp. vanilla
1   recipe Buttercream Frosting
2   cups coconut chips or flaked coconut

PREPARATION
1. Let egg whites stand at room temperature 30 minutes. Preheat oven to 350°F. Grease and flour two 9-inch round baking pans; set aside.
2. In large mixing bowl combine flour, sugar, baking powder, salt, and baking soda. Add buttermilk, shortening, and vanilla; beat on low until combined. Beat on medium 2 minutes more, scraping bowl. Add egg whites; beat 2 minutes more. (Batter will appear curdled.)
3. Spread in pans. Bake 25 to 30 minutes or until tops spring back when lightly touched and wooden pick inserted near centers comes out clean. Cool on wire rack for 10 minutes. Remove from pans; cool completely.
4. Prepare Buttercream Frosting. Place one layer, flat side down, on plate; spread top with some of the frosting. Stack second layer, flat side down; frost top and sides. Sprinkle coconut. Serve immediately or cover and refrigerate. **Makes 16 servings.**
Buttercream Frosting In 4-quart mixing bowl beat ¾ cup softened *butter* on medium until smooth. Gradually beat in 3 cups *powdered sugar* to combine. Beat in ¼ cup *buttermilk* or milk and 2 teaspoons *vanilla*. Gradually beat in enough additional *powdered sugar* (3¼ to 3¾ cups) to make spreading consistency.
***Sour milk** Pour 1 tablespoon lemon juice or vinegar in 1-cup glass measure; add milk to equal 1 cup. Let stand 5 minutes.

EACH SERVING *529 cal, 20 g fat (12 g sat. fat), 24 mg chol, 258 mg sodium, 85 g carbo, 1 g fiber, 3 g pro. Daily Values: 5% vit. A, 4% calcium, 4% iron.*

KID FRIENDLY

RED VELVET CAKE

For July 4th, this cake is a true-blue hit!

PREP 1 hr. 15 min. **BAKE** 25 min.
COOL 10 min. **OVEN** 350°F

INGREDIENTS
3   eggs
¾   cup butter
3   cups all-purpose flour
2   tsp. unsweetened cocoa powder
2¼   cups sugar
1½   tsp. vanilla
1   1-oz. bottle red food coloring (2 Tbsp.)
1½   cups buttermilk
1½   tsp. baking soda
1½   tsp. vinegar
1   recipe Buttercream Frosting

PREPARATION
1. Let eggs and butter stand 30 minutes. Preheat oven to 350°F. Grease and flour three 8×1½-inch round baking pans; set aside.
2. In bowl combine flour, cocoa powder, and ¾ teaspoon *salt*; set aside. In mixing bowl beat butter on medium-high 30 seconds. Add sugar and vanilla; beat until combined. Add eggs 1 at a time; beat on medium after each addition. Beat in food coloring on low.
3. Alternately add flour mixture and buttermilk to egg mixture; beat on medium-low after each just until combined. Stir together baking soda and vinegar. Add to batter; beat just until combined.
4. Spread in prepared pans. Bake 25 to 30 minutes or until pick inserted near centers comes out clean (cakes may appear marbled). Cool in pans on wire racks 10 minutes. Remove from pans; cool.
5. Prepare Buttercream Frosting. Place one layer, flat side up, on plate. Spread top with ¾ cup frosting. Stack layer, flat side up; spread top with ¾ cup frosting. Stack final layer, flat side down; spread remaining frosting on top and sides. **Makes 16 servings.**
Buttercream Frosting In saucepan whisk together 1½ cups *whole milk*, ⅓ cup *flour*, and dash *salt*. Cook and stir over medium heat until thickened and bubbly. Reduce heat; cook and stir 2 minutes more. Transfer to bowl; cover surface with plastic wrap. Refrigerate until cooled (do not stir). In bowl beat 1½ cups softened *butter*, 1½ cups *sugar*, and 2 teaspoons *vanilla* on medium 5 minutes until light and fluffy and sugar is almost dissolved. Add milk mixture, ¼ cup at a time; beat on low after each until smooth.

EACH SERVING *546 cal, 28 g fat (17 g sat. fat), 112 mg chol, 467 mg sodium, 69 g carbo, 0 g fiber, 4 g pro. Daily Values: 17% vit. A, 7% calcium, 8% iron.*

Hot Milk Sponge Cake with Tropical Topper

Beloved sponge cake gets sassy with toppings of citrusy syrup and colorful tropical fruit.

page 38

Poppy Seed Cake with Lemon Glaze

Wait, if you can, for the bold lemon glaze to soak into the poppy seed-flecked interior. Bake this one for Mother's Day or Sunday brunch.

page 39

Ginger-Carrot Cake

Freshly grated ginger updates this version of a truly American cake—delicious in any season.

page 39

Banana-Split Cake

Strawberry, banana, and chocolate flavors swirl throughout this sublime sundae of a cake.

page 39

BUTTERY YELLOW CITRUS CAKE

KID FRIENDLY

Use the extra egg whites for an egg-white omelet. Recipe pictured on page 34.

PREP 1 hr. 15 min. **BAKE** 20 min. **COOL** 10 min. **OVEN** 375°F

INGREDIENTS

3/4 cup butter
6 egg yolks or 3 whole eggs
2 2/3 cups all-purpose flour
2 tsp. baking powder
1/2 tsp. salt
1/4 tsp. baking soda
1 2/3 cups sugar
1 cup milk
2 tsp. finely shredded lemon or lime peel
1 tsp. finely shredded orange peel
2 Tbsp. lemon or lime juice
2 Tbsp. orange juice
1 recipe Lemony Whipped Cream Frosting

PREPARATION

1. Let butter and eggs stand at room temperature 30 minutes. Preheat oven to 375°F. Grease and lightly flour two 9×2-inch round baking pans; set aside.
2. In medium bowl combine flour, baking powder, salt, and baking soda; set aside. In large bowl beat butter on medium speed 30 seconds. Gradually beat in sugar until combined; beat 2 minutes more. Add yolks 1 at a time; beat well after each. Add flour mixture and milk alternately; beat on low after each just until combined. Stir in peels and juices. Spread batter in prepared pans.
3. Bake 20 to 25 minutes or until pick inserted near centers comes out clean. Cool in pans on racks 10 minutes. Remove from pans; cool.
4. Prepare Lemony Whipped Cream Frosting. Place one layer, flat side down, on plate; spread top with frosting. Stack second layer, flat side down; spread remaining frosting. Serve immediately or cover and refrigerate.
Makes 12 servings.
Lemony Whipped Cream Frosting In large chilled bowl beat 2 cups *whipping cream*, 2 tablespoons *powdered sugar*, and 1 tablespoon *instant vanilla pudding* on medium-high until stiff peaks form. Fold in 1 tablespoon *shredded lemon peel*. If made ahead, chill up to 24 hours; stir before spreading.

EACH SERVING *499 cal, 29 g fat (18 g sat. fat), 192 mg chol, 303 mg sodium, 55 g carbo, 1 g fiber, 4 g pro. Daily Values: 22% vit. A, 7% vit. C, 13% calcium, 9% iron.*

DATE-AND-SPICE CAKE

Flavorful spices, boosted by molasses, result in this delightful confection. Recipe pictured on page 34.

PREP 45 min. **STAND** 15 min. **BAKE** 25 min. **COOL** 10 min. **OVEN** 350°F

INGREDIENTS

3 eggs
2/3 cup butter
1 8-oz. pkg. chopped pitted dates
2 1/2 cups all-purpose flour
1 1/2 tsp. baking powder
3/4 tsp. baking soda
1/2 tsp. *each* ground cinnamon, nutmeg, allspice, and cloves
1/2 cup granulated sugar
1/2 cup packed brown sugar
1 tsp. vanilla
1 1/4 cups half-and-half or light cream
1/4 cup molasses
1 recipe Sour Cream Frosting
Vanilla ice cream (optional)
Ground cinnamon or ground nutmeg (optional)

PREPARATION

1. Let eggs and butter stand at room temperature 30 minutes. In small bowl combine dates and *boiling water* to cover. Let stand 15 minutes; drain and set aside.
2. Preheat oven to 350°F. Grease and flour two 9-inch round cake pans. In bowl combine flour, baking powder, baking soda, and spices; set aside.
3. In 4-quart bowl beat butter on medium to high speed 30 seconds. Beat in sugars and vanilla until combined. Add eggs, 1 at a time, beating 1 minute after each. In bowl stir together half-and-half and molasses. Alternately add flour mixture and molasses mixture to egg mixture; beat on low after each until combined (may appear curdled). Stir in dates. Spread batter in prepared pans.
4. Bake 25 to 30 minutes or until pick inserted near centers comes out clean. Cool in pans on rack 10 minutes. Remove from pans; cool.
5. Prepare Sour Cream Frosting. Place one layer, flat side up, on plate; spread 2/3 cup frosting. Stack second layer, flat side up; spread remaining frosting. Cover and refrigerate. Serve with ice cream lightly dusted with cinnamon or nutmeg.
Makes 16 servings.
Sour Cream Frosting Beat together one 8-ounce carton dairy *sour cream*, 1 cup *whipping cream*, 3/4 cup *powdered sugar*, and 1/4 teaspoon *almond extract* on medium until thick and nearly holds stiff peaks.

EACH SERVING *517 cal, 26 g fat (16 g sat. fat), 125 mg chol, 250 mg sodium, 67 g carbo, 2 g fiber, 4 g pro. Daily Values: 18% vit. A, 1% vit. C, 15% calcium, 13% iron.*

CHOCOLATE-ESPRESSO CHIFFON CAKE

This cake is lighter and airier than many thanks to beaten egg whites. Recipe pictured on page 34.

PREP 65 min. **BAKE** 1 hr. **OVEN** 325°F

INGREDIENTS

8 eggs
4 tsp. espresso powder or instant coffee crystals
3/4 cup water
2 cups all-purpose flour
1 1/2 cups sugar
1 Tbsp. baking powder
1 tsp. salt
1/2 cup cooking oil
1 tsp. vanilla
3 oz. bittersweet chocolate, grated
1/2 tsp. cream of tartar
1 recipe Espresso Whipped Cream

PREPARATION

1. Separate eggs, discarding 3 of the yolks or saving for another use. Let eggs stand at room temperature 30 minutes. Preheat oven to 325°F. Dissolve espresso in water; set aside.
2. In large bowl stir together flour, sugar, baking powder, and salt; make well in center. Add oil, the 5 egg yolks, dissolved espresso, and vanilla. Beat on low until moistened; beat on medium-high 4 to 5 minutes or until satin smooth. Stir in grated chocolate.
3. Wash and dry beaters. In 4-quart bowl beat egg whites and cream of tartar on medium-high until stiff peaks form (tips stand straight). Pour chocolate batter in thin stream over surface of whites; fold to blend. Spoon in ungreased 10-inch tube pan.
4. Bake 60 to 70 minutes or until top springs back when lightly touched near center. Invert pan to cool. Carefully loosen sides; remove from pan. Serve with Espresso Whipped Cream. **Makes 14 servings.**
Espresso Whipped Cream In chilled bowl combine 1 cup *whipping cream*, 1 tablespoon *sugar*, 1/2 to 1 teaspoon *espresso powder* or instant coffee crystals, and 1/2 teaspoon *vanilla*. Beat until soft peaks form.

EACH SERVING *354 cal, 19 g fat (7 g sat. fat), 99 mg chol, 286 mg sodium, 42 g carbo, 1 g fiber, 4 g pro. Daily Values: 7% vit. A, 10% calcium, 9% iron.*

CARAMEL-FROSTED HUMMINGBIRD CAKE

The frosting hardens to seal in moist goodness. Recipe pictured on page 34.

PREP 65 min. **BAKE** 30 min. **COOL** 2 hr. **OVEN** 350°F

INGREDIENTS

3	eggs, lightly beaten
3	cups all-purpose flour
2	cups sugar
1	Tbsp. baking powder
1	tsp. salt
¼	tsp. ground cloves
2	cups mashed bananas (5 medium)
1	cup cooking oil
1½	tsp. vanilla
2	cups peeled, shredded uncooked sweet potato (about ½ lb.)
1	8-oz. can crushed pineapple (juice pack), drained
1	recipe Caramel Butter Frosting

PREPARATION

1. Let eggs stand at room temperature 30 minutes. Preheat oven to 350°F. Grease three 9-inch round cake pans. Line bottoms with waxed or parchment paper. Grease and flour paper; set aside.

2. In bowl combine flour, sugar, baking powder, salt, and cloves. Stir in bananas, oil, eggs, and vanilla until moist and thick. Stir in sweet potato and pineapple. Spread evenly in prepared pans.

3. Bake 30 minutes or until pick inserted near centers comes out clean. Cool in pans on wire racks 10 minutes. Remove from pans. Peel off paper. Cool completely.

4. Prepare Caramel Butter Frosting. Place one layer, flat side up, on plate. Spread top only with 1¼ cups frosting. Stack and frost remaining layers. **Makes 16 servings.**

Caramel Butter Frosting In large saucepan melt 1 cup *butter*; add 2 cups packed *brown sugar*. Bring to boiling over medium heat; stir constantly. Cook and stir 1 minute; cool 5 minutes. Whisk in ½ cup *milk* until smooth. Whisk in 6 cups *powdered sugar* until smooth. Use at once; frosting stiffens as it cools.

EACH SERVING *741 cal, 27 g fat (9 g sat. fat), 71 mg chol, 310 mg sodium, 125 g carbo, 2 g fiber, 3 g pro. Values: 56% vit. A, 6% vit. C, 7% calcium, 11% iron.*

PECAN-LACED GERMAN CHOCOLATE CAKE

Chocolate is the star, but coffee is a key ingredient—it deepens the flavor of chocolate. Recipe pictured on page 34.

PREP 40 min. **BAKE** 25 min. **COOL** 10 min. **OVEN** 350°F

INGREDIENTS

4	eggs
¾	cup butter
1¾	cups all-purpose flour
¾	cup pecans, toasted and ground
1	tsp. baking soda
¼	tsp. baking powder
2	cups sugar
1	4-oz. pkg. sweet baking chocolate, chopped, melted, and cooled
1	cup buttermilk
½	cup strong coffee or water
1	recipe Coconut-Pecan Frosting

PREPARATION

1. Separate eggs. Let eggs and butter stand at room temperature 30 minutes. Preheat oven to 350°F. Grease bottoms of three 9-inch round cake pans. Line with waxed or parchment paper; grease and flour bottoms and sides. Set aside.

2. In large mixing bowl beat egg whites until stiff peaks form; set aside. In medium bowl stir together flour, pecans, baking soda, baking powder, and ¼ teaspoon *salt*. In 4-quart bowl beat butter on medium-high 30 seconds. Gradually add sugar; beat until light and fluffy. Add egg yolks, 1 at a time, beating after each. Beat in chocolate on low.

3. In bowl combine buttermilk and coffee. Alternately add with flour mixture to butter mixture; beat well after each. With spatula fold in egg whites. Spread batter in pans.

4. Bake 25 minutes or until pick inserted near centers comes out clean. Cool in pans 10 minutes. Remove; peel off paper. Cool on wire racks.

5. Prepare Coconut-Pecan Frosting. Spread 1 cup on rounded tops of two layers. Add third layer, flat side down; spread with remaining frosting. **Makes 16 servings.**

Coconut-Pecan Frosting In saucepan slightly beat 2 *eggs*. Stir in 1⅓ cups *half-and-half*, 1⅓ cups *sugar*, and ½ cup *butter*. Cook and stir over medium heat 10 minutes, until slightly thickened and bubbly. Remove from heat; stir in 7-ounce pkg. (2⅔ cups) *coconut* and 1 cup chopped toasted *pecans*. Cover and cool.

EACH SERVING *571 cal, 33 g fat (17 g sat. fat), 125 mg chol, 303 mg sodium, 65 g carbo, 3 g fiber, 6 g pro. Daily Values: 12% vit. A, 1% vit. C, 6% calcium, 8% iron.*

KID FRIENDLY

HOT MILK SPONGE CAKE WITH TROPICAL TOPPER

This is one of the most versatile cakes from the Better Homes and Gardens® Test Kitchen. Bake it for shortcakes, snack cakes, and trifles. Recipe pictured on page 36.

PREP 1 hr. **BAKE** 20 min. **OVEN** 350°F

INGREDIENTS

2	eggs
1	cup all-purpose flour
1	tsp. baking powder
1	cup sugar
½	cup milk
2	Tbsp. butter
1	recipe Lime Syrup with Tropical Fruit

PREPARATION

1. Let eggs stand at room temperature 30 minutes. Preheat oven to 350°F. Grease one 9×2-inch round cake pan (batter will overflow a shallower pan); set aside.

2. In small bowl stir together flour and baking powder; set aside. In large bowl beat eggs on high about 4 minutes until slightly thickened. Gradually add sugar; beat on medium 4 to 5 minutes until pale yellow and thickened. Add flour mixture; beat on low to medium just until combined.

3. In small saucepan over low heat stir milk and butter until butter is melted; add to batter; beat to combine. Pour batter in pan. Bake 20 to 25 minutes or until wooden pick inserted near center comes out clean. Cool in pan on wire rack. To serve, cut cake in wedges; top with Lime Syrup with Tropical Fruit. Serve immediately. To store, cover and refrigerate untopped cake. **Makes 9 servings.**

Lime Syrup with Tropical Fruit Shred 2 teaspoons *lime peel*; set aside. In pan combine ¼ cup each *lime juice* and *water* with ½ cup *sugar*; cook and stir to dissolve sugar. Increase heat; boil gently, uncovered, 3 minutes (don't stir). Cool 5 minutes. Stir in peel and 4 cups *fruit* (*mango, papaya,* and *carambola/star fruit*).

EACH SERVING *253 cal, 4 g fat (2 g sat. fat), 55 mg chol, 81 mg sodium, 52 g carbo, 1 g fiber, 2 g pro. Daily Values: 4% vit. A, 36% vit. C, 7% calcium, 6% iron.*

POPPY SEED CAKE WITH LEMON GLAZE

Have your poppy seeds been around a while? Replace them with a fresh container for this recipe. Recipe pictured on page 36.

PREP 1 hr. **BAKE** 40 min. **COOL** 10 min.
OVEN 350°F

INGREDIENTS

¾	cup butter
4	eggs
2	cups all-purpose flour
1	tsp. baking soda
½	tsp. salt
1½	cups granulated sugar
¼	cup poppy seeds (about 1 oz.)
1	8-oz. carton dairy sour cream
1	recipe Lemon Glaze

PREPARATION

1. Let butter and eggs stand 30 minutes. Preheat oven to 350°F. Grease and flour 10-inch fluted tube pan; set aside.

2. In medium bowl combine flour, baking soda, and salt; set aside. In large mixing bowl beat butter on medium 30 seconds. Gradually beat in sugar. Beat in eggs and poppy seeds. Alternately add flour mixture and sour cream to butter mixture; beat on low after each addition just until combined. Spread evenly in prepared pan.

3. Bake 40 to 45 minutes or until wooden pick inserted near center comes out clean. Cool in pan on rack 10 minutes. Meanwhile, prepare Lemon Glaze. Remove and invert cake on rack; poke all over with fork tines. Brush glaze over cake. Serve immediately or cover and refrigerate. **Makes 16 servings.**

Lemon Glaze In small saucepan heat ¼ cup *sugar*, ¼ cup *lemon juice*, and 2 tablespoons *butter* over medium-low heat until butter is melted and sugar is dissolved.

EACH SERVING *292 cal, 16 g fat (9 g sat. fat), 86 mg chol, 212 mg sodium, 36 g carbo, 1 g fiber, 3 g pro. Daily Values: 9% vit. A, 3% vit. C, 6% calcium, 6% iron.*

KID FRIENDLY

BANANA-SPLIT CAKE

Red food coloring intensifies the hue of the strawberry layer. Chocolate lovers: Drizzle with purchased chocolate sauce. Recipe pictured on page 36.

PREP 1 hr. 10 min. **BAKE** 30 min.
OVEN 350°F

INGREDIENTS

¾	cup butter
3	eggs
1	cup sugar
1	small ripe banana, mashed (⅓ cup)
⅓	cup dairy sour cream
⅓	cup milk
1	tsp. vanilla
2¼	cups all-purpose flour
1¼	tsp. baking powder
½	tsp. salt
¼	tsp. baking soda
½	cup strawberry jam
2	drops red food coloring (optional)
2	1-oz. squares semisweet chocolate, melted and cooled
¾	to 1 cup strawberry jam or preserves Strawberry ice cream (optional)

PREPARATION

1. Let butter and eggs stand at room temperature 30 minutes. Preheat oven to 350°F. Grease bottoms of two 8-inch round cake pans. Line bottoms with waxed or parchment paper. Grease and flour; set aside.

2. In large bowl beat butter on medium speed 30 seconds; gradually beat in sugar to combine. Add eggs, 1 at a time, beating well after each addition. In medium bowl combine banana, sour cream, milk, and vanilla. In another bowl combine flour, baking powder, salt, and soda. Alternately beat flour and banana mixtures into butter mixture on low.

3. In small bowl combine ⅔ cup batter, the ½ cup strawberry jam, and food coloring. In separate bowl combine ⅔ cup batter and melted chocolate. Spread plain batter in prepared pans. Spoon flavored batters on each plain batter; gently swirl with knife.

4. Bake 30 to 35 minutes or until wooden pick inserted near centers comes out clean. Cool in pans on racks 10 minutes. Remove from pans; peel off paper; cool. Place one, layer flat side, down on plate. Top with jam. Stack second layer, flat side down. Serve with strawberry ice cream. **Makes 12 servings.**

EACH SERVING *406 cal, 16 g fat (9 g sat. fat), 86 mg chol, 264 mg sodium, 62 g carbo, 1 g fiber, 3 g pro. Daily Values: 9% vit. A, 6% vit. C, 4% calcium, 10% iron.*

GINGER-CARROT CAKE

Recipe pictured on page 36.

PREP 1 hr. **BAKE** 30 min. **COOL** 10 min.
OVEN 350°F

INGREDIENTS

4	eggs, lightly beaten
2	cups all-purpose flour
1¾	cups sugar
2	tsp. baking powder
½	tsp. baking soda
¼	tsp. salt
4	cups finely shredded carrot
⅔	cup cooking oil
¼	cup orange juice
2	tsp. grated fresh ginger or ¾ tsp. ground ginger
1	cup walnuts, toasted and finely chopped (optional)
1	recipe Double Cream Cheese Frosting

PREPARATION

1. Let eggs stand at room temperature 30 minutes. Preheat oven to 350°F. Grease two 9-inch round cake pans; line bottoms with waxed or parchment paper; set aside.

2. In large bowl combine flour, sugar, baking powder, baking soda, and salt. In another bowl combine eggs, carrot, oil, orange juice, and ginger. Stir egg mixture into flour mixture; stir in nuts. Spread batter in prepared pans. Bake 30 to 35 minutes or until pick inserted near centers comes out clean. Cool in pans on wire rack 10 minutes. Remove from pans; cool thoroughly on racks.

3. Prepare Double Cream Cheese Frosting. Place one layer, flat side down, on plate; spread ¾ cup frosting. Stack second layer, flat side down; spread remaining frosting on top and sides. **Makes 12 servings.**

Double Cream Cheese Frosting In large bowl beat together on low speed one 8-ounce package *cream cheese*, softened; 2 tablespoons *whipping cream*; and ¼ teaspoon *salt* until fluffy. Gradually beat in 5 to 5½ cups *powdered sugar*.

EACH SERVING *607 cal, 22 g fat (7 g sat. fat), 95 mg chol, 316 mg sodium, 100 g carbo, 2 g fiber, 5 g pro. Daily Values: 131% vit. A, 8% vit. C, 10% calcium, 10% iron.*

CAKE STORAGE

■ To ensure that a frosted cake stays attractive before serving, refrigerate it for 1 hour to firm up the frosting.

■ Keep cakes, wrapped or covered, in the refrigerator for 1 week. On the counter under a cake dome or in a cake keeper, they will stay fresh for 3 days.

SWEETHEART CAKES

Adapt the Red Velvet Cake recipe (page 35) to make these cupcakes. Bake batter in 2½-inch cupcake pans 15 to 17 minutes, filling cups two-thirds full. Cool. Top with chocolate cookies cut out with 1- to 2-inch heart-shape cookie cutter. Dust with powdered sugar. **Makes 28.**

Make cakes to suit every occasion by substituting different-size pans. Just divide the batter according to this chart and follow recommended baking times. Dark pans absorb more heat than shiny bakeware and result in darker cakes.

	8-INCH ROUND	9-INCH ROUND	9×13	FLUTED TUBE PAN	2½-INCH CUPCAKE	JUMBO CUPCAKE
Chocolate-Sour Cream Cake	2 pans; 25–30 min.	2 pans; 25 min.	25–30 min.	40–45 min.	Makes 21; 16–18 min.	Makes 8; 22–25 min.
Buttermilk White Cake	2 pans; 30–35 min.	2 pans; 25–30 min.	25–30 min.	40–45 min.	Makes 22; 16–18 min.	Makes 8; 22–25 min.
Hot Milk Sponge Cake with Tropical Topper	NR*	9×2-inch pan; 20–25 min.	NR	NR	Makes 14; 12–14 min.	Makes 6; 18–20 min.
Poppy Seed Cake with Lemon Glaze	2 pans; 25–30 min.	2 pans; 20–25 min.	NR	40–45 min.	Makes 24; 15–17 min.	Makes 10; 20–25 min.
Banana-Split Cake	2 pans; 30–35 min.	NR	30–35 min.	40–45 min.	NR	NR
Ginger-Carrot Cake	2 pans; 30–35 min.	2 pans; 30–35 min.	40–45 min.	50–55 min.	Makes 22; 20–25 min.	Makes 11; 25–30 min.
Pecan-Laced German Chocolate Cake	4 pans; 20–25 min.	3 pans; 25–30 min.	NR	NR	NR	NR
Caramel-Frosted Hummingbird Cake	4 pans; 25–30 min.	3 pans; 30 min.	35–40 min.	55–65 min.	Makes 28; 18–20 min.	Makes 12; 28–30 min.
Chocolate-Espresso Chiffon Cake	NR	NR	NR	60–70 min.	NR	NR
Buttery Yellow Citrus Cake	2 pans; 30–35 min.	2 pans; 20–25 min.	25–30 min.	30–35 min.	Makes 26; 14–16 min.	Makes 12; 16–20 min.
Date-and-Spice Cake	3 pans; 15–20 min.	2 pans; 25–30 min.	30–35 min.	NR	Makes 24; 12–14 min.	Makes 10; 22–24 min.
Red Velvet Cake	3 pans; 25–30 min.	3 pans; 20–25 min.	30–35 min.	40–45 min.	Makes 28; 15–17 min.	Makes 12; 22–25 min.

NR=Not Recommended

Fondue Finale

Get cozy over an intimate dessert of bite-size dippers coated with warm chocolate sauce. This rum-laced fondue assembles in minutes.

CELEBRATE *with*
Pam Anderson

FAST!

RUM-LACED CHOCOLATE FONDUE

START TO FINISH 15 min.

INGREDIENTS

2	Tbsp. half-and-half
1	Tbsp. butter
2	Tbsp. dark or light rum
8	oz. bittersweet or semisweet chocolate, chopped

DIPPERS

Fortune cookies, petite croissants (heated according to package directions), brioche or challah bread (cut in bite-size chunks), whole fresh strawberries, raspberry or mango sorbet (use a 1-tablespoon scoop)

PREPARATION

1. In a small saucepan bring half-and-half, butter, and *1 tablespoon* of the rum to simmering. Remove from heat; whisk in chocolate until melted. Whisk in the remaining 1 tablespoon of rum (if necessary, add an additional tablespoon half-and-half to make dipping consistency). Transfer the chocolate mixture to a small fondue pot or a 10-ounce custard cup. Serve with dippers.

Makes 4 servings.

EACH SERVING (¼ CUP WITHOUT DIPPERS) *338 cal, 26 g fat (16 g sat. fat), 12 mg chol, 25 mg sodium, 31 g carbo, 1 g fiber, 3 g pro. Daily Values: 3% vit. A, 4% calcium, 22% iron.*

PAM'S TIPS

- No fondue pot? Fill a pretty little dish and set it on a complementary serving platter.

- Set the mood for romance in a cozy room with glowing candles and soft music.

- Spear food for dipping with long appetizer-style toothpicks or dainty seafood forks.

Eating In

Bye-bye, drive-thru. Hello, fresh, more healthful, never boring, and ready in a jiffy.

BY **PEG SMITH** PHOTOS **ANDY LYONS** RECIPES AND FOOD STYLING **JILL LUST**

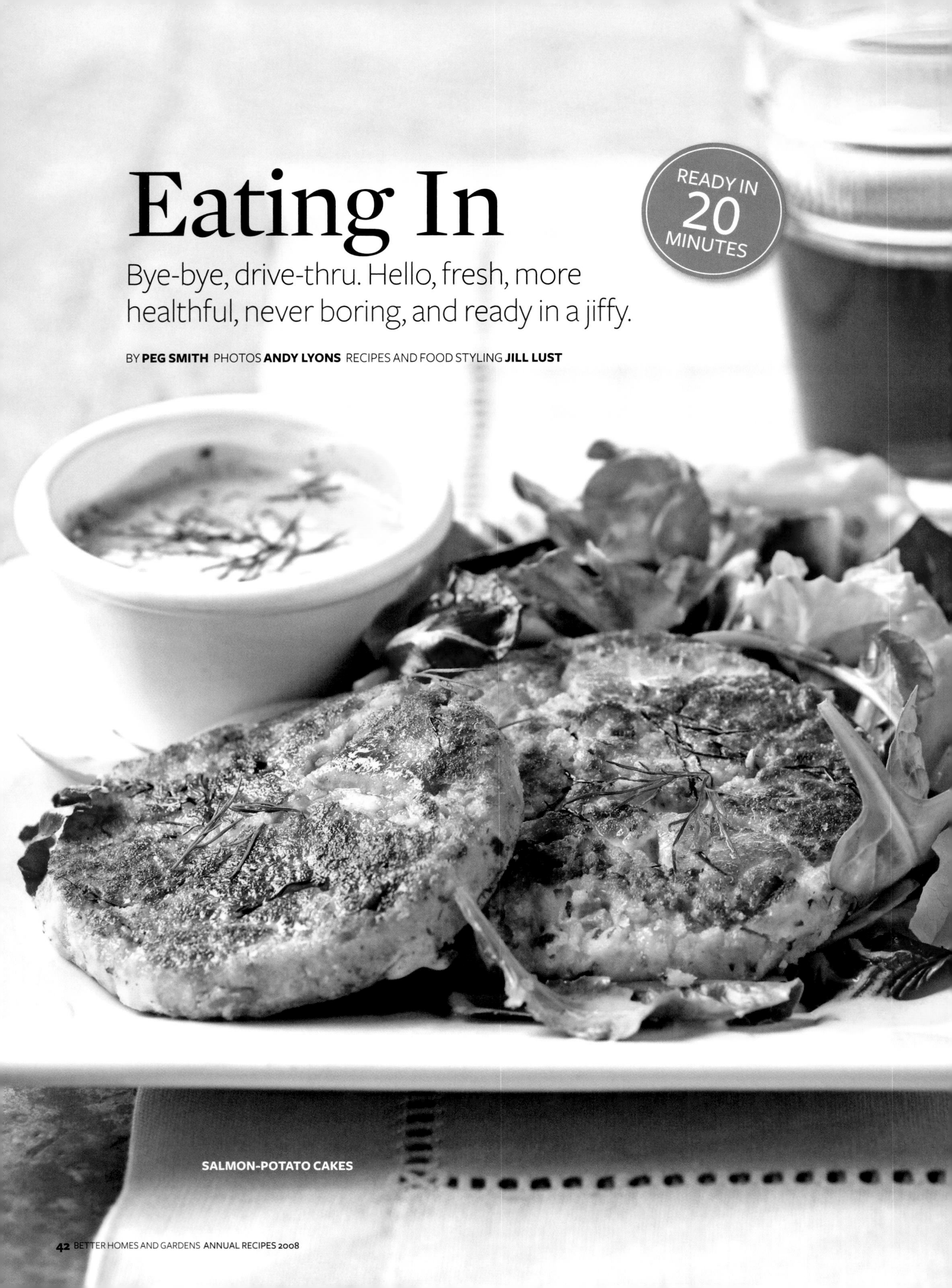

READY IN
20
MINUTES

SALMON-POTATO CAKES

FAST!

SALMON-POTATO CAKES

START TO FINISH 20 min.
INGREDIENTS

14	oz. fresh skinless salmon fillets
2	cups refrigerated sour cream and chive mashed potatoes
1/2	cup seasoned fine dry bread crumbs
3	Tbsp. snipped fresh dill
	Nonstick cooking spray
1	5-oz. pkg. mixed salad greens
1/2	cup bottled Honey-Dijon salad dressing

PREPARATION

1. Rinse and dry salmon. Place in 2-quart square microwave-safe baking dish; cover with vented plastic. Microcook on high (100% power) for 2 1/2 to 3 1/2 minutes or until salmon flakes easily with a fork. Break in pieces. In bowl combine salmon, potatoes, bread crumbs, and dill. Form salmon mixture in eight 3 1/2-inch cakes. Lightly coat a large nonstick skillet with cooking spray. Cook cakes over medium-high heat 3 to 4 minutes on each side until heated through and browned. Place salad greens on plates. Top with salmon-potato cakes; serve with salad dressing. **MAKES 4 SERVINGS.**

EACH SERVING *503 cal, 31 g fat (7 g sat. fat), 74 mg chol, 851 mg sodium, 31 g carbo, 2 g fiber, 25 g pro. Daily Values: 17% vit. A, 14% vit. C, 9% calcium, 9% iron.*

FAST!

CHORIZO-TOPPED PIZZAS

START TO FINISH 20 min.
INGREDIENTS

8	oz. chorizo sausage
1	cup deli-fresh chunky salsa with corn and beans
	Nonstick cooking spray
4	7- to 8-inch flour tortillas
1	cup shredded Mexican cheese blend (4 oz.)
1	avocado, halved, pitted, peeled, and sliced
4	green onions, chopped
1/4	cup snipped fresh cilantro
	Lime wedges

PREPARATION

1. Preheat broiler. In large skillet crumble and cook chorizo over medium heat until no pink remains. Drain in colander. In small saucepan heat salsa over medium heat until heated through.
2. Lightly coat large baking sheet with cooking spray. Arrange tortillas, 2 at a time, on baking sheet; top each with 1/4 cup of the cheese. Broil 3 to 4 inches from heat 2 to 3 minutes until cheese is melted. Top each pizza with one-fourth the warm salsa, cooked chorizo, avocado, green onion, and cilantro. Pass lime wedges.
Makes 16 servings.

EACH SERVING *588 cal, 41 g fat (15 g sat. fat), 75 mg chol, 1,242 mg sodium, 31 g carbo, 6 g fiber, 24 g pro. Daily Values: 2% vit. A, 22% vit. C, 20% calcium, 11% iron.*

CHORIZO-TOPPED PIZZAS

TUSCAN BEAN SOUP

FAST!

PINEAPPLE CHICKEN

START TO FINISH 20 min.

INGREDIENTS

1½ lb. skinless, boneless chicken thighs
½ tsp. curry seasoning blend
1 red sweet pepper, cut in strips
1 pineapple, peeled, cored, cut in large chunks
1 serrano pepper, thinly sliced (see Note, page 101)
¾ cup unsweetened coconut milk
1 Tbsp. packed brown sugar

PREPARATION

1. Sprinkle chicken with ½ teaspoon *salt* and curry seasoning. In 12-inch skillet quickly brown chicken on both sides in 1 tablespoon hot *olive oil* over high heat. Reduce heat to medium-high; cook 12 minutes until tender and no longer pink.
2. For sauce, in second skillet cook sweet pepper in 1 tablespoon hot *olive oil* over medium-high heat 3 minutes; set aside. Add pineapple; cook 5 minutes or until brown. Add serrano pepper; cook 1 minute. Stir in coconut milk and brown sugar; heat through. Serve sauce with peppers over chicken. **Makes 4 servings.**

 EACH SERVING *443 cal, 24 g fat (12 g sat. fat), 141 mg chol, 448 mg sodium, 23 g carbo, 3 g fiber, 35 g pro. Daily Values: 22% vit. A, 137% vit. C, 4% calcium, 17% iron.*

FAST! **LOW FAT**

TUSCAN BEAN SOUP

START TO FINISH 20 min.

INGREDIENTS

1 cup packaged peeled baby carrots, coarsely chopped
1 small onion, chopped
3 Tbsp. olive oil
2 15-oz. cans cannellini beans, rinsed and drained
1 32-oz. box reduced-sodium chicken broth
2 to 3 tsp. dried Italian seasoning, crushed
1 5-oz. pkg. baby spinach
 Freshly cracked black pepper
 Cracker bread (optional)

PREPARATION

1. In 4-quart Dutch oven cook and stir carrot and onion in *1 tablespoon* olive oil over medium-high heat 3 minutes. Add beans, broth, and seasoning. Bring to boiling; slightly mash beans. Reduce heat; simmer, uncovered, 8 minutes, stirring occasionally.
2. Meanwhile, in large skillet heat remaining oil over medium-high heat. Add spinach; toss with tongs 1 to 2 minutes, just until wilted. Remove from heat. Ladle soup; top with spinach, sprinkle with pepper. Serve with cracker bread. **Makes 4 servings.**

 EACH SERVING *254 cal, 11 g fat (2 g sat. fat), 0 mg chol, 919 mg sodium, 36 g carbo, 12 g fiber, 16 g pro. Daily Values: 169% vit. A, 22% vit. C, 11% calcium, 21% iron.*

PINEAPPLE CHICKEN

FAST!

PORK CHOPS PRIMAVERA

START TO FINISH 20 min.

INGREDIENTS

- 4 slices peppered bacon, cut in 1-inch pieces
- 12 oz. trimmed fresh young green beans
- 4 boneless pork chops, ½ inch thick
- 1 Tbsp. soy sauce
- ⅓ cup apple butter
- ¼ cup water
- 1 cup red or yellow cherry or grape tomatoes

PREPARATION

1. In 12-inch skillet cook bacon over medium-high heat until crisp; remove. Reserve *1 tablespoon* drippings in skillet. Drain bacon on paper towels.

2. Meanwhile, in 2-quart microwave-safe dish microcook beans in 2 tablespoons *water*, covered, on high (100% power) 4 minutes; stir once. Drain, set aside. Brush chops with soy sauce. In skillet brown chops on both sides. Add apple butter and the ¼ cup water; reduce heat. Simmer, covered, 5 minutes. Add beans, tomatoes, and bacon; cook, uncovered, 3 to 5 minutes until sauce thickens. **Makes 4 servings.**

EACH SERVING *402 cal, 16 g fat (5 g sat. fat), 80 mg chol, 534 mg sodium, 39 g carbo, 5 g fiber, 27 g pro. Daily Values: 20% vit. A, 35% vit. C, 7% calcium, 14% iron.*

PORK CHOPS PRIMAVERA

Taste of Success

The *Your Best Recipes* contest drew thousands of entries from cooks all over the country. The winning recipes share three things: ease, simplicity, and a delicious difference.

BY **RICHARD SWEARINGER** PHOTOS **ANDY LYONS** FOOD STYLING **JILL LUST**

GRAND PRIZE WINNER

GRILLED STEAK BRUSCHETTA SALAD

GRAND PRIZE
GRILLED STEAK BRUSCHETTA SALAD

Pretty presentation and clean flavors convinced the judges to award top prize to Devon Delaney of Princeton, New Jersey.

START TO FINISH 35 min.

INGREDIENTS

¼	cup apricot preserves
¼	cup prepared horseradish
¼	cup creamy Dijon-style mustard blend
2	Tbsp. lemon juice
4	6-oz. beef tenderloin steaks, 1 inch thick
12	¼-inch-thick slices baguette-style French bread
4	cups arugula
¼	cup bottled roasted red sweet peppers, chopped
¼	cup crumbled blue cheese

PREPARATION

1. Snip any large pieces in preserves. In bowl combine preserves, horseradish, mustard blend, and lemon juice. Set aside.

2. Sprinkle beef on both sides with ¼ teaspoon each *salt* and *ground black pepper*. For charcoal grill, grill steaks on the rack of uncovered grill directly over medium coals, turning once. Allow 10 to 12 minutes for medium-rare doneness (145°F), 12 to 15 minutes for medium (160°F). Grill bread slices with steaks during last 2 minutes or until bread is toasted; turn once. (For gas grill, preheat grill. Reduce to medium. Place steaks on rack over heat. Cover and grill as above.)

3. Divide arugula among 4 serving plates. Top with bread slices. Drizzle with dressing. Slice steak; arrange on bread. Top with red peppers and blue cheese. **Makes 4 servings.**

EACH SERVING *488 cal, 17 g fat (7 g sat. fat), 111 mg chol, 964 mg sodium, 39 g carbo, 2 g fiber, 43 g pro. Daily Values: 11% vit. A, 63% vit. C, 12% calcium, 35% iron.*

LOW FAT

SLOW COOKER CATEGORY
NEW WORLD CHILI

Roxanne Chan of Albany, California, was inspired to create this dish by pumpkins and squash in her garden. "The individual flavors really stand out," said judges.

PREP 25 min.   **COOK** 10 hr. on low or 5 hr. on high

INGREDIENTS

1	lb. turkey breast tenderloin, cut in 1-inch pieces
1	28-oz. can diced tomatoes
1	15-oz. can black beans, rinsed and drained
1	8-oz. can tomato sauce
1	cup peeled, seeded, and cubed butternut squash or pumpkin
1	medium onion, chopped
½	cup chicken broth
½	cup frozen whole kernel corn
½	cup dried cranberries
1	fresh jalapeño pepper, seeded and finely chopped (see Note, page 101)
1	Tbsp. chili powder
1	clove garlic, minced
	Chicken broth
2	cups shredded fresh spinach
4	oz. Monterey Jack cheese with jalapeño peppers, shredded (1 cup)

PREPARATION

1. In a 5-quart slow cooker combine turkey, undrained tomatoes, beans, tomato sauce, squash, onion, the ½ cup chicken broth, corn, cranberries, jalapeño pepper, chili powder, and garlic.

2. Cover and cook on low-heat setting for 10 to 12 hours or on high-heat setting for 5 to 6 hours. If desired, stir in additional broth to reach desired consistency. Stir in spinach just before serving. Sprinkle each serving with cheese. **Makes 6 servings.**

EACH SERVING *301 cal, 7 g fat (4 g sat. fat), 64 mg chol, 1,051 mg sodium, 35 g carbo, 8 g fiber, 29 g pro. Daily Values: 93% vit. A, 43% vit. C, 24% calcium, 20% iron.*

NEW WORLD CHILI

FAST!

20-MINUTE CATEGORY
CHICKEN-CORN PIZZA

"Innovative" said judges about this entry from Robin Haas of Cranston, Rhode Island.

START TO FINISH 20 min. **OVEN** 450°F

INGREDIENTS

1   12-inch packaged prebaked pizza crust
1   cup ricotta cheese
1   cup finely shredded Parmesan cheese
½   tsp. ground black pepper
1   10-oz. pkg. frozen whole kernel corn in butter sauce
1   6-oz. pkg. refrigerated cooked chicken breast strips
½   cup coarsely chopped red sweet pepper
1   Tbsp. finely shredded lemon peel
2   tsp. dried tarragon
1   tsp. bottled minced garlic
½   cup crumbled goat cheese
1   2¼-oz. can sliced pitted ripe olives, drained
¼   cup chopped fresh parsley

PREPARATION

1. Preheat oven to 450°F. Line baking sheet with foil. Coat foil with *nonstick cooking spray.* Place pizza crust on foil; set aside.
2. In bowl combine ricotta, Parmesan, and black pepper. Spread on crust, leaving ½-inch space around edge. Bake 5 minutes.
3. Transfer corn and sauce from package to microwave-safe bowl. Microcook on high (100% power) 3 minutes. Stir. Microcook 1 minute more. Stir in chicken, sweet pepper, lemon peel, tarragon, and garlic. Remove pizza from oven. Spoon corn mixture over ricotta mixture on crust.
4. Top with goat cheese and black olives. Bake 5 minutes more or until cheese and edges are lightly browned. Sprinkle parsley before serving. **Makes 4 servings.**

EACH SERVING *679 cal, 28 g fat (12 g sat. fat), 84 mg chol, 1,928 mg sodium, 69 g carbo, 4 g fiber, 41 g pro. Daily Values: 32% vit. A, 57% vit. C, 58% calcium, 26% iron.*

KID FRIENDLY

CASSEROLES CATEGORY
PESTO SHRIMP MAC AND CHEESE

Michael Cohen, a composer from Los Angeles, struck a chord with his entry. "If you took this to a potluck, it would be all gone," raved Gayle Butler, editor in chief.

PREP 20 min. **BAKE** 40 min. **STAND** 10 min.
OVEN 350°F

INGREDIENTS

1   lb. fresh or frozen medium shrimp in shells
8   oz. dried elbow macaroni (2 cups)
2   eggs, lightly beaten
¼   cup butter, melted
1   cup half-and-half
1¼   cups shredded fontina cheese (5 oz.)
½   cup grated Parmesan cheese
2   cloves garlic, minced
2   Tbsp. pine nuts, toasted
1½   cups lightly packed fresh basil leaves, chopped
   Fresh basil leaves

PREPARATION

1. Thaw shrimp, if frozen. Preheat oven to 350°F. Peel and devein shrimp, removing tails. Rinse shrimp; pat dry with paper towels. Chop shrimp and set aside.
2. Cook macaroni according to package directions. Drain and keep warm.
3. In large bowl stir together eggs, butter, half-and-half, *1 cup* of the fontina cheese, *¼ cup* of the Parmesan cheese, garlic, pine nuts, chopped basil, and ¼ teaspoon each *salt* and *ground black pepper.* Stir in shrimp and macaroni. Transfer to buttered 2-quart casserole. Top with remaining cheeses.
4. Bake, uncovered, 40 to 45 minutes or until heated through and shrimp pieces are opaque. Let stand for 10 minutes before serving. Top with fresh basil leaves.
Makes 6 servings.

EACH SERVING *509 cal, 27 g fat (14 g sat. fat), 254 mg chol, 694 mg sodium, 33 g carbo, 2 g fiber, 33 g pro. Daily Values: 30% vit. A, 7% vit. C, 33% calcium, 23% iron.*

KID FRIENDLY

PERSONAL FAVORITES CATEGORY
ROSEMARY-LEMON SANDWICH COOKIES

Judges ooohed and ahhed over this old family recipe from Kristina Vanni of Los Angeles.

PREP 30 min. **BAKE** 8 min. **STAND** 30 min.
COOL 30 min. **OVEN** 400°F

INGREDIENTS

1   cup unsalted butter, softened
¾   cup granulated sugar
2   tsp. snipped fresh rosemary
2   tsp. finely shredded lemon peel
½   tsp. baking powder
¼   tsp. salt
1   tsp. vanilla
2¼   cups all-purpose flour
½   cup lemon curd
½   cup mascarpone cheese
1   Tbsp. powdered sugar

PREPARATION

1. Preheat oven to 400° F. In mixing bowl beat butter with electric mixer on medium speed 30 seconds. Add granulated sugar, rosemary, lemon peel, baking powder, and salt. Beat until combined, scraping sides of bowl. Beat in vanilla. Beat in as much of the flour as you can. Stir in remaining flour.
2. Shape dough in 1-inch balls. Place 2 inches apart on parchment paper-lined cookie sheet. With bottom of glass dipped in granulated sugar flatten to ½-inch thickness. Bake 8 minutes or until bottoms are lightly browned. Cool 1 minute. Transfer to wire rack; cool.
3. Meanwhile, in small bowl combine lemon curd and mascarpone cheese. Spread on flat sides of half of cookies. Top with remaining cookies, flat sides to filling. Sprinkle with powdered sugar. Serve immediately or refrigerate, in layers separated by waxed paper, in airtight container up to 24 hours. Let stand at room temperature for 30 minutes before serving. Sprinkle with powdered sugar. **Makes 20 cookies.**

EACH COOKIE *215 cal, 12 g fat (8 g sat. fat), 38 mg chol, 49 mg sodium, 25 g carbo, 1 g fiber, 2 g pro. Daily Values: 6% vit. A, 0% vit. C, 1% calcium, 4% iron.*

HEALTHY CATEGORY
WHEAT BERRY SALAD WITH DRIED APRICOTS

*"My wife is always searching out new grains,"
said winner Jamaine Batson of Salt Lake City.
"This recipe gives wheat berries a nice light
touch," said the judges.*

PREP 15 min. **CHILL** overnight
COOK 45 min. **COOL** 1 hr.

INGREDIENTS
1   cup wheat berries, rinsed and drained
1   15-oz. can garbanzo beans
      (chickpeas), rinsed and drained
1   cup slivered fresh snow peas
½   cup dried apricots, sliced
½   cup dried cranberries
¼   cup chopped green onion
3   Tbsp. toasted walnut oil
1   Tbsp. lemon juice

PREPARATION
1. In a medium bowl combine wheat berries,
3 cups *water,* and ⅛ teaspoon *salt;* cover and
refrigerate overnight. Transfer to medium
saucepan; bring to boiling. Reduce heat;
simmer, covered, 45 to 60 minutes or until
tender. Drain; cool 1 hour.
2. In large bowl combine drained wheat
berries, garbanzo beans, snow peas, apricots,
cranberries, and green onion. In bowl whisk
together oil, lemon juice, and ½ teaspoon
each *salt* and *ground black pepper.* Pour over
wheat berry mixture; stir to coat. Serve at
once or cover and refrigerate up to 24 hours.
Makes 8 side-dish servings.

EACH SERVING *239 cal, 6 g total fat (1 g sat.
fat), 0 mg chol, 342 mg sodium, 43 g carbo,
7 g fiber, 6 g pro. Daily Values: 7% vit. A,
18% vit. C, 4% calcium, 14% iron.*

DESSERTS CATEGORY
BABY CHEESECAKES WITH TOFFEE PEARS

*This spin on a "classic flavor combo" ensured
that Janice Elder of Charlotte, North
Carolina, won this category.*

PREP 45 min. **BAKE** 28 min. **COOL** 30 min.
CHILL 2 hr. **OVEN** 375°F/325°F

INGREDIENTS
¾   cup quick-cooking rolled oats
¼   cup finely chopped walnuts
¼   cup packed brown sugar
3   Tbsp. butter, melted
1   8-oz. pkg. cream cheese, softened
1   egg
2   oz. crumbled blue cheese
¼   cup dairy sour cream
2   Tbsp. butter
½   cup packed brown sugar
2   Tbsp. whipping cream
4   pears, cored and sliced
¼   tsp. vanilla
½   cup lightly toasted broken walnuts

PREPARATION
1. Preheat oven to 375°F. Line eight 2½-inch
muffin cups with foil or paper bake cups;
set aside.
2. For crust, in bowl stir together oats,
¼ cup walnuts, ¼ cup brown sugar, and the
3 tablespoons butter until combined. Spoon
2 rounded tablespoons oat mixture into each
prepared muffin cup. With bottom of a
narrow glass press down lightly. Bake
8 minutes or until lightly browned. Cool
slightly on wire racks. Reduce oven
temperature to 325°F.
3. For cheesecake filling, in medium bowl beat
cream cheese with an electric mixer on
medium to high speed until smooth. Add egg
and beat just until combined. Stir in blue
cheese and sour cream.
4. Spoon well-rounded tablespoons of the
cheese mixture into each crust-lined muffin
cup. Bake 20 minutes or until slightly puffed
and set. Cool 30 minutes. Remove from cups.
Place on tray; cover and refrigerate at least

2 or up to 24 hours. Let stand at room
temperature for 30 minutes before serving.
5. For Toffee Pears, in large skillet melt the
2 tablespoons butter over medium heat.
Add the ½ cup brown sugar and cream.
Cook and stir until bubbly. Add pears. Cook,
stirring occasionally, 5 minutes or until
pears are tender. Remove from heat. Stir in
vanilla. Cool slightly.
6. To serve, remove foil or paper liners from
cheesecakes. Spoon about 1 tablespoon
brown sugar-cream mixture into each of
8 dessert dishes. Top with a cheesecake.
Spoon pears around cheesecakes. Sprinkle
each with toasted walnuts.
Makes 8 servings.

EACH SERVING *454 cal, 28 g total fat (15 g sat.
fat), 90 mg chol, 257 mg sodium, 45 g carbo,
5 g fiber, 9 g protein. Daily Values: 16% vit. A,
6% vit. C, 12% calcium, 11% iron.*

MALTED MOUSSE CAKE page 59

MARCH

JUST WHEN WE NEED IT, MARCH REVIVES OUR SPIRITS.
CELEBRATE SPRING RENEWAL WITH A BRIGHTLY FLAVORED
EASTER DINNER, THE SEASON'S FRESHEST VEGETABLES, AND
CITRUS-LADEN CUPCAKES AND BREAD.

Spring Fling

CITRUS-ROASTED ASPARAGUS page 55

PARMESAN-CRUSTED FISH page 63

ORANGE-RAISIN BRUNCH BREAD page 67

spring

BY **RICHARD SWEARINGER**
PHOTOS **CON POULOS**
PRODUCED BY **NANCY WALL HOPKINS**
RECIPES BY **MELANIE BARNARD**
FOOD STYLING **SUSAN SUGARMAN**
PROP STYLING **PAMELA DUNCAN SILVER**

fling
EASTER DINNER AS LIGHT AND BRIGHT AS THE SEASON

A splash of maple syrup and a dab of butter add an irresistible gleam to **MAPLE-GLAZED NEW POTATOES,** *above left* (*page 55*). Just before serving, the potatoes are tossed with lemon zest and fresh parsley. **PEPPERCORN-CRUSTED HAM,** *above* (*page 55*), begins with an easy-to-serve spiral-sliced ham that's generously slathered with a mustard-based glaze updated with apricot preserves and pink peppercorns. Lighthearted place settings, *opposite,* announce the theme of rebirth. In each bowl a decorative nest, purchased from a crafts store, cradles egg-shape malted milk balls.

CITRUS-ROASTED ASPARAGUS,
MAPLE-GLAZED NEW POTATOES, AND
PEPPERCORN-CRUSTED HAM

MAPLE-GLAZED NEW POTATOES

Just before serving, sprinkle potatoes with sliced green onion, lemon zest, and Italian parsley for added freshness and flavor.

PREP 20 min. **ROAST** 55 min. **OVEN** 325°F

INGREDIENTS

3	lb. tiny new potatoes
¼	cup butter, melted
	Salt and cracked black pepper
3	Tbsp. white balsamic vinegar
2	Tbsp. pure maple syrup
3	cloves garlic, thinly sliced
¼	cup chopped green onion
2	Tbsp. chopped fresh Italian (flat-leaf) parsley
1	Tbsp. finely shredded lemon peel

PREPARATION

1. Preheat oven to 325°F. Halve or quarter any large potatoes. In shallow dish large enough to hold potatoes in a single layer, toss potatoes with butter; season with salt and pepper. Spread in single layer. Roast potatoes, uncovered, 45 minutes, stirring once or twice during roasting.
2. Meanwhile, in small dish stir together vinegar, maple syrup, and sliced garlic. Drizzle potatoes with vinegar mixture; gently toss with spoon or spatula to coat. Continue to roast about 10 to 20 minutes more until potatoes are fork-tender and glazed, stirring once or twice.
3. To serve, sprinkle potatoes with green onion, Italian parsley, and lemon peel. **Makes 6 servings.**

EACH SERVING *275 cal, 8 g fat (5 g sat. fat), 20 mg chol, 265 mg sodium, 47 g carbo, 5 g fiber, 3 g pro. Daily Values: 6% vit. A, 81% vit. C, 5% calcium, 12% iron.*

LOW FAT

PEPPERCORN-CRUSTED HAM

Buy national brands or regional boutique smoked hams. Warm, rather than cook, fully cooked hams; overcooking dries them.

PREP 15 min. **ROAST** 1 hr. 20 min. **STAND** 15 min. **OVEN** 325°F

INGREDIENTS

1	6- to 8-lb. cooked bone-in spiral-sliced ham
1	12-oz. jar apricot preserves
¾	cup Dijon-style mustard
1	to 2 Tbsp. pink or mixed peppercorns
½	cup snipped dried apricots
	Dried apricots (optional)
	Boston lettuce leaves (optional)

PREPARATION

1. Preheat oven to 325°F. Place ham on rack in shallow roasting pan. Tent with foil; crimp foil to pan edges. Roast 1 to 1¾ hours until internal temperature is 130°F.
2. Remove foil from ham. In medium bowl stir together preserves and mustard; set aside ¾ cup. Brush remaining on top and sides of ham. Sprinkle with peppercorns. Cover cut side of ham with foil to prevent drying. Roast 20 to 30 minutes or until internal temperature is 140°F. Remove from oven; remove foil. Let stand at least 15 minutes.

3. Meanwhile, for sauce, in small saucepan combine reserved apricot mixture and snipped apricots; heat through. Slice ham; serve warm or at room temperature with sauce. Garnish with apricots and lettuce. **Makes 16 to 20 servings.**

EACH SERVING *249 cal, 5 g fat (2 g sat. fat), 85 mg chol, 1,862 mg sodium, 19 g carbo, 1 g fiber, 30 g pro. Daily Values: 11% vit. A, 4% vit. C, 2% calcium, 8% iron.*

CITRUS-ROASTED ASPARAGUS

PREP 15 min. **ROAST** 12 min. **OVEN** 400°F

INGREDIENTS

2	seedless oranges
2	lemons
5	Tbsp. extra virgin olive oil
2	lb. asparagus spears
2	cloves garlic, thinly sliced
2	tsp. fresh tarragon leaves
	Sea salt and coarsely ground black pepper

PREPARATION

1. Preheat oven to 400°F. From *one* orange and *one* lemon cut ⅛×2-inch strips avoiding bitter white pith; set aside. From same orange and lemon squeeze a total of *2 tablespoons* juice; set aside.
2. Thinly slice remaining orange and lemon; drizzle slices with *1 tablespoon* of the olive oil. Place on baking sheet lined with parchment paper; set aside.
3. Wash asparagus; break off woody bases. Place spears in 15×10×1-inch baking pan. Sprinkle with garlic, tarragon, and citrus strips. Drizzle 2 tablespoons of the olive oil; toss to coat spears. Spread in single layer. Season with salt and pepper.
4. Roast asparagus and citrus slices 12 to 15 minutes, turning once or twice with tongs, until asparagus is tender and citrus begins to brown. Transfer to serving platter.
5. Meanwhile, for vinaigrette, in small dish whisk together reserved juices and remaining 2 tablespoons oil; season with salt and pepper. Drizzle over roasted asparagus, citrus, and garlic. Sprinkle with roasted citrus slices. Serve warm. **Makes 8 servings.**

EACH SERVING *87 cal, 7 g fat (1 g sat. fat), 0 mg chol, 53 mg sodium, 6 g carbo, 2 g fiber, 2 g pro. Daily Values: 12% vit. A, 41% vit. C, 3% calcium, 9% iron.*

IT'S A SNAP

For the best asparagus flavor, select crisp, colorful spears with tightly closed tips that are similar in size (for uniform cooking). To remove the woody base, hold a spear in two hands and bend it. Snap off the base at the point where the spear easily bends. If the stem still seems tough, use a vegetable peeler to remove the outer layer.

BISCUIT BLOSSOMS

Stack these heavenly biscuits in a pretty basket lined with a pastel cloth. Serve with dinner or as a treat to energize a morning egg hunt. Buttermilk, butter, and shortening ensure the richest, flakiest biscuits.

PREP 20 min. **BAKE** 10 min. **OVEN** 450°F

INGREDIENTS

	Nonstick cooking spray
2	cups all-purpose flour
1	Tbsp. baking powder
½	tsp. salt
¼	tsp. baking soda
4	Tbsp. cold unsalted butter, cut in small pieces
3	Tbsp. cold shortening, cut in small pieces
3	Tbsp. finely chopped green onion
¾	cup cold buttermilk
12	small yellow pear or grape tomatoes
	Olive oil

PREPARATION

1. Preheat oven to 450°F. Lightly coat a pan of twelve 2½-inch muffin cups with nonstick cooking spray; set aside.

2. In medium bowl stir together flour, baking powder, salt, and baking soda. With pastry blender or two knives cut in butter and shortening until flour mixture resembles coarse crumbs. Stir in green onion. Make a well in center; add buttermilk all at once. Toss with fork to moisten all ingredients.

3. Turn out dough onto lightly floured surface. Quickly knead 10 to 12 strokes until dough is nearly smooth. Divide dough in 36 walnut-size pieces; pat into balls. Place 3 balls in each muffin cup. Press 1 tomato in center of each; brush with oil.

4. Bake 10 to 12 minutes until golden brown. Cool slightly on rack. Serve warm. To reheat, wrap in foil; warm in 350°F oven 8 to 10 minutes. **Makes 12 biscuits.**

EACH BISCUIT *166 cal, 10 g fat (4 g sat. fat), 11 mg chol, 233 mg sodium, 17 g carbo, 1 g fiber, 1 g pro. Daily Values: 3% vit. A, 2% vit. C, 11% calcium, 7% iron.*

BISCUIT BLOSSOMS

GARDEN SOUP

Celebrate a most welcome hue of the season with creamy pureed soup flavored by green onions, watercress, and tarragon.

PREP 30 min. **COOK** 23 min. **COOL** 15 min.

INGREDIENTS

1¼	lb. russet potatoes (3 medium), peeled, cut in 1-inch pieces
1½	cups sliced green onion (2 to 3 bunches)
2	Tbsp. butter
6	cups reduced-sodium chicken broth
6	cups watercress (about 3 bunches), tough stems removed, or fresh baby spinach leaves
3	Tbsp. snipped fresh tarragon
½	cup dry white wine or reduced-sodium chicken broth
	Salt and freshly ground black pepper
½	cup sour cream (optional)

PREPARATION

1. In 4- to 5-quart Dutch oven cook potato and onion in hot butter over medium heat 3 to 5 minutes or until onion is tender but not brown, stirring occasionally. Add 6 cups broth; bring to boiling. Reduce heat. Simmer, covered, 20 minutes or until potatoes are tender.

2. Stir in watercress; return broth to simmering. Simmer, covered, for 3 to 5 minutes until greens are tender. Remove soup from heat; cool 15 minutes. Stir in tarragon. Puree soup using immersion blender or in batches using a blender.

3. Stir wine or broth into soup; season with salt and pepper. Heat through over low heat. Top servings with sour cream.
Makes 8 side-dish servings.

EACH SERVING *125 cal, 6 g fat (3 g sat. fat), 13 mg chol, 617 mg sodium, 13 g carbo, 1 g fiber, 5 g pro. Daily Values: 33% vit. A, 44% vit. C, 7% calcium, 5% iron.*

HAVE A BALL

Working with dough can be therapeutic and relaxing, and the results merit rave reviews. Be gentle when patting the balls for these biscuits to avoid squeezing out the air bubbles that make the biscuits flaky and tender. To shape, use ungreased hands to lightly pat and gently roll each ball until the dough forms uniform-size balls.

CUCUMBER-YOGURT DIP
SMOKED SALMON DIP

CUCUMBER-YOGURT DIP

For a thick and rich dip, use the Greek yogurt now available in many supermarkets around the country or make Yogurt Cheese (recipe, below) with plain whole-milk yogurt.

PREP 15 min. **STAND** 15 min.

INGREDIENTS

1½ cups Greek yogurt or Yogurt Cheese
3 Tbsp. snipped fresh dill
2 Tbsp. snipped fresh mint
2 Tbsp. snipped fresh chives
1 Tbsp. lemon juice
1 to 2 cloves garlic, minced
½ tsp. salt
½ seedless English cucumber, chopped (about 2 cups)
  Salt and cracked black pepper
  Fresh dill sprig
  Assorted vegetable dippers: baby zucchini, baby carrots, tender young green beans, small radishes

PREPARATION

1. In bowl stir together yogurt, dill, mint, chives, juice, garlic, and salt. Let stand 15 minutes or refrigerate up to 12 hours.
2. Before serving, stir in cucumber. Season with salt and pepper. Top with dill sprig. Serve with assorted vegetables. Cover and refrigerate leftovers; stir well before serving. **Makes about 3 cups.**
YOGURT CHEESE Suspend a small colander over a bowl. Line colander with three layers cotton cheesecloth or a paper coffee filter. Spoon in 2 cups *yogurt.* (Use yogurt without gums, gelatin, or fillers to ensure whey and curd separate.) Cover with plastic wrap; refrigerate at least 24 hours. Discard liquid.

EACH SERVING (2 TBSP. DIP) *21 cal, 1 g fat (1 g sat. fat), 3 mg chol, 65 mg sodium, 1 g carbo, 0 g fiber, 1 g pro. Daily Values: 2% vit. A, 2% vit. C, 2% calcium, 1% iron.*

SMOKED SALMON DIP

PREP 10 min. **STAND** 15 min.

INGREDIENTS

4 oz. smoked salmon, skin and bones removed, or lox-style salmon
⅓ cup finely chopped red onion
1 to 2 Tbsp. prepared horseradish
1 8-oz. carton sour cream or whipped cream cheese
  Salt and ground black pepper
  Snipped fresh chives, cucumber slice
  Assorted vegetable dippers

PREPARATION

1. In bowl finely flake salmon; add onion, horseradish, and sour cream. Season with salt and pepper. Let stand at least 15 minutes or refrigerate up to 24 hours.
2. Stir before serving. Top with chives and cucumber. Serve with dippers. **Makes 1⅔ cups.**

EACH SERVING (2 TBSP. DIP) *46 cal, 4 g fat (2 g sat. fat), 9 mg chol, 117 mg sodium, 1 g carbo, 0 g fiber, 2 g pro. Daily Values: 3% vit. A, 1% vit. C, 2% calcium, 1% iron.*

MALTED MOUSSE CAKE

Amaretti are crisp macaroon cookies, frequently sold in tins labeled Amaretti di Saronna. They contribute to the crisp crust for this light-as-air and richly satisfying dessert—a cross between panna cotta and tiramisu. Make the cake a day before serving and store, lightly covered, in the refrigerator. To serve, top with pastel candy eggs. Recipe pictured on page 50.

PREP 45 min. **BAKE** 10 min. **COOL** 45 min.
CHILL 3 hr. **OVEN** 350°F

INGREDIENTS

6 oz. amaretti (about 3 cups) or shortbread cookies
½ cup hazelnuts
5 Tbsp. butter, melted
2 oz. white chocolate
1¼ cups whipping cream
1 envelope unflavored gelatin
⅓ cup milk
2 8-oz. pkg. cream cheese, softened
⅓ cup sugar
3 Tbsp. plain malted milk powder
¼ tsp. salt
6 to 8 pastel malted milk candy eggs or malted milk balls

PREPARATION

1. Preheat oven to 350°F. For crust, in food processor bowl combine amaretti and nuts; process to fine crumbs. Add butter; process just until combined. Pat in bottom of 9-inch springform pan. Bake 10 minutes or until golden brown. Completely cool in pan on rack about 45 minutes.
2. Meanwhile, in small saucepan melt white chocolate with ¼ cup of the whipping cream; set aside.
3. In small microwave-safe bowl sprinkle gelatin over milk; let stand until gelatin is softened, about 3 minutes. Microcook gelatin mixture, uncovered, on 50% power 15 seconds, just until gelatin is completely dissolved. Stir gelatin mixture into white chocolate mixture. Refrigerate, stirring often, until chocolate-gelatin mixture is chilled and begins to thicken.
4. Meanwhile, in extra-large mixing bowl beat cream cheese, sugar, malted milk powder, and salt on medium until light and fluffy. Gradually add gelatin mixture; beat just until combined. In medium mixing bowl beat remaining 1 cup whipping cream until stiff peaks form. Fold whipped cream into cream cheese mixture until blended. Spoon into cooled crust. Refrigerate until firm, at least 3 hours or up to 8 hours.
5. To serve, remove sides of pan; place on serving plate. Top with malted milk eggs; slice cake. **Makes 12 to 16 servings.**

EACH SERVING *354 cal, 26 g fat (14 g sat. fat), 67 mg chol, 205 mg sodium, 26 g carbo, 1 g fiber, 5 g pro. Daily Values: 16% vit. A, 6% calcium, 3% iron.*

Hop to the Table

Rouse appetites for spring-fresh meals brightened with carrots, pineapple, greens, and herbs.

READY IN 20 MINUTES!

BY **PEG SMITH** PHOTOS **ANDY LYONS** RECIPES AND FOOD STYLING **JILL LUST**

LOW FAT **FAST!**

HERB-GARLIC BEEF ROAST

START TO FINISH 20 min.

INGREDIENTS

1 17-oz. pkg. refrigerated cooked beef roast au jus
1 lb. small round red potatoes
3 medium carrots
1 Tbsp. cooking oil
   Freshly ground black pepper
3 Tbsp. chopped fresh Italian (flat-leaf) parsley
3 to 6 cloves garlic, minced
1 Tbsp. finely shredded lemon peel

PREPARATION

1. In large skillet cook beef roast, covered, over medium heat for 10 minutes. Uncover; simmer 5 minutes more until juices are slightly reduced. Meanwhile, quarter potatoes. Peel and diagonally slice carrots in ³/₄-inch pieces. Place vegetables in microwave-safe dish. Drizzle with cooking oil and sprinkle with pepper; toss to coat. Tightly cover with lid or plastic wrap. Microcook on high (100% power) for 10 minutes or until tender.
2. For herb-garlic mixture, in small bowl combine parsley, garlic, and lemon peel. To serve, stir vegetables into skillet with beef and juices. Divide among serving dishes. Sprinkle with herb-garlic mixture. **Makes 4 servings.**

EACH SERVING *311 cal, 12 g fat (5 g sat. fat), 64 mg chol, 465 mg sodium, 28 g carbo, 4 g fiber, 25 g pro. Daily Values: 159% vit. A, 52% vit. C, 4% calcium, 18% iron.*

FAST!

POLENTA-SAUSAGE BOWL

START TO FINISH 20 min.

INGREDIENTS

1 16-oz. tube refrigerated polenta with sun-dried tomatoes
2 medium zucchini, halved lengthwise
1 Tbsp. cooking oil
1 lb. bulk Italian sausage
1 8-oz. pkg. sliced mushrooms
1 cup grape tomatoes
1 tsp. dried Italian seasoning, crushed
   Finely shredded Parmesan cheese

PREPARATION

1. Preheat broiler. Lightly grease baking sheet. Cut polenta in 12 slices. Place polenta and zucchini on baking sheet. Brush with oil; sprinkle with *salt* and *ground black pepper*. Broil 4 to 5 inches from heat 8 to 10 minutes until polenta is lightly browned and zucchini is crisp-tender; turning once.
2. Meanwhile in large skillet cook and break up sausage over medium heat until sausage begins to brown. Drain off fat. Add mushrooms, tomatoes, and seasoning to skillet; cook 5 minutes until meat is no longer pink. Slice zucchini crosswise. Spoon sausage mixture and zucchini over polenta. Sprinkle with cheese. **Makes 4 servings.**

EACH SERVING *547 cal, 40 g fat (13 g sat. fat), 86 mg chol, 1,340 mg sodium, 26 g carbo, 3 g fiber, 23 g pro. Daily Values: 18% vit. A, 55% vit. C, 5% calcium, 15% iron.*

POLENTA-SAUSAGE BOWL

SPINACH SALAD WITH
ANCHO CHILE PEPPER CHOPS

FAST!

SPINACH SALAD WITH ANCHO CHILE PEPPER CHOPS

START TO FINISH 20 min.
INGREDIENTS

1 ¼ Tbsp. ground ancho chile pepper
4   boneless pork sirloin chops, ½-inch cuts (about 1½ lb.)
4   slices bacon, chopped
½   cup thinly sliced red onion
⅓   cup cider vinegar
1   Tbsp. sugar
1   5- to 6-oz. pkg. fresh baby spinach

PREPARATION

1. Preheat extra-large skillet over medium-high heat. Meanwhile, in bowl combine *1 tablespoon* ancho chile pepper and ½ teaspoon each *salt* and *ground black pepper*. Rub into chops. Add chops and bacon to hot skillet; reduce heat to medium. Cook 6 to 8 minutes, turning chops and stirring bacon, until chops are pink in center (160°F) and bacon is crisp. Remove and set aside.
2. For dressing, cook onion in hot skillet for 1 minute. Remove from heat; stir in vinegar, sugar, and remaining ¼ teaspoon ancho chile pepper. Slice pork; divide pork and spinach among 4 plates. Drizzle dressing; sprinkle bacon. **Makes 4 servings.**

EACH SERVING *429 cal, 25 g fat (8 g sat. fat), 133 mg chol, 745 mg sodium, 8 g carbo, 2 g fiber, 42 g pro. Daily Values: 80% vit. A, 23% vit. C, 7% calcium, 17% iron.*

CHICKEN-PINEAPPLE FAJITAS

FAST! **LOW FAT**

CHICKEN-PINEAPPLE FAJITAS

START TO FINISH 20 min.
INGREDIENTS

8   6-inch flour tortillas
4   1-inch slices peeled fresh pineapple (about half)
1   lb. skinless, boneless chicken breast halves
2   small red or orange sweet peppers, seeded, cut in strips
2   tsp. Jamaican jerk seasoning
⅛   tsp. ground black pepper
1   Tbsp. cooking oil
     Fresh cilantro and lime wedges

PREPARATION

1. Preheat oven to 350°F. Wrap tortillas in foil and heat in oven. Meanwhile, coat 12-inch nonstick skillet with *nonstick cooking spray*; heat over medium-high. Add pineapple slices; cook 4 to 6 minutes until browned, turning once. Remove.
2. Cut chicken in strips; toss with sweet peppers strips, jerk seasoning, and black pepper. Heat oil in skillet; add chicken and pepper strips. Cook and stir over medium-high heat 4 to 6 minutes, until chicken is no longer pink. Core and chop pineapple. Serve with chicken, tortillas, cilantro, and lime. **Makes 4 servings.**

EACH SERVING *393 cal, 10 g fat (2 g sat. fat), 66 mg chol, 633 mg sodium, 43 g carbo, 4 g fiber, 32 g pro. Daily Values: 26% vit. A, 122% vit. C, 11% calcium, 18% iron.*

PARMESAN-CRUSTED FISH

START TO FINISH 20 min.

INGREDIENTS

4   skinless cod fillets (1½ lb.)
⅓   cup panko (Japanese-style) bread crumbs
¼   cup finely shredded Parmesan cheese
1   10-oz. pkg. julienned carrots (3 cups)
1   Tbsp. butter
¾   tsp. ground ginger
     Mixed fresh salad greens

PREPARATION

1. Preheat oven to 450°F. Lightly coat a baking sheet with *nonstick cooking spray*. Rinse and pat fish dry; place on baking sheet. Season with *salt* and *ground black pepper*. In small bowl stir together crumbs and cheese; sprinkle on fish. Bake, uncovered, 4 to 6 minutes for each ½-inch thickness of fish, until crumbs are golden and fish flakes easily when tested with a fork.

2. Meanwhile, in large skillet bring ½ cup *water* to boiling; add carrots. Reduce heat. Cook, covered, 5 minutes. Uncover; cook 2 minutes more. Add butter and ginger; toss. Serve fish and carrots with greens. **Makes 4 servings.**

EACH SERVING *233 cal, 6 g fat (3 g sat. fat), 84 mg chol, 407 mg sodium, 11 g carbo, 2 g fiber, 34 g pro. Daily Values: 242% vit. A, 9% vit. C, 12% calcium, 5% iron.*

Spring Baking

Using fresh ingredients is the surest route to the most delectable cakes and breads.

BY **PEG SMITH** PHOTOS **ANDY LYONS** FOOD STYLING **JILL LUST** RECIPES **DAVID BONOM**

KID FRIENDLY

FRESH ROSEMARY AND LEMON CUPCAKES

If you have more batter than fits one muffin pan, refrigerate remaining batter while first batch is baking. After pans cool, bake remaining batter. It's OK to bake a pan with unfilled muffin cups as long as the empty cups are not greased or lined with paper. Use this recipe for mini and jumbo cupcakes.

PREP 30 min. **BAKE** 22 min. **COOL** 5 min.
OVEN 350°F

INGREDIENTS

½ cup butter, softened
2 eggs
1¾ cups cake flour
2 tsp. finely snipped fresh rosemary
1½ tsp. baking powder
½ tsp. salt
1 cup granulated sugar
1½ tsp. lemon extract
½ tsp. vanilla
⅔ cup milk
2 tsp. finely shredded lemon peel
3 Tbsp. lemon juice
1 recipe Lemon Glaze

PREPARATION

1. Let butter and eggs stand at room temperature 30 minutes. Line fifteen 2½-inch muffin cups with paper bake cups; set aside. In medium bowl combine cake flour, rosemary, baking powder, and salt; set aside.

2. Preheat oven to 350°F. In large mixing bowl beat butter on medium-high 30 seconds. Add granulated sugar, lemon extract, and vanilla. Beat on medium-high 2 minutes until light and fluffy, scraping bowl.

3. Add eggs, 1 at a time, beating well after each addition. Alternately add flour mixture and milk to butter mixture; beat on low after each just until combined. Stir in lemon peel and lemon juice.

4. Spoon batter in prepared cups to three-fourths full. Bake 22 to 25 minutes until a wooden pick inserted in centers comes out clean. (Bake 36 mini cakes 15 to 18 minutes; 6 jumbo cakes 25 to 30 minutes.) Cool in muffin cups on rack 5 minutes. Remove from pan; cool completely.

5. Spoon Lemon Glaze on cupcakes. Let stand 10 minutes. **Makes 15 (2½-inch) cupcakes.**

Lemon Glaze In small bowl combine 1 cup *powdered sugar* and enough *lemon juice* (5 to 5½ teaspoons) for spreading consistency. Stir in finely shredded *lemon peel*.

EACH 2½-INCH CUPCAKE *213 cal, 7 g fat (4 g sat. fat), 45 mg chol, 159 mg sodium, 35 g carbo, 0 g fiber, 3 g pro. Daily Values: 5% vit. A, 4% vit. C, 3% calcium, 7% iron.*

**CARROT-PINEAPPLE
UPSIDE-DOWN CAKE**

CARROT-PINEAPPLE UPSIDE-DOWN CAKE

Find fresh pineapple—peeled, cored, sliced, and packed in its own juice—in the produce section of grocery stores.

PREP 30 min. **BAKE** 45 min. **COOL** 35 min. **OVEN** 350°F

INGREDIENTS

⅓	cup packed brown sugar
2	Tbsp. butter
1	Tbsp. water
6	to 8¼-inch-thick slices fresh pineapple, cored and halved
2	cups all-purpose flour
1	Tbsp. baking powder
½	tsp. salt
¼	tsp. ground nutmeg
½	cup butter, softened
1	cup granulated sugar
2	eggs
1	tsp. vanilla
¾	cup milk
3	carrots, finely shredded (1½ cups)

PREPARATION

1. Preheat oven to 350°F. Lightly coat a 9×9×2-inch baking pan with *nonstick cooking spray;* set aside.

2. In small saucepan combine brown sugar, the 2 tablespoons butter, and the water. Cook and stir over medium heat until mixture comes to boiling and is smooth. Pour sugar mixture in prepared pan; tilt to evenly coat bottom. Arrange pineapple slices over top of mixture.

3. In medium bowl combine flour, baking powder, salt, and nutmeg; set aside.

4. In large mixing bowl beat ½ cup butter on medium-high 30 seconds. Gradually add granulated sugar, beat until combined; beat 2 minutes more. Add eggs, 1 at a time, beating well after each addition. Beat in vanilla. Alternately add flour mixture and milk; beat on low after each just until combined. Stir in carrot. Spread batter over pineapple.

5. Bake 45 minutes or until golden and wooden pick inserted in center comes out clean. Cool in pan on rack 5 minutes. Invert on platter. Cool 30 minutes. **Makes 9 servings.**

EACH SERVING *374 cal, 15 g fat (9 g sat. fat), 82 mg chol, 341 mg sodium, 56 g carbo, 2 g fiber, 5 g pro. Daily Values: 78% vit. A, 12% vit. C, 8% calcium, 9% iron.*

ORANGE-RAISIN BRUNCH BREAD

This yeast bread, or brioche (BREE-ohsh), has a lightly sweet and rich flavor. Braided and shaped, it encircles fruit or a container of spread for serving.

PREP 30 min. **RISE** 1½ hr. 40 min.
REST 5 min. **BAKE** 25 min. **OVEN** 350°F

INGREDIENTS

2 ¾ to 3 ¼ cups all-purpose flour
1   pkg. active dry yeast
½   cup butter
¼   cup milk
¼   cup water
2   Tbsp. sugar
½   tsp. salt
2   eggs
1   Tbsp. finely shredded orange peel
¾   cup golden raisins
    Milk
    Apricot jam

PREPARATION

1. In large mixing bowl combine 1½ cups of the flour and yeast; set aside.
2. In medium saucepan heat butter, the ¼ cup milk, water, sugar, and salt over medium heat until very warm (120°F to 130°F) and butter is almost melted. Add butter mixture, eggs, and orange peel to flour mixture. Beat on low until combined; beat on high 3 minutes. With wooden spoon stir in raisins and as much remaining flour as you can.

3. Turn out dough on lightly floured surface. Knead in enough remaining flour for moderately soft dough that is smooth and elastic (3 to 5 minutes). Place in greased bowl; turn to grease surface. Cover; let rise in warm place 1 hour or until nearly double in size.
4. Punch dough down; turn onto work surface. Cover; let rest 5 minutes. Equally divide dough into three portions; roll each portion into a 26-inch length. Lay side by side 1 inch apart; braid. Pinch each end of braid together. Transfer to large greased baking sheet. Shape in ring and pinch both ends together. Cover with plastic wrap; let rise 40 minutes; dough will rise slightly.
5. Meanwhile, preheat oven to 350°F. Lightly brush bread ring with milk. Place a foil ball or oven-safe glass measure or jar in center to preserve shape. Bake 25 to 30 minutes or until golden and bread sounds hollow when tapped. Remove from oven; cool. Place on platter; cut into slices. Serve with apricot jam. **Makes 8 to 10 servings.**

EACH SERVING *343 cal, 13 g fat (8 g sat. fat), 84 mg chol, 252 mg sodium, 49 g carbo, 2 g fiber, 4 g pro. Daily Values: 9% vit. A, 3% vit. C, 4% calcium, 15% iron.*

BRAIDING DOUGH If it's been a while since you've braided, practice a bit first, perhaps with some rope. Then with three lengths of dough side by side and leaving short tails at each end, alternately cross one outer length between the two adjacent lengths.

ORANGE-RAISIN BRUNCH BREAD

Easy Irish Dinner

Rich flavors and a fast one-skillet meal update the traditional meat-and-potatoes St. Patrick's Day dinner.

CELEBRATE *with*
Pam Anderson

ST. PAT'S BEEF AND VEGGIES
Another time, try the salmon version, below.

PREP 25 min. **COOK** 35 min. **OVEN** 170°F

INGREDIENTS

1/2	cup sour cream
2	Tbsp. coarse-grain brown mustard
1 1/2	lb. boneless beef rib-eye steak, 1 1/4 to 1 1/2 inch thick
2	Tbsp. cooking oil
4	medium carrots, peeled
1	large red onion, peeled, cut in wedges
32	oz. reduced-sodium chicken broth
1	lb. new potatoes, halve if large
1	lb. packaged fresh spinach

PREPARATION

1. Stir together sour cream and mustard; cover and refrigerate. Heat oven to 170°F. Heat 12-inch skillet over medium-high. Coat beef with *1 tablespoon* of the oil; season with *salt, ground black pepper,* and 1 teaspoon *sugar.* Brown in hot skillet 4 minutes, turning once. Transfer to platter; set aside.

2. Add remaining oil, carrots, and onion to skillet. Cook and stir 5 minutes until browned. Add broth and potatoes; bring to boiling. Reduce heat; cook, covered, 15 minutes until tender. Return beef to skillet. Simmer, covered, 8 minutes for medium (10 minutes for medium-well).

3. Reserving broth in skillet, transfer vegetables and beef to oven-safe platter; keep warm in oven. Simmer broth; add spinach. Cook and toss with tongs 3 to 4 minutes.

4. To serve, ladle broth in bowls; reserve some to drizzle over meat and vegetables. Divide beef and vegetables among plates. Serve with mustard sauce. **Makes 4 servings.**

EACH SERVING *557 cal, 27 g fat (10 g sat. fat), 111 mg chol, 1,269 mg sodium, 35 g carbo, 7 g fiber, 44 g pro. Daily Values: 421% vit. A, 80% vit. C, 20% calcium, 44% iron.*

Salmon Dinner Use four 6-ounce *salmon fillets;* substitute 16 ounce *clam juice* for 2 cups chicken broth. Simmer vegetables 15 minutes. Add salmon; simmer 5 to 7 minutes. Stir in 1 tablespoon lemon juice. Pass lemon wedges.

PHOTO **ANDY LYONS**
PRODUCED BY **JILL LUST**

Although Diane Okerson, of Yorba Linda, California, had never entered a recipe contest before, her Deviled Egg Salad beat entries from thousands of other cooks to win the 2007 Grand Prize in our Prize Tested Recipe Contest for cash and prizes worth up to $10,000.

GRAND PRIZE WINNER

Beginner's Luck

FAST!

DEVILED EGG SALAD

START TO FINISH 30 min.

INGREDIENTS

7	hard-cooked eggs*
3	Tbsp. salad dressing or mayonnaise
1	Tbsp. chopped fresh dill
1	clove garlic, minced
5	dashes bottled hot pepper sauce
⅛	tsp. salt
6	cups torn Boston or Bibb lettuce
2	cups grape or cherry tomatoes, halved if desired
1	medium red sweet pepper, chopped
4	slices bacon, crisp-cooked, drained, and crumbled
3	green onions, sliced
1	recipe Dill Vinaigrette

PREPARATION

1. Remove shells and halve hard-cooked eggs lengthwise; remove yolks. Set aside whites. Place yolks in a small bowl; mash with a fork. Add salad dressing, dill, garlic, hot pepper sauce, and salt. Spoon yolk mixture into egg white halves. Set aside.

2. On a large serving platter arrange lettuce, tomatoes, sweet pepper, bacon, and green onion. Arrange stuffed eggs on greens, vegetables, and bacon. Drizzle with Dill Vinaigrette.

Makes 6 to 8 servings.

Dill Vinaigrette In a screw-top jar combine ⅓ cup *olive oil*; 2 tablespoons *tarragon vinegar*; 1 tablespoon chopped *fresh dill*; 2 teaspoons *Dijon-style mustard*; 1 clove *garlic*, minced; ¼ teaspoon *salt*; and ¼ teaspoon bottled *hot pepper sauce*. Cover and shake well.

EACH SERVING *269 cal, 22 g total fat (4 g sat. fat), 254 mg chol, 427 mg sodium, 8 g carbo, 2 g fiber, 11 g pro. Daily Values: 67% vit. A, 82% vit. C, 7% calcium, 11% iron.*

*TEST KITCHEN TIP To hard-cook eggs, place in single layer (do not stack) in large saucepan. Add cold water to cover eggs by at least 1 inch. Bring water to rapid boiling over high heat. Remove from heat, cover; let stand 15 minutes (18 minutes for extra-large); drain. Run cold water over eggs or place them in ice water until cool enough to handle; drain. To peel, gently tap egg on countertop, then roll between the palms of your hands. Peel off shell, beginning at large end.

APRIL

DRUMSTICKS WITH PEAS AND RICE
page 81

THIS MONTH SEVEN FAVORITE COOKS PUT A SPRING-FRESH SPIN ON CHICKEN, SUNNY SCRAMBLED EGGS ARE DRESSED 10 WAYS, QUICK ONE-DISH MEALS GET A MARKET MAKEOVER, AND GUACAMOLE GETS MADE TO ORDER.

Project Chicken

**HERBED LAMB
STEAK SALADS**
page 84

SLOW COOKER RISOTTO
page 87

PUFFY SHORTCAKES WITH MERINGUE
page 91

project chicken

The challenge: Create easy, delicious dishes with one of America's favorite ingredients. **The team:** our favorite cooks, *from left,* Susan Sugarman, Melanie Barnard, Rocco DiSpirito, Jackie Newgent, Scott Peacock, Pam Anderson, and David Bonom. **The results:** braised, grilled, sauteed, and awesome.

BY **RICHARD SWEARINGER** FOOD PHOTOS **ANDY LYONS** FOOD STYLING **JILL LUST** PROP STYLING **KAREN JOHNSON**
PORTRAIT PHOTOS **MATTHEW RODGERS** PRODUCED BY **NANCY WALL HOPKINS**

<A QUICK SAUTE FOLLOWED BY A BRIEF BRAISING KEEPS CHICKEN BREASTS MOIST—THE GARLIC, FRESH LEMON, AND PARSLEY STAY BRIGHT TOO.
—**MELANIE BARNARD,** COOKBOOK AUTHOR

DRUMSTICKS WITH PEAS AND RICE
page 81

∧ SLOW SIMMERING MAKES DRUMSTICKS EXTRA TENDER; A LIGHT ONION GRAVY MAKES THEM IRRESISTIBLE.
—**SCOTT PEACOCK,** CHEF AND SOUTHERN FOOD GURU

MY FORTE IS HEALTHFUL, >
MY FOCUS IS FAST.
PRECOOKED CHICKEN
BREAST STRIPS
LET ME HAVE BOTH—
A 400-CALORIE DISH
READY IN 20 MINUTES.

—JACKIE NEWGENT,
NUTRITIONIST

**SESAME CHICKEN
AND NOODLES**

**CHICKEN THIGHS
WITH ARTICHOKES**

FAST! **LOW FAT**

JACKIE NEWGENT'S
SESAME CHICKEN AND NOODLES

Sesame oil, which is extracted from sesame seeds, adds a nutty taste to this dish. Find it in the Asian section of the supermarket or substitute canola oil and add 2 tablespoons of toasted sesame seeds at serving time.

START TO FINISH 20 min.

INGREDIENTS

⅓	cup rice vinegar
⅓	cup thinly sliced green onion
2	Tbsp. honey
1	Tbsp. reduced-sodium soy sauce
1	Tbsp. grated fresh ginger
2	tsp. Asian garlic-chili sauce
2	6-oz. pkg. refrigerated grilled chicken breast strips
12	oz. dried udon noodles or whole wheat spaghetti
3	Tbsp. toasted sesame oil
2	medium yellow, red, and/or orange sweet peppers, cut in bite-size strips
	Fresh cilantro

PREPARATION

1. In medium bowl stir together vinegar, green onion, honey, soy sauce, ginger, and garlic-chili sauce. Add chicken; stir to coat. Set aside to allow flavors to meld.
2. Meanwhile, in large saucepan cook noodles in boiling water about 8 minutes until just tender. Drain noodles well and return to saucepan. Drizzle with oil and toss to coat. Add chicken mixture and toss to combine.
3. Transfer to bowls. Top each with pepper strips and cilantro.
Makes 6 servings.

EACH SERVING *391 cal, 11 g total fat (2 g sat. fat), 37 mg chol, 718 mg sodium, 51 g carbo, 4 g fiber, 21 g pro. Daily Values: 6% vit. A, 195% vit. C, 4% calcium, 16% iron.*

PAM ANDERSON'S
CHICKEN THIGHS WITH ARTICHOKES

Fuss-free boneless, skinless chicken thighs are readily available in most supermarkets at a lower cost than chicken breasts.

START TO FINISH 40 min.

INGREDIENTS

2	tsp. plus 1 Tbsp. olive oil
2	oz. prosciutto, cut in thin strips
1½	lb. boneless, skinless chicken thighs
1	9-oz. pkg. frozen artichoke hearts, thawed and drained
1	6-oz. pkg. cremini mushrooms, sliced
2	cloves garlic, minced
1	Tbsp. snipped fresh tarragon
2	Tbsp. all-purpose flour
1	14-oz. can reduced-sodium chicken broth
1	Tbsp. white balsamic vinegar
	Fresh tarragon sprigs (optional)

PREPARATION

1. In skillet cook prosciutto in the *2 teaspoons* hot oil over medium-high heat 2 minutes or until crisp. Remove. Sprinkle chicken with *salt* and *ground black pepper*. Cook in same skillet 8 to 10 minutes or until browned, turning once. Transfer to bowl; set aside.
2. Add remaining olive oil and artichokes to skillet. Cook and stir 3 minutes until golden brown. Transfer to bowl with chicken. Add mushrooms to skillet. Cook 3 minutes, stirring up browned bits, until golden. Stir in garlic and tarragon; cook 1 minute.
3. In second bowl whisk together flour, broth, and vinegar. Remove skillet from heat. Add broth mixture. Add chicken and artichokes. Return to heat. Bring to boiling; reduce heat. Simmer, uncovered, until thickened. Top with prosciutto and tarragon sprigs.
Makes 4 to 6 servings.

EACH SERVING *346 cal, 14 g total fat (3 g sat. fat), 151 mg chol, 955 mg sodium, 11 g carbo, 4 g fiber, 42 g pro. Daily Values: 5% vit. A, 12% vit. C, 6% calcium, 15% iron.*

< WHAT OTHER CUT COULD PRODUCE A COMPANY-READY MEAL WITH JUST A FEW MINUTES OF STEWING? THAT'S WHY I LOVE THIGHS.
—PAM ANDERSON,
BETTER HOMES AND GARDENS FOOD COLUMNIST

FAST! **LOW FAT**

MELANIE BARNARD'S
CHICKEN BREASTS WITH HERBS

The herb mixture used in this recipe is a variation on the traditional Italian condiment gremolata. Recipe pictured on page 72.

PREP 15 min. **COOK** 14 min.

INGREDIENTS
⅓	cup chopped fresh Italian (flat-leaf) parsley
1	Tbsp. chopped fresh oregano
1	Tbsp. finely shredded lemon peel
1	Tbsp. finely chopped garlic (3 cloves)
3	Tbsp. butter
4	skinless, boneless chicken breast halves
¼	cup chicken broth

PREPARATION
1. In small bowl stir together parsley, oregano, lemon peel, and garlic. Set aside. Season chicken with *salt* and *ground black pepper*.
2. In 10-inch skillet over medium-high heat cook chicken in butter 6 minutes or until browned, turning once. Transfer to plate. Remove skillet from heat; stir in half of the herb mixture. Return to heat. Add broth; bring to boiling, stirring to scrape up browned bits. Return chicken to skillet; reduce heat. Simmer, covered, 8 minutes or until chicken is no longer pink.
3. Serve with pan sauce; sprinkle with remaining herb mixture.
Makes 4 servings.

EACH SERVING *275 cal, 11 g total fat (6 g sat. fat), 122 mg chol, 356 mg sodium, 2 g carbo, 40 g pro. Daily Values: 15% vit. A, 21% vit. C, 4% calcium, 9% iron.*

DAVID BONOM'S
CHICKEN WITH ASPARAGUS AND PEAS

Chicken thighs and legs are great for grilling. The heat of the grill sears the outside, keeping the meat moist and tender.

PREP 25 min. **GRILL** 35 min.

INGREDIENTS
¼	cup ketchup
3	Tbsp. hoisin sauce
4	whole chicken legs, about 2½ lb.
4	slices bacon
2	bunches small carrots with tops, trimmed, or 12 oz. baby carrots
¾	lb. sugar snap peas
8	oz. asparagus, trimmed and cut in 2-inch lengths
1	Tbsp. small fresh mint leaves

PREPARATION
1. For sauce, in bowl stir together ketchup and hoisin sauce; set aside.
2. Sprinkle chicken with ¼ teaspoon each *salt* and *ground black pepper*. For charcoal grill, place chicken on rack, bone sides up, directly over medium coals. Grill, uncovered, 35 to 45 minutes or until no longer pink (180°F), turning once halfway through and brushing with sauce last 10 minutes. (For gas grill, preheat grill. Reduce heat to medium. Place chicken on rack over heat. Cover; grill as above.)
3. Meanwhile, for vegetables, in 12-inch skillet cook bacon over medium-low heat until crisp. Drain on paper towels, reserving drippings in skillet. Add carrots to drippings; cook and stir 5 minutes. Add peas and asparagus; cook and stir 6 to 8 minutes or until vegetables are tender. Remove from heat. Crumble bacon. Stir in mint and bacon. Serve with chicken. **Makes 4 servings.**

EACH SERVING *674 cal, 43 g fat (13 g sat. fat), 198 mg chol, 1,056 mg sodium, 25 g carbo, 5 g fiber, 46 g pro. Daily Values: 299% vit. A, 32% vit. C, 11% calcium, 21% iron.*

CHICKEN WITH
ASPARAGUS AND PEAS

THE WHOLE LEG IS DELICIOUS WHEN GRILLED,
SO I KEPT THE RECIPE SIMPLE WITH A
TWO-INGREDIENT GLAZE.
—**DAVID BONOM,** RECIPE DEVELOPER

TO SAVE TIME, BUY CHICKEN CUTLETS, THEN PULL
TOGETHER AN EASY SALSA WHILE THE CHICKEN GRILLS.
—**ROCCO DISPIRITO,** TV CHEF AND COOKBOOK AUTHOR

FAST!

ROCCO DISPIRITO'S
CHICKEN WITH LIME AND AVOCADO SALSA

PREP 20 min. **COOK** 4 min.

INGREDIENTS
4   chicken cutlets
3   Tbsp. extra virgin olive oil
3   large avocados, halved, pitted, peeled, and chopped
1   large tomato, chopped
1   medium red onion, cut in thin strips
1   fresh jalapeño pepper, seeded and sliced (see Note, page 101)
3   Tbsp. lime juice
¼   cup packed fresh cilantro leaves
     Lime wedges

PREPARATION
1. Preheat grill pan over high heat. Coat chicken with *2 tablespoons* olive oil; sprinkle generously with *salt* and *ground black pepper*. Add to grill pan; cook 2 to 3 minutes each side or until no pink remains.
2. Meanwhile, in large bowl combine avocados, tomato, onion, jalapeño, lime juice, and remaining 1 tablespoon olive oil. Season to taste with *salt* and *pepper*. Serve with chicken. Garnish with cilantro and lime wedges. **Makes 4 servings.**

EACH SERVING *496 cal, 33 g fat (5 g sat. fat), 82 mg chol, 254 mg sodium, 18 g carbo, 11 g fiber, 36 g pro. Daily Values: 19% vit. A, 55% vit. C, 5% calcium, 13% iron.*

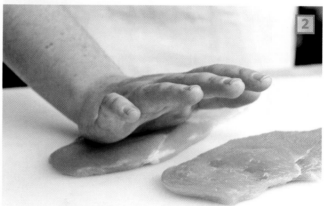

MAKING CHICKEN CUTLETS
If chicken cutlets are unavailable, make your own using boneless, skinless chicken breasts. Steady the meat by placing your hand on top of the thickest part of the chicken breast. Cut in half horizontally, being sure to hold your fingers up and away from the blade. Once you have cut through a few inches of the breast, pull the sliced part back to open and cut down the middle, forming two pieces. If needed, gently flatten the cutlet with the heel of your hand until it is about a half inch thick.

CHICKEN WITH
SUMMER SQUASH

PREPARED ROTISSERIE CHICKEN IS A SHORTCUT
TO HOMEMADE STYLE—JUST QUARTER THE CHICKEN
AND SERVE IT ON A BED OF SAUTEED VEGETABLES.
—**SUSAN SUGARMAN,** FOOD STYLIST

FAST!

SUSAN SUGARMAN'S
CHICKEN WITH SUMMER SQUASH

Arugula is a peppery salad green; baby spinach leaves also work well in this recipe.

START TO FINISH 25 min.

INGREDIENTS

1	2¼-lb. purchased roasted chicken
3	Tbsp. olive oil
4	small or 2 medium yellow summer squash, cut in quarters lengthwise
2	cloves garlic, thinly sliced
1	cup yellow grape or cherry tomatoes
	Small fresh arugula leaves

PREPARATION

1. Remove string from chicken, if present, and quarter chicken. Heat oil in 12-inch skillet over medium-high heat. Cook chicken quarters, skin sides down, 3 to 4 minutes or until brown. Remove from skillet. Add squash, garlic, and ¼ teaspoon each *salt* and *ground black pepper* to drippings in skillet. Cook 2 minutes, stirring occasionally.

2. Return chicken to skillet, skin side up. Cook, covered, over medium heat about 10 minutes or until chicken is heated through and squash is tender, adding tomatoes the last 2 minutes of cooking. Transfer chicken and squash mixture to platter and sprinkle with arugula.
Makes 4 servings.

EACH SERVING *385 cal, 21 g total fat (4 g sat. fat), 125 mg chol, 277 mg sodium, 6 g carbo, 2 g fiber, 42 g pro. Daily Values: 6% vit. A, 22% vit. C, 6% calcium, 14% iron.*

KID FRIENDLY

SCOTT PEACOCK'S
DRUMSTICKS WITH PEAS AND RICE

Recipe pictured on page 73.

PREP 30 min. **COOK** 1 hr. 10 min.

INGREDIENTS

8	chicken drumsticks
½	tsp. kosher salt or salt
3	Tbsp. butter
1	Tbsp. olive or cooking oil
2	medium onions, chopped
1	shallot, finely chopped
2	cloves garlic, minced
1	bay leaf
¾	tsp. dried thyme, crushed
¼	tsp. freshly ground black pepper
½	cup dry white wine or chicken broth
1	14-oz. can reduced-sodium chicken broth
	Fresh mint leaves
1	recipe Peas and Rice

PREPARATION

1. Sprinkle chicken with salt. In 12-inch skillet cook chicken in hot butter and oil over medium-high heat for 10 minutes, turning often. Using tongs, remove chicken, keeping butter and oil in skillet. Set chicken aside.

2. Add onion, shallot, garlic, and bay leaf to skillet. Cook 5 minutes or until onion is tender, stirring to scrape up browned bits.

3. Return chicken to pan. Sprinkle with thyme and pepper. Add wine and broth. Bring to boiling; reduce heat. Simmer, covered, 45 to 60 minutes or until tender, spooning juices over chicken. Remove chicken. Cover; keep warm. Simmer onion mixture in pan, uncovered, 10 minutes. Season with additional salt and pepper. Remove bay leaf.

4. To serve, transfer chicken to platter. Sprinkle with mint. Serve with onion mixture and Peas and Rice. **Makes 4 servings.**

Peas and Rice In saucepan cook 2 cups fresh or frozen *peas* in boiling salted water, covered, until tender (10 minutes for fresh, 3 minutes for frozen). Drain. Plunge in ice water; drain. In 12-inch skillet cook ½ cup sliced *green onion* in 3 tablespoons melted *butter* for 1 minute. Add cooked peas, ¼ cup torn *mint leaves*, ¼ teaspoon *salt*, and ⅛ teaspoon *sugar*. Cook and stir 1 minute. Stir in 3 cups cooked *rice* and 2 tablespoons *reduced-sodium chicken broth* or water; heat through.

EACH SERVING *691 cal, 34 g fat (15 g sat. fat), 164 mg chol, 874 mg sodium, 51 g carbo, 7 g fiber, 38 g pro. Daily Values: 29% vit. A, 69% vit. C, 12% calcium, 37% iron.*

READY IN 20 MINUTES!

Market-Fresh Suppers

Short on time? Beat the clock—without sacrificing variety and great taste—with these one-dish meals.

BY **PEG SMITH** PHOTOS **ANDY LYONS** RECIPES AND FOOD STYLING **JILL LUST**

SALMON AND NOODLE BOWL

START TO FINISH 20 min.

INGREDIENTS

- 1   9-oz. pkg. refrigerated fettuccine
- 2   Tbsp. olive oil
- 1   lb. skinless, boneless 1-inch-thick salmon,
       cut in 8 pieces
       Salt and ground black pepper
- 6   cups packaged fresh baby spinach
- ½   cup bottled roasted red or yellow sweet peppers
- ½   cup reduced-calorie balsamic vinaigrette
       salad dressing

PREPARATION

1. Prepare pasta according to package directions.

2. Meanwhile, brush *1 tablespoon* of the olive oil on salmon. Sprinkle with salt and pepper. Heat an extra-large skillet over medium heat; add salmon. Cook 8 to 12 minutes or until salmon flakes, turning once. Remove salmon; cover and keep warm. Add spinach, sweet peppers, and remaining oil to skillet. Cook and stir 1 to 2 minutes until spinach is wilted. Drain pasta; add to skillet. Add dressing; toss to coat. Season with salt and pepper. Divide spinach-pasta mixture among four bowls. Top with salmon. **Makes 4 servings.**

EACH SERVING *508 cal, 25 g fat (5 g sat. fat), 108 mg chol, 733 mg sodium, 39 g carbo, 3 g fiber, 31 g pro. Daily Values: 86% vit. A, 113% vit. C, 7% calcium, 18% iron.*

TURKEY BURGERS AND HOME FRIES

START TO FINISH 20 min.

INGREDIENTS

- ½   cup mayonnaise
- 2   tsp. curry powder
- 2   cups refrigerated sliced potatoes
- 1   lb. ground turkey breast
- 2   oz. feta cheese with basil and tomato, crumbled
- 4   Greek pita flatbread
       Red onion slices
       Spinach
       Feta cheese

PREPARATION

1. Heat broiler. Stir together mayonnaise and curry; set aside. In extra-large skillet heat 2 tablespoons *olive oil* over medium-high. Add potatoes; sprinkle with *salt* and *ground black pepper*. Cook 6 minutes, turn; cook 6 minutes more or until crisp.

2. Meanwhile, combine turkey, 2 tablespoons of curry-mayonnaise, feta, and ¼ teaspoon *salt*. Shape mixture into four ½-inch-thick patties. Broil 4 inches from heat 11 to 13 minutes (165°F); turn once. Spread remaining curry-mayonnaise on bread; layer patties, onion, spinach, and feta. Serve with potatoes. **Makes 4 servings.**

EACH SERVING *658 cal, 33 g fat (6 g sat. fat), 91 mg chol, 1,033 mg sodium, 51 g carbo, 3 g fiber, 38 g pro. Daily Values: 4% vit. A, 8% vit. C, 11% calcium, 20% iron.*

TURKEY BURGERS AND HOME FRIES

HERBED LAMB STEAK SALADS

START TO FINISH 20 min.

INGREDIENTS

1	lb. lamb arm steaks, ½ inch thick
1	Tbsp. olive oil
	Salt and ground black pepper
1	5-oz. pkg. mixed salad greens with herbs
⅔	cup sliced fresh radishes
1	6-oz. carton plain yogurt
1	to 2 Tbsp. snipped fresh mint
	Herbed feta cheese

PREPARATION

1. Heat grill pan over medium-high heat. Brush steaks with oil; sprinkle lightly with salt and pepper. Cook steaks for 8 to 12 minutes or until desired doneness (160°F for medium), turning once halfway through cooking. Transfer to cutting board; cover and let rest 2 minutes.

2. Meanwhile, divide salad greens and radishes among four plates. For dressing, in a bowl combine yogurt and mint; season to taste with salt and pepper.

3. Remove bone from lamb. Cut lamb in strips; place meat on greens. Sprinkle with feta; pass yogurt-mint dressing. **Makes 4 servings.**

EACH SERVING *344 cal, 26 g fat (10 g sat. fat), 82 mg chol, 258 mg sodium, 5 g carbo, 1 g fiber, 22 g pro. Daily Values: 10% vit. A, 11% vit. C, 12% calcium, 13% iron.*

HERBED LAMB STEAK SALADS

CREAMY SHRIMP AND TOMATO CHOWDER

CREAMY SHRIMP AND TOMATO CHOWDER

START TO FINISH 20 min.

INGREDIENTS

2	stalks celery, chopped (1 cup)
1	medium onion, chopped (½ cup)
1	Tbsp. olive oil
2	14.5-oz. cans diced tomatoes with basil, garlic, and oregano, undrained
8	oz. medium peeled cooked shrimp
½	cup whipping cream
½	cup water
	Ground black pepper
	Slivered fresh basil
	Focaccia wedges

PREPARATION

1. In saucepan cook celery and onion in hot oil just until tender. Stir in tomatoes; heat through. Add shrimp, whipping cream, and water. Cook over medium heat just until hot. Season to taste with pepper.

2. Ladle chowder into bowls; top with basil. Serve with focaccia wedges. **Makes 4 (1 ½-cup) servings.**

EACH SERVING *245 cal, 15 g fat (8 g sat. fat), 152 mg chol, 1,056 mg sodium, 14 g carbo, 2 g fiber, 15 g pro. Daily Values: 23% vit. A, 40% vit. C, 12% calcium, 14% iron.*

FAST!

SESAME AND GINGER CHICKEN

START TO FINISH 20 min.

INGREDIENTS

1   lb. skinless, boneless chicken breasts, cut in bite-size pieces
¼   cup bottled light Asian-style dressing with sesame and ginger
2   cups packaged julienned carrots
⅛   tsp. crushed red pepper
1   head butterhead lettuce, leaves separated
¼   cup honey-roasted peanuts, chopped
Lime wedges

PREPARATION

1. Sprinkle chicken with *salt* and *ground black pepper*. Lightly coat a large skillet with *nonstick cooking spray;* heat over medium-high heat. Add chicken; cook and stir for 3 minutes or until browned. Add *1 tablespoon* of the dressing and the carrots to skillet; cook and stir for 2 to 3 minutes more or until carrots are crisp-tender and chicken is no longer pink. Stir in red pepper.

2. Stack lettuce on plates. Top with chicken-carrot mixture. Sprinkle with chopped nuts. Serve with remaining dressing and lime wedges.

Makes 4 servings.

EACH SERVING *231 cal, 7 g fat (1 g sat. fat), 66 mg chol, 436 mg sodium, 12 g carbo, 3 g fiber, 29 g pro. Daily Values: 212% vit. A, 10% vit. C, 5% calcium, 9% iron.*

SESAME AND GINGER CHICKEN

Risotto

This flavorful side dish from Italy creates its own creamy sauce as it cooks. The technique is simple: Stir hot broth into rice—and keep on stirring. These recipes will open a world of variations.

SPINACH-PEA RISOTTO

BY **RICHARD SWEARINGER**
PHOTOS **ANDY LYONS**
FOOD STYLING **JILL LUST**
RECIPES BY **MARYELLEN KRANTZ**

SPINACH-PEA RISOTTO

This is our best basic risotto recipe. Tuck it away to use year-round with your choice of other lightly cooked seasonal vegetables.

START TO FINISH 40 min.

INGREDIENTS

2	cloves garlic, minced
2	Tbsp. olive oil
1	cup Arborio rice
½	cup thinly sliced carrot
2	14-oz. cans vegetable broth or reduced-sodium chicken broth (3½ cups)
2	cups fresh spinach leaves, coarsely chopped
1	cup frozen baby or regular peas
2	oz. Parmigiano-Reggiano cheese, shredded
⅓	cup thinly sliced green onion
¼	cup thin wedges fresh radishes
2	tsp. snipped fresh tarragon
	Parmigiano-Reggiano cheese, cut in shards

PREPARATION

1. In 3-quart saucepan cook garlic in hot oil over medium heat for 30 seconds. Add the rice. Cook about 5 minutes or until rice is golden brown, stirring frequently. Remove from heat. Stir in carrot.

2. Meanwhile, in a 1½-quart saucepan bring broth to boiling. Reduce heat and simmer.

3. Carefully stir *1 cup* of the hot broth into rice mixture. Cook, stirring frequently, over medium heat until liquid is absorbed. Then add ½ cup of the broth at a time, stirring frequently until broth is absorbed before adding more broth (about 22 minutes).

4. Stir in any remaining broth. Cook and stir just until rice is tender and creamy.

5. Stir in spinach, peas, shredded cheese, green onion, radishes, and tarragon; heat through. Top with cheese shards. Serve immediately.
Makes 6 servings.

EACH SERVING *191 cal, 7 g fat (2 g sat. fat), 7 mg chol, 723 mg sodium, 25 g carbo, 2 g fiber, 7 g pro. Daily Values: 71% vit. A, 16% vit. C, 14% calcium, 14% iron.*

SLOW COOKER RISOTTO

Find wheat berries in the supermarket's natural food aisle, health food stores, or at bobsredmill.com or kingarthurflour.com.

PREP 40 min. **COOK** 4 hr. **STAND** 15 min.

INGREDIENTS

½	cup wheat berries
1¼	lb. fresh mushrooms (cremini, button, and/or shiitake), sliced
3	14-oz. cans reduced-sodium chicken broth
1⅔	cups converted rice (no substitution)
½	cup chopped shallot
3	cloves garlic, minced
1	tsp. dried oregano, crushed
¼	tsp. *each* salt and ground black pepper
4	oz. Asiago cheese, finely shredded
3	Tbsp. butter, cut up
1	cup sliced fresh mushrooms
1	small yellow sweet pepper, chopped
	Fresh Italian (flat-leaf) parsley

PREPARATION

1. In a small saucepan combine wheat berries and 1½ cups *water*; bring to boiling. Reduce heat. Simmer, covered, 30 minutes. Drain.

2. Lightly coat inside of 4- to 5-quart slow cooker with *nonstick cooking spray*. Place wheat berries, mushrooms, broth, rice, shallots, garlic, oregano, salt and pepper in cooker. Cover; cook on low-heat setting 4 hours or until rice is tender.

3. Stir cheese and butter into rice. Turn off cooker. Let stand, covered, 15 minutes. Stir in additional broth if risotto is too dry.

4. Meanwhile, saute the 1 cup sliced mushrooms in a small amount of *olive oil;* set aside. To serve risotto, top with sweet pepper, sauteed mushrooms, and parsley.
Makes 12 to 14 side-dish servings.

EACH SERVING *212 cal, 7 g fat (4 g sat. fat), 18 mg chol, 413 mg sodium, 31 g carbo, 1 g fiber, 8 g pro. Daily Values: 4% vit. A, 35% vit. C, 10% calcium, 9% iron.*

RISOTTO BASICS
Focus on these steps:
- Lightly toast the raw rice in oil. This builds the first flavor layer and helps rice absorb liquid evenly.
- After the initial cup of broth, add additional broth only ½ cup at a time.
- Taste-test as you go and stop cooking when the rice is tender yet firm and the mixture has a creamy look.

SLOW COOKER RISOTTO

ASPARAGUS–LEEK RISOTTO

ASPARAGUS-LEEK RISOTTO

To save time, while the asparagus is roasting, cook the leeks, brown the rice, and heat the broth to simmering.

START TO FINISH 45 min. **OVEN** 450°F

INGREDIENTS

¾ lb. asparagus spears, trimmed
2 Tbsp. olive oil
1½ cups sliced leek
1 cup Arborio rice
3 cups reduced-sodium chicken broth
⅓ cup freshly grated Parmesan cheese
2 Tbsp. snipped fresh parsley
½ tsp. finely shredded lemon peel
1 Tbsp. lemon juice
¼ tsp. freshly ground coarse black pepper
Lemon slices
Lemon peel

PREPARATION

1. Place asparagus in single layer on baking sheet. Brush with *1 tablespoon* of the olive oil; lightly sprinkle *salt* and *ground black pepper*. Bake, uncovered, in 450°F oven about 10 minutes or until crisp-tender. Cool slightly. Cut *two-thirds* of the spears into 2-inch pieces; set aside all asparagus.
2. Meanwhile, in large saucepan cook leek in remaining olive oil until tender. Stir in uncooked rice. Cook and stir over medium heat about 5 minutes or until rice begins to turn golden brown.
3. In another saucepan bring broth to boiling. Reduce heat and simmer. Carefully stir *1 cup* of the hot broth into rice mixture. Cook, stirring frequently, over medium heat until liquid is absorbed. Then add ½ cup of the broth at a time, stirring frequently until broth is absorbed before adding more broth (about 22 minutes).
4. Stir in any remaining broth. Cook and stir just until rice is tender and creamy.
5. Stir in asparagus pieces, cheese, parsley, lemon peel, lemon juice, and coarse pepper. Top with asparagus spears, lemon slices, and peel. **Makes 4 servings.**

EACH SERVING *256 cal, 9 g fat (2 g sat. fat), 6 mg chol, 683 mg sodium, 36 g carbo, 3 g fiber, 10 g pro. Daily Values: 28% vit. A, 22% vit. C, 12% calcium, 27% iron.*

ROSY BEET RISOTTO

For a quicker version, substitute one 15-ounce can of beets for the roasted beets. Reserve the liquid from the canned beets to use in making the broth.

PREP 15 min. **ROAST** 1 hr. 15 min. **COOL** 30 min. **COOK** 25 min.
OVEN 350°F

INGREDIENTS

2 medium beets (about 12 oz.)
3 Tbsp. olive oil
1 medium red onion, chopped
1½ cups Arborio or short grain rice
2 Tbsp. snipped fresh basil or 1 tsp. dried basil, crushed
2 14-oz. cans reduced-sodium chicken broth
½ cup crumbled blue cheese (2 oz.)
Salt and freshly ground black pepper
Fresh basil leaves

PREPARATION

1. Preheat oven to 350°F. Place beets in center of 18-inch square of heavy foil. Drizzle with *1 tablespoon* of the olive oil. Fold together opposite edges of foil in double folds, allowing room for steam to build. Roast 1 hour and 15 minutes or until tender. Cool 30 minutes. Carefully open packet. Remove beets; gently transfer liquid to measuring cup; add water to equal ½ cup. Pour liquid in medium saucepan. Cut beets in wedges.
2. In 3-quart saucepan cook onion in remaining oil over medium heat until tender; add rice. Cook and stir 5 minutes. Stir in dried basil, if using.
3. Meanwhile, add broth to beet liquid in saucepan. Bring to boiling. Reduce heat and simmer. Carefully stir *1 cup* of the hot broth into rice mixture. Cook, stirring frequently, over medium heat until liquid is absorbed. Then add ½ cup of the broth at a time, stirring frequently until broth is absorbed before adding more broth (about 22 minutes).
4. Stir in any remaining broth. Cook and stir just until rice is tender and creamy.
5. Add beets; heat through. Remove rice from heat; stir in *half* of the cheese, snipped basil (if using), and salt and pepper to taste. Sprinkle remaining cheese and fresh basil leaves.
Makes 8 (¾-cup) side-dish servings.

EACH SERVING *185 cal, 7 g fat (2 g sat. fat), 5 mg chol, 441 mg sodium, 26 g carbo, 1 g fiber, 5 g pro. Daily Values: 2% vit. A, 5% vit. C, 5% calcium, 11% iron.*

TEST KITCHEN TIP
We call for reduced-sodium broth for two reasons: It allows people to adjust seasoning to their tastes and accommodates folks who need to cut sodium from their diets.

ROSY BEET RISOTTO

Sage Advice

Wedding showers tempt you to offer advice on married life. Offer this fanciful nibble instead.

PHOTO **HELEN NORMAN**

FAST!

SAGE BISCUITS

PREP 15 min. **BAKE** 10 min. **OVEN** 425°F

INGREDIENTS
½   cup cold whole milk
1   egg
2   cups unbleached all-purpose flour
1½   tsp. baking powder
1   tsp. salt
1   Tbsp. finely chopped fresh sage
¼   tsp. freshly ground black pepper
¾   cup (1½ sticks) chilled unsalted butter, cut in small pieces

PREPARATION
1. Preheat oven to 425°F. In small bowl whisk together milk and egg until blended; set aside. Blend flour, baking powder, salt, sage, and pepper in food processor or large bowl. Add cold butter and pulse or quickly blend with fingertips until mixture resembles coarse meal. Do not overmix. Add milk mixture and process just until moist clumps begin to form. Transfer dough to floured surface.
2. Knead dough until it holds together, about 6 turns. Roll out dough to ½-inch thickness. Using floured 2½- to 3-inch biscuit or cookie cutter, cut out biscuits. Reroll scraps and cut remaining biscuits. Transfer to large nonstick or lightly greased baking sheet.
3. Bake until golden brown, 10 to 12 minutes. Serve warm.
Makes 12 to 15 biscuits.

EACH BISCUIT *190 cal, 12 g fat (8 g sat. fat), 49 mg chol, 251 mg sodium, 17 g carbo, 1 g fiber, 3 g pro. Daily Values: 8% vit. A, 1% vit. C, 6% calcium, 6% iron.*

CHICKEN SALAD

PREP 30 min. **CHILL** 2 hr.

INGREDIENTS
1   cup mayonnaise
1   8-oz. carton dairy sour cream
3   lb. skinless, boneless chicken breast halves, cooked and diced
1   cup diced celery
1   cup seedless red or green grapes, halved or quartered
       Salt and ground black pepper

PREPARATION
1. In small bowl stir together mayonnaise and sour cream. In a very large bowl stir together chicken, celery, grapes, and sour cream mixture. Add salt and pepper to taste. Cover; chill 2 to 24 hours. To serve, split Sage Biscuits, spoon in Chicken Salad. **Makes 8 cups (12 to 16 servings).**

EACH SERVING (WITHOUT BISCUIT) *304 cal, 20 g fat (5 g sat. fat), 81 mg chol, 273 mg sodium, 2 g carbo, 0 g fiber, 27 g pro. Daily Values: 4% vit. A, 3% vit. C, 4% calcium, 4% iron.*

Spotlight Spring

The first rosy berries of the season are reason enough to celebrate, especially if dessert just *feels* superrich.

PHOTO **ANDY LYONS** PRODUCED BY **JILL LUST**

CELEBRATE EVERY DAY *with*
Pam Anderson

PAM'S TIPS

- Set the table with seasonal crisp linens to make even weeknights feel elegant.
- Choose a few lush, plump berries with leaves intact; perch those as toppers.
- Dab a bit of sauce on the meringues to hold the whole berries in place.

PUFFY SHORTCAKES WITH MERINGUE [KID FRIENDLY]

This triple-berry sauce is built on the convenience of frozen berries and jelly—for a luscious, inexpensive any-day dessert.

PREP 30 min. **BAKE** 25 min. **OVEN** 425°F/325°F

INGREDIENTS

1	16-oz. pkg. frozen strawberries, partially thawed
½	cup strawberry jelly
2	cups fresh strawberries, hulled and sliced
½	a 17.3-oz. pkg. (1 sheet) frozen puff pastry, thawed
1	Tbsp. cornstarch
¾	cup sugar
½	tsp. cream of tartar
6	egg whites
1	tsp. vanilla
8	fresh whole strawberries

PREPARATION

1. Preheat oven to 425°F. Blend or process frozen strawberries and jelly until smooth. Stir in sliced berries; cover and refrigerate.

2. Roll pastry into a 12×10-inch rectangle; cut in eight rectangles. Place pastry rectangles 1 inch apart on large baking sheet; pierce with fork tines. Cover with second baking sheet. Bake 6 minutes. Remove top baking sheet; bake 4 minutes more. Remove from oven; let stand on sheet. Reduce oven to 325°F.

3. For meringue, in small saucepan cook and stir ½ cup *water* and the cornstarch over medium heat until thickened and bubbly. Remove from heat; cool slightly. In bowl combine sugar and cream of tartar; set aside. In large mixing bowl beat egg whites and vanilla on medium to high speed until frothy. Gradually beat in sugar mixture until soft peaks form. Add cornstarch mixture; beat to stiff peaks. Spoon on pastry; bake meringue 15 minutes. Serve pastries warm with sauce; top each with fresh whole strawberry. **Makes 8 servings.**

EACH SERVING *351 cal, 12 g fat (3 g sat. fat), 0 mg chol, 127 mg sodium, 58 g carbo, 2 g fiber, 6 g pro. Daily Values: 64% vit. C, 2% calcium, 6% iron.*

BUILD A BETTER

Guacamole

For made-to-order taste and vivid color, combine fresh ingredients and mash gently.

BY **PEG SMITH**
PHOTO **ANDY LYONS**
FOOD STYLING **JILL LUST**

AVOCADOS
Allow at least a quarter of an avocado per person. To determine ripeness, gently squeeze them in the palm of your hand; ripe fruits yield to slight pressure. Use a knife to cut around the fruit, then twist and pull apart. Pierce the pit with edge of knife and twist it out. Scoop out flesh with spoon. Mash with fork, leaving chunks.

LIME JUICE
Freshly squeezed juice adds tartness and keeps avocado's color bright. Stir in a tablespoon per avocado—more if you love the taste.

ONION AND GARLIC
Finely chop a quarter of an onion (red, yellow, white, or green) and a clove of garlic per avocado. Stir, taste, and add more if needed.

TOPPINGS
Dust with ground cumin; stir in or sprinkle chopped tomatoes and cilantro.

HEAT
Add finely chopped serrano chile peppers and/or hot pepper sauce for a little fire.

TEST KITCHEN TIP For the best color and flavor, plan to make guacamole right before serving— even at the table. If you must store, cover surface tightly with plastic wrap; refrigerate 1 hour or less.

Scrambled Eggs

Vary flavorful add-ins to create appetizing choices for breakfast, lunch, and dinner.

1. BRUNCH SKILLET
Lox (brined salmon), sour cream, dill

2. VEGGIE CRUNCH
Brussels sprouts, snap peas, carrots

3. HERB GARDEN
Basil, Italian (flat-leaf) parsley, thyme, tarragon, freshly ground black pepper

4. DENVER-STYLE
Bacon, mushrooms, green onions

5. TUSCAN SUN
Olive medley with pepperoncini, sun-dried tomatoes, feta cheese

6. CALIFORNIAN
Avocado, red onion, grape tomatoes, fresh cilantro

7. BEEFY BLUES
Leftover steak slices, blue cheese

8. POPEYE'S PUNCH
Tomatoes, spinach, hollandaise sauce

9. SWEET SPICE
Sausage (cooked, crumbled), roasted sweet peppers

10. HAM 'N' CHEESE
Ham, cheddar cheese, sliced jalapeño peppers

BHG BASICS

Cook beaten eggs in a hot skillet with melted butter. As eggs begin to set, lift with spatula to let uncooked portion flow beneath. Cook just until glossy and moist.

BY **PEG SMITH**
PHOTO **ANDY LYONS**
PRODUCED BY **JILL LUST**

MAY

CLASSIC CASSEROLES STAND CENTER STAGE WITH THEIR CONTEMPORARY COUNTERPARTS THIS MONTH, ALONG WITH STACKS OF BAR COOKIES, HEALTHY SALADS, AND A PRETTY DESSERT FOR TWO TO SHARE WITH MOM.

TUNA NOODLE CASSEROLE
page 103

Take It from Mom

SAUSAGE-FRUIT KABOBS
page 108

SALSA, BLACK BEAN, AND RICE SALAD
page 111

CHERRY REVEL BARS
page 119

take it from mom

WHEN IT COMES TO COMFORT COOKING, MOM KNOWS BEST. HERE ARE FOUR OF HER UNFORGETTABLE CASSEROLES— WITH A CLASSIC SPIN AND A MODERN TWIST FOR EACH.

BY **RICHARD SWEARINGER** PHOTOS **ANDY LYONS** RECIPES **JULI HALE** AND **MARYELLYN KRANTZ** FOOD STYLING **JILL LUST** AND **SUSAN BROWN DRAUDT** PROP STYLING **KAREN JOHNSON** AND **SUE MITCHELL**

modern
Savor the nutty flavor of Gruyère cheese and the smokiness of Black Forest ham in **CREAMY POTATO CASSEROLE,** *above.*
page 104

classic
Time-tested **POTATO-HAM BAKE,** *opposite,* features the season's best asparagus, fresh tarragon, and peppery chives.

HAM AND POTATO CASEROLES
ARE TIMELESS FAVORITES—ADAPT THEM
TO ANY SEASON OR OCCASION.

CHICKEN AND RICE CASSEROLE IS THE CROWD-PLEASER YOU GREW UP WITH. SO SIMPLE, IT MAKES EVERY MOM A SUCCESS IN THE KITCHEN.

modern

HERBED CHICKEN AND ORZO goes together in 30 minutes, thanks to a purchased rotisserie chicken. Completing the combo: a creamy sauce made from soft cheese with garlic and herbs, and rice-shape pasta.

HERBED CHICKEN AND ORZO

Orzo is small, flat, rice-shape pasta. Combining the hot cooked orzo with the cheese mixture helps the cheese to melt.

PREP 30 min. **BAKE** 30 min. **STAND** 5 min. **OVEN** 350°F

INGREDIENTS

8	oz. dried orzo
$1\frac{1}{2}$	cups 1-inch pieces fresh green beans (6 oz.)
1	whole roasted deli chicken
2	5.2-oz. containers semisoft cheese with garlic and herbs
$\frac{1}{2}$	cup milk
$1\frac{1}{2}$	cups shredded carrot
2	Tbsp. snipped fresh Italian (flat-leaf) parsley

PREPARATION

1. Preheat oven to 350°F. Grease a 3-quart oval or rectangular baking dish; set aside.
2. Cook orzo according to package directions, adding green beans during last 3 minutes of cooking; drain. Meanwhile, cut chicken in 6 pieces; set aside.
3. In large bowl whisk together cheese and milk until combined. Add hot orzo mixture; stir until coated. Stir in shredded carrot. Spoon into prepared baking dish. Top with chicken pieces.
4. Bake, covered, 30 to 40 minutes or until heated through. Let stand 5 minutes. Sprinkle parsley. **Makes 6 servings.**

COST PER SERVING $4.01/$24.06 total
EACH SERVING *566 cal, 32 g fat (16 g sat. fat), 147 mg chol, 685 mg sodium, 37 g carbo, 3 g fiber, 31 g pro. Daily Values: 99% vit. A, 13% vit. C, 8% calcium, 17% iron.*

CHICKEN ALFREDO AND RICE CASSEROLE

The first recipe for chicken and rice casserole appeared in the 1896 edition of Fannie Farmer's The Boston Cooking-School Cookbook. *If you don't have cooked rice on hand, prepare 1 cup uncooked rice, which will give you about 3 cups cooked.*

PREP 25 min. **BAKE** 50 min. **STAND** 5 min. **OVEN** 350°F

INGREDIENTS

1	10-oz. container refrigerated light Alfredo pasta sauce
$\frac{1}{2}$	cup milk
$2\frac{1}{2}$	cups cooked white rice or wild rice
2	cups cubed cooked chicken
1	cup frozen peas
$\frac{1}{3}$	cup chopped bottled roasted red sweet peppers
$\frac{1}{4}$	cup slivered almonds, toasted (optional)
1	Tbsp. snipped fresh basil or $\frac{1}{2}$ tsp. dried basil, crushed
1	cup soft bread crumbs
1	Tbsp. butter, melted

PREPARATION

1. Preheat oven to 350°F. In large bowl combine pasta sauce and milk. Stir in rice, chicken, peas, sweet peppers, almonds, and basil. Transfer to $1\frac{1}{2}$-quart baking dish.
2. Bake, covered, 30 minutes. Uncover and stir. Combine bread crumbs and melted butter; sprinkle on top. Bake, uncovered, 20 to 25 minutes more or until heated through and crumbs are golden brown. Let stand 5 minutes before serving. **Makes 4 servings.**

COST PER SERVING $2.50/$10 total
EACH SERVING *456 cal, 16 g fat (8 g sat. fat), 97 mg chol, 672 mg sodium, 45 g carbo, 3 g fiber, 32 g pro. Daily Values: 22% vit. A, 68% vit. C, 22% calcium, 21% iron.*

classic
Refrigerated pasta sauce trades places with soup as a rich, no-fuss base for homey **CHICKEN ALFREDO AND RICE CASSEROLE,** while leftover cubed chicken—roasted or fried—keeps the whole dish simple.

classic Homemade corn bread batter spooned over **MEXICALI HAMBURGER CASSEROLE** seals in the flavor of beef, corn, and cheese. Spoon a Fresh Tomato Toss over the top.

TAMALE PIE—POPULARIZED IN THE '30s AND '40s—HELPED AMERICA FALL IN LOVE WITH BEEF AND CORN CASSEROLES

KID FRIENDLY

MEXICALI HAMBURGER CASSEROLE

Hamburger, salsa, and corn are covered with corn bread for a bake that's homey and quick.

PREP 30 min. **BAKE** 30 min. **STAND** 5 min. **OVEN** 350°F

INGREDIENTS

1½   lb. lean ground beef
1   15-oz. can Mexican-style diced tomatoes
1½   cups frozen whole kernel corn, thawed
½   cup plus 2 Tbsp. finely shredded Mexican cheese blend
½   cup all-purpose flour
½   cup yellow cornmeal
1   Tbsp. sugar
1¼   tsp. baking powder
1   egg, beaten
⅔   cup milk
2   Tbsp. cooking oil
1   recipe Fresh Tomato Toss

PREPARATION

1. Preheat oven to 350°F. In 12-inch skillet cook and brown beef; drain off fat. Stir in undrained tomatoes and *1 cup* of the corn; heat through. Transfer to greased 2-quart baking dish. Sprinkle with *½ cup* of the cheese.
2. For corn bread topping, in medium bowl combine flour, cornmeal, sugar, baking powder, and ½ teaspoon *salt*. Stir in egg, milk, and oil. Evenly spread on beef mixture. Sprinkle remaining 2 tablespoons cheese. Bake, uncovered, 30 minutes or until topping is set. Let stand 5 minutes.
Fresh Tomato Toss In bowl stir together 1 cup *red grape tomatoes*, halved; ¼ cup coarsely chopped *cilantro*; remaining ½ cup *corn*, and, if desired, ⅓ cup *green olives*, halved; spoon over servings.
Makes 6 servings.

COST PER SERVING $1.75/$10.50 total
EACH SERVING *506 cal, 27 g fat (10 g sat. fat), 125 mg chol, 603 mg sodium, 38 g carbo, 2 g fiber, 30 g pro. Daily Values: 95% vit. A, 9% vit. C, 239% calcium, 4% iron.*

ROAST BEEF TAMALE CASSEROLE

A mild poblano chile pepper provides a hint of heat in this modern dish. When buying, look for peppers that are firm and dark green.

PREP 30 min. **BAKE** 25 min. **OVEN** 350°F

INGREDIENTS

1   17-oz. pkg. refrigerated cooked beef roast au jus
1   medium fresh poblano or Anaheim pepper, seeded and sliced*
1   medium onion, chopped
2   Tbsp. butter
2   Tbsp. all-purpose flour
1   15-oz. can pinto beans, rinsed, drained
1½   cups 1-inch pieces zucchini and/or yellow summer squash
1   cup grape tomatoes, halved if desired
¾   a 16-oz. tube refrigerated cooked polenta, cut in ½-inch slices
4   oz. Monterey Jack cheese with jalapeño peppers, shredded (1 cup)
½   cup sour cream
1   Tbsp. snipped fresh cilantro
   Lime wedges

PREPARATION

1. Preheat oven to 350°F. Heat beef according to package directions. Pour juice into 2-cup glass measure; add *water* to equal 1 cup. Coarsely shred beef with two forks.
2. In large skillet cook pepper and onion in hot butter over medium heat until tender. Stir in flour. Add juice mixture; cook until thickened and bubbly. Stir in beef, beans, zucchini, and tomatoes. Transfer to lightly greased 2-quart (8×8×2-inch) baking dish. Arrange polenta slices around edges.
3. Bake, uncovered, 20 minutes. Sprinkle cheese. Bake 5 to 10 minutes more until cheese is melted. Let stand 5 minutes.
4. In bowl combine sour cream and cilantro. Serve with casserole; pass lime wedges. **Makes 4 to 6 servings.**
***NOTE** Hot peppers contain oils that can burn skin and eyes. Wear kitchen gloves while handling peppers, then wash hands well after.

COST PER SERVING $3.78/$15.12 total
EACH SERVING *578 cal, 31 g fat (18 g sat. fat), 125 mg chol, 1,155 mg sodium, 40 g carbo, 8 g fiber, 41 g pro. Daily Values: 30% vit. A, 153% vit. C, 33% calcium, 26% iron.*

modern
In this new **ROAST BEEF TAMALE CASSEROLE,** it's all about convenience. Prepackaged polenta rounds substitute for the classic corn bread topping, and precooked beef pot roast replaces ground beef. Start to finish is less than an hour.

TUNA AND NOODLES IGNITED THE CASSEROLE CRAZE IN THE 1930s. BRINGING NEW FLAVORS TO THE COMBO IS OUR WAY OF KEEPING THE TRADITION GOING.

modern

Pickley little capers dot the top of this fresh-tasting combination.
LEMONY TUNA AND PASTA includes olive oil packed tuna, rigatoni, fresh dill, and lemon peel.

LEMONY TUNA AND PASTA

The definitive "cupboard casserole" gets fresh with dashes of lemon and dill, rich olive oil packed tuna, and the crunch of coarsely chopped celery. Top with lemon slices and capers and it's ready for company.

PREP 30 min. **BAKE** 20 min. **STAND** 5 min. **OVEN** 375°F

INGREDIENTS

2	cups dried rigatoni or penne pasta (6 oz.)
1	cup coarsely chopped celery
1/4	cup chopped onion
2	cloves garlic, minced
1/4	cup olive oil
1/4	cup all-purpose flour
2	Tbsp. Dijon-style mustard
1	Tbsp. snipped fresh dill or 1 tsp. dried dill
1	tsp. finely shredded lemon peel
1/4	tsp. ground black pepper
2	cups reduced-sodium chicken broth
2	5.5-oz. cans chunk tuna (packed in olive oil), drained
1/2	cup finely crushed herb-seasoned croutons
2	Tbsp. butter, melted
1	small lemon, thinly sliced
1	Tbsp. capers (optional)
	Fresh dill sprigs (optional)

PREPARATION

1. Preheat oven to 375°F. Grease 1 1/2-quart baking dish; set aside. Cook pasta according to package directions; drain.
2. In medium saucepan cook celery, onion, and garlic in hot oil until tender. Stir in flour, mustard, dill, lemon peel, and pepper. Add broth all at once. Cook and stir until thickened and bubbly, whisking to remove any lumps. Stir in tuna and pasta. Transfer to prepared baking dish.
3. In small bowl stir together croutons and melted butter. Sprinkle on tuna mixture. Bake, covered, for 15 minutes. Uncover. Top with lemon slices; bake, uncovered, 5 minutes more or until heated through. Let stand 5 minutes. Sprinkle with capers and dill sprigs.
Makes 4 to 6 servings.

COST PER SERVING $1.95/$7.80 total
EACH SERVING *565 cal, 27 g fat (7 g sat. fat), 30 mg chol, 868 mg sodium, 47 g carbo, 4 g fiber, 32 g pro. Daily Values: 7% vit. A, 24% vit. C, 6% calcium, 3% iron.*

TUNA NOODLE CASSEROLE

Give this childhood comfort food grown-up appeal with Dijon-style mustard and roasted red sweet peppers. For a nostalgic touch, top the casserole with uncrushed potato chips.

PREP 25 min. **BAKE** 30 min. **STAND** 5 min. **OVEN** 375°F

INGREDIENTS

3	cups medium dried noodles (4 oz.)
1	cup chopped celery
1/4	cup chopped onion
1/4	cup butter
1/4	cup all-purpose flour
2	to 3 Tbsp. Dijon-style mustard
2 1/4	cups milk
1	12-oz. can chunk tuna, drained
1/2	cup bottled roasted red sweet peppers, chopped
	Potato chips (optional)

PREPARATION

1. Preheat oven to 375°F. In large saucepan cook noodles according to package directions. Drain; return noodles to pan.
2. For sauce, in medium saucepan cook celery and onion in hot butter until tender. Stir in flour, mustard, and 1/4 teaspoon *ground black pepper*. Add milk all at once; cook and stir until slightly thickened and bubbly, whisking to remove any lumps.
3. Gently fold sauce, tuna, and sweet peppers into noodles. Transfer to lightly greased 1 1/2-quart baking dish. Top with chips. Bake, uncovered, 30 to 35 minutes, until heated through. Let stand 5 minutes. **Makes 4 servings.**

COST PER SERVING $1.89/$7.56 total
EACH SERVING *419 cal, 16 g fat (10 g sat. fat), 110 mg chol, 720 mg sodium, 36 g carbo, 2 g fiber, 29 g pro. Daily Values: 15% vit. A, 88% vit. C, 20% calcium, 15% iron.*

classic
It wouldn't be Mom's without them: Whole potato chips set sail atop **TUNA NOODLE CASSEROLE.** Additions include roasted red peppers and Dijon mustard.

POTATO-HAM BAKE

CREAMY POTATO CASSEROLE

Gruyère cheese (pronounced groo-YEHR) is a dense, hard cheese with a creamy, nutty, earthy taste. It is comparable to Swiss cheese but sharper and not as sweet. Find it in the specialty cheese section of the supermarket.

PREP 30 min. **BAKE** 1 hr. 10 min. **STAND** 10 min. **OVEN** 350°F

INGREDIENTS
1   medium onion, chopped
2   Tbsp. butter
2   Tbsp. all-purpose flour
2   Tbsp. Dijon-style mustard
1³/₄   cups milk
¹/₂   of an 8-oz. pkg. reduced-fat cream cheese (Neufchâtel), cut up
1   cup Gruyère cheese, shredded (4 oz.)
1   Tbsp. snipped fresh chives or green onion
1¹/₂   lb. Yukon gold or round red potatoes, cut in thin wedges
8   oz. sliced cooked Black Forest ham or country ham, coarsely chopped
¹/₂   cup coarsely crushed bagel chips
         Fresh thyme and/or Italian (flat-leaf) parsley leaves

PREPARATION
1. Preheat oven to 350°F. Grease a 2-quart rectangular baking dish; set aside.
2. For sauce, in medium saucepan cook onion in hot butter over medium heat 5 minutes or until tender; stirring occasionally. Stir in flour and mustard. Add milk all at once. Cook and stir over medium heat until slightly thickened and bubbly. Reduce heat to low. Whisk in Neufchâtel cheese until smooth. Gradually add ¹/₂ cup of the Gruyère cheese until cheese is melted. Stir in chives.
3. In bowl combine potatoes, ham, and sauce; toss gently to combine. Transfer to prepared baking dish.
4. Bake, covered, 1 hour or until potatoes are tender. Uncover; stir carefully. Sprinkle with crushed chips and remaining cheese. Bake, uncovered, 10 to 15 minutes more or until cheese is melted. Let stand 10 minutes before serving. Sprinkle herbs. **Makes 6 servings.**

COST PER SERVING $2.00/$12.00 total
EACH SERVING *381 cal, 20 g fat (11 g sat. fat), 73 mg chol, 846 mg sodium, 31 g carbo, 3 g fiber, 19 g pro. Daily Values: 14% vit. A, 23% vit. C, 317% calcium, 9% iron.*

POTATO-HAM BAKE

Asparagus and tarragon give this modern bake a touch of showmanship.

PREP 25 min. **BAKE** 30 min. **STAND** 5 min. **OVEN** 400°F

INGREDIENTS

1 lb. Yukon gold potatoes, sliced
1 8-oz. tub light cream cheese spread with chives and onion
¾ cup milk
¼ cup finely shredded Parmesan cheese
1 Tbsp. snipped fresh tarragon or ½ tsp. dried tarragon, crushed
8 oz. cooked boneless ham, cut in bite-size slices
1 lb. fresh asparagus spears, trimmed, cut in 2- to 3-inch pieces
Fresh tarragon sprigs (optional)

PREPARATION

1. Preheat oven to 400°F. In medium saucepan cook potatoes, covered, in small amount of lightly salted boiling water 5 to 7 minutes, just until tender. Drain; transfer to bowl and set aside.
2. For sauce, in same pan combine cream cheese, milk, *2 tablespoons* of the Parmesan, and ¼ teaspoon *ground black pepper*. Heat and whisk until smooth and cheese is melted. Remove from heat; stir in tarragon.
3. Layer potatoes, ham, asparagus, and sauce in 1½-quart baking dish. Bake, covered, 20 minutes. Uncover; sprinkle remaining Parmesan. Bake 10 to 12 minutes. Let stand 5 minutes. Top with tarragon and freshly ground *black pepper*. **Makes 4 servings.**

COST PER SERVING $1.99/$7.96 total
EACH SERVING *346 cal, 16 g fat (9 g sat. fat), 67 mg chol, 1,162 mg sodium, 30 g carbo, 5 g fiber, 22 g pro. Daily Values: 20% vit. A, 49% vit. C, 34% calcium, 16% iron.*

meet the team

A casserole is a baking dish or pan in which food is baked and served. The term also refers to the food baked in the dish. Casserole cookery has been around for centuries, but the convenient one-dish meals known as casseroles became popular in America during the 1930s. They continue to be favorites. Two casserole makers in the *Better Homes and Gardens®* Test Kitchen share their tips for making the popular dishes.

■ **MARYELLYN KRANTZ** (*above, left*) put her 35 years in the Test Kitchen to good use in developing the Classic casserole recipes in this chapter. Growing up in a Catholic family, she remembers her mother's Tuna Noodle Casserole as a "fish on Friday" dinner. Maryellyn replaced the condensed soup that's typically in the recipe with an easy homemade white sauce. She says in a pinch a can of cream of celery soup thinned with a little milk can be substituted in Tuna Noodle Casserole. She recommends reheating casseroles in the microwave at 50% to 70% power or in the oven with the dish covered.

■ **JULI HALE** created the Modern casseroles. From starting to cook at age 9, and through culinary school and beyond, she's made plenty of casseroles over the years. When it comes to cheese, she prefers cheddar, Swiss, Gruyère, or Monterey Jack for a melted, cheesy texture. To add thickness to sauce, cream cheese or processed cheese works well. For crunchy toppers, Juli uses buttered bread crumbs as a standby—tortilla chips, chow mein noodles, sliced almonds, and canned french-fried onions are alternatives.

Springtime Suppers

These one-dish meals are full of the season's best—fresh veggies, bright flavors, and cheery colors—all prepared fast!

BY **PEG SMITH** PHOTOS **ANDY LYONS** RECIPES AND FOOD STYLING **JILL LUST**

READY IN 20 MINUTES!

VEGGIE FISH CHOWDER

FAST! **LOW FAT**

VEGGIE FISH CHOWDER

START TO FINISH 20 min.

INGREDIENTS

1   lb. firm-texture white fish, cut in 4 pieces
    Freshly ground black pepper
2   medium carrots, thinly sliced
1   cup sugar snap peas, halved diagonally
1   Tbsp. olive oil
1   14-oz. can vegetable broth
2¼ cups water
1   4-oz. pkg. (or half a 7.2-oz. box) butter-and-herb-flavored mashed potatoes
    Shaved Parmesan cheese

PREPARATION

1. Season fish lightly with pepper. In 4-quart Dutch oven cook fish, carrot, and peas in hot oil over medium-high heat for 3 minutes.
2. Add broth and water; bring to boiling. Reduce heat. Simmer, covered, for 3 minutes or until fish flakes when tested with a fork.
3. Place mashed potatoes in small bowl. Carefully remove *1¼ cups* broth from Dutch oven; stir broth into potatoes (mixture will be thick).
4. Divide mashed potato mixture among four bowls. Break fish in bite-size pieces. Ladle hot fish and vegetable mixture over potatoes. Season to taste with *salt* and pepper. Serve with Parmesan cheese. **Makes 4 servings.**

EACH SERVING *264 cal, 7 g fat (2 g sat. fat), 49 mg chol, 1,001 mg sodium, 27 g carbo, 3 g fiber, 23 g pro. Daily Values: 108% vit. A, 14% vit. C, 6% calcium, 7% iron.*

FAST! **LOW FAT**

SPICY BEEF AND NOODLE SALAD

START TO FINISH 20 min.

INGREDIENTS

1   lb. beef flank steak
1   Tbsp. soy sauce
8   oz. rice noodles
1   medium English cucumber
½   cup Asian sweet chili sauce
½   cup water
1   cup packaged fresh julienned carrots
    Fresh cilantro leaves

PREPARATION

1. Preheat broiler. Brush steak with soy sauce. Place on rack of unheated broiler pan. Broil 4 to 5 inches from heat for 15 to 18 minutes or to desired doneness (160°F for medium), turning once halfway through broiling. Thinly slice beef across the grain.
2. Meanwhile, cook noodles according to package directions; drain in colander. Rinse with cold water.
3. Slice cucumber crosswise in three sections. Using a vegetable peeler, cut lengthwise ribbons from sections.
4. Combine chili sauce and water. Divide steak, noodles, cucumber, and carrots among bowls. Drizzle with chili sauce mixture; sprinkle cilantro. **Makes 4 servings.**

EACH SERVING *477 cal, 9 g fat (4 g sat. fat), 40 mg chol, 839 mg sodium, 70 g carbo, 3 g fiber, 27 g pro. Daily Values: 93% vit. A, 6% vit. C, 6% calcium, 18% iron.*

SPICY BEEF AND NOODLE SALAD

FAST!

CHICKEN AND ASPARAGUS
SKILLET SUPPER

START TO FINISH 20 min.

INGREDIENTS

8   skinless, boneless chicken thighs
3   slices bacon, coarsely chopped
½   cup chicken broth
1   lb. asparagus spears, trimmed
1   small yellow summer squash, halved crosswise and
     cut in ½-inch strips
4   green onions, cut in 2-inch pieces

PREPARATION

1. Sprinkle chicken with *salt* and *ground black pepper.* In 12-inch skillet cook chicken and bacon over medium-high heat 12 minutes, turning to brown evenly. Carefully add broth; cover and cook 3 to 5 minutes more or until chicken is tender and no longer pink (180°F).
2. Meanwhile, in microwave-safe 2-quart dish combine asparagus, squash, and 2 tablespoons *water.* Sprinkle *salt* and *pepper.* Cover with vented plastic wrap. Microcook on 100% power (high) 3 to 5 minutes until vegetables are crisp-tender, stirring once. Transfer to plates. Drizzle cooking liquid; top with chicken, bacon, and onion. **Makes 4 servings.**

  EACH SERVING *320 cal, 18 g fat (6 g sat. fat), 134 mg chol, 626 mg sodium, 5 g carbo, 2 g fiber, 32 g pro. Daily Values: 15% vit. A, 13% vit. C, 5% calcium, 18% iron.*

**CHICKEN AND ASPARAGUS
SKILLET SUPPER**

SAUSAGE-FRUIT KABOBS

FAST! **KID FRIENDLY**

SAUSAGE-FRUIT KABOBS

START TO FINISH 20 min.

INGREDIENTS

3   Tbsp. spicy brown or Dijon-style mustard
3   Tbsp. honey
12   oz. cooked smoked sausage, bias cut in ½-inch slices
1   apple, cored, cut in ½-inch wedges
1   medium zucchini, halved and cut in ¼-inch slices
6   oz. crusty bread, cut in 1-inch pieces

PREPARATION

1. Preheat broiler. In bowl stir mustard into honey.
2. On four 12-inch skewers alternately thread sausage, apple wedges, and zucchini, leaving ¼ inch between pieces. Brush with some of the honey-mustard; reserve remaining honey-mustard. Place on rack of unheated broiler pan. Broil 4 to 5 inches from heat for 4 minutes.
3. Meanwhile, thread bread on four 12-inch skewers; lightly brush with *olive oil.* Add bread skewers to broiler; turn sausage skewers. Broil 3 minutes more or until sausage is heated through and bread is toasted, turning bread once. Serve with reserved honey-mustard. **Makes 4 servings.**

EACH SERVING *527 cal, 32 g fat (9 g sat. fat), 52 mg chol, 1,138 mg sodium, 33 g carbo, 3 g fiber, 11 g pro. Daily Values: 2% vit. A, 17% vit. C, 5% calcium, 11% iron.*

FAST! LOW FAT

CUBAN FRIED RICE

START TO FINISH 20 min.

INGREDIENTS

1   fresh pineapple, peeled, packed in juice
1   Tbsp. olive oil
1   14.8-oz. pouch cooked long grain rice
12   oz. cooked ham, coarsely chopped
1   cup chopped or sliced sweet pepper
1   fresh jalapeño pepper, seeded, if desired, and sliced (see Note, page 101)
½   15-oz. can black beans, rinsed and drained (¾ cup)
     Lime wedges

PREPARATION

1. Remove pineapple from container, reserving juice. Cut pineapple in ¾-inch slices; discard core if present. Heat oil in 12-inch skillet over medium-high heat; add pineapple slices. Cook 3 to 4 minutes or until beginning to brown. Divide pineapple among four plates.
2. Meanwhile, prepare rice according to package directions. Add ham and peppers to skillet; cook 3 minutes, stirring occasionally. Add beans and rice. Cook, stirring occasionally, 3 minutes or until heated through. Stir in reserved pineapple juice. Serve with lime wedges.
Makes 4 servings.

EACH SERVING *375 cal, 9 g fat (1 g sat. fat), 38 mg chol, 1,549 mg sodium, 58 g carbo, 6 g fiber, 24 g pro. Daily Values: 6% vit. A, 146% vit. C, 4% calcium, 8% iron.*

CUBAN FRIED RICE

Brilliant Salads

Supercharge the nutrition in main-dish meals
with the power of color.

BY **MARGE PERRY**

GRILLED TUNA SALAD

High in heart-healthy fats that fight inflammation, olives and olive oil also have antioxidants that fight cancer.

PREP 30 min. **BROIL** 8 min.

INGREDIENTS
1	lb. fresh or frozen tuna steaks, cut 1 inch thick
3	Tbsp. sherry vinegar
2	Tbsp. finely chopped shallot
1	Tbsp. Dijon-style mustard
2	Tbsp. olive oil
1	anchovy fillet, rinsed and mashed
	Salt and ground black pepper
8	oz. tiny new potatoes, quartered
6	oz. fresh green beans
6	cups Bibb or romaine lettuce leaves
¾	cup thinly sliced radishes
½	cup niçoise olives or ripe olives, pitted
	Finely chopped red onion (optional)
	Cracked black pepper (optional)

PREPARATION

1. Thaw fish, if frozen. Rinse fish; pat dry with paper towels. For dressing, in bowl combine vinegar and shallot. Whisk in mustard. Whisking constantly, add oil in steady thin stream. Stir in anchovy; season to taste with salt and pepper. Remove *1 tablespoon* of the dressing to brush fish; set aside remaining dressing.

2. Preheat broiler on high setting. Brush the 1 tablespoon dressing over all sides of fish. Place fish on greased unheated rack of broiler pan. Broil about 4 inches from heat 8 to 12 minutes or until fish flakes easily when tested with a fork, gently turning once halfway through broiling. (Or grill fish on greased rack of uncovered grill directly over medium coals 8 to 12 minutes, turning once halfway through grilling.) Slice fish.

3. Meanwhile, in covered medium saucepan cook potatoes in large amount of boiling water for 7 minutes. Add green beans; cook about 2 minutes more or until potatoes are tender. Drain and cool slightly.

4. Arrange fish, potatoes, green beans, lettuce leaves, radishes, and olives on platter. Sprinkle with red onion and cracked black pepper. Serve with remaining dressing. **Makes 4 servings.**

EACH SERVING *282 cal, 10 g fat (1 g sat. fat), 51 mg chol, 408 mg sodium, 17 g carbo, 4 g fiber, 30 g pro. Daily Values: 63% vit. A, 40% vit. C, 9% calcium, 20% iron.*

SALSA, BLACK BEAN, AND RICE SALAD

Beans are loaded with fiber that lowers blood sugar. For even more fiber and nutrients, substitute brown rice for the white in this recipe.

START TO FINISH 30 min.

INGREDIENTS
2	cups cooked long grain rice, chilled
1	15-oz. can black beans, rinsed and drained
2	cups chopped tomato
1	cup chopped yellow or red sweet pepper
1	cup frozen whole kernel corn, thawed
2	green onions, thinly sliced
2	Tbsp. snipped fresh cilantro
1	cup bottled picante sauce or salsa
4	oz. Monterey Jack cheese with jalapeño chile peppers, cut in ¼-inch cubes (optional)
	Lettuce leaves
½	cup fat-free or reduced-fat sour cream

PREPARATION

1. In large bowl stir together chilled rice, beans, tomato, sweet pepper, corn, onion, and cilantro; add picante sauce or salsa. Toss to coat. Stir in cheese, if using.

2. Line six salad bowls or plates with lettuce leaves. Top with rice mixture. Serve with sour cream. **Makes 6 servings.**

EACH SERVING *196 cal, 3 g fat (1 g sat. fat), 6 mg chol, 662 mg sodium, 39 g carbo, 7 g fiber, 9 g pro. Daily Values: 76% vit. A, 71% vit. C, 8% calcium, 12% iron.*

SALSA, BLACK BEAN, AND RICE SALAD

Choose Bibb over iceberg lettuce. The darker and more vibrant the color, the more concentrated the nutrients.

STRIKING OIL

Mix vinaigrettes yourself to control calories and types of fats. For heart health, choose oils high in monounsaturated or polyunsaturated fats, such as olive, canola, safflower, sunflower, corn, and soybean oils. Combine equal parts oil and vinegar, adjusting amounts, along with seasonings, to suit your taste.

GREEK CHICKEN SALAD

Feta can be a good source of calcium—including at least some calcium at every meal makes it easier to reach your daily goal.

PREP 30 min. **MARINATE** 4 hr. **GRILL** 12 min.

INGREDIENTS

4	skinless, boneless chicken breast halves (1¼ to 1½ lb. total)
1	Tbsp. lemon juice
1	Tbsp. olive oil
1	Tbsp. snipped fresh oregano or 1 tsp. dried oregano, crushed
2	cloves garlic, minced
¼	tsp. ground black pepper
3	medium cucumbers, seeded and coarsely chopped
2	medium red and/or yellow tomatoes, coarsely chopped
½	cup sliced red onion
	Mixed salad greens
⅓	cup bottled reduced-calorie creamy cucumber salad dressing
½	cup crumbled feta cheese (2 oz.)
¼	cup pitted kalamata olives or ripe olives

PREPARATION

1. Place chicken in resealable plastic bag set in shallow dish. For marinade, in small bowl combine lemon juice, oil, oregano, garlic, and pepper. Pour over chicken. Seal bag; turn to coat chicken. Marinate, refrigerated, 4 to 24 hours, turning bag occasionally.
2. Meanwhile, in medium bowl combine cucumber, tomato, and onion; set aside.
3. Drain chicken, discarding marinade. Place chicken on rack of uncovered grill directly over medium coals. Grill 12 to 15 minutes or until chicken is tender and no longer pink (170°F), turning once.
4. Transfer chicken to cutting board; cut in bite-size pieces. Toss with cucumber mixture. Serve on salad greens. Drizzle with salad dressing. Sprinkle feta cheese and olives. **Makes 4 servings.**

EACH SERVING *331 cal, 12 g fat (3 g sat. fat), 95 mg chol, 631 mg sodium, 17 g carbo, 3 g fiber, 38 g pro. Daily Values: 27% vit. A, 38% vit. C, 16% calcium, 12% iron.*

ROAST PORK SALAD WITH GINGER-PINEAPPLE DRESSING

Pork tenderloin has fewer calories and slightly less fat than skinless chicken breast. Plus it's a good source of the B vitamins thiamine and riboflavin—both are essential for growth and healthy red blood cells.

PREP 25 min. **ROAST** 25 min. **OVEN** 425°F

INGREDIENTS

12	oz. pork tenderloin
⅛	tsp. salt
⅛	tsp. freshly ground black pepper
2	Tbsp. honey mustard
6	cups torn romaine and/or spinach
2	cups fresh or canned pineapple chunks and/or sliced fresh nectarine or peach
	Cracked black pepper (optional)
1	recipe Ginger-Pineapple Dressing

PREPARATION

1. Preheat oven to 425°F. Trim fat from pork; sprinkle salt and pepper. Place pork on rack set in shallow roasting pan. Roast pork for 20 minutes.
2. Spoon mustard on pork. Roast 5 to 10 minutes longer or until instant-read thermometer inserted in thickest part registers 160°F.
3. Thinly slice pork. In four salad bowls arrange greens, pork, and fruit. Sprinkle with cracked black pepper. Stir Ginger-Pineapple Dressing; drizzle on salads. **Makes 4 servings.**
Ginger-Pineapple Dressing In small bowl combine ¼ cup *low-fat mayonnaise dressing*, ¼ cup *unsweetened pineapple juice* or orange juice, 1 tablespoon *honey mustard*, and 1 teaspoon grated fresh *ginger*. Cover; chill until serving time.

EACH SERVING *226 cal, 6 g fat (1 g sat. fat), 60 mg chol, 220 mg sodium, 22 g carbo, 3 g fiber, 19 g pro. Daily Values: 98% vit. A, 55% vit. C, 4% calcium, 10% iron.*

ROAST PORK SALAD WITH GINGER-PINEAPPLE DRESSING

CALORIE-FRIENDLY COLESLAW

Make this summer side salad more calorie-friendly by replacing regular mayo or sour cream with reduced-fat or fat-free versions. Use red and green cabbages and stir in crunchy, colorful carrots, red and yellow sweet peppers, and green onions.

Bar Cookies

Easy, impressive, and full of fresh flavor, these one-pan desserts are ideal for gatherings from graduations to wedding showers.

BY **RICHARD SWEARINGER**
PHOTOS **ANDY LYONS**
FOOD STYLING **JILL LUST**

KID FRIENDLY

LEMON-LIME BARS

A random scatter of Candied Citrus Slices and Strips on top of the bars adds a festive touch.

PREP 20 min. **BAKE** 40 min. **COOL** 2 hr. **CHILL** 2 hr. **OVEN** 350°F

INGREDIENTS

	Candied Citrus Slices or Candied Citrus Strips (optional)
⅔	cup butter, softened
½	cup packed brown sugar
2½	cups all-purpose flour
4	tsp. finely shredded lemon peel
6	eggs
2¼	cups granulated sugar
½	cup lemon juice
¾	tsp. baking powder
⅛	tsp. ground nutmeg
1	tsp. finely shredded lime peel
2	Tbsp. sifted powdered sugar

PREPARATION

1. If using, prepare Candied Citrus Slices or Strips. Preheat oven to 350°F. Line 13×9×2-inch pan with heavy foil; set aside.

2. For crust, in large mixing bowl beat butter on medium to high 30 seconds. Add brown sugar; beat until combined. Beat in *2 cups* of the flour until crumbly. Stir in *2 teaspoons* of the lemon peel. Evenly press on bottom of prepared pan. Bake 20 minutes.

3. Meanwhile, for filling, in medium bowl combine eggs, granulated sugar, the remaining ½ cup flour, lemon juice, baking powder, and nutmeg. Beat on medium 2 minutes. Stir in remaining lemon peel and the lime peel. Pour over hot crust. Bake 20 minutes more or until edges are browned and center appears set. Remove to rack; cool 1 hour. Refrigerate, covered, 2 hours.

4. To serve, sprinkle evenly with powdered sugar. Lift from pan using foil; cut into bars. Add Candied Citrus Slices or Strips. Store, covered, in refrigerator up to 3 days. **Makes 16 to 20 bars.**

Candied Citrus Slices In large skillet combine ¼ cup *water* and ¾ cup *sugar*; bring to boiling. Add 2 *lemons* or 10 key limes, thinly sliced. Simmer gently, uncovered, for 1 to 2 minutes or until just softened. Transfer to rack; cool.

Candied Citrus Strips Cut strips of peel from 2 *lemons* or 2 limes. With spoon scrape away white pith. Cut into thin strips and cook in sugar mixture as above.

EACH BAR *307 cal, 10 g fat (5 g sat. fat), 100 mg chol, 96 mg sodium, 52 g carbo, 0 g fiber, 4 g pro. Daily Values: 7% vit. A, 7% vit. C, 3% calcium, 8% iron.*

A dusting of powdered sugar makes an easy topping for the bars.

TIPS FOR BAR COOKIE SUCCESS

■ Start by lining the baking pan with foil or parchment paper that extends beyond pan edges. That way, after baking, the bars will lift out in one piece, making them easy to cut neatly.

■ Butter is better for flavor, richness, texture, and color, which is why these recipes call for it. Margarine can be substituted for butter, but not all margarines are created equally. To ensure the best results, choose margarine made with at least 80% vegetable oil or that is at least 100 calories per tablespoon.

■ When measuring flour, stir it, then lightly spoon it into the appropriate cup size and level off with the straight edge of a knife or spatula. Do not pack the flour or tap the cup when filling it. Brown sugar, on the other hand, should be pressed firmly into the measuring cup; it will hold the shape of the cup when turned out.

■ Pay close attention to pan sizes in bar recipes. Too large may result in dry bars, especially around the edges. Too small, and the centers may be underbaked and doughy.

■ It's best to allow enough time for the bars to cool completely in the pan before cutting them. Cooling helps the bars set up and hold their shape. Cutting too early will cause them to fall apart and not cut neatly.

■ If you're shipping or toting bars, keep them looking good by layering them between sheets of parchment or waxed paper.

OATY RHUBARB STREUSEL BARS

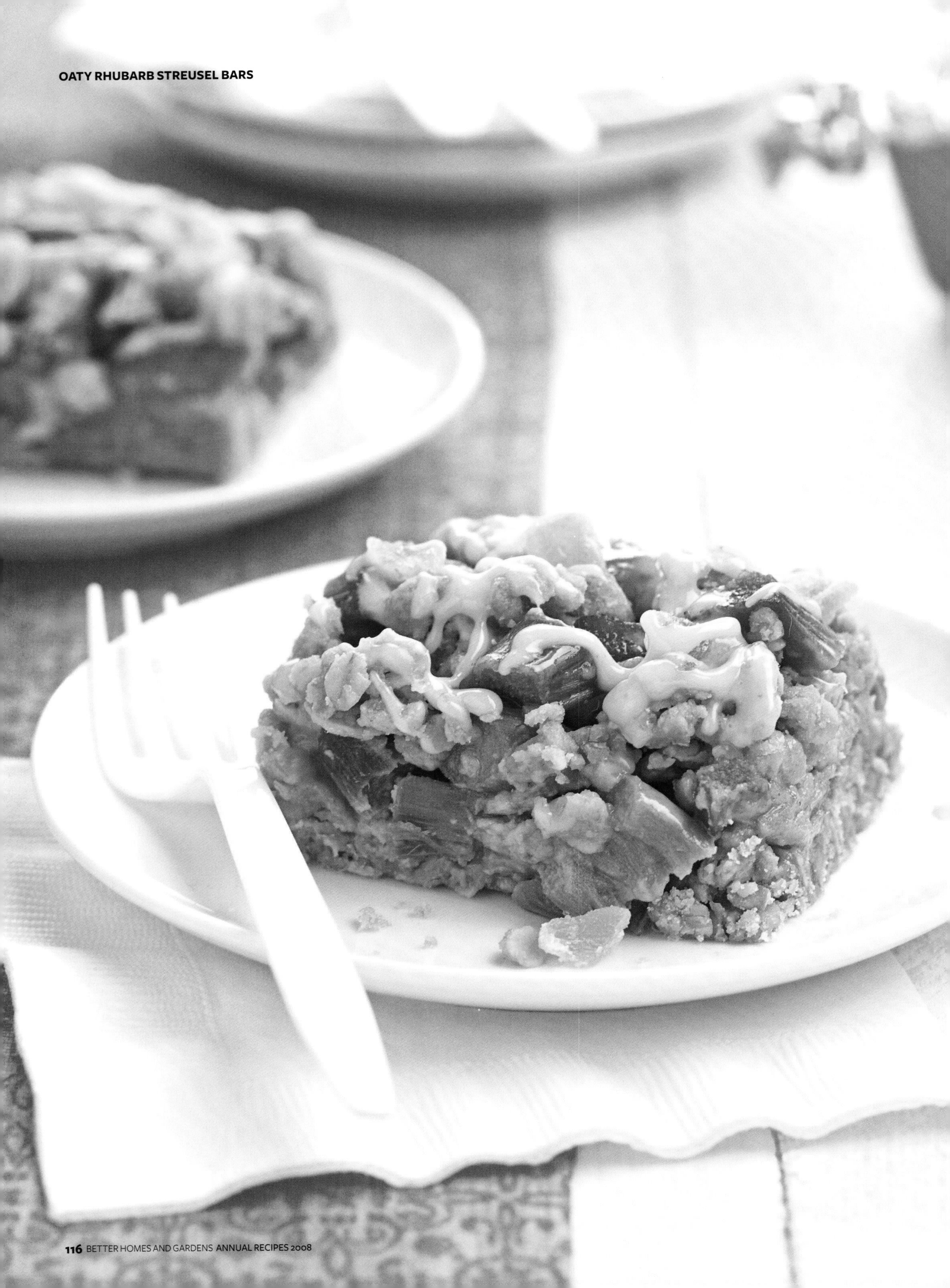

OATY RHUBARB STREUSEL BARS

PREP 25 min. **BAKE** 55 min. **COOL** 2 hr. **OVEN** 350°F

INGREDIENTS

1½ cups quick-cooking rolled oats
1 cup all-purpose flour
¾ cup packed brown sugar
¾ cup butter
¼ cup granulated sugar
2 Tbsp. all-purpose flour
½ tsp. ground ginger
2 cups fresh or frozen unsweetened sliced rhubarb
1 recipe Ginger Icing
1 Tbsp. finely chopped crystallized ginger (optional)

PREPARATION

1. Preheat oven to 350°F. Line 8×8×2-inch baking pan with heavy foil extended beyond pan edges.
2. In large bowl stir together oats, the 1 cup flour, and brown sugar. Cut in butter until mixture resembles coarse crumbs. Set aside 1 cup oats mixture. Press remaining on bottom of prepared pan. Bake 25 minutes.
3. Meanwhile, in medium bowl stir together granulated sugar, the 2 tablespoons flour, and ground ginger. Add rhubarb; toss to coat. Spread on hot crust. Sprinkle reserved oats mixture; press lightly.
4. Bake 30 to 35 minutes until top is golden and filling is bubbly. Cool on rack. Drizzle icing, sprinkle crystallized ginger. Lift from pan; cut into bars. Store, covered, in refrigerator up to 2 days. **Makes 16 bars.**
Ginger Icing In small bowl stir together ¾ cup sifted *powdered sugar*, ¼ teaspoon *ground ginger*, and 3 to 4 teaspoons *apricot nectar*, orange juice, or milk.

EACH BAR *221 cal, 10 g fat (5 g sat. fat), 24 mg chol, 70 mg sodium, 32 g carbo, 1 g fiber, 2 g pro. Daily Values: 7% vit. A, 3% vit. C, 2% calcium, 5% iron.*

RHUBARB Select uniform-size stalks, ½ to 1 inch in diameter, with bright, shiny reddish skins and fresh-looking leaves. Before slicing, remove any coarse fibers.

If you've never had rhubarb, it's a treat. The flavor is a sweet-tart cross between grapefruit and watermelon.

BERRY GOOD Perfect bars deserve perfect blueberries. Look at the underside of the box and avoid those with bruised or moldy berries. The light coating of white, or bloom, on the berries seals in moisture. Refrigerate, unwashed, until ready to use.

COCONUT-BLUEBERRY CHEESECAKE BARS

PREP 30 min. **BAKE** 26 min. **CHILL** 3 hr. **OVEN** 350°F

INGREDIENTS
½ cup butter
¾ cup finely crushed graham crackers
½ cup all-purpose flour
½ cup flaked coconut
½ cup ground pecans
¼ cup sugar
1½ 8-oz. pkg. cream cheese, softened
⅔ cup sugar
4 eggs
1 Tbsp. brandy or milk
1 tsp. vanilla
2 cups blueberries

PREPARATION
1. Preheat oven to 350°F. Lightly grease 13×9×2-inch baking pan; set aside.
2. For crust, in small saucepan heat butter over medium heat until the color of light brown sugar. Remove from heat; set aside.
3. In medium bowl stir together graham crackers, flour, coconut, pecans, and ¼ cup sugar. Stir in butter until combined. Evenly press on bottom of prepared pan. Bake 8 to 10 minutes or until lightly browned.
4. Meanwhile, in large mixing bowl beat cream cheese and ⅔ cup sugar on medium until combined. Add eggs, brandy, and vanilla. Beat until combined. Pour over hot crust. Sprinkle blueberries.
5. Bake 18 to 20 minutes or until center appears set. Cool in pan on rack. Cover and refrigerate. Cut into bars. Store, covered, in refrigerator. **Makes 32 bars.**

EACH BAR *136 cal, 9 g fat (5 g sat. fat), 46 mg chol, 78 mg sodium, 11 g carbo, 1 g fiber, 2 g pro. Daily Values: 5% vit. A, 1% vit. C, 2% calcium, 3% iron.*

KID FRIENDLY

CHERRY REVEL BARS

Frozen cherries, thawed and drained, can be substituted for fresh.

PREP 35 min. **BAKE** 25 min. **COOL** 1 hr. **CHILL** 2 hr. **OVEN** 350°F

INGREDIENTS
1 cup butter, softened, divided
2½ cups packed brown sugar, divided
½ tsp. baking soda
¼ tsp. salt
4 eggs, divided
1½ tsp. vanilla, divided
2½ cups all-purpose flour, divided
1½ cups quick-cooking rolled oats
6 oz. bittersweet chocolate, chopped
2 cups (10 oz.) fresh sweet cherries (such as Bing or Royal Ann), pitted
½ cup slivered toasted almonds

PREPARATION
1. Preheat oven to 350°F. Line 13×9×2-inch baking pan with foil; set aside. In mixing bowl beat *½ cup* of the butter on medium to high 30 seconds. Add *1 cup* of the brown sugar, the baking soda, and salt. Beat until combined, occasionally scraping bowl. Beat in 1 egg and *½ teaspoon* of the vanilla. Beat or stir in *1¼ cups* of the flour. Stir in oats; set aside.
2. For filling, in saucepan stir remaining 1½ cups brown sugar and ½ cup butter over medium heat until combined; cool slightly. Stir in remaining 3 eggs and 1 teaspoon vanilla; lightly beat with wooden spoon. Stir in remaining 1¼ cups flour and the chocolate.
3. Set aside ¾ cup oats mixture; press remaining in pan. Spread filling, top with cherries, dot with reserved oats mixture, and sprinkle nuts. Bake 25 minutes until top is light brown and filling is moist. Cool on rack 1 hour. Cover and refrigerate at least 2 hours.
4. Lift from pan; cut with serrated knife. Store, covered, at room temperature. **Makes 25 bars.**

EACH BAR *280 cal, 13 g fat (6 g sat. fat), 54 mg chol, 124 mg sodium, 40 g carbo, 2 g fiber, 4 g pro. Daily Values: 6% vit. A, 1% vit. C, 4% calcium, 10% iron.*

CHERRY REVEL BARS

Happy Mother's Day

Mom always said to share. This pretty dessert comes together quickly, so you'll soon be enjoying cake and conversation while making more delicious memories.

PHOTOS **ANDY LYONS** FOOD STYLING **JILL LUST**

RASPBERRY CAKES FOR TWO

CELEBRATE EVERY DAY *with*
Pam Anderson

RASPBERRY CAKES FOR TWO

Each cake makes two servings.

START TO FINISH 30 min.

INGREDIENTS

½   an 8-oz. pkg. cream cheese, softened
2   Tbsp. butter, softened
¼   cup lemon curd
3   Tbsp. powdered sugar
1   4.5-oz. pkg. prepared shortcakes
½   cup fresh raspberries
2   Tbsp. low-sugar raspberry preserves
    Fresh raspberries
    Small fresh mint leaves

PREPARATION

1. For frosting, in small bowl beat cream cheese and butter with electric mixer on medium until smooth. Beat in lemon curd. Add powdered sugar; beat until smooth and fluffy. Set aside.
2. Place two cakes, well sides up, on two dessert plates. Divide berries, in a single layer, between wells of two cakes. Spoon ½ tablespoon of the preserves over each. Place remaining cakes, well sides down, over filling. Spread frosting on cakes. Serve immediately or refrigerate, loosely covered, up to 48 hours.
3. To serve, stir remaining raspberry preserves; spoon on cakes. Top with additional raspberries and mint leaves.
Makes 2 cakes (4 servings).

EACH SERVING *307 cal, 14 g fat (8 g sat. fat), 61 mg chol, 99 mg sodium, 43 g carbo, 3 g fiber, 2 g pro. Daily Values: 7% vit. A, 4% vit. C, 2% calcium, 3% iron.*

> **PAM'S TIPS**
>
> To build this dessert quickly, use packaged shortcakes from a grocery store. Place one shortcake right side up. Fill with berries and preserves. Stack second cake upside down over filling. Frost as you would a layer cake. Guests will be pleasantly surprised to discover the berry filling.

JUNE

LIGHT THE GRILL, GRAB THE TONGS, AND GET READY TO ENJOY A SUMMER OF GREAT EATING. THE IDEAS YOU NEED ARE HERE: SEVEN UNIQUE STEAK RECIPES, EASY SIDE DISHES, AND TIPS FOR A BETTER CHEESEBURGER.

TENDERLOIN WITH GRILLED CORN RELISH
page 126

The Steaks of Summer

CHIMICHURRI CHICKEN
page 136

GREEK PASTA SALAD
page 139

**WALNUT-FETA YOGURT DIP AND
PINE NUT-WHITE BEAN DIP**
pages 142 and 143

THE STEAKS OF SUMMER

"COME ON OVER—WE'LL THROW A STEAK ON THE GRILL"
IS AN OFFER THAT'S EASY TO MAKE AND HARD TO RESIST.
THESE SEVEN SIMPLE RECIPES FROM GRILL GURU
JAMIE PURVIANCE MAKE STEAK FOOLPROOF AND DELICIOUS.

PORTERHOUSE

BY **RICHARD SWEARINGER**
RECIPES **JAMIE PURVIANCE** PHOTOS **ANDY LYONS**
FOOD STYLING **JILL LUST** PROP STYLING **KAREN JOHNSON** AND **SUE MITCHELL**

When company's coming **ROSEMARY PORTERHOUSE STEAKS,** *opposite,* is a showstopper. Add simple go-withs: creamy **Olive Mayo** and **Herbed Potatoes and Squash.**

page 131

You can smell the smoky paprika rub when **MEDITERRANEAN STRIP STEAKS** hit the fire. Just before serving, squeeze grilled lemons over the feta cheese, avocado, steak, and oregano.

page 133

TOP LOIN STRIP

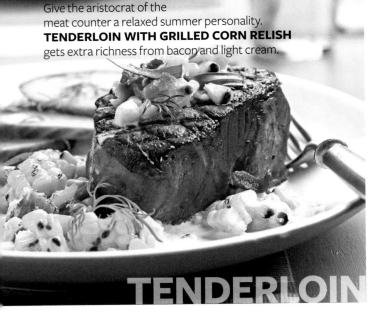

Give the aristocrat of the meat counter a relaxed summer personality. **TENDERLOIN WITH GRILLED CORN RELISH** gets extra richness from bacon and light cream.

TENDERLOIN

TENDERLOIN WITH GRILLED CORN RELISH

PREP 30 min. **GRILL** 28 min. **STAND** 10 min.

INGREDIENTS

3   ears corn, husks and silks removed
4   center-cut beef tenderloin steaks, cut 2 inches thick (about 2 lb. total)
4   slices bacon
½   cup finely chopped yellow onion
¾   cup half-and-half or light cream
2   Tbsp. finely chopped fresh dill
1   Tbsp. finely chopped fresh tarragon

PREPARATION

1. Lightly coat corn and steaks with *extra virgin olive oil*. Season steaks with ½ teaspoon *salt* and ¼ teaspoon *ground black pepper*. Let steaks stand at room temperature while grilling corn.
2. For charcoal grill, place corn on rack over medium-hot coals. Cover; grill 10 minutes or until golden, turning occasionally. (For gas grill, preheat grill to medium-high. Grill as above.) Set corn aside. With grilling tongs, carefully push coals to one side of grill and, if necessary, add more coals for medium-hot heat.
3. Place steaks on rack directly over coals. Cover and lightly sear on both sides, 5 to 6 minutes. Move to unheated side of grill. Cover and grill 13 to 15 minutes more for medium rare (145°F); remove. Cover with foil; set aside.
4. For corn relish, in skillet over medium coals cook bacon. Drain on paper towels; reserve drippings in skillet. Cut kernels from cob. Cook onion in drippings over medium coals until tender, 3 minutes, stirring often. Add corn and half-and-half. Bring to boiling; reduce heat. Simmer 3 minutes or until thickened. Add crumbled bacon and herbs; spoon over steaks. **MAKES 4 SERVINGS.**

EACH SERVING *701 cal, 42 g fat (15 g sat. fat), 189 mg chol, 699 mg sodium, 17 g carbo, 2 g fiber, 62 g pro. Daily Values: 8% vit. A, 13% vit. C, 9% calcium, 23% iron.*

WE TESTED AND TASTED TO FIND THE SEVEN BEST STEAKS FOR SUMMER GRILLING. THIS COLLECTION HAS SOMETHING FOR EVERY BUDGET AND OCCASION.

FRUIT-AND-FIRE FLAT IRON STEAKS

For easy slicing keep your steak knives sharp. We like Chef'sChoice model 130 Professional Sharpening Station for our serrated knives.

PREP 20 min. **MARINATE** 12 hr. **GRILL** 20 min.

INGREDIENTS

2   stalks fresh lemon grass or 1 Tbsp. finely shredded lemon peel
½   cup reduced-sodium soy sauce
⅓   cup bottled hoisin sauce
3   Tbsp. lemon juice
4   cloves garlic, minced
¼   to ½ tsp. crushed red pepper
4   boneless beef shoulder top blade (flat iron) steaks, cut 1 to 1¼ inches thick (about 1½ lb. total)
½   peeled, cored fresh pineapple, sliced
2   nectarines, halved, pitted, cut in wedges
2   plums, pitted, cut in wedges
1   bunch green onions (about 8), trimmed

PREPARATION

1. For marinade, trim ends of lemon grass; halve lengthwise. Remove two or three layers of tough outer stalk. Remove tender inner stalks; wrap, refrigerate, and reserve to garnish grilled steaks. Finely chop *1 tablespoon* remaining lemon grass. In bowl combine chopped lemon grass, soy sauce, hoisin sauce, lemon juice, garlic, and crushed red pepper. Transfer *½ cup* marinade to airtight container; refrigerate.
2. Place steaks in large self-sealing plastic bag set in shallow dish. Pour remaining marinade over steaks; seal bag. Refrigerate 12 to 24 hours; turn occasionally.
3. Remove steaks from marinade; discard marinade. Let steaks stand at room temperature 30 minutes.
4. For charcoal grill, place pineapple slices, nectarines, and plums on rack over hot coals. Cover; grill 4 to 6 minutes until fruit is lightly seared, turning once. Brush with refrigerated marinade the last 2 minutes of grilling. Transfer fruit to platter; set aside.
5. For charcoal grill, place steaks on rack directly over medium coals. Cover; grill 15 to 18 minutes for medium rare (145°F); turning once and brushing with refrigerated marinade the last 2 minutes of grilling. Place green onions on rack over coals; grill, uncovered, 1 minute, turning occasionally. (For gas grill, preheat grill to medium-high. Place fruit on rack over heat. Cover; grill fruit. Reduce heat to medium. Grill steaks and onions as above.)
6. Slice steaks. Serve with fruit, onions, and reserved lemon grass. **MAKES 4 SERVINGS.**

EACH SERVING *415 cal, 18 g fat (6 g sat. fat), 111 mg chol, 962 mg sodium, 29 g carbo, 3 g fiber, 36 g pro. Daily Values: 8% vit. A, 66% vit. C, 4% calcium, 25% iron.*

FRUIT-AND-FIRE FLAT IRON STEAKS is made with one of the newest, most affordable cuts at the meat counter. Start prep in the morning so the steak has all day to soak up a marinade of soy sauce, lemon juice, garlic, and red pepper.

FLAT IRON

TOP SIRLOIN

Cut and skewered into **TOP SIRLOIN KABOBS,** more of the steak's surface is exposed to heat, developing caramelized flavor. Serve with a creamy avocado-lime-mint sauce.

GIVE STEAKS A FRESH LOOK WITH THE PRODUCE OF SUMMER: PLUMP, JUICY TOMATOES; CRISP LETTUCE; SPICY PEPPERS; AND JUST-SNIPPED HERBS.

A 30-minute dinner, **RIBEYES WITH GARDEN TOMATOES** combines steak and tender butterhead lettuce splashed with balsamic-basil dressing and a sprinkle of sea salt.

RIBEYE

TOP SIRLOIN KABOBS AND AVOCADO SAUCE

Granulated garlic and garlic powder are made from ground dehydrated garlic; the granulated version is simply more coarsely ground. If substituting, use half as much powdered garlic as granulated. The same is true for granulated onion.

PREP 30 min. **MARINATE** 30 min. **GRILL** 10 min.

INGREDIENTS

3   Tbsp. extra virgin olive oil
1   Tbsp. granulated garlic
1   Tbsp. granulated onion
1½   tsp. dried oregano, crushed
1   tsp. freshly ground black pepper
½   tsp. kosher salt or salt
3   lb. beef top sirloin steak, about 1 inch thick
1   medium ripe avocado, pitted, peeled, and coarsely chopped
½   cup seedless (English) cucumber, coarsely chopped
⅓   cup lightly packed fresh mint leaves
¼   cup sour cream
2   Tbsp. lime juice
1   tsp. kosher salt or salt
1   tsp. ground cumin
1   recipe Grilled Peppers and Onions (optional)
     Fresh mint leaves (optional)

PREPARATION

1. In large bowl combine oil, granulated garlic and onion, oregano, pepper, and ½ teaspoon salt; set aside. Trim fat from meat. Cut meat in 1-inch cubes. Add meat to oil mixture; toss to coat evenly. Let stand at room temperature 30 minutes.
2. Meanwhile, for Avocado Sauce, in food processor combine avocado, cucumber, mint, sour cream, lime juice, 1 tablespoon *water*, 1 teaspoon salt, and cumin. Cover; process until nearly smooth, stopping to scrape sides as necessary. Transfer to serving bowl.
3. Thread meat on skewers, leaving ¼ inch between pieces.* For charcoal grill, place steaks on rack directly over medium coals. Cover; grill 10 to 12 minutes for medium rare (145°F), turning to brown evenly. (For gas grill, preheat grill. Grill as directed above.) Serve steaks with Avocado Sauce and Grilled Peppers and Onions. Sprinkle fresh mint. **MAKES 6 SERVINGS.**
Grilled Peppers and Onions Brush *whole peppers* and *onion slices* with *oil*. Cover and grill directly over hot coals, 8 minutes or until tender, turning occasionally.
*Test Kitchen Tip Soak bamboo skewers in water for 30 minutes before using.

EACH SERVING *353 cal, 19 g fat (5 g sat. fat), 73 mg chol, 569 mg sodium, 6 g carbo, 2 g fiber, 38 g pro. Daily Values: 2% vit. A, 8% vit. C, 6% calcium, 18% iron.*

RIBEYES WITH GARDEN TOMATOES

Extremely flavorful heirloom tomatoes start popping up at farmers' markets and large supermarkets in June. Intriguing in shape and size, they range in color from green striped to orange and deep purple-red.

PREP 25 min. **STAND** 35 min. **GRILL** 12 min.

INGREDIENTS

2   Tbsp. balsamic vinegar
2   Tbsp. finely chopped fresh basil
2   tsp. minced garlic
6   Tbsp. extra virgin olive oil
2   1¼-inch-thick beef ribeye steaks (about 2 lb. total)
1   head butterhead lettuce, cored, leaves separated (about 6 oz.)
1½   lb. assorted fresh heirloom or desired tomatoes, sliced or cut in wedges
½   cup whole basil leaves
     Coarse sea salt

PREPARATION

1. For dressing, in bowl whisk together vinegar, chopped basil, garlic, 1 teaspoon *salt*, and ½ teaspoon *ground black pepper*. Slowly whisk in oil until smooth. Remove *2 tablespoons* to marinate steaks; set remaining dressing aside. Brush steaks with the 2 tablespoons dressing; let stand at room temperature for 30 minutes.
3. For charcoal grill, arrange medium-hot coals on one side of grill. Place steaks on rack directly over coals. Cover; lightly sear on both sides, 8 minutes. Move to unheated side of grill. Cover; grill 4 to 6 minutes more for medium rare (145°F). Remove; let stand 5 minutes. (For gas grill, preheat to medium-high. Adjust for indirect grilling. Grill as above.)
4. Diagonally slice steaks; arrange on lettuce leaves with tomatoes and basil. Drizzle dressing; season with salt. **MAKES 4 TO 6 SERVINGS.**

EACH SERVING *605 cal, 37 g fat (9 g sat. fat), 167 mg chol, 624 mg sodium, 10 g carbo, 3 g fiber, 56 g pro. Daily Values: 64% vit. A, 42% vit. C, 8% calcium, 29% iron.*

TRI-TIP STEAKS WITH TEXAS TOAST makes a casual meal for family and friends. Molasses-bourbon sauce soaks the spicy meat, which is heaped with pickled jalapeño rings and billowy romaine lettuce.

TRI-TIP STEAKS WITH TEXAS TOAST

Top steaks with shredded romaine, slivered onion, and jalapeño slices. If Texas toast is unavailable, use any thick-sliced white bread.

PREP 30 min. **MARINATE** 2 hr. **STAND** 30 min. **GRILL** 16 min.

INGREDIENTS
- ⅔ cup bourbon
- ⅓ cup reduced-sodium soy sauce
- ¼ cup molasses
- 2 Tbsp. cider vinegar
- 2 tsp. chili powder
- 1½ to 2 lb. beef tri-tip steaks, cut 1 inch thick
- ½ cup ketchup
- 6 Tbsp. butter, softened
- 6 to 8 slices Texas toast

PREPARATION

1. For marinade, whisk together bourbon, soy sauce, molasses, vinegar, and chili powder. Remove ¼ cup for sauce. Prick both sides of steaks with fork. Place in self-sealing plastic bag set in shallow dish. Pour marinade over. Seal; marinate refrigerated, 2 to 3 hours, turning occasionally.

2. For sauce, in saucepan combine ketchup, ½ cup *water*, ¼ cup reserved marinade, *2 tablespoons* of the butter, and ¼ teaspoon *ground black pepper*. Bring to boiling over medium; set aside.

3. Remove steaks from marinade; discard marinade. Brush meat with 1 tablespoon *cooking oil*. Let stand at room temperature 30 minutes.

4. For charcoal grill, arrange medium-hot coals on one side of grill. Place steaks on rack directly over coals. Cover; lightly sear on both sides, 4 minutes. Move to unheated side of grill. Cover and grill 12 to 15 minutes more for medium rare (145°F). Remove; let stand 5 minutes. Butter bread; place on hot grill. (For gas grill, preheat grill to medium-high. Adjust for indirect grilling. Grill as above.)

5. Reheat sauce. Thinly slice steak and arrange on toast; pass sauce.

MAKES 6 TO 8 SERVINGS.

EACH SERVING *513 cal, 27 g fat (11 g sat. fat), 169 mg chol, 970 mg sodium, 31 g carbo, 1 g fiber, 35 g pro. Daily Values: 19% vit. A, 6% vit. C, 8% calcium, 23% iron.*

JAMIE SAYS SEAR AND SLIDE

Thick steaks often require two types of heat. First sear both sides over direct medium-high heat to develop flavors on the surface. Then slide the meat to a less hot (medium) section of the grill to finish cooking. The medium heat will cook the steak through to the center without overbrowning the top or bottom.

JAMIE SAYS HOT OR NOT?

Coals are ready for grilling when they are glowing and covered with gray ash. To check the temperature of your coals, carefully place the palm of your hand about 5 inches above the grill rack at cooking level and count the number of seconds you can hold it there: 2 seconds for high, 4 seconds for medium-high, 6 seconds for medium.

ROSEMARY PORTERHOUSE STEAKS WITH OLIVE MAYO

A porterhouse typically serves 2 to 3 people. If you're feeding big appetites, plan for one each and expect leftovers. The Olive Mayo serves 8 to 10. Recipe pictured on page 124.

PREP 25 min. **STAND** 30 min. **GRILL** 9 min.

INGREDIENTS
- 1 cup mayonnaise
- ¼ cup pitted kalamata olives, chopped
- 1 Tbsp. finely chopped fresh dill
- 1 clove garlic, minced
- 2 porterhouse steaks, cut 1 to 1¼ inches thick (about 1 lb. each)
- 1 Tbsp. extra virgin olive oil
- 1 Tbsp. finely chopped fresh rosemary
- ¾ tsp. kosher salt or salt
- ½ tsp. freshly ground black pepper
  Snipped fresh rosemary (optional)
- 1 recipe Herbed Potatoes and Squash

PREPARATION

1. For Olive Mayo, in bowl combine mayonnaise, olives, dill, and garlic. Cover; refrigerate up to 1 week.

2. Brush steaks with oil. Combine the 1 tablespoon rosemary, salt, and pepper; rub on steaks. Let stand at room temperature 30 minutes.

3. For charcoal grill, place steaks on rack directly over medium-hot coals. Cover; grill 9 to 11 minutes for medium rare (145°F), turning once. (For gas grill, preheat; set to medium-high. Cover; grill as above.)

4. Sprinkle steaks with fresh rosemary; cut in serving portions. Serve with Olive Mayo and Herbed Potatoes and Squash.

MAKES 4 TO 6 SERVINGS.

EACH SERVING *589 cal, 46 g fat (11 g sat. fat), 112 mg chol, 667 mg sodium, 1 g carbo, 0 g fiber, 40 g pro. Daily Values: 1% vit. C, 1% calcium, 29% iron.*

HERBED POTATOES AND SQUASH

Recipe pictured on page 124.

PREP 20 min. **GRILL** 25 min.

INGREDIENTS
- 2 Tbsp. extra virgin olive oil
- 2 tsp. finely chopped fresh rosemary
- 1 lb. red and/or white tiny new potatoes, halved
- 2 small yellow summer squash, cut in thick diagonal slices (about 2 cups)
  Snipped fresh rosemary and/or dill

PREPARATION

1. In bowl stir together oil, rosemary, and ½ teaspoon *salt*. Add potatoes; toss.

2. For charcoal grill, arrange medium-hot coals around drip pan. Place grill wok, basket, or foil pan directly on rack above drip pan; heat 5 minutes. Add potatoes; cover and grill 10 minutes, stirring once. Add squash. Cover; grill 15 minutes more until potatoes are tender, stirring once. Transfer to serving dish. Sprinkle with remaining fresh rosemary. **MAKES 4 TO 6 SERVINGS.**

EACH SERVING *147 cal, 7 g fat (1 g sat. fat), 0 mg chol, 249 mg sodium, 20 g carbo, 3 g fiber, 3 g pro. Daily Values: 1% vit. A, 22% vit. C, 2% calcium, 6% iron.*

THE STEAKS OF SUMMER

A CUT ABOVE THE REST

1. RIBEYE Juicy, tender, and flavorful. "Generous marbling makes it a worry-free choice for a crowd," says grilling expert Jamie Purviance.

2. TENDERLOIN The most tender of all steaks, it's also known as filet mignon.

3. FLAT IRON Not only is it a budget steak, it's the second-most tender cut. Takes rubs well.

4. TOP LOIN STRIP Also called a New York steak or a KC strip, "the beefy flavor of its rosy interior defines the essence of a great steak," says Jamie.

5. TOP SIRLOIN These flat, firmly grained steaks are easy to slice into cubes for kabobs. "As long as you don't grill past medium rare, the meat will be juicy to the core," Jamie says.

6. TRI-TIP Flavorful beef at an affordable price, it works very well with marinades and when sliced thin is tender and juicy; great for salads and sandwiches.

7. PORTERHOUSE "This is the power steak—a highly successful merger of a tenderloin and a strip. Cooks best over consistent medium-high heat," Jamie says.

MEDITERRANEAN STRIP STEAKS

Mediterranean ingredients—lemon, olive oil, feta, and oregano—complement paprika and brown sugar-rubbed steaks. Recipe pictured on page 125.

PREP 20 min. **STAND** 30 min. **GRILL** 9 min.

INGREDIENTS

- 2   tsp. smoked paprika
- 1   tsp. packed brown sugar
- 2   Tbsp. extra virgin olive oil
- 4   top loin (strip) steaks, cut 1 inch thick (about 12 oz. each)
- 2   lemons, halved
- 1   avocado, pitted, peeled, and sliced
    Feta cheese wedges (optional)
- 4   oz. feta cheese, crumbled
    Fresh oregano
- 1   tsp. finely shredded lemon peel

PREPARATION

1. For rub, stir together paprika, sugar, 1 teaspoon *salt,* and ½ teaspoon *ground black pepper.* Coat steaks with *1 tablespoon* of the oil; rub mixture on both sides. Let stand at room temperature 30 minutes.

2. For charcoal grill, arrange medium-hot coals on one side of grill. Place steaks on rack directly over coals. Cover and lightly sear on both sides, 5 to 6 minutes. Move to unheated side of grill. Cover and grill 4 to 5 minutes more for medium rare (145°F). Remove; let stand 5 minutes. Grill lemon halves, cut sides down, directly over coals, 2 minutes. (For gas grill, preheat grill. Adjust heat for indirect cooking. Grill as above.)

3. Serve with lemons, avocado, and feta cheese wedges. Sprinkle feta, oregano, and lemon peel; drizzle remaining oil. **MAKES 8 SERVINGS.**

EACH SERVING *340 cal, 18 g fat (6 g sat. fat), 97 mg chol, 479 mg sodium, 5 g carbo, 2 g fiber, 40 g pro. Daily Values: 7% vit. A, 38% vit. C, 12% calcium, 16% iron.*

JAMIE SAYS GET THE MARKS

For diamond-shape grill marks, think of the grill as a clock and the steak as a hand on its face. Once the grill is hot, place the steak on the rack so one end points toward 10 o'clock. Leave in place a few minutes. Rotate one-fourth turn, so the end points toward 2. Leave each steak in that position a few minutes more. Turn the steaks over, then pat yourself on the back.

MEET JAMIE

We chose the perfect cuts; then turned to freelance grilling guru **JAMIE PURVIANCE** to make them the best steaks of summer. As an expert in outdoor cooking, Jamie appears on national TV shows and judges several major barbecue competitions. He

sums up his time around the grill this way: "People have been grilling meat over fire for so long that it must be hardwired into our DNA. Once the meat juices start dripping into the flames and vaporizing into aromatic smoke, I am locked in to the whole delicious process. I was meant to be doing this."

Jamie's most recent book is *Weber's Charcoal Grilling: The Art of Cooking with Live Fire* (Sunset, $19.95).

ALLEN BROTHERS

The steaks in this story were supplied by Allen Brothers, a family-owned business based in Chicago since 1893.
800/957-0111 OR allenbrothers.com

JAMIE SAYS MAKING THE GRADE

All beef sold in the U.S. must, by law, be inspected for safety. Meat packers can also choose to have beef graded for quality based on marbling—the flecks of fat distributed within the beef that provide flavor and juiciness. **PRIME,** the top grade, has the most marbling; it's sold to restaurants and some specialty retailers. **CHOICE** has moderate marbling and is commonly sold in supermarkets. **SELECT** is the leanest, but is less juicy and tender than the top two grades.

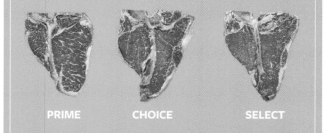

PRIME   CHOICE   SELECT

JAMIE SAYS GRASS VS. GRAIN-FED

Grass-fed cattle spend nearly all their lives in pastures, eating only grass. Grain-fed cattle typically spend most of their lives eating grass in pastures before moving to a feedlot where they are fed a high-energy grain diet for 4 to 6 months. Grass-fed beef is leaner and tends to have a stronger, "beefier" flavor.

Grilling Season

READY IN
20
MINUTES

Ready, set, get outdoors! These weeknight suppers
are simple, fresh, and quick to the table.

BY **PEG SMITH** PHOTOS **ANDY LYONS** RECIPES **JULIANA HALE** FOOD STYLING **JILL LUST**

FAST!

SPICE-RUBBED SALMON

START TO FINISH 20 min.

INGREDIENTS

2   tsp. chili powder
1   tsp. ground cumin
1   tsp. packed brown sugar
4   5-oz. skinless salmon fillets
1   small cabbage, cut in 6 wedges
2   to 3 Tbsp. cooking oil
1   large carrot
      Orange wedges

PREPARATION

1. In small bowl mix chili powder, cumin, brown sugar, ¼ teaspoon *salt,* and ⅛ teaspoon *ground black pepper.* Rub spice mixture on salmon. Brush cabbage wedges with *1 tablespoon* of the oil.
2. On charcoal grill place salmon and cabbage on greased rack of uncovered grill directly over medium coals. Grill salmon 4 to 6 minutes for each ½ inch of thickness or until it flakes when tested with a fork, turning once halfway through cooking time. Grill cabbage 6 to 8 minutes, turning once.
3. Meanwhile, peel carrot and cut in wide strips. Remove fish and cabbage from grill. Coarsely cut cabbage; combine with carrot and 1 to 2 tablespoons remaining oil. Season with *salt* and *pepper.* Serve with oranges. **MAKES 4 SERVINGS.**

EACH SERVING *380 cal, 23 g fat (4 g sat. fat), 84 mg chol, 284 mg sodium, 14 g carbo, 5 g fiber, 31 g pro. Daily Values: 64% vit. A, 122% vit. C, 10% calcium, 9% iron.*

FAST!

PITA, CHEESE, AND VEGGIE GRILL

START TO FINISH 20 min.

INGREDIENTS

1   8-oz. block feta cheese, quartered
1   medium zucchini, halved lengthwise
1   medium red onion, cut in ½-inch slices
¼   cup Italian salad dressing
4   pita bread rounds
2   medium tomatoes, cut in wedges
1   Tbsp. honey

PREPARATION

1. Drizzle cheese, zucchini, and onion slices with *half* the salad dressing. Sprinkle *salt* and *ground black pepper.*
2. On rack of charcoal grill place zucchini, onion slices, and 6-inch cast-iron skillet (to heat for softening cheese) directly over medium coals. Grill zucchini and onion 8 minutes or until tender, turning once halfway through cooking time. Remove vegetables. Grill pita bread and tomatoes on grill rack 2 minutes or until bread is toasted and tomatoes are lightly charred. Place cheese in hot skillet; heat 1 to 2 minutes to soften.
3. To serve, cut zucchini in chunks. Drizzle cheese, vegetables, pitas, and tomatoes with honey and remaining salad dressing.
MAKES 4 SERVINGS.

EACH SERVING *404 cal, 17 g fat (9 g sat. fat), 50 mg chol, 1,352 mg sodium, 48 g carbo, 3 g fiber, 15 g pro. Daily Values: 17% vit. A, 30% vit. C, 35% calcium, 14% iron.*

PITA, CHEESE, AND VEGGIE GRILL

BRATS WITH MANGO RELISH

CHIMICHURRI CHICKEN

START TO FINISH 20 min.

INGREDIENTS

4	skinless, boneless chicken breast halves
3	Tbsp. cooking oil
12	oz. fresh young green beans
¾	cup packed Italian (flat-leaf) parsley
1	Tbsp. cider vinegar
2	cloves garlic, halved
¼	tsp. crushed red pepper
	Shredded peel and and juice from one lemon

PREPARATION

1. Brush chicken with *1 tablespoon* of the oil; sprinkle ¼ teaspoon each *salt* and *ground black pepper.* On charcoal grill, cook chicken on rack directly over medium coals 12 to 15 minutes or until no longer pink, turning once halfway through grilling time.
2. Place beans in microwave-safe 1½-quart dish. Add 1 tablespoon *water.* Cover with vented plastic wrap. Cook on high 3 minutes; drain.
3. For chimichurri sauce, in small food processor bowl combine parsley, the remaining oil, the vinegar, garlic, ¼ teaspoon *salt,* and red pepper. Process until nearly smooth. Serve chicken and beans topped with chimichurri sauce, lemon peel, and juice.
MAKES 4 SERVINGS.

EACH SERVING *281 cal, 12 g fat (2 g sat. fat), 82 mg chol, 376 mg sodium, 8 g carbo, 3 g fiber, 35 g pro. Daily Values: 32% vit. A, 57% vit. C, 7% calcium, 14% iron.*

BRATS WITH MANGO RELISH

START TO FINISH 20 min.

INGREDIENTS

1	large fresh mango, seeded, peeled, and halved
1	small red onion, cut in ½-inch slices
4	cooked smoked bratwurst (12 oz.)
4	buns, split
2	hearts of romaine lettuce, halved
½	tsp. Jamaican jerk seasoning

PREPARATION

1. Brush mango and onion with 1 tablespoon *cooking oil.*
2. On rack of uncovered charcoal grill place mango halves, onion, and brats directly over medium coals. Grill 8 minutes or until mango and brats are browned and heated through and onion is crisp-tender, turning once halfway through cooking. Lightly toast buns 1 to 2 minutes on grill. Set aside mango, onion, and brats.
3. Lightly brush romaine with *cooking oil.* Grill 1 to 2 minutes, directly over medium coals, until lightly browned and wilted, turning once.
4. For relish, chop grilled mango and onion. Combine in bowl with 1 tablespoon *cooking oil,* jerk seasoning, and *salt* and *ground black pepper.* Serve brats in buns with relish and romaine.
MAKES 4 SERVINGS.

EACH SERVING *478 cal, 31 g fat (6 g sat. fat), 66 mg chol, 1,112 mg sodium, 35 g carbo, 2 g fiber, 15 g pro. Daily Values: 8% vit. A, 27% vit. C, 8% calcium, 13% iron.*

CHIMICHURRI CHICKEN

FAST!

PORTOBELLO BURGERS

START TO FINISH 20 min.

INGREDIENTS

4	portobello mushrooms
2	Tbsp. olive oil
1	tsp. dried Italian seasoning, crushed
4	slices provolone cheese
4	ciabatta rolls, split
¼	cup mayonnaise
4	to 8 pieces bottled roasted red sweet pepper
¾	cup fresh basil leaves

PREPARATION

1. Scrape gills from mushroom caps, if desired. Drizzle mushrooms with oil. Sprinkle *salt, ground black pepper,* and crushed Italian seasoning.

2. On charcoal grill cook mushrooms on rack of uncovered grill directly over medium coals 6 to 8 minutes, turning once halfway through cooking. Top each mushroom with a cheese slice. Place rolls, split sides down, on grill rack. Grill 2 minutes more until cheese is melted, mushrooms are tender, and rolls are toasted.

3. Serve mushrooms on rolls. Pass mayonnaise, sweet pepper pieces, and basil leaves. **MAKES 4 SERVINGS.**

EACH SERVING *520 cal, 29 g fat (9 g sat. fat), 25 mg chol, 972 mg sodium, 49 g carbo, 4 g fiber, 17 g pro. Daily Values: 13% vit. A, 88% vit. C, 31% calcium, 22% iron.*

PORTOBELLO BURGERS

Barbecue Sides

When burgers, brats, or ribs are on the grill, these crowd-pleasers round out dinner with ease.

BY **ERIN SIMPSON** PHOTOS **ANDY LYONS** FOOD STYLING **JILL LUST**

GREEK PASTA SALAD

GREEK PASTA SALAD

The fresh herbs, vegetables, and olives that characterize Greek cuisine are tossed with pasta in this sprightly salad. Feta cheese gives it a tangy finish.

PREP 40 min. **CHILL** 2 hr.

INGREDIENTS
12   oz. dried mostaccioli or penne (about 4 cups uncooked)
2   cups cherry tomatoes, quartered
1   medium cucumber, halved lengthwise and sliced
4   green onions, sliced
⅓   cup pitted Kalamata olives, halved
½   cup olive oil
½   cup lemon juice
2   Tbsp. snipped fresh basil or 2 tsp. dried basil, crushed
2   Tbsp. snipped fresh oregano or 2 tsp. dried oregano, crushed
1   Tbsp. anchovy paste (optional)
4   to 6 cloves garlic, minced
¼   tsp. salt
¼   tsp. ground black pepper
1   cup crumbled feta cheese (4 oz.)
      Fresh oregano leaves

PREPARATION

1. Cook pasta according to package directions. Drain in colander. Rinse with cold water; drain again.
2. In large bowl toss together cooked pasta, tomatoes, cucumber, green onion, and olives.
3. In screw-top jar combine olive oil, lemon juice, basil, 2 tablespoons oregano, anchovy paste, garlic, salt, and pepper. Cover; shake well. Drizzle over pasta mixture; toss to coat.
4. Cover; chill in refrigerator at least 2 hours or up to 24 hours. To serve, add feta cheese; toss. Sprinkle fresh oregano leaves. **MAKES 12 TO 16 SIDE-DISH SERVINGS.**

EACH SERVING *231 cal, 12 g fat (3 g sat. fat), 8 mg chol, 200 mg sodium, 26 g carbo, 2 g fiber, 6 g pro. Daily Values: 8% vit. A, 18% vit. C, 7% calcium, 7% iron.*

QUICK SALADS TO TRY

■ **GARDEN PASTA** To 4 cups cooked pasta, add a cupful of steamed asparagus pieces and green peas, and ample pinches of snipped chives, mint, and dill. Hit with a squeeze of lemon juice and extra virgin olive oil.
■ **CURRY BEAN** Throw together two cans of garbanzo beans (chickpeas), a handful of shredded carrot, sliced green onion, chopped red sweet pepper, and a few halved grapes. Toss in a dressing of plain yogurt combined with generous dashes of curry powder, a spoonful of honey, and a touch of cayenne pepper.

FAST!

GREEN BEAN SALAD

PREP 10 min. **COOK** 5 min. **STAND** up to 30 min.

INGREDIENTS
12   oz. fresh green beans, trimmed
⅓   cup fresh parsley, coarsely chopped
4   green onions, sliced
2   stalks celery, chopped
2   Tbsp. olive oil
2   Tbsp. lime juice
      Lime wedges (optional)

PREPARATION

1. In 2-quart microwave-safe dish add green beans and 2 tablespoons *water.* Cover; microcook on 100% power (high) 5 minutes or until tender, stirring halfway. Drain; rinse with cold water. Drain again. Transfer to serving dish. Toss with parsley, green onion, celery, oil, and juice. Cover; let stand at room temperature up to 30 minutes.
2. To serve, sprinkle with *salt* and *ground black pepper;* squeeze lime wedges over top. **MAKES 4 TO 6 SIDE-DISH SERVINGS.**

EACH SERVING *96 cal, 7 g total fat (1 g sat. fat), 0 mg chol, 134 mg sodium, 8 g carbo, 4 g fiber, 2 g pro. Daily Values: 24% vit. A, 36% vit. C, 6% calcium, 8% iron.*

GREEN BEAN SALAD

KID FRIENDLY **LOW FAT**

SKILLET WHITE BEANS

Baked beans are a summer staple. This streamlined version develops the same deep, rich flavor without heating up the oven.

PREP 25 min. **COOK** 25 min.

INGREDIENTS

1	large sweet onion, halved lengthwise and thinly sliced (2 cups)
3	Tbsp. butter
½	cup maple or maple-flavored syrup
⅓	cup white balsamic vinegar or lemon juice
2	Tbsp. packed brown sugar
2	Tbsp. snipped fresh sage
2	Tbsp. tomato paste
1	tsp. salt
½	tsp. freshly ground black pepper
2	15 ½- or 16-oz. cans navy beans, rinsed and drained
2	15 ½- or 16-oz. cans butter beans, rinsed and drained
1	15 ½- to 16-oz. can garbanzo beans (chickpeas), rinsed and drained
	Dairy sour cream or crème frâiche
	Yellow, red, and/or green tomatoes, chopped (optional)
	Sage leaves (optional)

PREPARATION

1. In 12-inch skillet cook onion in hot butter over medium heat about 15 minutes or until tender and browned, stirring occasionally. Stir in maple syrup, balsamic vinegar, brown sugar, 2 tablespoons sage, tomato paste, salt, and pepper. Add beans; stir to coat.

2. Cover and cook over medium heat 10 to 15 minutes or until heated through, stirring occasionally. Transfer to a serving bowl. Top with sour cream. Garnish with tomatoes and sage leaves.

MAKES 12 TO 14 SIDE-DISH SERVINGS.

EACH SERVING *246 cal, 7 g total fat (4 g sat. fat), 21 mg chol, 570 mg sodium, 43 g carbo, 9 g fiber, 10 g pro. Daily Values: 9% vit. A, 8% vit. C, 6% calcium, 13% iron.*

MORE BAKED BEANS

■ SLOW COOKER In a slow cooker combine three cans pinto beans, a chopped large onion and yellow sweet pepper, a few hefty spoonfuls of barbecue sauce, brown sugar, and a teaspoon of dried mustard. Cook 4 hours on low or 2 hours on high.

■ SOUTHERN Start with two cans Great Northern beans. Toss in a sliced large peach, crumbled bacon, a diced medium onion, half a shot of bourbon, and a splash of peach nectar or apple juice. Drizzle molasses. Simmer until thickened.

Cheeseburger

Fully loaded, this backyard classic brings summertime to the table.

BY **ERIN SIMPSON** PHOTO **ANDY LYONS** FOOD STYLING **JILL LUST**

ON A ROLL
A whole wheat bun, lightly toasted on the grill, can stand up to a juicy burger. Substitute a bagel, English muffin, or flatbread.

VARY THE VEGGIES
Replace ho-hum iceberg with baby greens, like spinach and romaine, or even fresh basil leaves. A variety of heirloom tomatoes provide summer-fresh taste and color.

BEEF IT UP
A mix of 90% lean ground sirloin and 80% lean ground chuck gives the best balance of flavor and juiciness. Then fold in diced onion and chopped herbs. Or add crumbled bacon.

CHEESE, PLEASE
We love classic sharp cheddar on our burger. Or try creamy Muenster, nutty Gruyère, or tangy blue cheese.

WELL SPREAD
Mix mayo with ground horseradish, brown mustard, or chili powder. Or drizzle on Thousand Island dressing or barbecue sauce.

HANDLE WITH CARE
For a tender burger, do not pack or squeeze ground beef into shape. Lightly press meat together to form a ball, then flatten gently into a patty. Press the center of the burger slightly thinner than the edge to ensure even cooking.

TEST KITCHEN TIP
Play it safe and use a meat thermometer to check meat for doneness. Insert thermometer stem at least 2 inches into side of burger. It will register temperature in 15 to 20 seconds. Cook to 160°F (medium): for a ¾-inch-thick burger grill over medium coals 14 to 18 minutes, turning halfway through.

**WALNUT-FETA
YOGURT DIP AND
PINE NUT-WHITE BEAN DIP**

40 CALORIES PER SERVING

Skinny Dips

Dive right in. With sensible nibbling, you can control the urge to overeat.

BY **MARGE PERRY** PHOTOS **SCOTT LITTLE**

LAURA SAYS

Stirring fresh herbs into dips adds flavor and may also be beneficial to your health. Researchers are investigating whether oregano, for example, may help in the fight against heart disease, diabetes, and cancer. Of course, herbs are only a small part of your diet, but in nutrition, a smidgen here and a nibble there can add up to real benefits.

LAURA MARZEN, RD, TEST KITCHEN NUTRITION SPECIALIST

PINE NUT-WHITE BEAN DIP

Substitute other beans and nuts; the health benefits will be similar.

PREP 15 min. **CHILL** 2 hr.

INGREDIENTS
¼ cup soft bread crumbs
2 Tbsp. fat-free milk
1 15-oz. can cannellini or Great Northern beans, rinsed and drained
¼ cup fat-free or light sour cream
3 Tbsp. pine nuts, toasted
2 tsp. lemon juice
¼ tsp. salt-free garlic and herb seasoning blend
⅛ tsp. cayenne pepper
2 tsp. snipped fresh oregano or basil
Pine nuts, toasted (optional)
Fresh oregano leaves (optional)
Assorted vegetable dippers

PREPARATION
1. In small bowl combine crumbs and milk; cover. Let stand 5 minutes.
2. Meanwhile, in blender or food processor combine beans, sour cream, pine nuts, lemon juice, seasoning, and pepper. Cover and blend or process until nearly smooth. Add crumb mixture. Cover and blend or process until smooth. Stir in herbs. Cover; refrigerate 2 to 24 hours. To serve, sprinkle dip with pine nuts and oregano. Serve with vegetable dippers. **MAKES 1½ CUPS.**

EACH SERVING (2 TBSP.) *40 cal, 1 g fat (0 g sat. fat), 1 mg chol, 70 mg sodium, 7 g carbo, 2 g fiber, 3 g pro. Daily Values: 1% vit. A, 1% vit. C, 2% calcium, 4% iron.*

WALNUT-FETA YOGURT DIP

PREP 25 min. **CHILL** 25 hr.

INGREDIENTS

4	cups plain low-fat or fat-free yogurt*
½	cup crumbled feta cheese (2 oz.)
⅓	cup chopped walnuts or pine nuts
2	Tbsp. snipped dried tomatoes (not oil packed)
2	tsp. snipped fresh oregano or 1 tsp. dried oregano, crushed
¼	tsp. salt
⅛	tsp. freshly ground black pepper
	Walnut halves (optional)
	Assorted vegetable dippers

PREPARATION

1. To prepare yogurt for the dip, line a strainer or small colander with three layers of 100%-cotton cheesecloth or a clean paper coffee filter and suspend lined strainer over a bowl. Spoon in yogurt. Cover with plastic wrap and refrigerate at least 24 hours, up to 48 hours. Remove from refrigerator; discard liquid in bowl.

2. Transfer yogurt cheese to medium bowl. Stir in feta cheese, nuts, tomatoes, oregano, salt, and pepper. Cover; refrigerate at least 1 hour, up to 24 hours. Top with walnut halves. Serve with vegetable dippers. **MAKES 2 CUPS (SIXTEEN 2-TBSP. SERVINGS).**

*Note Use yogurt that contains no gums, gelatin, or fillers, which may prevent curd and whey from separating.

EACH SERVING *68 cal, 4 g fat (1 g sat. fat), 8 mg chol, 140 mg sodium, 5 g carbo, 0 g fiber, 4 g pro. Daily Values: 1% vit. A, 1% vit. C, 14% calcium, 1% iron.*

CURRIED CARROT SPREAD

PREP 20 min. **COOK** 15 min. **CHILL** 4 hr.

INGREDIENTS

3	cups sliced carrot
¾	cup chopped onion
3	cloves garlic, minced
2	Tbsp. olive oil or cooking oil
1	Tbsp. curry powder
1	tsp. ground cumin
1	15-oz. can cannellini beans, rinsed and drained
¾	tsp. salt
	Thinly sliced green onion (optional)
	Whole wheat crackers and/or assorted vegetable dippers

PREPARATION

1. In medium covered saucepan cook carrot in small amount of boiling water about 15 minutes or until very tender. Drain.

2. Meanwhile, in small skillet cook onion and garlic in hot oil until tender. Stir in curry powder and cumin. Transfer carrot and onion mixture to food processor; add beans and salt. Cover and process until smooth. Transfer to serving bowl. Cover and refrigerate at least 4 hours, up to 3 days. To serve, top with green onion. Serve with crackers or vegetable dippers. **MAKES 3 CUPS.**

EACH SERVING (2 TBSP.) *40 cal, 1 g fat (0 g sat. fat), 0 mg chol, 84 mg sodium, 6 g carbo, 2 g fiber, 2 g pro. Daily Values: 46% vit. A, 2% vit. C, 1% calcium, 2% iron.*

CURRIED CARROT SPREAD

40 CALORIES PER SERVING

PLATE IT UP

Resist the urge to overdip by spooning a 2-tablespoon serving (about the size of a golf ball) onto a small plate instead of grazing. You will be able to keep track of how much you have eaten and are less likely to end up with dip on your shirt.

TANGY LEMON-CAPER DIP

32 CALORIES PER SERVING

FAST! | LOW FAT

TANGY LEMON-CAPER DIP

Thanks to two different dairy products, this dip is a good source of calcium.

START TO FINISH: 10 min.

INGREDIENTS

1	8-oz. carton light sour cream
½	cup plain low-fat yogurt
1	Tbsp. drained capers, finely chopped
2	tsp. snipped fresh dill or thyme, or ½ tsp. dried dill or dried thyme, crushed
½	tsp. finely shredded lemon peel
	Finely shredded lemon peel (optional)
	Fresh dill or thyme (optional)
	Assorted vegetable dippers

PREPARATION

1. In small bowl stir together sour cream, yogurt, capers, the 2 teaspoons snipped dill, and the ½ teaspoon lemon peel. To serve, top with additional lemon peel and fresh dill or thyme. Serve with vegetable dippers.
MAKES 1½ CUPS.

EACH SERVING (2 TBSP.) *32 cal, 2 g fat (2 g sat. fat), 8 mg chol, 36 mg sodium, 2 g carbo, 0 g fiber, 1 g pro. Daily Values: 1% vit. A, 1% vit. C, 5% calcium.*

DIPPERS GO LIGHTLY

Give the veggie platter a fresh face with asparagus spears, endive leaves, green beans, sliced fresh fennel, jicama strips, mushrooms, and sugar snap and snow peas. Accompany with a colorful fruit, such as watermelon or grapes.

Sunset Sangria

Invite friends over to enjoy a celebratory pitcher of sangria. This one is an intriguing blend of ruby red wine and pale green limeade.

PHOTO **ANDY LYONS** FOOD STYLING **JILL LUST**

CELEBRATE EVERY DAY *with* *Pam Anderson*

SUNSET SANGRIA

PREP 25 min. **CHILL** 2 hr.

INGREDIENTS
- 2 tsp. finely shredded lime peel
- 1 cup lime juice
- ¾ cup sugar
  Ice
- 1 750-ml. bottle Pinot Noir or Syrah, chilled
- 1 nectarine, pitted and sliced

PREPARATION

1. In a 1-quart glass measuring cup combine lime peel, lime juice, and sugar; add *water* to equal 4 cups. Stir to dissolve sugar. Cover and refrigerate at least 2 hours.

2. To serve, place ice in six 16-ounce glasses. Add ⅔ cup of the lime juice mixture to each glass. Pouring along side of glass, slowly add ½ cup of the wine. Thread nectarine slices on skewers and add to glasses. **MAKES 6 SERVINGS.**

EACH SERVING *220 cal, 0 g fat, 0 mg chol, 2 mg sodium, 34 g carbo, 1 g fiber, 1 g pro. Daily Values: 2% vit. A, 24% vit. C, 1% calcium, 1% iron.*

Pam Anderson, winner of a Julia Child Award, is the author of several cookbooks. Look for her most recent book, The Perfect Recipe for Losing Weight & Eating Great.

PAM'S TIPS

Peak season for nectarines, a firm relative of peaches, is late June through August. Look for firm, fragrant ripe fruit, golden yellow with blushes of red, that gives to light pressure; avoid hard or green nectarines. Let slightly unripe fruit ripen at room temperature for a couple of days. Refrigerate ripe fruit up to 5 days.

JULY

JULY BECKONS YOU TO COME OUTSIDE AND ENJOY FRESH SUMMER FLAVORS. PULL UP A CHAIR TO SHARE A PORCH SUPPER WITH FRIENDS, 20-MINUTE GRILLED SUPPERS, AND HEALTHFUL SUMMERTIME SANDWICHES.

SHRIMP AND SAUSAGE BOIL page 155

Plates to Share

BLACKBERRY SANGRIA page 151

BARBEQUED SALMON WITH FRESH NECTARINE SALSA page 160

BACON, SPINACH, AND TOMATO SALSA SANDWICH page 163

plates
to share

AN EASY PORCH SUPPER FROM CHEF SCOTT PEACOCK
LETS YOU LAZE AWAY A SUMMER AFTERNOON

BY **MIKE BUTLER** PRODUCED BY **NANCY WALL HOPKINS**
RECIPES **SCOTT PEACOCK** PHOTOS **ALISON MIKSCH**
FOOD STYLING **SUSAN SUGARMAN** PROP STYLING **ANNETTE JOSEPH**

Butter Lettuce Salad page 151

Blackberry Sangria page 151

Starting with a crisp **BUTTER LETTUCE SALAD,** serve the meal in stages from generous platters and encourage friends to take and eat at their own pace. Courses build to a spicy Lowcountry-style **SHRIMP AND SAUSAGE BOIL,** *left.*

On a warm Atlanta afternoon, Scott, *above left,* cools friends off with **BLACKBERRY SANGRIA,** *above right,* a casual rendezvous of sun-ripe fruit and wine.

MENU

BLACKBERRY SANGRIA

EGGPLANT RELISH

BUTTER LETTUCE SALAD

TOMATO AND RED ONION SALAD

SHRIMP AND SAUSAGE BOIL

GARLIC-HERBED BREAD

CORNMEAL SANDIES AND
LEMON ICE CREAM

BUTTER LETTUCE SALAD

Scott's guests choose what they want, then he seasons, dresses, and tosses it for them. Crème fraîche adds a delicate tang to the dressing. Recipe pictured on page 148.

START TO FINISH 25 min.

INGREDIENTS

1	tsp. garlic (about 2 cloves)
½	tsp. salt
1	Tbsp. lemon juice
¾	cup crème fraîche or sour cream
2	Tbsp. whipping cream
12	oz. green beans, trimmed (3 cups)
3	or 4 large heads butterhead (Boston or Bibb) lettuce, torn (12 to 14 cups)
2	medium cucumbers, halved lengthwise, seeded, and thinly bias-sliced (1½ cups)*
3	to 4 Tbsp. thinly sliced chives

PREPARATION

1. For crème fraîche dressing, on cutting board finely chop garlic. Sprinkle with a pinch of *salt* and rub with side of a knife to form a paste. Transfer paste to glass bowl. Mix in the ½ teaspoon salt and lemon juice; let stand 10 minutes. Whisk in crème fraîche and whipping cream. Season to taste with *salt* and *ground black pepper*.
2. Place green beans in a large pan of rapidly boiling, lightly salted water. Cook, uncovered, 5 to 7 minutes or until just tender. Drain and place in bowl of lightly salted ice water to quickly chill. Let sit 3 to 5 minutes or until cold; drain.
3. Arrange lettuce, green beans, and cucumbers on platter. Season with *salt* and *freshly ground black pepper*. Lightly toss with dressing and chives. Pass additional dressing. **MAKES 6 TO 8 SERVINGS.**
*NOTE If cucumber peel is waxed or thick, peel before slicing.

EACH SERVING *163 cal, 13 g fat (8 g sat. fat), 47 mg chol, 336 mg sodium, 10 g carbo, 3 g fiber, 3 g pro. Daily Values: 81% vit. A, 15% vit. C, 7% calcium, 11% iron.*

BLACKBERRY SANGRIA

Recipe pictured on page 149.

PREP 20 min. **CHILL** 4 hr.

INGREDIENTS

4	cups fresh blackberries
¾	cup sugar
1½	cups water
2	750-ml. bottles rosé wine
1	cup cognac
¼	cup lemon or lime juice
3	cups sliced peaches and/or plums
	Fresh basil sprigs (optional)

PREPARATION

1. For the syrup, in saucepan* combine *2 cups* berries, sugar, water, and dash *salt*. Bring to boiling; reduce heat. Simmer 10 minutes, stirring occasionally. Remove from heat; cool slightly. Strain in colander, pressing gently (do not crush fruit); discard berries. Cool syrup.
2. For sangria, in gallon jar or pitcher combine blackberry syrup, rosé wine, cognac, lemon juice, fruit, and a few sprigs of basil. Cover and refrigerate 4 to 24 hours. Serve with ice, additional fruit, and basil. **MAKES 13 CUPS.**
*TEST KITCHEN TIP Use a nonreactive saucepan (Teflon-lined, enamel, stainless steel, or silver). The acid in berries may react with metal.

EACH SERVING (4 OZ.) *109 cal, 0 g fat, 0 mg chol, 6 mg sodium, 11 g carbo, 1 g fiber, 1 g pro. Daily Values: 2% vit. A, 12% vit. C, 1% calcium, 1% iron.*

SCOTT SAYS TAKE THE BITE OUT

"Pairing raw onion with fresh, ripe tomatoes just tastes like summertime out on the porch. Soak the onion slices in salted ice water before adding to the salad to make them less harsh and more sociable. Soaking also firms the texture and makes the onion pleasantly crisp."

The best the season has to offer, **TOMATO AND RED ONION SALAD** can be made ahead or in a few minutes after guests arrive—just toss with the sweet-sour vinegar dressing and serve.

LOW FAT

TOMATO AND RED ONION SALAD

Choose a variety of heirloom and farmstead tomatoes for a colorful salad.

PREP 25 min. **STAND** 25 min.

INGREDIENTS

1	medium red onion, sliced ¼ inch thick
½	cup cider vinegar
¼	cup sugar
8	cups tomatoes, cut (about 3 lb.)

PREPARATION

1. In medium bowl combine 4 cups *ice cold water* and 2 teaspoons *salt*; stir to dissolve salt. Add onion slices; stir gently to separate rings. Let stand 20 minutes; drain.
2. Meanwhile, for sweet-sour dressing, in small bowl whisk together vinegar, sugar, and ¾ teaspoon each *salt* and *ground black pepper*. In extra-large bowl combine tomatoes and drained onions. Add dressing; gently toss to coat. Let stand 5 minutes.
MAKES 6 TO 8 SERVINGS.

EACH SERVING *88 cal, 1 g fat (0 g sat. fat), 0 mg chol, 401 mg sodium, 20 g carbo, 3 g fiber, 2 g pro. Daily Values: 40% vit. A, 53% vit. C, 3% calcium, 4% iron.*

Whatever happened to
GARLIC-HERBED BREAD?
This freshened-up recipe,
right, revives memories of
the version Mom made
and is perfect for sopping
up the boil's juices.

FAST!

GARLIC-HERBED BREAD

Here's the classic you grew up with, updated with fresh garlic, parsley, and kosher salt. Look for a soft, plump baguette that is easy to pull apart.

PREP 15 min. **BAKE** 15 min. **OVEN** 375°F

INGREDIENTS
½	cup butter, softened
2	Tbsp. snipped Italian (flat-leaf) parsley
1½	tsp. minced garlic (about 3 cloves)
¾	tsp. kosher salt or ½ tsp. salt
1	14- to 18-oz. baguette or Italian bread

PREPARATION

1. Preheat oven to 375°F. In a small bowl combine butter, parsley, garlic, salt, and a dash of *ground black pepper*.
2. Without cutting through bottom crust, slice baguette in 1½-inch slices. Generously spread butter mixture between slices. Wrap baguette in heavy foil. Bake 15 minutes or until heated through. Serve warm. **MAKES 10 TO 12 SLICES.**

EACH SLICE *192 cal, 11 g fat (6 g sat. fat), 24 mg chol, 443 mg sodium, 20 g carbo, 1 g fiber, 4 g pro. Daily Values: 7% vit. A, 2% vit. C, 4% calcium, 7% iron.*

LOW FAT

EGGPLANT RELISH

Scott prefers roasting the eggplant whole, which keeps it from getting too dry while bringing out its sweetness.

PREP 30 min. **ROAST** 1 hr. **CHILL** 8 hr. **STAND** 30 min. **OVEN** 375°F

INGREDIENTS
¼	cup golden raisins
3	Tbsp. cider vinegar
1	large eggplant (about 1½ lb.)
1	large yellow onion, chopped
1	medium green or red sweet pepper, chopped
3	Tbsp. olive oil
1	fresh jalapeño pepper, seeded and finely chopped (see Note, page 101)
1½	tsp. finely chopped garlic
1	medium tomato, chopped
4	tsp. honey
2	Tbsp. finely chopped Italian (flat-leaf) parsley
	Toasted baguette slices (optional)

PREPARATION

1. Preheat oven to 375°F. In nonreactive saucepan combine raisins and vinegar. Bring to boiling; remove from heat; cover and set aside.
2. With tip of knife pierce eggplant in five or six places. Place on foil-lined 15×10×1-inch baking pan. Roast 1 to 1½ hours or until eggplant is soft to touch and collapsing. Remove from oven; cool on baking sheet. When cool enough to handle, cut eggplant in half lengthwise; scoop out flesh. Coarsely chop flesh; set aside.
3. In 10-inch skillet cook onion and sweet pepper in hot oil 5 minutes or until tender. Stir in jalapeño, garlic, ½ teaspoon *salt,* and ¼ teaspoon *ground black pepper.* Cook and stir 3 minutes. Stir in raisin-vinegar mixture, eggplant, tomato, and honey. Bring to simmer and cook 5 minutes; cool. Season with *salt* and *pepper.* Cover and refrigerate at least 8 hours or overnight.
4. To serve, let stand at room temperature 30 minutes. Stir in parsley. Serve with toasted baguette slices. **MAKES 3 CUPS.**

EACH SERVING (2 TBSP.) *37 cal, 2 g fat (0 g sat. fat), 75 mg sodium, 5 g carbo, 1 g fiber, 0 g pro. Daily Values: 5% vit. A, 15% vit. C, 1% calcium, 1% iron.*

GARLIC MAYONNAISE

Scott loves a classic mayonnaise and uses two fresh egg yolks in his recipe; we opted for the pasteurized product in this version.

START TO FINISH 15 min.

INGREDIENTS
2	Tbsp. refrigerated or frozen egg product, thawed
1	Tbsp. cider or white wine vinegar
1	Tbsp. fresh lemon juice
1	tsp. kosher salt or ¾ tsp. salt
1	tsp. ground mustard
1½	cups peanut oil
1	tsp. garlic (about 2 cloves)
1	Tbsp. boiling water

PREPARATION

1. In glass bowl combine egg product, vinegar, lemon juice, salt, and mustard; whisk until smooth. Whisk in *1 tablespoon* of the oil a few drops at a time. Gradually add remaining oil in thin steady stream, whisking constantly until mixture is thickened, about 7 minutes.
2. On cutting board finely chop garlic. Sprinkle with pinch of *salt;* rub with side of knife to form paste. Transfer paste to glass bowl. Add boiling water; let stand 2 minutes. Stir into mayonnaise. Refrigerate, covered, up to 3 days. **MAKES ABOUT 1¾ CUPS.**
BLENDER METHOD In blender combine egg product, vinegar, lemon juice, salt, and mustard. Cover and blend 5 seconds. With blender on low, add *1 cup* of the peanut oil in a thin steady stream through opening in lid, stopping blender to scrape down sides with rubber spatula. Gradually blend in enough hot water to thin to a saucelike consistency. Prepare garlic as above; stir into mayonnaise.

EACH SERVING (1 TBSP.) *104 cal, 12 g fat (2 g sat. fat), 0 mg chol, 75 mg sodium, 0 g carbo, 0 g fiber, 0 g pro. Daily Values: 1% vit. C.*

EGGPLANT RELISH encourages between-course nibbling with intriguing sweet heat that comes from raisins and chile peppers.

A one-pot wonder, **SHRIMP AND SAUSAGE BOIL** combines fresh seafood with earthy corn and potatoes; sausage adds a hint of smoke. Pass the garlic mayonnaise, cocktail sauce—and napkins.

SHRIMP AND SAUSAGE BOIL

Bring an easy-to-share platter of this Lowcountry favorite to the table and everyone will be impressed. Let guests nibble on Eggplant Relish and salad as the boil cooks. Toss in lemon halves last to squeeze over the shrimp.

PREP 1 hr. **COOK** 30 min.

INGREDIENTS

1	3-oz. bag shrimp or crab boil
3	Tbsp. Old Bay Seasoning
2¼	to 3 lb. small new potatoes
4	or 5 ears corn, husked and cut in 1½- to 3-inch pieces
1	2-lb. spicy smoked link sausage (kielbasa or andouille), diagonally sliced in 1-inch pieces
3	to 4 lb. medium to large unpeeled shrimp (preferably heads on)
3	to 4 lemons, halved
	Snipped fresh Italian (flat-leaf) parsley
	Garlic Mayonnaise (page 153) and Cocktail Sauce

PREPARATION

1. In 12- to 16-quart pot bring 2 gallons water to boiling. Add shrimp or crab boil and Old Bay Seasoning; reduce heat. Simmer, uncovered, 10 minutes. Add potatoes, a few at a time, allowing water to continue simmering. Simmer 7 to 10 minutes until nearly tender. Add corn; simmer, uncovered, 5 minutes. Add sausage and shrimp. Simmer 3 to 5 minutes until shrimp are opaque (do not overcook shrimp) and sausage is heated through; drain.
2. Transfer to large platter. Add lemon halves and sprinkle parsley. Serve hot or within 1 hour of cooking. Pass Garlic Mayonnaise and Cocktail Sauce. **MAKES 6 TO 8 SERVINGS.**

EACH SERVING *678 cal, 34 g fat (11 g sat. fat), 339 mg chol, 1,356 mg sodium, 41 g carbo, 5 g fiber, 53 g pro. Daily Values: 12% vit. A, 97% vit. C, 14% calcium, 36% iron.*

COCKTAIL SAUCE

START TO FINISH 5 min.

INGREDIENTS

1	cup bottled chili sauce
¼	cup prepared horseradish
1	Tbsp. fresh lemon juice
1	tsp. bottled hot pepper sauce (optional)

PREPARATION

1. In small bowl combine chili sauce, horseradish, lemon juice, and hot pepper sauce. Season to taste with *salt* and *ground black pepper*. Store, refrigerated, up to 1 week. **MAKES ABOUT 1¼ CUPS.**

EACH SERVING (2 TBSP.) *28 cal, 0 g fat (0 g sat. fat), 0 mg chol, 398 mg sodium, 6 g carbo, 2 g fiber, 1 g pro. Daily Values: 3% vit. A, 10% vit. C, 1% calcium, 1% iron.*

THE SUN MELTS TOWARD THE HORIZON AND A GENTLE BREEZE KICKS UP—TIME FOR EVERYONE'S FAVORITE SUMMER DESSERT.

Cap the afternoon with a bowl of **LEMON ICE CREAM** and sugary **CORNMEAL SANDIES.** Have the ice cream ready to go, or make it on the porch and let everyone take a turn on the crank.

LEMON ICE CREAM

The ice cream and Cornmeal Sandies are both flavored with lemon peel. Take care when shredding citrus peels to use only the colored outside and to avoid the bitter white pith.

PREP 20 min. **CHILL** 4 hr. **FREEZE** according to manufacturer's directions

INGREDIENTS
5   to 6 lemons
2   cups milk
1¼ cups granulated sugar
¼   tsp. salt
12 egg yolks
2   cups whipping cream
1   recipe Blueberry Sauce

PREPARATION
1. Finely shred 2 tablespoons peel from lemons. Squeeze juice to equal ¾ cup. Set aside peel; cover and refrigerate juice.
2. In small saucepan heat milk over medium heat just until tiny bubbles begin to appear around the edge of the saucepan.
3. In large saucepan whisk sugar, salt, and lemon peel into egg yolks until well blended. Gradually whisk in warmed milk. Cook and stir continuously with wooden spoon or heatproof rubber spatula over medium heat until mixture thickens and coats back of clean metal spoon, about 15 minutes (do not boil). Remove pan from heat. Transfer mixture to large bowl. Quickly cool by placing the bowl of custard in very large bowl of ice water about 5 to 7 minutes, stirring constantly. Once completely cool, stir in whipping cream. Cover; chill 4 to 24 hours.
4. Just before freezing stir in lemon juice. Strain through fine-mesh strainer; discard peel. Freeze in 4- or 5-quart ice cream freezer according to directions. If desired, ripen 4 hours. Serve with Blueberry Sauce. **MAKES ABOUT 7 CUPS.**

EACH SERVING (½ CUP) *374 cal, 20 g fat (11 g sat. fat), 268 mg chol, 187 mg sodium, 48 g carbo, 3 g fiber, 6 g pro. Daily Values: 19% vit. A, 66% vit. C, 13% calcium, 5% iron.*

BLUEBERRY SAUCE

PREP 15 min. **COOL** 1 hr.

INGREDIENTS
⅔   cup sugar
1   tsp. cornstarch
¼   tsp. salt
⅓   cup water
1   tsp. lemon juice
4   cups fresh or frozen blueberries

PREPARATION
1. In saucepan combine sugar, cornstarch, and salt; stir in water and lemon juice and mix well. Add blueberries. Cook over medium heat, stirring often, until mixture is slightly thickened and bubbly. Cook and stir 2 minutes more.
2. Transfer to bowl; cool. Serve at room temperature. Or cover and refrigerate 1 hour or up to 2 days. If chilled, let stand at room temperature 30 minutes before serving. **MAKES 3 CUPS.**

EACH SERVING (¼ CUP) *72 cal, 0 g fat, 0 mg chol, 49 mg sodium, 18 g carbo, 1 g fiber, 0 g pro. Daily Values: 1% vit. A, 8% vit. C, 1% iron.*

CORNMEAL SANDIES

Tender and crisp, these cookies are keepers. Go ahead, dip them into the melting ice cream.

PREP 30 min. **BAKE** 10 min. per batch
COOL 2 min. per batch **OVEN** 350°F

INGREDIENTS
1   cup butter, softened
¼   cup sugar
3   tsp. finely shredded orange peel
2   tsp. finely shredded lemon peel
1   tsp. vanilla
1½   cups unbleached all-purpose flour
½   cup yellow cornmeal
¼   tsp. salt
     Sugar

PREPARATION
1. Preheat oven to 350°F. Line baking sheets with parchment paper. Set aside.
2. In large mixing bowl beat butter with electric mixer on medium to high speed for 30 seconds. Beat in the ¼ cup sugar and fruit peels; beat in vanilla.
3. In separate bowl combine flour, cornmeal, and salt; gradually add to and mix with butter mixture until cohesive ball of dough forms.
4. Using a 1-ounce scoop or tablespoon, roll dough in ¾-inch balls. Place 1 inch apart on prepared baking sheets. Flatten slightly with palm of hand.
5. Bake 10 to 12 minutes until edges are lightly browned. Cool 2 minutes on baking sheet. Place additional sugar in shallow dish; gently toss warm cookies in sugar. Cool on rack.
MAKES 3 DOZEN COOKIES.

EACH COOKIE *83 cal, 5 g fat (3 g sat. fat), 14 mg chol, 53 mg sodium, 9 g carbo, 0 g fiber, 1 g pro. Daily Values: 3% vit. A, 2% iron.*

MEET SCOTT

As executive chef at Watershed Restaurant in Decatur, Georgia, Scott Peacock was awarded Best Chef in the Southeast by the James Beard Foundation in 2007. He's also coauthor of *The Gift of Southern Cooking: Recipes and Revelations from Two Great American Cooks* (Knopf, $29.95).

Summertime

And the cooking is easy. Suppers are jumping with fresh flavors, sunset colors, and tasty combinations.

BY **PEG SMITH** PHOTOS **ANDY LYONS** RECIPES **MARYELLYN KRANTZ** FOOD STYLING **JILL LUST**

READY IN 20 MINUTES!

GRILLED CHICKEN AND CREAMY CORN

FAST! **KID FRIENDLY**

GRILLED CHICKEN AND CREAMY CORN

START TO FINISH 20 min.

INGREDIENTS

2   Tbsp. olive oil
1   tsp. smoked paprika
3   fresh ears of sweet corn
4   skinless, boneless chicken breast halves
⅓   cup sour cream
¼   cup shredded fresh basil

PREPARATION

1. In small bowl combine oil and paprika. Brush corn and chicken with oil mixture. Lightly sprinkle *salt* and *ground black pepper*. Grill directly over medium coals 12 to 15 minutes or until chicken is no longer pink (170°F), turning once.
2. Carefully cut kernels from cob by firmly holding the corn at the top (using a kitchen towel to grip, if necessary) and slicing downward with a sharp knife. Transfer to bowl; stir in sour cream. Season with additional *salt* and *pepper*. Stir in *milk* to desired creaminess. Slice chicken breasts. Serve with corn; sprinkle shredded basil.
MAKES 4 SERVINGS.

EACH SERVING *309 cal, 13 g fat (4 g sat. fat), 89 mg chol, 238 mg sodium, 14 g carbo, 2 g fiber, 36 g pro. Daily Values: 13% vit. A, 12% vit. C, 4% calcium, 9% iron.*

FAST!

SHRIMP AND WATERMELON SALAD

START TO FINISH 20 min.

INGREDIENTS

2   Tbsp. olive oil
1   lb. peeled, deveined medium shrimp
2   tsp. snipped fresh thyme
4   cups sliced bok choy or napa cabbage
1   cup grape tomatoes, halved
2   1-inch slices seedless watermelon, halved
    Small limes, halved
    Feta cheese (optional)
    Fresh thyme sprigs

PREPARATION

1. Heat *1 tablespoon* of the oil in large skillet over medium-high heat. Add shrimp; cook and stir 3 to 4 minutes until shrimp are opaque. Transfer shrimp to bowl; stir in thyme. Add remaining olive oil, bok choy, and tomatoes to skillet; cook and stir 1 minute. Return shrimp to skillet; cook and stir 1 minute more. Season with *salt* and *ground black pepper*.
2. Serve shrimp and vegetables with watermelon. Squeeze lime juice on salads; sprinkle feta and thyme sprigs. **MAKES 4 SERVINGS.**

EACH SERVING *241 cal, 9 g fat (1 g sat. fat), 172 mg chol, 363 mg sodium, 16 g carbo, 2 g fiber, 25 g pro. Daily Values: 91% vit. A, 88% vit. C, 15% calcium, 22% iron.*

SHRIMP AND WATERMELON SALAD

**SAUSAGE AND
SUMMER SQUASH**

FAST!

BARBECUED SALMON WITH FRESH NECTARINE SALSA

START TO FINISH 20 min.

INGREDIENTS

4   4- to 5-oz. fresh skinless salmon fillets, about 1 inch thick
3   Tbsp. bottled barbecue sauce
2   nectarines, pitted and chopped
¾   cup fresh blueberries
¼   cup coarsely chopped toasted pecans
      Lemon wedges

PREPARATION

1. Rinse fish; pat dry with paper towels. Lightly sprinkle salmon with *salt* and *ground black pepper.* Place *2 tablespoons* of the barbecue sauce in bowl; brush sauce on both sides of salmon.
2. For charcoal grill, cook salmon on greased grill rack directly over medium coals 8 to 12 minutes or until salmon flakes when tested with fork, turning once halfway through grilling. (For gas grill, preheat grill. Reduce heat to medium. Place salmon on greased grill rack over medium heat. Cover and grill as above.)
3. For nectarine salsa, in medium bowl combine nectarines, blueberries, pecans, and remaining 1 tablespoon barbecue sauce. Season with *salt.* Serve salmon with salsa and lemon wedges.
MAKES 4 SERVINGS.

EACH SERVING *318 cal, 17 g fat (3 g sat. fat), 66 mg chol, 344 mg sodium, 17 g carbo, 3 g fiber, 24 g pro. Daily Values: 6% vit. A, 20% vit. C, 3% calcium, 5% iron.*

**BARBECUED SALMON WITH
FRESH NECTARINE SALSA**

FAST!

SAUSAGE AND SUMMER SQUASH

START TO FINISH 20 min.

INGREDIENTS

⅓   to ½ cup bottled Italian salad dressing
2   cloves garlic, minced
12   oz. cooked Polish sausage links, halved lengthwise, sliced diagonally
3   small yellow summer squash and/or zucchini, quartered lengthwise
4   wedges Italian flatbread, split
¼   cup sliced green onion
      Fresh oregano leaves
¼   cup coarsely shredded Parmesan cheese (optional)

PREPARATION

1. Preheat broiler. In small bowl combine dressing and garlic. In extra-large skillet cook sausage and squash in *2 tablespoons* of the dressing mixture for 8 to 10 minutes or until sausage is heated through and squash is almost tender, stirring occasionally.
2. Meanwhile, place bread on broiler pan; brush with remaining 1 tablespoon of the dressing mixture. Broil 3 to 4 inches from heat 1 to 2 minutes until lightly toasted.
3. Serve sausage and squash with toasted bread. Drizzle remaining dressing; sprinkle green onion and oregano. Pass Parmesan cheese. **MAKES 4 SERVINGS.**

EACH SERVING *412 cal, 31 g fat (10 g sat. fat), 62 mg chol, 1,182 mg sodium, 19 g carbo, 1 g fiber, 15 g pro. Daily Values: 3% vit. A, 13% vit. C, 7% calcium, 10% iron.*

FAST! **LOW FAT**

CHOPS AND PINEAPPLE WITH CHILI SLAW

START TO FINISH 20 min.

INGREDIENTS

8	½ inch cuts boneless top loin pork chops (1½ lb. total)
1½	tsp. chili powder
½	of a cored fresh pineapple, sliced
3	Tbsp. cider vinegar
2	Tbsp. orange juice
2	Tbsp. olive oil
1	Tbsp. sugar
⅓	of small green cabbage, cored and sliced (about 5 cups)
½	of a red onion, thinly sliced
1	small red sweet pepper, cut in strips

PREPARATION

1. Sprinkle chops with *salt* and *1 teaspoon* of the chili powder. For charcoal grill, cook chops and pineapple on uncovered grill directly over medium coals 6 to 8 minutes until chops are done (160°F), turning once. (For gas grill, preheat; reduce to medium. Grill chops and pineapple, covered.)

2. Meanwhile, for chili slaw, in large bowl whisk together vinegar, juice, oil, sugar, and remaining ½ teaspoon chili powder. Add cabbage, onion, and sweet pepper; toss. Season with *salt* and *ground black pepper.* Serve chops with pineapple pieces and slaw.

MAKES 4 SERVINGS.

EACH SERVING *357 cal, 12 g fat (3 g sat. fat), 112 mg chol, 392 mg sodium, 20 g carbo, 4 g fiber, 40 g pro. Daily Values: 27% vit. A, 165% vit. C, 5% calcium, 9% iron.*

CHOPS AND PINEAPPLE WITH CHILI SLAW

Salad on a Slice

Whether you're lunching on the run or at your desk, supercharged sandwiches deliver the nutrition you need.

BY **MARGE PERRY** PHOTOS **ANDY LYONS** FOOD STYLING **JILL LUST** RECIPES **LAURA MARZEN**

250 CALORIES PER SERVING

OPEN-FACE RATATOUILLE SANDWICHES

LOW FAT

OPEN-FACE RATATOUILLE SANDWICH

PREP 25 min. **ROAST** 45 min. **OVEN** 400°F

INGREDIENTS

1	small eggplant, cut in 1-inch pieces
1	small zucchini or yellow summer squash, cut in ¾-inch slices
1	medium red sweet pepper, cut in strips
½	of a small red onion, cut in ½-inch wedges
1	Tbsp. olive oil
½	tsp. herbes de Provence or dried thyme, crushed
2	medium Roma tomatoes, each cut lengthwise in 6 wedges
8	small or 4 large ½-inch slices whole wheat or white French bread, toasted (about 8 oz. total)
1	clove garlic, halved
2	Tbsp. balsamic vinegar
	Fresh thyme sprigs (optional)

PREPARATION

1. Preheat oven to 400°F. Coat a large shallow roasting pan with *nonstick cooking spray*. Add eggplant, zucchini, sweet pepper, and onion to prepared pan. Drizzle olive oil; sprinkle herbes de Provence, ⅛ teaspoon *salt*, and ⅛ teaspoon *ground black pepper*. Toss to coat. Roast vegetables 30 minutes, tossing once. Add tomatoes to roasting pan. Roast 15 to 20 minutes more or until vegetables are tender and some surface areas are lightly browned.

2. Meanwhile, rub toasted bread with cut sides of garlic clove. Place two small slices or one large slice bread on each of 4 plates. Sprinkle balsamic vinegar over vegetables; toss gently to coat. Spoon warm vegetables on bread. Garnish with fresh thyme sprigs.

MAKES 4 SERVINGS.

EACH SERVING *250 cal, 7 g fat (1 g sat. fat), 0 mg chol, 328 mg sodium, 43 g carbo, 8 g fiber, 7 g pro. Daily Values: 31% vit. A, 90% vit. C, 5% calcium, 14% iron.*

SALAD NIÇOISE SANDWICH

START TO FINISH 25 min.

INGREDIENTS

4	oz. fresh green beans, trimmed and cut in 1-inch pieces (about 1 cup)
1	12-oz. can chunk white or light tuna (water pack), drained and flaked
1	cup halved cherry tomatoes
⅓	cup chopped pitted niçoise or kalamata olives
¼	cup finely chopped sweet onion
2	Tbsp. chopped fresh mint
1	Tbsp. lemon juice
2	tsp. olive oil
3	cups packaged mixed salad greens
3	Greek pita flatbreads
6	short wooden skewers
	Cherry tomatoes, pitted niçoise or kalamata olives, fresh mint leaves

PREPARATION

1. In medium covered saucepan cook green beans in boiling water about 4 minutes until crisp-tender. Drain; rinse under cold water; drain again.

2. Place beans in bowl. Stir in tuna, 1 cup halved tomatoes, the ⅓ cup olives, onion, and 2 tablespoons mint. Add lemon juice, oil, and ⅛ teaspoon *ground black pepper*; toss to combine. Stir in salad mix.

3. To serve, cut pitas in half crosswise. Cut each half horizontally. Fill pitas with about ½ *cup* tuna mixture. On each wooden skewer, thread a whole cherry tomato, whole olive, and mint leaf; spear filled pitas. **MAKES 6 SERVINGS.**

EACH SERVING *210 cal, 5 g fat (1 g sat. fat), 24 mg chol, 527 mg sodium, 23 g carbo, 3 g fiber, 17 g pro. Daily Values: 13% vit. A, 23% vit. C, 6% calcium, 13% iron.*

BACON, SPINACH, AND TOMATO SALSA SANDWICH

START TO FINISH 25 min.

INGREDIENTS

2	large ripe tomatoes, seeded, coarsely chopped (about 1¾ cups)
¼	cup finely chopped red onion
¼	cup chopped fresh cilantro
1	Tbsp. finely chopped fresh jalapeño chile pepper (see Note, page 101)
1	Tbsp. lime juice
⅛	tsp. kosher salt or salt
8	slices turkey bacon
¼	cup light mayonnaise
4	10-inch vegetable-flavor flour tortillas or flour tortillas
2	cups fresh baby spinach

INGREDIENTS

1. For tomato salsa, in medium bowl combine tomato, onion, cilantro, and chile pepper. Stir in lime juice and salt. Set aside.

2. Cook bacon according to package directions. Drain well on paper towels; cut bacon in large pieces.

3. For sandwiches, spread mayonnaise on tortillas; top with spinach. With slotted spoon scoop salsa on spinach. Top with bacon. Roll up tortillas to enclose filling. Cut each tortilla in half. **MAKES 4 SERVINGS.**

EACH SERVING *227 cal, 9 g fat (3 g sat. fat), 30 mg chol, 625 mg sodium, 27 g carb, 2 g fiber, 8 g pro. Daily Values: 45% vit. A, 28% vit. C, 8% calcium, 12% iron.*

210 CALORIES PER SERVING

SALAD NIÇOISE SANDWICH

227 CALORIES PER SERVING

BACON, SPINACH, AND TOMATO SALSA SANDWICH

AUGUST

THINK GARDEN-FRESH THIS MONTH WITH TASTY NEW
TAKES ON CLASSIC SALADS, CREATIVE IDEAS FOR A BUMPER
CROP OF CORN, AND A FAST STOVE-TOP PEACH DESSERT,
SERVED À LA MODE, OF COURSE.

**CRISPY CHOPPED
CHICKEN SALAD** page 171

Salad Redefined

BACON AND EGG SALAD SANDWICHES page 175

FRESH CORN-RICE SALAD page 179

SKILLET PEACHES À LA MODE page 181

salad
redefined

Stacked, tossed, or arranged, salad takes on a new definition in these fresh, sassy main dishes from PBS star chef Joanne Weir.

BY **RICHARD SWEARINGER** AND **ERIN SIMPSON** PHOTOS **ALISON MIKSCH**
RECIPES **JOANNE WEIR** FOOD STYLING **JILL LUST** PROP STYLING **KAREN JOHNSON**

MINTY PASTA SALAD WITH LAMB page 173

LAYERED TUNA SALAD page 173

Arugula and mint tossed with pasta create a bed for peppery lamb chops, *opposite*. The chops go on the plate still sizzling from the grill.

Planks of fresh corn, *above*, top a layered salad built of Yukon gold potatoes and grilled tuna dressed with lime juice, cumin, and extra virgin olive oil.

salad \ˈsa-ləd\

n 1: Mix of greens topped or tossed with vegetables and/or meat.
2: Everyday warm-weather fare often served cold and on the side.

salad redefined \ˈsa-ləd re-di-ˈfīnd\

n 1: Classic combos with fresh and bold flavor twists (as in grilled meats, chilled pasta, garden vegetables, and crusty bread). 2: A highly desirable summer supper.

Roasted potatoes and grilled ribeye steak are served with steak-house flair on a raft of cool romaine lettuce.

STEAK AND POTATO SALAD

STEAK AND POTATO SALAD

PREP 30 min. **ROAST** 50 min. **OVEN** 375°F **GRILL** 10 min.

INGREDIENTS
2   lb. small new Yukon gold potatoes, halved or quartered
2   Tbsp. extra virgin olive oil
1½   to 2 lb. ribeye steaks, cut 1 inch thick
2   heads romaine lettuce
1   recipe Salsa Verde
5   green onions, thinly sliced

PREPARATION
1. Preheat oven to 375°F. Place potatoes in a 15×10×1-inch baking pan. Drizzle with *1 tablespoon* of the olive oil; sprinkle with *salt* and *ground black pepper*. Toss to combine. Roast, uncovered, 50 to 60 minutes or until tender. Cool slightly.
2. Meanwhile, brush remaining olive oil on steaks. Season with *salt* and *pepper*. For charcoal grill, grill steaks on rack of uncovered grill directly over medium coals, 10 to 12 minutes (145°F for medium-rare), turning once. (For gas grill, preheat grill. Reduce heat to medium. Place steaks on rack over heat. Cover; grill as above.)
3. Slice romaine into six 2-inch-thick slices, reserving tops for another use. Prepare Salsa Verde.
4. Place slice of romaine on each serving plate; drizzle with *half* of the Salsa Verde. Toss warm potatoes with remaining sauce and green onions. Spoon onto romaine. Thinly slice steak and place on top of potatoes. **MAKES 6 SERVINGS.**
Salsa Verde In bowl combine ½ cup chopped *Italian (flat-leaf) parsley*, ¼ cup *extra virgin olive oil*, 3 tablespoons chopped *chives*, 3 tablespoons drained *capers*, 2 teaspoons chopped *oregano*, 1 teaspoon chopped *thyme*, and 2 cloves minced *garlic*. Season with *salt* and *ground black pepper*.

EACH SERVING *453 cal, 24 g fat (6 g sat. fat), 67 mg chol, 419 mg sodium, 33 g carbo, 7 g fiber, 28 g pro. Daily Values: 186% vit. A, 128% vit. C, 10% calcium, 33% iron.*

GAZPACHO SHRIMP SALAD

PREP 40 min. **COOK** 1 min. **STAND** 1 min.

INGREDIENTS
1½   lb. fresh or frozen extra-large or jumbo shrimp, unpeeled
1   recipe Red Pepper-Tomato Dressing
5   large ripe tomatoes, chopped
1   medium green sweet pepper, chopped
1   medium red onion, chopped
1   English cucumber, chopped
2   cups purchased croutons
     Italian (flat-leaf) parsley

PREPARATION
1. Thaw shrimp, if frozen. Peel and devein. Fill large skillet half full with *lightly salted water*; bring to boiling. Add shrimp. Cook, uncovered, 1 minute. Remove skillet from heat. Let shrimp sit in water 1 to 2 minutes or until opaque. Remove with slotted spoon; set aside to cool.
2. Prepare Red Pepper-Tomato Dressing. In large bowl toss together vegetables. Season with *salt* and *ground black pepper*.
3. Divide dressing among six bowls. Top with vegetables, shrimp, croutons, and parsley. **MAKES 6 SERVINGS.**

EACH SERVING (WITH DRESSING) *285 cal, 14 g fat (2 g sat. fat), 115 mg chol, 371 mg sodium, 21 g carbo, 4 g fiber, 19 g pro. Daily Values: 35% vit. A, 237% vit. C, 8% calcium, 19% iron.*

RED PEPPER-TOMATO DRESSING

INGREDIENTS
1   12-oz. jar roasted red sweet peppers
2   large ripe tomatoes, quartered
⅓   cup extra virgin olive oil
2   to 3 Tbsp. sherry or white wine vinegar
1   clove garlic, minced
1   tsp. smoked paprika

PREPARATION
1. Drain peppers. In blender combine peppers, tomatoes, olive oil, *2 tablespoons* vinegar, garlic, and paprika. Cover; blend until very smooth. Season with remaining vinegar, *salt,* and *ground black pepper*.

The red pepper-tomato dressing is poured into the bowl, then the gazpacho salad is set on top and finished with quick-cooked shrimp and crunchy croutons.

GAZPACHO SHRIMP SALAD

dressing \'dre-sing\

n **1:** A sauce for greens (as in oil and vinegar, creamy fix-up, or blue cheese-laden classic). **2:** Store-bought salad condiment, typically from a bottle.

dressing redefined \'dre-sing re-di-'find\

n Standout blend of fiery roasted peppers and tomatoes, snappy drizzles of lime juice and olive oil, or a quick whirled-together vinaigrette with fragrant herbs.

EDAMAME BREAD SALAD

This adaptation of an Italian bread salad is meatless but—thanks to high-protein edamame—seriously hearty. The dressing gets plenty of punch from extra virgin olive oil, balsamic vinegar, and fresh basil.

EDAMAME BREAD SALAD

PREP 30 min. **COOK** 6 min.

INGREDIENTS

¾   cup feta cheese
½   cup Greek yogurt or plain low-fat yogurt
2   Tbsp. snipped fresh basil
1   small clove garlic, minced
2   12-oz. pkgs. frozen soybeans (edamame)
1½   lb. fresh green beans, trimmed
1   recipe Balsamic Dressing
2   cups yellow cherry tomatoes, halved
12   slices crusty country bread, toasted
    Fresh basil leaves

PREPARATION

1. In bowl combine feta cheese and yogurt. Using fork, mash into paste. Add basil and garlic; mash to blend. Season with *salt* and *ground black pepper*. Refrigerate, covered, up to 8 hours.
2. In saucepan bring 8 cups *lightly salted water* to boiling. Add soybeans and green beans; return to boiling. Reduce heat; cook, covered, 6 to 8 minutes or until tender. Drain; cool. Prepare Balsamic Dressing.
3. Add tomatoes to bean mixture. Drizzle *half* of dressing; toss to coat. Refrigerate, covered, up to 8 hours. Toss before serving.
4. Spread feta mixture on bread slices; place slice on serving plate; mound bean mixture on top. Drizzle remaining dressing; sprinkle basil. **MAKES 6 SERVINGS.**

EACH SERVING (WITH DRESSING) *398 cal, 22 g fat (6 g sat. fat), 25 mg chol, 420 mg sodium, 35 g carbo, 11 g fiber, 20 g pro. Daily Values: 32% vit. A, 58% vit. C, 24% calcium, 27% iron.*

BALSAMIC DRESSING

INGREDIENTS

¼   cup extra virgin olive oil
2   Tbsp. balsamic vinegar
2   Tbsp. red wine vinegar
¼   cup basil leaves, lightly packed
2   Tbsp. whipping cream

PREPARATION

1. In blender combine first 4 ingredients; blend. Add cream; blend to mix. Season to taste with *salt* and *ground black pepper*.

CRISPY CHOPPED CHICKEN SALAD

PREP 45 min. **BAKE** 8 min. **COOK** 8 min. **OVEN** 400°F

INGREDIENTS

6   thin slices prosciutto (about 4 oz.)
½   cup extra virgin olive oil
4   skinless, boneless chicken breast halves
    Paprika
2   lemons
1   shallot, finely chopped
2   small carrots, peeled and thinly sliced
2   medium zucchini, chopped
1   medium red sweet pepper, chopped
1   medium yellow sweet pepper, chopped
½   of a small red onion, chopped
5   oz. blue cheese, crumbled
    Romaine lettuce leaves

PREPARATION

1. Preheat oven to 400°F. Place prosciutto in single layer on large baking sheet. Bake until crisp 8 to 10 minutes; set aside.
2. In large nonstick skillet heat *1 tablespoon* of the oil over medium heat. Sprinkle chicken with *salt, ground black pepper,* and paprika; add to skillet. Cook 8 to 10 minutes or until chicken is no longer pink (170°F), turning once. Cool slightly; slice.
3. For dressing, finely shred peel from one lemon; squeeze lemons to make ⅓ cup juice. In small bowl whisk together remaining olive oil, lemon juice, shredded peel, and shallot. Season with *salt* and *pepper;* set aside.
4. In large bowl combine carrot slices, zucchini, sweet peppers, onion, and chicken. Toss with dressing. Add blue cheese.
5. Line salad bowls with romaine. Spoon in chicken mixture. Top with prosciutto. **MAKES 6 SERVINGS.**

EACH SERVING *425 cal, 28 g fat (8 g sat. fat), 86 mg chol, 965 mg sodium, 10 g carbo, 2 g fiber, 34 g pro. Daily Values: 87% vit. A, 178% vit. C, 17% calcium, 10% iron.*

Crispy, wafer-thin slices of prosciutto and a lemony dressing top this mix of sauteed chicken, vegetables, and blue cheese.

CRISPY CHOPPED CHICKEN SALAD

GRILLED PORK,
PLUMS, AND GREENS

GRILLED PORK, PLUMS, AND GREENS

PREP 15 min. **GRILL** 10 min.

INGREDIENTS

1½ lb. pork tenderloin, cut ¾ inch thick
3 Tbsp. extra virgin olive oil
3 to 6 nectarines, halved and pitted
3 plums, halved and pitted
4 cups mixed salad greens
1 recipe Cayenne Mayonnaise

PREPARATION

1. Brush pork with *1 tablespoon* of the oil. Sprinkle with ½ teaspoon *salt* and 2 teaspoons *ground black pepper.* For charcoal grill, grill pork slices on rack of uncovered grill directly over medium coals 6 minutes, turning once, or until pork is done (160°F).
2. Toss fruit with remaining oil. Grill directly over medium coals 2 minutes per side or until grill marks form.
3. Arrange greens, pork, and fruit on serving plates. Serve with Cayenne Mayonnaise. **MAKES 6 SERVINGS.**

EACH SERVING (WITH MAYONNAISE) *397 cal, 27 g fat (4 g sat. fat), 73 mg chol, 325 mg sodium, 13 g carbo, 2 g fiber, 26 g pro. Daily Values: 16% vit. A, 17% vit. C, 3% calcium, 11% iron.*

CAYENNE MAYONNAISE

INGREDIENTS

2 Tbsp. refrigerated or frozen egg product, thawed
1 Tbsp. lemon juice
1 tsp. Dijon-style mustard
¼ tsp. cayenne pepper
½ cup extra virgin olive oil
½ cup canola oil

PREPARATION

1. In glass bowl combine egg product, lemon juice, mustard, and cayenne. Whisk until smooth. Whisk in *1 tablespoon* olive oil, a few drops at a time. Gradually add remaining olive oil and canola oil in a thin stream, whisking constantly until mixture is thickened (about 8 minutes). Season with *salt, ground black pepper,* and additional cayenne. Gradually whisk in *warm water* (up to ¼ cup) to make a sauce. Store in refrigerator up to 3 days.

MINTY PASTA SALAD WITH LAMB

PREP 20 min. **GRILL** 10 min. **CHILL** 2 hr.

INGREDIENTS

5	oz. dried fettuccine
1	Tbsp. extra virgin olive oil
1	tsp. finely shredded lemon peel
1	recipe Mint-Herb Pesto
12	small lamb double rib chops
3	cups arugula
1	cup fresh mint leaves
	Pine nuts, toasted

PREPARATION

1. Cook pasta according to package directions; drain. Rinse; drain. Transfer to bowl; toss with oil and lemon peel. Prepare Mint-Herb Pesto. Add to pasta; toss. Set aside. (Pasta may be chilled up to 24 hours.)
2. Meanwhile, sprinkle lamb with *salt* and *ground black pepper*. For charcoal grill, place chops on rack directly over medium coals. Grill, uncovered, 10 minutes (145°F for medium rare), turning once. (For gas grill, preheat grill. Reduce heat to medium. Place chops on rack over heat. Cover; grill as above.)
3. Toss pasta with arugula and mint. Top with grilled chops; sprinkle with pine nuts.
MAKES 6 SERVINGS.

EACH SERVING (WITH PESTO) *365 cal, 22 g fat (5 g sat. fat), 53 mg chol, 218 mg sodium, 21 g carbo, 3 g fiber, 21 g pro. Daily Values: 10% vit. A, 12% vit. C, 14% calcium, 29% iron.*

MINT-HERB PESTO

INGREDIENTS

1/2	cup lightly packed arugula
1/2	cup lightly packed mint
1/2	cup lightly packed basil
1/4	cup extra virgin olive oil
2	Tbsp. pine nuts, toasted
1	Tbsp. lemon juice
2	cloves garlic, minced
1	oz. shredded pecorino cheese (1/4 cup)
1/2	tsp. crushed red pepper

PREPARATION

1. In blender or food processor combine arugula, mint, basil, olive oil, pine nuts, lemon juice, and garlic. Cover; blend or process until smooth, scraping down sides as needed. Add cheese and red pepper. Cover; blend or process until just combined. Season with *salt* and *ground black pepper*.

LAYERED TUNA SALAD

Recipe pictured above.

PREP 50 min. **GRILL** 8 min. **CHILL** 2 hr.

INGREDIENTS

1 1/2	lb. fresh ahi tuna fillets, cut 1 inch thick
1	Tbsp. extra virgin olive oil
1 1/4	lb. small new Yukon gold potatoes, thinly sliced
6	ears fresh sweet corn
1	cup chopped fresh cilantro
12	green onions, sliced
1	fresh jalapeño pepper, seeded, sliced (see Note, page 101)
1	recipe Lime Dressing
1	medium red sweet pepper, chopped
	Chili powder

PREPARATION

1. Rinse tuna; pat dry. Brush tuna with olive oil; sprinkle with *salt* and *ground black pepper*. For charcoal grill, grill tuna on greased rack of uncovered grill directly over medium coals 8 to 12 minutes or until fish flakes easily when tested with fork and center is slightly pink, turning once. (For gas grill, preheat grill. Reduce heat to medium. Place tuna on greased rack over heat. Cover; grill as above.)
2. Meanwhile, cook potato slices in boiling *salted water* 5 to 8 minutes or until tender. Drain; set aside. Cut corn from cob (see tip for planking corn, *page 179*).
3. In bowl combine cilantro, green onion, and jalapeño; cover; chill. Prepare dressing; set aside. Break tuna into 3/4-inch pieces.

4. Place tuna evenly on bottom of 3-quart rectangular baking dish. Drizzle with *one-third* of dressing. Add potatoes; drizzle with another third of the dressing. Add corn; drizzle with remaining dressing. Sprinkle lightly with *salt* and *ground black pepper*. Cover and chill in refrigerator 2 to 3 hours.
5. To serve, top with cilantro mixture and sweet pepper. Sprinkle with chili powder.
MAKES 6 SERVINGS.

EACH SERVING (WITH DRESSING) *492 cal, 23 g fat (3 g sat. fat), 51 mg chol, 371 mg sodium, 43 g carbo, 8 g fiber, 33 g pro. Daily Values: 44% vit. A, 142% vit. C, 9% calcium, 21% iron.*

LIME DRESSING

3	limes
1/2	cup extra virgin olive oil
2	cloves garlic, minced
2	tsp. *each* ground coriander and cumin
1/2	tsp. salt
1/8	tsp. freshly ground pepper

PREPARATION

1. Finely shred *2 teaspoons* of peel from the limes. Squeeze enough lime juice to equal *1/2 cup*.
2. In small bowl whisk together the lime peel, lime juice, olive oil, garlic, coriander, cumin, salt, and pepper.

MEET JOANNE

Awardwinning cookbook author and TV chef Joanne Weir used her passion for fresh seasonal cooking to create these redefined salads. "Salads are a personal favorite, and there are so many options. The sky—or the garden—is the limit." Her latest book is Wine Country Cooking (Ten Speed Press 2008).

Weekday Wonders

These fresh and fast dishes are just right for dining on the deck.

BY **ERIN SIMPSON**   PHOTOS **ANDY LYONS**   RECIPES AND FOOD STYLING **JILL LUST**

READY
IN 20
MINUTES!

**BACON AND EGG
SALAD SANDWICHES**

BACON AND EGG SALAD SANDWICHES

START TO FINISH 20 min.

INGREDIENTS

6   eggs
8   slices applewood-smoked bacon
8   slices brioche
½   cup mayonnaise
2   tsp. yellow mustard
12   to 16 basil leaves
½   of an English cucumber, chopped

PREPARATION

1. Place eggs in medium saucepan; cover with water. Bring to boiling over high heat; cover and remove from heat. After 6 minutes, remove 2 eggs. Rinse with cold water; peel and set aside. Let remaining eggs stand in hot water 4 minutes more. Drain; rinse with cold water. Peel and coarsely chop the 10-minute eggs.

2. Meanwhile, in 12-inch skillet cook bacon until crisp; drain. Discard drippings; wipe pan with paper towel. Lightly toast both sides of bread slices in skillet. In bowl combine mayonnaise and mustard.

3. Top 4 of the bread slices with basil leaves, chopped egg, and cucumber. Halve the remaining 2 eggs and place one half on each sandwich. Top with mayonnaise mixture, bacon, and remaining bread slices. **MAKES 4 SERVINGS.**

EACH SERVING *614 cal, 40 g fat (10 g sat. fat), 391 mg chol, 38 g carbo, 2 g fiber, 22 g pro. Daily Values: 19% vit. A, 3% vit. C, 7% calcium, 20% iron.*

SUMMER STEW

START TO FINISH 20 min.

INGREDIENTS

1   17-oz. pkg. refrigerated cooked beef roast au jus
1   8-oz. pkg. peeled fresh baby carrots, sliced
3½   cups water
½   of 16-oz. pkg. refrigerated rosemary- and roasted garlic-seasoned diced red-skinned potatoes (about 2 cups)
1   14.5-oz. can diced fire-roasted tomatoes with garlic
2   Tbsp. snipped fresh oregano

PREPARATION

1. Pour juices from beef roast into saucepan; set meat aside. Add carrots and *1 cup* water to saucepan; bring to boiling. Reduce heat and simmer, covered, 3 minutes. Add remaining water, potatoes, tomatoes, and *1 tablespoon* of the oregano. Return to boiling; cover. Simmer 3 minutes or until vegetables are tender. Break beef into bite-size pieces. Add to stew; heat through. Season with *salt*.

2. Spoon into shallow bowls; top with freshly *ground black pepper* and remaining oregano. **MAKES 4 SERVINGS.**

EACH SERVING *253 cal, 9 g fat (4 g sat. fat), 64 mg chol, 948 mg sodium, 20 g carbo, 3 g fiber, 25 g pro. Daily Values: 166% vit. A, 52% vit. C, 6% calcium, 20% iron.*

SUMMER STEW

ZUCCHINI CAKES WITH MUSHROOM RAGOUT

START TO FINISH 20 min.

INGREDIENTS

	Nonstick cooking spray
1/2	of medium zucchini, shredded (1 cup)
1	8½-oz. pkg. corn muffin mix
1	cup shredded cheddar cheese (4 oz.)
1/4	cup milk
1	egg
1/4	tsp. cayenne pepper
12	oz. assorted mushrooms, quartered (4½ cups)
1	cup drained bottled roasted red sweet peppers

PREPARATION

1. Preheat oven to 400°F. Lightly coat twelve 2½-inch muffin cups with cooking spray; set aside.

2. In bowl combine zucchini, muffin mix, cheese, milk, egg, and cayenne pepper; spoon evenly into prepared muffin cups. Bake for 11 to 14 minutes or until golden.

3. Meanwhile, heat 1 tablespoon *olive oil* in skillet over medium-high heat. Add mushrooms; cook 3 to 4 minutes or until tender, stirring occasionally. Season with *salt* and *ground black pepper*. Place roasted peppers in blender. Cover; blend until nearly smooth.

4. Arrange 3 cakes on each plate with some of the mushrooms and pepper sauce. **MAKES 4 SERVINGS.**

EACH SERVING *443 cal, 21 g fat (7 g sat. fat), 84 mg chol, 701 mg sodium, 49 g carbo, 2 g fiber, 16 g pro. Daily Values: 9% vit. A, 180% vit. C, 24% calcium, 15% iron.*

ZUCCHINI CAKES WITH MUSHROOM RAGOUT

CAJUN SNAPPER WITH RED BEANS AND RICE

CAJUN SNAPPER WITH RED BEANS AND RICE

START TO FINISH 20 min.

INGREDIENTS

2	10-oz. fresh red snapper fillets
2	tsp. Creole or Cajun seasoning
1	14.8-oz. pouch cooked long grain rice
1	15-oz. can red beans, rinsed and drained
2	lemons
	Italian (flat-leaf) parsley (optional)
2	Tbsp. butter, melted

PREPARATION

1. Rinse fish; pat dry. Cut each fillet in half crosswise. Sprinkle snapper with *1 teaspoon* of the Creole seasoning. Heat 12-inch heavy nonstick skillet over medium-high heat. Add fish, skin sides up; cook 4 minutes; turn. Cook 2 to 4 minutes more or until fish flakes when tested with fork.

2. Meanwhile, in microwave-safe bowl combine rice, beans, and remaining seasoning. Cover and microcook on high (100% power) 3 to 3½ minutes or until heated through, stirring twice.

3. Finely shred *2 teaspoons* peel from one lemon; cut other lemon into wedges.

4. Serve fish with rice and beans. Drizzle melted butter over top; sprinkle lemon peel and parsley. Pass lemon wedges.
MAKES 4 SERVINGS.

EACH SERVING *447 cal, 11 g fat (4 g sat. fat), 68 mg chol, 1,055 mg sodium, 51 g carbo, 6 g fiber, 38 g pro. Daily Values: 6% vit. A, 18% vit. C, 11% calcium, 8% iron.*

FAST! LOW FAT

PAN-FRIED CHICKEN WITH TOMATO JAM

START TO FINISH 20 min.

INGREDIENTS

1	pint grape or cherry tomatoes
1	Tbsp. packed brown sugar
¾	cup quick-cooking polenta mix
½	cup all-purpose flour
¼	cup buttermilk
4	skinless, boneless chicken breast halves
1	9-oz. pkg. fresh spinach

PREPARATION

1. Pierce tomatoes with knife. Place in microwave-safe bowl; sprinkle with brown sugar. Cover loosely. Microcook on high (100% power) 3 minutes or until skins burst and tomatoes are soft, stirring once; set aside.

2. In saucepan bring 2½ cups *water* and 1 teaspoon *salt* to boiling; stir in polenta. Reduce heat; cook 5 minutes, stirring often.

3. In shallow dish combine flour with ½ teaspoon each *salt* and *ground black pepper;* add buttermilk to another dish. Dip chicken in buttermilk, then flour mixture. Heat 3 tablespoons *cooking oil* in large skillet over medium-high heat; add chicken. Cook 4 minutes per side or until no pink remains (170°F); remove.

4. Drain pan drippings. Add spinach; cook until just wilted. Season to taste. Serve chicken with spinach, polenta, and tomato jam.

MAKES 4 SERVINGS.

EACH SERVING *448 cal, 9 g fat (1 g sat. fat), 66 mg chol, 869 mg sodium, 56 g carbo, 8 g fiber, 34 g pro. Daily Values: 135% vit. A, 51% vit. C, 11% calcium, 21% iron.*

**PAN-FRIED CHICKEN
WITH TOMATO JAM**

All Ears

Sweet summer corn is ripe and ready to enjoy fresh, grilled, or baked in a tart.

BY **ERIN SIMPSON**
PHOTOS **ANDY LYONS**
FOOD STYLING **JILL LUST**

MARGARITA GRILLED CORN

Shred lime peel on a fine grater or zester. Leftover lime salt can be used to sprinkle over grilled meats or veggies.

PREP 25 min. **SOAK** 2 hr. **GRILL** 25 min.

INGREDIENTS
8   ears fresh corn in husks
4   tsp. finely shredded lime peel (peel from 2 to 3 limes)
2   tsp. kosher salt or sea salt
⅓   cup butter, melted
1   tsp. chili powder
     Small limes (optional)

PREPARATION
1. Carefully peel back corn husks but do not remove. Scrub ears with stiff brush to remove silks. Rinse ears. Pull husks back up around corn. Place in large pot; cover with water. Soak 2 to 4 hours; drain well. Peel back husks and pat corn dry with paper towels.
2. For lime salt, in small bowl stir together lime peel and salt. Brush some of the butter on corn. Sprinkle lightly with lime salt and chili powder. Fold husks back around ears. Tie husk tops with strips of corn husk or 100%-cotton kitchen string.
3. For charcoal grill, grill corn on rack of uncovered grill directly over medium coals 25 to 30 minutes or until tender, turning and rearranging occasionally. (For gas grill, preheat grill. Reduce heat to medium. Place corn on grill rack over heat. Cover; grill as above.)
4. To serve, remove ties from corn; peel back husks. Pass remaining butter, lime salt, chili powder, and limes for squeezing.
MAKES 8 SERVINGS.

EACH SERVING *147 cal, 9 g fat (5 g sat. fat), 20 mg chol, 553 mg sodium, 17 g carbo, 3 g fiber, 3 g pro. Daily Values: 10% vit. A, 13% vit. C, 1% calcium, 3% iron.*

FAST! **LOW FAT**

FRESH CORN-RICE SALAD

This salad is a great way to use leftover rice. If none is on hand, prepare ¹/₂ cup uncooked long grain rice and let cool before using.

PREP 20 min. **COOK** 3 min. **CHILL** 1 hr.

INGREDIENTS
4   ears fresh corn
1½   cups cooked rice, cooled
1   pint cherry or grape tomatoes, halved
1   cup fresh arugula
1   small red onion, cut in thin wedges
1   fresh jalapeño pepper, thinly sliced (see Note, page 101)
2   Tbsp. rice vinegar or red wine vinegar
2   Tbsp. olive oil

PREPARATION
1. Husk corn and remove silk with a stiff brush; rinse. Cook corn in boiling, lightly salted water for 3 minutes. Remove corn; let cool. Cut corn off the cob in planks (see box, *below*).
2. Combine cooked rice, tomatoes, arugula, onion, and jalapeño pepper. Transfer to serving bowl; top with corn.
3. Drizzle with vinegar and olive oil. Season to taste with *salt* and *ground black pepper*. Serve at room temperature.
MAKES 10 TO 12 SERVINGS.

EACH SERVING *123 cal, 1 g fat (0 g sat. fat), 0 mg chol, 332 mg sodium, 28 g carbo, 2 g fiber, 3 g pro. Daily Values: 12% vit. A, 16% vit. C, 2% calcium, 6% iron.*

PLANKING CORN

To cut planks, place an ear on its side on a cutting board. Holding the corn firmly with fingers away from the blade, cut off a side of the corn. Rotate and repeat until all sides are removed. Use a spatula to gently move planks to salad.

FRESH CORN-RICE SALAD

CORN AND BASIL TART

PREP 25 min. **CHILL** 30 min. **BAKE** 49 min.
COOL 10 min. **OVEN** 350°F

- ⅓ cup butter, softened
- 2 Tbsp. sugar
- ½ tsp. salt
- 3 eggs
- ⅔ cup yellow cornmeal
- ⅔ cup all-purpose flour
- 1 cup half-and-half or light cream
- 1½ cups fresh corn kernels (about 3 ears)
- ½ cup coarsely snipped fresh basil
- ½ tsp. salt
- ¼ tsp. ground black pepper
  Chopped tomato and basil (optional)

PREPARATION

1. For cornmeal crust, in medium bowl beat butter with electric mixer on medium to high speed for 30 seconds. Add sugar and ½ teaspoon salt. Beat until combined. Beat in 1 egg until combined. Beat in cornmeal and as much of the flour as you can with the mixer; stir in any remaining flour. Form dough into a disk and wrap in plastic. Chill 30 to 60 minutes or until easy to handle.

2. Preheat oven to 350°F. Pat dough onto bottom and sides of 9-inch tart pan with removable bottom. Press evenly onto bottom and sides with a small glass (see box). Line pastry with double thickness of foil and bake 10 minutes; remove foil. Bake 4 to 6 minutes more.

3. Meanwhile, in medium bowl whisk together the 2 eggs and half-and-half. Stir in corn, basil, ½ teaspoon salt, and the pepper. Pour into pastry shell. Bake 35 to 40 minutes or until set. Let stand 10 minutes. Remove sides of pan to serve. Sprinkle tomato and additional basil.

MAKES 8 SERVINGS.

EACH SERVING *251 cal, 13 g fat (7 g sat. fat), 111 mg chol, 401 mg sodium, 30 g carbo, 1 g fiber, 6 g pro. Daily Values: 11% vit. A, 2% vit. C, 5% calcium, 8% iron.*

MAKING THE TART CRUST

To ensure even baking, lightly press dough on bottom and up sides of the tart pan. Using the side of a small glass, roll the crust smooth on the bottom. Holding the glass upright, gently press dough to sides of pan for a uniform edge.

Easy as Pie

Top off summer's juiciest peaches with a brown sugar syrup and a flaky lattice pastry top.

SKILLET PEACHES À LA MODE

FAST! **KID FRIENDLY**

SKILLET PEACHES À LA MODE

Use half of the Sugared Pastry to top the Skillet Peaches and freeze the rest to have on hand for serving with bowls of other summer fruits.

PREP 10 min. **BAKE** 10 min. **COOK** 5 min. **OVEN** 375°F

INGREDIENTS

1	recipe Sugared Pastry
⅓	cup butter
6	to 8 peaches or nectarines, pitted and halved or quartered (about 2 lb.)
¼	cup peach or apricot nectar
2	Tbsp. packed brown sugar
1	cup fresh raspberries or blueberries
	Fresh mint leaves (optional)
	Vanilla ice cream

PREPARATION

1. Prepare Sugared Pastry. Melt butter in 12-inch skillet over medium-high heat. Add peaches, skin sides up. Reduce heat to medium; cook 4 to 5 minutes, turning once. Remove peaches to bowls. Add nectar and brown sugar to skillet. Cook and stir over medium heat 1 to 2 minutes or until sugar is dissolved and syrup forms.

2. Spoon syrup on peaches. Top with berries, mint, and Sugared Pastry. Serve with ice cream. **MAKES 4 TO 6 SERVINGS.**

Sugared Pastry Preheat oven to 375°F. Let one 15-ounce rolled *refrigerated piecrust* stand at room temperature 15 minutes. Line baking sheet with nonstick foil or parchment paper. Unroll crust onto lightly floured surface. Brush with 1 tablespoon melted *butter*. Sprinkle with 1 tablespoon *coarse decorating sugar* or granulated sugar and ¼ teaspoon *cinnamon*. Cut pastry in half. Cut halves into strips, stars, or desired shapes. Place on prepared sheet. Bake 10 to 12 minutes or until lightly browned. Cool on baking sheet on wire rack. Pastry can be frozen up to 3 months. Makes about 40 strips.

EACH SERVING *557 cal, 32 g fat (18 g sat. fat), 79 mg chol, 289 mg sodium, 66 g carbo, 6 g fiber, 6 g pro. Daily Values: 32% vit. A, 41% vit. C, 13% calcium, 6% iron.*

SEPTEMBER

NINE TALENTED READERS STRUT THEIR STUFF THIS MONTH BY SHARING THEIR FAVORITE PIE RECIPES, AND WINNERS FROM THE *YOUR BEST RECIPES* CONTEST SHOW WHAT THEY CAN DO WITH A FAST AND FRESH OUTLOOK. FALL COOKING GETS UNDERWAY WITH ONE-DISH DINNERS SLOW-SIMMERED ON THE STOVE.

CRANBERRY CHOCOLATE NUT PIE
page 191

American Pie

SPICY SHRIMP PASTA
page 197

**MUSTARD-HERB
BEEF STEW**
page 201

**CHOCOLATE-HAZELNUT
ICE CREAM SANDWICHES**
page 203

No matter the time
of year or the occasion, our
readers love playing in the dough.
So we sent out a call asking you to
share your flakiest homespun favorites.

american pie

The result: a collection of praiseworthy pies
as pleasing to make as they are to eat. Take
it from apple pie innovator Catherine
Wilkinson: "What's better to
make than pie?"

BY **ERIN SIMPSON** PHOTOS **ANDY LYONS**
FOOD STYLING **SUSAN SUGARMAN** PROP STYLING **SUE MITCHELL**

ROSEMARY APPLE PIE
CATHERINE WILKINSON
DEWEY, ARIZ.
Reader for 15 years

page 189

A rosemary-flecked sugar syrup adds just the right sweetness to tart Granny Smith apples. It's an aromatic spin on Mom's classic.

MAPLE-NUT PIE
ROBIN HAAS
CRANSTON, R.I.
Reader for 10 years
page 191

Pies are like their makers—each has its own personality. Whether nutty and sweet, simple and good, or spicy and decadent, they all bring something special to the table.

BUTTERMILK PIE
HILLARY BARZILLA
HOUSTON, TEXAS
Reader for 1 year
page 193

This sticky Maple-Nut Pie, *opposite above*, is similar to pecan but features toasty walnuts. Hints of light rum and nutmeg round out the flavor. Cobbler-like Blackberry Swirl aPie, *left*, will have you savoring the last of the summer berries. Sweet Potato Pie, *below*, is a lightly spiced, lemony version of the autumn classic. Snickerdoodle Pie is cakey and cinnamon-laden, *opposite center*, with all the charm of the cookie in pie form. Silky and sweet, Buttermilk Pie, *opposite bottom*, has a delicate tang. The fast-cooked filling is poured into a pastry shell, baked, and chilled for an easy-to-slice custard pie.

BLACKBERRY SWIRL PIE
KRISTA MERRIMAN
CLAREMORE, OKLA.
Reader for 14 years
page 193

SNICKERDOODLE PIE
SUZANNE CONRAD
FINDLAY, OHIO
Reader for 12 years
page 191

SWEET POTATO PIE
BETSY AUSTIN
MARDELA SPRINGS, MD.
Longtime reader
page 194

The quick toss-together filling is laced with bourbon. A sprinkling of brown sugar adds extra crunchy sweetness to the lattice top.

PEACH-BLUEBERRY PIE

"My mom was a baker and always made fresh peach pie when peaches were in season." —Diane Disbrow

PREP 30 min. **BAKE** 50 min. **OVEN** 375°F

INGREDIENTS

2   recipes Single-Crust Pie Pastry, page 194, or 2 rolled refrigerated unbaked piecrusts (15-oz. pkg.)
5   cups peeled, sliced fresh peaches or frozen peach slices, thawed
1   cup fresh or frozen blueberries, thawed
1/3 cup packed brown sugar
2   Tbsp. cornstarch
2   Tbsp. bourbon (optional)
1/2 tsp. ground cinnamon
2   Tbsp. packed brown sugar

PREPARATION

1. Preheat oven to 375°F. Prepare pastries. Line 9-inch pie plate with one crust. Trim edge of crust to 1/2 inch beyond pie plate. Set aside.
2. In large bowl combine peaches, blueberries, 1/3 cup brown sugar, cornstarch, bourbon, and cinnamon. Place filling in prepared crust. On lightly floured surface, roll remaining crust to circle 12 inches in diameter. Cut in 1-inch-wide strips. Weave strips over filling in lattice pattern. Press strip ends into bottom pastry. Fold bottom pastry over strips' ends; seal and crimp. Sprinkle lattice with 2 tablespoons brown sugar.
3. Cover edges with foil. Bake on baking sheet 25 minutes. Remove foil. Bake 25 minutes more or until filling is thickened and crust is golden. Cool on rack. **MAKES 8 SERVINGS.**

EACH SERVING *319 cal, 13 g fat (3 g sat. fat), 0 mg chol, 120 mg sodium, 47 g carbo, 3 g fiber, 4 g pro. Daily Values: 9% vit. A, 12% vit. C, 2% calcium, 9% iron.*

ROSEMARY APPLE PIE

"My mother has Alzheimer's disease and can no longer bake. Each week when I visit, I bring a different pie for my father to 'test.' It is sort of like a challenge. This was one I came up with when I had a lot of rosemary in the garden." —Catherine Wilkinson
Recipe pictured on page 185.

PREP 1 hr. **STAND** 30 min. **BAKE** 55 min. **OVEN** 375°F

INGREDIENTS

1/4 cup granulated sugar
1/4 cup water
2   large sprigs fresh rosemary plus 1 tsp. finely snipped fresh rosemary
1/2 cup packed brown sugar
1/4 cup all-purpose flour
1/4 tsp. salt
6   cups cored, peeled, and sliced Granny Smith apples
1   Tbsp. lemon juice
3   Tbsp. whipping cream
1   tsp. vanilla
1/4 cup butter
1   recipe Rosemary Pastry
1   egg white, beaten
2   tsp. granulated sugar

PREPARATION

1. For rosemary syrup, in small microwave-safe bowl combine the 1/4 cup granulated sugar, the water, and 2 sprigs rosemary. Microcook, uncovered, on 100% power (high) for 2 minutes. Let stand 30 minutes; remove rosemary sprigs and discard.
2. In small bowl combine brown sugar, flour, salt, and the 1 teaspoon finely snipped rosemary; set aside. In very large bowl toss apples with lemon juice. Add brown sugar mixture; toss to coat. Add whipping cream, vanilla, and rosemary syrup.
3. In large skillet melt butter over medium heat; add apple mixture. Cook over medium heat for 8 minutes, stirring occasionally. Remove from heat and set aside.
4. Preheat oven to 375°F. On lightly floured surface, slightly flatten one Rosemary Pastry ball. Roll it from center to edges into a circle 12 inches in diameter. Wrap pastry circle around the rolling pin. Unroll pastry into 9-inch pie pan or plate. Trim pastry even with rim of pie pan; spoon in apple mixture.
5. Roll remaining ball of pastry into a circle 12 inches in diameter. Cut large slits in pastry. Place pastry circle on apple filling; trim to 1/2 inch beyond edge of pan. Fold top pastry under bottom pastry.

Crimp edge as desired. Brush with egg white and sprinkle with the 2 teaspoons granulated sugar.
6. To prevent overbrowning, cover edge of pie with foil. Place on foil-lined baking sheet. Bake 35 minutes. Remove foil. Bake 20 to 25 minutes more or until fruit is tender and filling is bubbly. Cool on wire rack; serve slightly warm.
MAKES 10 SERVINGS.

EACH SERVING *487 cal, 26 g fat (9 g sat. fat), 39 mg chol, 336 mg sodium, 57 g carbo, 2 g fiber, 5 g pro. Daily Values: 5% vit. A, 6% vit. C, 3% calcium, 12% iron.*

ROSEMARY PASTRY

PREP 10 min. **CHILL** 30 min.

INGREDIENTS

3   cups all-purpose flour
1   tsp. salt
1   tsp. sugar
1/2 tsp. finely snipped fresh rosemary leaves
1   cup shortening, chilled
1/3 cup ice water
1   egg yolk, lightly beaten
1   Tbsp. vinegar

PREPARATION

1. In large bowl combine flour, salt, sugar, and rosemary; cut in shortening until mixture resembles cornmeal.
2. In bowl combine ice water, egg yolk, and vinegar. Add liquid mixture, *1 tablespoon* at a time, to flour mixture using a fork to mix until flour mixture is moistened. Divide in half; form into balls. Wrap in plastic wrap; chill 30 minutes.
Food processor method In food processor combine flour, salt, sugar, and rosemary leaves. Add shortening. Pulse until mixture resembles cornmeal. Add liquid mixture, 1 tablespoon at a time, until moistened. Proceed as above.

The gooey mix of white chocolate, walnuts, and brandy-soaked cranberries looks like a blonde brownie, but eats like a pie.

CRANBERRY CHOCOLATE NUT PIE
REBECCA WALCH, ORLAND, CALIF. *Reader for 7 years*

CRANBERRY CHOCOLATE NUT PIE

KID FRIENDLY

"I like to serve this pie on the first really chilly fall day, still warm from the oven."
—Rebecca Walch

PREP 30 min. **CHILL** 1 hr. **BAKE** 65 min.
OVEN 325°F

INGREDIENTS

¾ cup dried cranberries
½ cup brandy or orange juice
1 recipe Single-Crust Pie Pastry, page 194, or 1 rolled refrigerated unbaked piecrust (½ of a 15-oz. pkg.)
⅓ cup butter, melted and cooled
1½ cups sugar
3 eggs
⅛ tsp. salt
1 cup chopped walnuts
¾ cup all-purpose flour
2 oz. white baking bars, chopped
1 recipe Sweetened Whipped Cream (optional)

1. In small bowl combine dried cranberries and brandy. Cover and chill for at least 1 hour. Drain and reserve *1 tablespoon* of the brandy.
2. Preheat oven to 325°F. Prepare pastry and line 9-inch pie plate.
3. In medium bowl whisk together butter, sugar, eggs, and salt. Stir in walnuts, flour, and chopped baking bars until just combined. Stir in drained cranberries and the 1 tablespoon reserved brandy mixture. Spoon into crust-lined pie plate. Bake for 65 minutes, loosely covering the pie with foil the last 30 minutes of baking. Cool on rack.
4. Top with Sweetened Whipped Cream.
MAKES 10 SERVINGS.
Sweetened Whipped Cream In chilled mixing bowl combine 1 cup *whipping cream*, 2 tablespoons *sugar*, and ½ teaspoon *vanilla*. Beat with electric mixer on medium speed until soft peaks form. Refrigerate until ready to use.

EACH SERVING *507 cal, 24 g fat (8 g sat. fat), 81 mg chol, 160 mg sodium, 61 g carbo, 2 g fiber, 7 g pro. Daily Values: 5% vit. A, 3% calcium, 10% iron.*

MAPLE-NUT PIE

KID FRIENDLY

"This recipe was created in honor of my father, who passed away when I was a little girl. We shared a love of maple walnut ice cream." —Robin Haas

Recipe pictured on page 186.

PREP 30 min. **BAKE** 13 min./35 min.
COOK 10 min. **OVEN** 450°F/350°F

INGREDIENTS

1 recipe Single-Crust Pie Pastry, page 194, or 1 rolled refrigerated unbaked piecrust (½ of a 15-oz. pkg.)
1½ cups pure maple syrup
3 eggs
6 Tbsp. butter, softened
⅓ cup granulated sugar
¼ cup packed brown sugar
2 cups coarsely chopped walnuts, toasted
1 Tbsp. vanilla
2 Tbsp. light rum (optional)
¼ tsp. freshly ground nutmeg
Rum raisin or vanilla ice cream

PREPARATION

1. Preheat oven to 450°F. Prepare pastry and line 9-inch pie plate. Prick bottom and sides of pastry with fork. Line pastry with double thickness of foil. Bake 8 minutes. Remove foil. Bake 5 minutes more or until crust is lightly browned; cool. Reduce oven to 350°F.
2. In saucepan bring maple syrup to boiling. Reduce heat. Simmer, uncovered, for 10 to 12 minutes or until reduced to 1 cup.
3. In medium bowl beat eggs with electric mixer on medium to high speed until thick and lemon colored, about 5 minutes.
4. In large bowl beat butter with electric mixer on medium to high speed for 30 seconds. Add granulated and brown sugars; beat to combine. Beat in reduced syrup and eggs. Fold in walnuts, vanilla, rum, and nutmeg. Pour into prebaked crust.
5. Bake pie on baking sheet in lower third of oven 35 minutes or until set around edges; cool. Serve with ice cream. **MAKES 10 SERVINGS.**

EACH SERVING *526 cal, 30 g fat (8 g sat. fat), 82 mg chol, 135 mg sodium, 60 g carbo, 2 g fiber, 7 g pro. Daily Values: 6% vit. A, 1% vit. C, 7% calcium, 13% iron.*

SNICKERDOODLE PIE

KID FRIENDLY

"My grandmother made a 'funny cake'— a cake baked in a pie shell. This is a variation on that recipe."—Suzanne Conrad

Recipe pictured on page 186.

PREP 40 min. **BAKE** 45 min. **COOL** 30 min.
OVEN 350°F

INGREDIENTS

1 recipe Single-Crust Pie Pastry, page 194, or 1 rolled refrigerated unbaked piecrust (½ of a 15-oz. pkg.)
1 Tbsp. raw sugar or coarse sugar
½ tsp. plus ¼ tsp. ground cinnamon
2 tsp. butter, melted
½ cup packed brown sugar
½ cup butter, softened
2 Tbsp. light-colored corn syrup
½ tsp. plus 1 tsp. vanilla
½ cup granulated sugar
¼ cup powdered sugar
1 tsp. baking powder
¼ tsp. cream of tartar
1 egg
½ cup milk
1¼ cups all-purpose flour

PREPARATION

1. Preheat oven to 350°F. Prepare pastry and line 9-inch pie plate. In bowl combine raw sugar and ½ *teaspoon* cinnamon. Brush melted butter over crust. Sprinkle with 1 teaspoon of sugar mixture. Set aside.
2. For syrup, in saucepan combine brown sugar, ¼ *cup* butter, 3 tablespoons *water*, corn syrup, and ¼ teaspoon cinnamon. Heat to boiling over medium heat, stirring to dissolve sugar. Boil gently 2 minutes. Remove from heat. Stir in ½ *teaspoon* vanilla. Set aside.
3. In mixing bowl beat remaining ¼ cup butter with electric mixer on medium speed 30 seconds. Beat in granulated and powdered sugars, baking powder, ½ teaspoon *salt*, and cream of tartar until well combined. Beat in egg and 1 teaspoon vanilla. Gradually beat in milk until combined. Beat in flour. Spread evenly in crust-lined pie plate.
4. Slowly pour syrup over filling. Sprinkle remaining sugar mixture. Cover edges with foil.
5. Bake pie 25 minutes; carefully remove foil. Bake 20 minutes more or until top is puffed and golden brown and a toothpick inserted near center comes out clean. Cool 30 minutes on wire rack. Serve warm.
MAKES 10 SERVINGS.

EACH SERVING *385 cal, 17 g fat (8 g sat. fat), 49 mg chol, 289 mg sodium, 53 g carbo, 1 g fiber, 4 g pro. Daily Values: 7% vit. A, 4% calcium, 9% iron.*

Egg whites are beaten until fluffy, then folded into the filling. The pie's light and airy texture is perfect for soaking up the tart-sweetness of candied lemon slices.

LEMON SPONGE PIE
VICTORIA MALANEY
FLINTSTONE, MD.
Longtime reader

page 193

LEMON SPONGE PIE

"My aunt gave me this recipe when I was 16 years old. I make piecrusts by hand—without measuring but by feel. Use a giant spatula to transfer the dough to pie plate."
—Victoria Malaney

PREP 25 min. **BAKE** 42 min. **COOL** 1 hr.
CHILL 3 hr. **OVEN** 450°F/425°F/ 350°F

INGREDIENTS

1	recipe Single-Crust Pie Pastry, page 194, or 1 rolled refrigerated unbaked piecrust (½ of a 15-oz. pkg.)
2	eggs
⅓	cup butter, softened
1	cup granulated sugar
2	tsp. finely shredded lemon peel
¼	cup lemon juice
2	Tbsp. all-purpose flour
1	cup milk
1	recipe Candied Lemon Slices (optional)

PREPARATION

1. Preheat oven to 450°F. Prepare pastry and line 9-inch pie plate. Line with double thickness of foil. Bake 8 minutes; remove foil. Bake 4 to 6 minutes more or until lightly browned. Cool on rack. Reduce oven temperature to 425°F.
2. Separate egg yolks from whites; place whites in medium bowl and set aside. In large bowl beat butter with electric mixer until fluffy. Beat in sugar until combined. Beat in egg yolks, lemon peel, lemon juice, flour, and ⅛ teaspoon *salt* until just combined. Add milk; beat until just combined (mixture will be thin and appear curdled).
3. Thoroughly wash beaters. In medium bowl beat egg whites with mixer on medium speed until stiff peaks form (tips stand straight). Fold egg whites into beaten yolk mixture. Transfer mixture to prebaked crust.
4. Loosely tent top of pie with foil to prevent overbrowning, making sure the foil does not touch filling. Bake 10 minutes. Reduce heat to 350°F. Bake 20 to 25 minutes more or until set in the center.
5. Cool 1 hour on wire rack. Cover and refrigerate 3 hours. To serve, top with Candied Lemon Slices. **MAKES 8 SERVINGS.**
Candied Lemon Slices In small saucepan combine ¼ cup *sugar* and ¼ cup *water*; bring to boiling. Add 1 *lemon*, very thinly sliced. Simmer gently, uncovered, for 12 to 15 minutes or until syrupy. Transfer slices to waxed paper. Discard remaining syrup.

EACH SERVING *351 cal, 18 g fat (8 g sat. fat), 75 mg chol, 194 mg sodium, 44 g carbo, 1 g fiber, 5 g pro. Daily Values: 7% vit. A, 7% vit. C, 5% calcium, 7% iron.*

BUTTERMILK PIE

"People who have tasted this say it reminds them of when they were kids, of something their grandmothers made."—Hillary Barzilla
Recipe pictured on page 186.

PREP 25min. **BAKE** 12 min./50 min.
COOL 1 hr. **CHILL** 4 hr. **OVEN** 450°F/350°F

INGREDIENTS

1	recipe Single-Crust Pie Pastry, page 194, or 1 rolled refrigerated unbaked piecrust (½ of a 15-oz. pkg.)
½	cup butter
1	cup sugar
3	Tbsp. all-purpose flour
3	eggs
1	cup buttermilk
1	tsp. vanilla

PREPARATION

1. Preheat oven to 450°F. Prepare pastry and line 9-inch pie plate. Line pastry with double thickness of foil. Bake 8 minutes. Remove foil. Bake 4 to 6 minutes more or until crust is lightly browned; cool. Reduce oven temperature to 350°F.
2. In saucepan, melt butter over medium-low heat. Stir in sugar and flour. Remove from heat; set aside. In mixing bowl beat eggs with electric mixer on medium speed just until fluffy (about 1 minute). Stir in buttermilk and vanilla. Gradually whisk buttermilk mixture into butter mixture until smooth. Pour into prebaked crust.
3. Place pie on oven rack; carefully tent whole pie with foil. Bake 50 to 55 minutes or until center is set when gently shaken. Cool on wire rack for 1 hour. Cover; refrigerate at least 4 hours before serving.
MAKES 8 SERVINGS.

EACH SERVING *394 cal, 22 g fat (10 g sat. fat), 111 mg chol, 214 mg sodium, 44 g carbo, 1 g fiber, 6 g pro. Daily Values: 9% vit. A, 1% vit. C, 5% calcium, 8% iron.*

KID FRIENDLY

BLACKBERRY SWIRL PIE

"With four small children I don't have time to do much baking. This pie is something I can make that is simple and guaranteed to taste great." —Krista Merriman
Recipe pictured on page 187.

PREP 20 min. **BAKE** 12 min. /45 min.
COOL 2 hr. **OVEN** 450°F/350°F

INGREDIENTS

3	cups fresh blackberries or 1 (16-oz.) pkg. frozen blackberries
1	recipe Single-Crust Pie Pastry, page 194, or 1 rolled refrigerated unbaked piecrust (½ of a 15-oz. pkg.)
1	8-oz. carton dairy sour cream
¾	cup sugar
3	Tbsp. all-purpose flour
⅛	tsp. salt

PREPARATION

1. Preheat oven to 450°F. Let frozen berries stand at room temperature for 15 minutes. Meanwhile, prepare pastry and line 9-inch pie plate. Line pastry with double thickness of foil. Bake 8 minutes. Remove foil. Bake 4 minutes more or until lightly browned. Cool on wire rack. Reduce oven to 350°F.
2. In bowl combine sour cream, sugar, flour, and salt. Add blackberries and gently stir to combine. Spoon into prebaked crust. To prevent overbrowning, cover edge of pie with foil. Bake 25 minutes (50 minutes for frozen berries). Remove foil. Bake 20 minutes more or until filling is bubbly and appears set. Cool on wire rack for 2 hours. Serve or cover and refrigerate. **MAKES 8 SERVINGS.**

EACH SERVING *311 cal, 14 g fat (6 g sat. fat), 12 mg chol, 125 mg sodium, 42 g carbo, 3 g fiber, 4 g pro. Daily Values: 6% vit. A, 19% vit. C, 5% calcium, 8% iron.*

SWEET POTATO PIE

"This recipe comes from my aunt Lucille. When she made sweet potato pie, she always used lemon to flavor it instead of vanilla."
—Betsy Austin

Recipe pictured on page 187.

PREP 30 min. **BAKE** 50 min. **OVEN** 350°F

INGREDIENTS

1	recipe Single-Crust Pie Pastry or 1 rolled refrigerated unbaked piecrust (½ of a 15-oz. pkg.)
2	eggs
¾	cup sugar
1	5-oz. can evaporated milk
3	Tbsp. butter, melted
1	tsp. finely shredded lemon peel
	Dash ground nutmeg
2	medium sweet potatoes peeled, cooked, and mashed (1⅓ cups)

PREPARATION

1. Preheat oven to 350°F. Prepare pastry and line 9-inch pie plate.

2. In bowl beat eggs with whisk. Whisk in sugar, evaporated milk, butter, lemon peel, and nutmeg. Whisk in sweet potatoes until combined. Pour into crust-lined pie plate.

3. To prevent overbrowning, cover edges of crust with foil. Bake 30 minutes. Uncover edges and bake 20 to 30 minutes more or until filling is set and knife inserted in center comes out clean. Cool completely. Cover and refrigerate within 2 hours after it cools. **MAKES 8 SERVINGS.**

EACH SERVING *338 cal, 15 g fat (6 g sat. fat), 69 mg chol, 155 mg sodium, 45 g carbo, 2 g fiber, 6 g pro. Daily Values: 176% vit. A, 13% vit. C, 7% calcium, 9% iron.*

SINGLE-CRUST PIE PASTRY

With this sure-fire recipe you can have a homemade crust in just 10 minutes. Learn how to pretty-up your pie edges on page 195.

PREP 10 min.

INGREDIENTS

1¼	cups all-purpose flour
¼	teaspoon salt
⅓	cup shortening
	Cold water

PREPARATION

1. In medium bowl stir together all-purpose flour and salt. Using pastry blender, cut in shortening until pieces are pea size. Sprinkle *1 tablespoon* cold water over part of the flour mixture; gently toss with a fork to mix. Push moistened pastry to side of bowl. Repeat moistening flour mixture, using 1 tablespoon of water at a time, until all of the flour mixture is moistened. Form dough into a ball.

2. On lightly floured surface, use your hands to slightly flatten pastry. Roll pastry from center to edges into a circle about 12 inches in diameter, lightly dusting with flour as needed.

TO LINE PIE PLATE wrap pastry around rolling pin. Unroll into a 9-inch pie plate or pan. Ease into pie plate without stretching the dough. Trim edges of crust to ½ inch beyond pie plate. Flute edge as desired.

Food processor method In food processor combine flour, salt, and shortening. Pulse until mixture resembles cornmeal but a few larger pieces remain. With processor running, quickly add *3 tablespoons* water through feed tube. Stop processor as soon as all water is added; scrape down sides. Process with two pulses (mixture may not look completely moistened). Remove pastry and form into a ball. Proceed as directed, *left*.

ON THE EDGE

SPOON FLUTE
Fold edge under. Pinch dough around your thumb to form scallops. Use tip of a spoon to make indentation.

UP AND DOWN
Fold edge under even with pie plate. Use kitchen scissors to snip dough about every inch. Fold every other piece up toward pie's center.

FREE FORM
Trim pastry ¾ inch wider than pie plate, lift, and form into large scallops, allowing pastry to fall over plate's edge.

ROUND THE RIM
Trim pastry to edge of pie plate. With a small cookie cutter, cut small circles from pastry scraps. Use a little water to attach circles.

PIE MAKERS

Out of hundreds of reader-submitted pies, we found these bakers served up the most delicious American slices.

Catherine Wilkinson from Dewey, Ariz., bakes a pie every week. Her Rosemary Apple Pie was a way to try out a new flavor pairing.

Robin Haas has fun making new recipes in her Cranston, R.I., home. A love of nut desserts led her to create Maple-Nut Pie.

Suzanne Conrad, from Findlay, Ohio, came up with Snickerdoodle Pie as a way to enjoy her favorite cinnamon-rich fall cookie.

Hillary Barzilla, of Houston, was hesitant to try her grandmother's Buttermilk Pie at first. She now makes it year-round.

Krista Merriman, from Claremore, Okla., had to share her Blackberry Swirl Pie—it's easy to make and her favorite.

Betsy Austin Each fall **Betsy Austin** gets busy making Sweet Potato Pie with potatoes grown in her hometown of Mardela Springs, Md.

Before making her Peach-Blueberry Pie, **Diane Disbrow** likes to pick her own peaches at local orchards in Collinsville, Ill.

Rebecca Walch's Cranberry Chocolate Nut Pie resulted from a craving for a chewy pie on a chilly day in Orland, Calif.

Victoria Malaney, of Flintstone, Md., has been making her Lemon Sponge Pie for more than 60 years.

CALIFORNIA TUNA PARMESAN
KAREEN BURNS LOS ALTOS, CALIF.

READY IN 20 MINUTES!

Get Fresh!

These winning 20-minute dishes from our *Your Best Recipes* contest promise great taste, ease, and speed.

CALIFORNIA TUNA PARMESAN

START TO FINISH 20 min.

INGREDIENTS

2 lemons
⅓ cup extra virgin olive oil
½ tsp. freshly ground black pepper
¼ tsp. salt
12 oz. asparagus, trimmed
4 4-oz. fresh tuna steaks
1 5-oz. pkg. mixed baby greens
⅓ cup freshly shaved Parmesan cheese

PREPARATION

1. Preheat oven to 450°F. Finely shred *2 teaspoons* peel from 1 lemon. Squeeze juice from lemon. For dressing, in small bowl whisk together oil, lemon peel and juice, pepper, and salt; set aside. Cut remaining lemon in wedges; set aside.
2. Place asparagus in single layer in shallow baking pan. Drizzle 2 tablespoons dressing. Bake, uncovered, 8 minutes.
3. Meanwhile, heat *1 tablespoon* dressing in skillet. Add tuna; cook 4 to 6 minutes each side until browned and center is slightly pink.
4. Divide greens among 4 plates; top with tuna and asparagus. Drizzle remaining dressing. Sprinkle Parmesan; pass lemon wedges. **MAKES 4 SERVINGS.**

EACH SERVING *377 cal, 26 g fat (5 g sat. fat), 48 mg chol, 312 mg sodium, 9 g carbo, 4 g fiber, 31 g pro. Daily Values: 66% vit. A, 79% vit. C, 16% calcium, 16% iron.*

SPICY SHRIMP PASTA

START TO FINISH 20 min.

INGREDIENTS

8 oz. dried angel hair pasta
3 cups fresh broccoli florets
1 6.5-oz. jar oil-packed dried tomato strips with Italian herbs
2 shallots, finely chopped
1 lb. frozen, peeled, and deveined shrimp with tails, thawed and drained
¼ to ½ tsp. crushed red pepper
¼ cup snipped fresh basil

PREPARATION

1. In 4-quart Dutch oven cook pasta with broccoli according to pasta package directions. Drain; return to Dutch oven. Cover to keep warm.
2. Meanwhile, drain tomatoes, reserving oil. If necessary, add *olive oil* to equal ¼ cup. In extra-large skillet heat oil over medium-high heat. Add shallot; cook and stir 1 to 2 minutes or until tender. Add shrimp and crushed red pepper; cook and stir 2 minutes. Add dried tomatoes; cook and stir 1 minute more or until shrimp are opaque.
3. Toss shrimp mixture with cooked pasta. Season with *salt* and *ground black pepper*. Drizzle additional olive oil. Transfer to serving bowls. Sprinkle snipped fresh basil. **MAKES 4 SERVINGS.**

EACH SERVING *526 cal, 19 g fat (3 g sat. fat), 172 mg chol, 394 mg sodium, 55 g carbo, 5 g fiber, 34 g pro. Daily Values: 20% vit. A, 141% vit. C, 12% calcium, 28% iron.*

SPICY SHRIMP PASTA
JESSICA CROLEY LEXINGTON, KY.

FAST! **KID FRIENDLY** **LOW FAT**

MAPLE-GLAZED CHICKEN WITH SWEET POTATOES

START TO FINISH 20 min.

INGREDIENTS

1	1-lb. 8-oz. pkg. refrigerated mashed sweet potatoes
1	lb. chicken breast tenderloins
2	tsp. steak grilling seasoning blend, such as Montreal
2	Tbsp. butter
¼	cup maple syrup
½	cup sliced green onion (about 4)

PREPARATION

1. Prepare sweet potatoes in microwave oven according to package directions.
2. Meanwhile, lightly coat chicken with steak seasoning. Heat butter in large skillet over medium-high heat; add chicken. Cook 5 to 6 minutes until no longer pink (170°F), turning once halfway through cooking. Remove from skillet; cover and keep warm. Stir maple syrup into hot skillet; cook 2 minutes. Stir in green onion.
3. Divide chicken and potatoes among 4 plates. Drizzle with maple syrup mixture. **MAKES 4 SERVINGS.**

EACH SERVING *384 cal, 7 g fat (4 g sat. fat), 81 mg chol, 505 mg sodium, 50 g carbo, 6 g fiber, 30 g pro. Daily Values: 660% vit. A, 61% vit. C, 10% calcium, 13% iron.*

MAPLE-GLAZED CHICKEN WITH SWEET POTATOES
CHARLENE CHAMBERS ORMOND BEACH, FLA.

SKILLET-SEARED SALMON
LAURA McALLISTER MORGANTON, N.C.

FAST!

SKILLET-SEARED SALMON

START TO FINISH 20 min.

INGREDIENTS

4	5- to 6-oz. skinless salmon fillets, about 1 inch thick
1	Tbsp. olive oil
4	large Roma tomatoes, seeded and coarsely chopped
1	jalapeño pepper, seeded and thinly sliced (see Note, page 101)
1	Tbsp. butter
¼	cup fresh cilantro

PREPARATION

1. Lightly season salmon with *salt* and *ground black pepper*. Heat olive oil in large nonstick skillet over medium-high heat. Add salmon; cook 8 to 10 minutes or until salmon flakes easily when tested with a fork, turning once halfway through cooking. If salmon browns too quickly, adjust heat to medium.
2. Transfer salmon to serving platter. Add tomatoes, jalapeño, and butter to skillet; cook and stir 1 minute. Spoon over salmon; sprinkle cilantro. **MAKES 4 SERVINGS.**

EACH SERVING *339 cal, 22 g fat (5 g sat. fat), 91 mg chol, 258 mg sodium, 5 g carbo, 2 g fiber, 29 g pro. Daily Values: 31% vit. A, 46% vit. C, 4% calcium, 6% iron.*

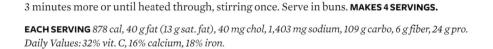

FAST! **KID FRIENDLY**

MEATBALL AND PINEAPPLE HOAGIES

START TO FINISH 20 min.

INGREDIENTS
- 1 large sweet onion, halved and sliced (2 cups)
- 2 Tbsp. olive oil
- 1 16-oz. pkg. frozen cooked meatballs, thawed
- 1 cup peeled, cored pineapple, chopped (about one-quarter pineapple)
- 1 cup desired chutney
- ¼ tsp. crushed red pepper
- 4 hoagie buns, split and toasted

PREPARATION
1. In large skillet cook onion in hot oil over medium heat for 8 minutes or until tender, stirring frequently. Stir in meatballs, pineapple, chutney, and crushed red pepper. Cover skillet; cook 3 minutes more or until heated through, stirring once. Serve in buns. **MAKES 4 SERVINGS.**

EACH SERVING *878 cal, 40 g fat (13 g sat. fat), 40 mg chol, 1,403 mg sodium, 109 g carbo, 6 g fiber, 24 g pro. Daily Values: 32% vit. C, 16% calcium, 18% iron.*

MEATBALL AND PINEAPPLE HOAGIES
MARY ANN LEE CLIFTON PARK, N.Y.

Set to Simmer

Slow cooking in robust liquids gives these one-pot suppers their hearty taste. They're good for busy days— once cooking is under way, they need no tending.

BY **RICHARD SWEARINGER**
PHOTOS **ANDY LYONS**
RECIPES AND FOOD STYLING **JILL LUST**

MUSTARD-HERB BEEF STEW

MUSTARD-HERB BEEF STEW

Basic meat and potatoes get bold flavor after simmering in this heady combination of dark beer, onions, thyme, and parsley.

PREP 30 min. **COOK** 1 hr.

INGREDIENTS

⅓	cup all-purpose flour
1	Tbsp. snipped fresh Italian (flat-leaf) parsley
1	tsp. snipped fresh thyme or ½ tsp. dried thyme, crushed
1½	lb. boneless beef chuck, cut in 1- to 1½-inch pieces
2	Tbsp. olive oil
1	8- to 10-oz. pkg. cipollini onions, peeled, or 1 medium onion, peeled and cut in wedges
4	carrots, peeled, cut in 1-inch pieces
1	8-oz. pkg. cremini mushrooms, halved if large
8	tiny Yukon gold potatoes, halved
3	Tbsp. tomato paste
2	Tbsp. spicy brown mustard
1	14-oz. can beef broth
1	12-oz. bottle dark porter beer or nonalcoholic beer
1	to 2 bay leaves
	Crusty bread slices

PREPARATION

1. In large bowl combine flour, parsley, thyme, 1 teaspoon *ground black pepper,* and ½ teaspoon *salt.* Add beef, a few pieces at a time; stir to coat. Reserve leftover flour mixture.

2. In 6-quart Dutch oven heat oil over medium-high heat. Brown beef. Stir in onions, carrots, mushrooms, and potatoes. Cook and stir 3 minutes. Stir in tomato paste, mustard, and remaining flour mixture. Add broth, beer, and bay leaves. Bring to boiling; reduce heat. Cover and simmer 1 to 1¼ hours until beef is tender. Remove and discard bay leaves. Serve with bread.

MAKES 6 (1½-CUP) SERVINGS.

EACH SERVING *426 cal, 11 g fat (3 g sat. fat), 50 mg chol, 880 mg sodium, 43 g carbo, 5 g fiber, 33 g pro. Daily Values: 140% vit. A, 32% vit. C, 9% calcium, 26% iron.*

MARTINI BRISKET

A splash of vodka and vermouth plus green olives gives this pepper-crusted beef its martini flavors. You may omit the alcohol; the flavor will be different but just as good.

PREP 25 min. **COOK** 3 hr. **STAND** 10 min.

INGREDIENTS

1	3- to 4-lb. beef brisket
1	Tbsp. mixed peppercorns, coarsely crushed
1	Tbsp. cooking oil
2	medium onions, sliced
1	28-oz. can crushed tomatoes
1	cup lower-sodium beef broth
1	Tbsp. Worcestershire sauce
1	Tbsp. fines herbes, crushed
½	cup whipping cream
2	Tbsp. dry vermouth (optional)
1	Tbsp. vodka (optional)
½	cup pimiento-stuffed green olives

PREPARATION

1. Trim fat from beef. Sprinkle beef with *salt* and peppercorns. In large heavy skillet brown brisket on both sides in hot oil. Remove beef. Add onions to skillet. Cook and stir until tender. Add brisket to skillet; add tomatoes, broth, Worcestershire, and fines herbes. Bring to boiling; reduce heat. Spoon some of onion mixture over brisket. Simmer, covered, 3 hours or until brisket is tender.

2. To serve, remove brisket from skillet; let stand 10 minutes. Meanwhile, skim fat from sauce in skillet. Stir in cream, vermouth, and vodka. Bring just to boiling. Remove from heat. Slice brisket; top with olives. Serve with sauce. **MAKES 8 SERVINGS.**

EACH SERVING *364 cal, 17 g fat (7 g sat. fat), 123 mg chol, 607 mg sodium, 10 g carbo, 2 g fiber, 37 g pro. Daily Values: 4% vit. A, 21% vit. C, 6% calcium, 24% iron.*

WHAT *IS* A SIMMER?

"Simmer" is a just-for-fun noun that has sprung up in the food world to mean cooking in a bold-flavored sauce. Think of it as braising with a twist. It's too new to be in dictionaries as a noun, but you'll see it used on restaurant menus, sauce labels, and in recipes. There are "simmer sauces," "simmer dinners," and just plain "simmers."

MARTINI BRISKET

GINGER CURRY CHICKEN WITH LENTILS AND LEEKS

All by itself, the cooking liquid—chicken broth flavored with ginger, oranges, and leeks—would be a great soup. Poultry, lentils, and bok choy make it a meal.

PREP 25 min. **COOK** 55 min.

INGREDIENTS

3	lb. meaty chicken pieces
2	Tbsp. curry powder
½	tsp. sea salt or salt
2	Tbsp. cooking oil
1	Tbsp. grated fresh ginger
2	large leeks, halved lengthwise, rinsed, and sliced
1	small orange, cut in wedges
1	cup dry French lentils, rinsed and drained
1	14-oz. can reduced-sodium chicken broth
1	cup dry white wine (optional)
1	to 2 heads baby bok choy, separated into individual leaves

PREPARATION

1. Skin chicken, if desired. Sprinkle chicken with *1 tablespoon* curry powder and salt. Brown chicken pieces, half at a time if necessary, in 4-quart Dutch oven in hot oil over medium-high heat. Remove from pan. Add ginger, leeks, orange wedges, and remaining curry powder. Cook and stir 2 to 3 minutes or until leeks are tender.

2. Stir in lentils, broth, and wine. Return chicken pieces to pan. Bring to boiling; reduce heat. Cook, covered, for 55 to 60 minutes or until chicken is tender and no longer pink (170°F).

3. Remove chicken; stir bok choy into lentil mixture. Use slotted spoon to serve.

MAKES 4 TO 6 SERVINGS.

EACH SERVING *527 cal, 26 g fat (7 g sat. fat), 132 mg chol, 409 mg sodium, 28 g carbo, 12 g fiber, 45 g pro. Daily Values: 27% vit. A, 41% vit. C, 9% calcium, 29% iron.*

READYMADE FLAVOR

Ready-to-use simmer sauces are on the market. Flavors include Scandinavian Dill Simmer Sauce by Maine-based Good Clean Food, $7; goodcleanfood.com, and Wine Country Simmer Sauce with Cabernet by Made in Napa Valley, Tulocay & Co., $6.95; 888/627-2859. There are global-inspired sauces as well, such as Red Curry 10-Minute Simmer Sauce from Thai Kitchen, $3.79; thaikitchen.com.

With most simmer sauces, all you do is brown meat and/or vegetables, pour on the sauce, and cook until meat is tender.

Summer Finale

Keep the carefree spirit of summer going into fall with these homemade triple-chocolate ice cream sandwiches.

PHOTO **ANDY LYONS** FOOD STYLING **JILL LUST**

KID FRIENDLY

CHOCOLATE-HAZELNUT ICE CREAM SANDWICHES
PREP 25 min. **FREEZE** 3 hr.

INGREDIENTS

16 chocolate wafer cookies (such as Nabisco Famous Chocolate Wafers)
⅓ cup chocolate hazelnut spread (such as Nutella)
1 pint premium chocolate ice cream
⅓ cup chopped toasted hazelnuts (see Tip, below)

PREPARATION

1. Spread flat side of each wafer with hazelnut spread; set aside. Scoop 8 ice cream balls, about 3 tablespoons each; keep in freezer until ready to assemble.
2. To assemble sandwiches, remove ice cream balls from freezer; let stand 1 minute to soften. Place 1 ice cream ball on each of 8 hazelnut-spread wafers. Top with remaining wafers; press gently together.
3. Sprinkle edges with nuts. Place sandwiches on baking sheet lined with waxed paper; freeze 3 hours or until firm. To store, freeze up to two weeks in self-sealing plastic bags. **MAKES 8 SANDWICHES.**

EACH SANDWICH *215 cal, 12 g fat (3 g sat. fat), 14 mg chol, 127 mg sodium, 26 g carbo, 1 g fiber, 4 g pro. Daily Values: 3% vit. A, 1% vit. C, 4% calcium, 6% iron.*

CELEBRATE EVERY DAY *with*
Pam Anderson

PAM'S TIP

To toast and skin hazelnuts, spread nuts in single layer on baking sheet. Bake at 350°F for 10 to 15 minutes until skins crackle. Wrap hazelnuts in clean towel; let steam 5 to 10 minutes. Vigorously rub hazelnuts in towel until skins flake off. Any skins that remain add color and flavor. For this somewhat messy job, consider taking the towel-wrapped nuts outdoors.

Green Giant

Fresh soybeans—also called edamame—offer big nutritional benefits.

BY **MARGE PERRY** PHOTOS **ANDY LYONS** RECIPES AND FOOD STYLING **JILL LUST**

TOMATO-EDAMAME GRILLED CHEESE

The leftover spread is a great dip for crisp fresh vegetables. Refrigerate, tightly covered, up to three days.

PREP 20 min. **ROAST** 15 min. **OVEN** 425°F

INGREDIENTS

1   bulb garlic
1   tsp. canola oil
1   12-oz. pkg. frozen shelled sweet soybeans (edamame)
¼   cup lemon juice
½   tsp. ground cumin
⅓   cup snipped fresh Italian (flat-leaf) parsley
8   slices whole grain bread
4   oz. reduced-fat Monterey Jack cheese, sliced
1   tomato, thinly sliced

LOW FAT

PREPARATION

1. For spread preheat oven to 425°F. Slice off top ½ inch of garlic bulb. Leaving bulb whole, remove loose outer layers. Place bulb, cut side up, in custard cup. Drizzle with oil. Cover with foil; roast 15 minutes until soft. Cool.

2. Meanwhile cook soybeans according to package directions. Drain; rinse with cold water. Squeeze 3 garlic cloves from bulb into food processor. Wrap and refrigerate remaining garlic for other use.

3. Add cooked soybeans, lemon juice, ¼ cup *water*, ½ teaspoon *salt*, and cumin to garlic in food processor. Cover and process until smooth. Transfer to bowl. Stir in parsley.

4. For each sandwich spread *2 tablespoons* soybean mixture on two slices whole grain bread. Top one bread slice with 1 ounce thinly sliced cheese and tomato slices. Add second bread slice. On nonstick griddle or nonstick skillet toast over medium-high heat, turning once.

MAKES 4 SANDWICHES PLUS 1 CUP SPREAD.

EACH SANDWICH WITH ¼ CUP SPREAD *332 cal, 12 g fat (4 g sat. fat), 20 mg chol, 685 mg sodium, 38 g carbo, 11 g fiber, 22 g pro. Daily Values: 16% vit. A, 27% vit. C, 30% calcium, 18% iron.*

EDAMAME SOUP WITH FETA CROUTONS

PREP 20 min. **COOK** 13 min.

INGREDIENTS

¾ cup chopped sweet onion
4 tsp. canola oil
2 medium carrots, thinly sliced
2 cloves garlic, minced
2 14-oz. cans reduced-sodium chicken broth or vegetable broth
1 12-oz. pkg. frozen shelled sweet soybeans (edamame)
1½ tsp. snipped fresh thyme
1 egg white
1 Tbsp. water
½ cup panko (Japanese-style) bread crumbs
4 oz. reduced-fat feta cheese, cut in ¾-inch cubes
  Fresh thyme leaves (optional)

PREPARATION

1. In saucepan cook onion in *2 teaspoons* of hot oil over medium heat 5 minutes or until tender, stirring occasionally. Add carrot slices and garlic; cook and stir 1 minute more. Add broth and edamame. Bring to boiling; reduce heat. Simmer, uncovered, 5 minutes or until edamame and carrot are tender. Stir in thyme.
2. Meanwhile, in small bowl beat egg white and water with fork until frothy. Place bread crumbs in another small bowl. Dip feta cubes, one at a time, into egg white to coat. Allow excess egg white mixture to drip off; coat feta cubes with bread crumbs. In large skillet, heat remaining 2 teaspoons oil over medium-high heat. Add feta cubes. Cook 2 to 3 minutes or until browned but not softened, turning carefully to brown all sides of cubes. Drain on paper towels.
3. Ladle soup into bowls. Top with feta croutons and additional thyme. **MAKES 6 (¾ CUP) SIDE-DISH SERVINGS.**

EACH SERVING *193 cal, 9 g fat (2 g sat. fat), 6 mg chol, 621 mg sodium, 15 g carbo, 4 g fiber, 14 g pro. Daily Values: 74% vit. A, 22% vit. C, 14% calcium, 8% iron.*

FAST! LOW FAT

SWEET AND SPICY EDAMAME-BEEF STIR-FRY

PREP 20 min. **COOK** 10 min.

INGREDIENTS

4 tsp. canola oil
2 tsp. finely chopped fresh ginger
3 cups packaged fresh cut-up stir-fry vegetables
8 oz. beef sirloin steak trimmed of fat and cut in very thin bite-size strips
1 cup frozen shelled sweet soybeans (edamame)
3 Tbsp. hoisin sauce
2 Tbsp. rice vinegar
1 tsp. red chili paste
1 8.8-oz. pouch cooked whole grain brown rice

PREPARATION

1. In nonstick wok or skillet heat *half* of oil over medium-high heat. Cook and stir ginger 15 seconds. Add vegetables. Cook and stir 4 minutes or until crisp-tender. Remove vegetables.
2. Add remaining oil to wok. Cook and stir beef and edamame 2 minutes or until beef is browned. Return vegetables to wok. In bowl combine hoisin, vinegar, and chili paste. Add to beef mixture, tossing to coat. Heat through.
3. Meanwhile, heat rice according to package directions. Serve beef over rice. **MAKES 4 SERVINGS.**

EACH SERVING *330 cal, 12 g fat (2 g sat. fat), 24 mg chol, 272 mg sodium, 34 g carbo, 5 g fiber, 22 g pro. Daily Values: 113% vit. A, 57% vit. C, 10% calcium, 18% iron.*

EDAMAME SOUP WITH FETA CROUTONS

SWEET AND SPICY EDAMAME-BEEF STIR-FRY

OCTOBER

THE CHANGE OF SEASON PUTS A NEW FOCUS ON THE KITCHEN. TAKE ADVANTAGE OF FALL VEGETABLES AND FRUITS WITH RECIPES THAT DOUBLE AS SIDES OR MAIN DISHES, AND HEARTY SUPPERS FROM THE SLOW COOKER. THERE ARE SOME SPOOKY TRICKS FOR CUPCAKE TREATS TOO.

CURRY PUMPKIN SOUP page 213

Fall Into Flavor

BALSAMIC PORK AND DUMPLINGS
page 219

BIG-BATCH PUTTANESCA SAUCE
page 223

BREAD PUDDING WITH CHOCOLATE AND CHERRIES page 227

fall into flavor

THAT CHILL IN THE AIR MEANS
IT'S TIME FOR A DIFFERENT KIND OF FRESH.
LET ONIONS, SQUASH, GRAPES,
PEARS, AND APPLES TAKE A SEAT
AT YOUR DINNER TABLE.

BY **RICHARD SWEARINGER** PHOTOS **ANDY LYONS**
RECIPES **DAVID BONOM** FOOD STYLING **JILL LUST** PROP STYLING **SUE MITCHELL**

Nestled beneath the chicken as it cooks, onions are both roasting rack and flavorful side dish. A rustic rub of cinnamon, paprika, cumin, and coriander gives **Spice-Rubbed Chicken** bold color.

SPICE-RUBBED CHICKEN
page 213

CELEBRATE THE ABUNDANCE OF FALL FRUIT
WITH RECIPES THAT PUT IT FRONT AND CENTER.

SAVORY PLUM SALAD
page 213

A warm raspberry-mustard dressing lightly coats baby spinach leaves and radicchio in **Savory Plum Salad.** The salad can also be a light dinner thanks to the bacon, nuts, and Gorgonzola.

GRAPE AND ROSEMARY FOCACCIA page 215

BUTTERNUT SQUASH BAKE page 215

CHERRY-POMEGRANATE CHUTNEY page 216

The convenience of refrigerated pizza dough cuts prep time to 20 minutes for Grape and Rosemary Focaccia, above. Serve it as a hearty appetizer or accompaniment to a meal.

Add a salad and dinner's done. Butternut Squash Bake includes noodles, shallots, and squash, above right. It's also a good side dish with beef.

Cherry-Pomegranate Chutney, right, can be used several ways. For company, serve it alongside crackers and a wedge or two of cheese. For family, try it as a topping for roasted turkey or sandwiches.

Using canned pumpkin makes this **Curry Pumpkin Soup,** *below,* quick to prepare. Pumpkin pie spice and a hit of curry give the dish bright seasonal flavor.

CURRY PUMPKIN SOUP

CURRY PUMPKIN SOUP

This recipe can be prepared through Step 3, then refrigerated up to 3 days or frozen up to 3 months. To serve, thaw, reheat, and proceed with Step 4.

PREP 20 min. **COOK** 30 min.

INGREDIENTS

1	recipe Orange-Cranberry Topper
2	Tbsp. butter
2	medium onions, chopped (1 cup)
1	medium carrot, chopped (½ cup)
1	stalk celery, chopped (½ cup)
1	tsp. curry powder
1	tsp. pumpkin pie spice
2	15-oz. cans pumpkin
2	14-oz. cans reduced-sodium chicken broth
⅔	cup water
1	cup half-and-half or light cream
½	tsp. salt
¼	tsp. ground black pepper

PREPARATION

1. Prepare Orange-Cranberry Topper.
2. In 4-quart Dutch oven melt butter over medium heat. Add onion, carrot, and celery. Cook 10 minutes, stirring occasionally, until softened. Add curry powder and pumpkin pie spice. Cook and stir 1 minute. Add pumpkin, broth, and water. Increase heat to medium-high; bring to boiling. Reduce heat to medium-low. Simmer, covered, 15 minutes. Remove from heat; cool slightly.
3. In food processor or blender, add one-third of the pumpkin mixture at a time, cover, and process or blend until smooth. Return all pumpkin mixture to Dutch oven.
4. Stir half-and-half, salt, and pepper into pumpkin mixture; heat through. Sprinkle each serving with Orange-Cranberry Topper. **MAKES 8 SERVINGS.**
ORANGE-CRANBERRY TOPPER In small bowl combine ½ cup *dried cranberries*, 1 tablespoon finely shredded *orange peel*, and 2 tablespoons snipped fresh *Italian (flat-leaf) parsley*.

EACH SERVING (1 cup) *145 cal, 7 g fat (4 g sat. fat), 19 mg chol, 433 mg sodium, 20 g carbo, 4 g fiber, 4 g pro. Daily Values: 363% vit. A, 15% vit. C, 8% calcium, 10% iron.*

SPICE-RUBBED CHICKEN

Roasting chickens are larger than broiler/fryer chickens and tend to be juicier. They're ideal for whole-roasting and rotisserie cooking. Recipe pictured on page 209.

PREP 20 min. **ROAST** 2 hr. **OVEN** 350°F

INGREDIENTS

4	cups thickly sliced or quartered red, white, and/or yellow onions, and/or boiling or cipollini onions, peeled
1	5- to 6-lb. whole roasting chicken
1	tsp. sugar
1	tsp. garlic powder
1	tsp. ground cumin
1	tsp. paprika
1	tsp. ground coriander
½	tsp. salt
¼	tsp. ground cinnamon
¼	tsp. ground black pepper
⅛	tsp. ground nutmeg
2	Tbsp. olive oil
	Chard leaves (optional)

PREPARATION

1. Preheat oven to 350°F. In large shallow roasting pan place *half* the onions in an even layer. Sprinkle with ¼ teaspoon *salt;* set aside. Fold chicken neck skin onto chicken back; secure with small skewer; tie legs to tail with kitchen string. Tie wings close to body or twist wing tips up and tuck under back of the chicken.
2. In small bowl combine sugar and remaining seasonings. Brush chicken all over with oil. Sprinkle spice mixture and rub in with fingers. Place chicken, breast side up, on onions in pan. If desired, insert meat thermometer into center of inside thigh muscle. (Thermometer should not touch bone.) Loosely cover with foil.
3. Roast 1 hour. Remove foil. Add remaining onions to pan. Roast, uncovered, 30 minutes; cut strings on legs and wings. Roast 30 to 45 minutes more or until drumsticks move easily in their sockets and chicken is no longer pink (180°F in thigh). Cover with foil. Let stand 15 minutes before carving. Serve chicken with roasted onions and chard leaves. **MAKES 6 TO 8 SERVINGS.**

EACH SERVING *618 cal, 42 g fat (11 g sat. fat), 191 mg chol, 438 mg sodium, 9 g carbo, 2 g fiber, 49 g pro. Daily Values: 9% vit. A, 14% vit. C, 5% calcium, 13% iron.*

FAST!

SAVORY PLUM SALAD

Crisp and peppery radicchio can vary in size. Use two medium heads (about softball size) or one large one. Find the purple-red heads in the salad greens section of the supermarket. Recipe pictured on page 210.

START TO FINISH 25 min.

INGREDIENTS

1	or 2 heads radicchio (about 4 cups)
½	of 6-oz. bag baby spinach (4 cups)
4	plums, quartered and pitted
½	cup pecan halves, toasted
6	slices bacon, crisp-cooked and crumbled
2	Tbsp. raspberry vinegar
1	Tbsp. Dijon-style mustard
½	tsp. salt
¼	tsp. ground black pepper
⅓	cup extra virgin olive oil
¼	cup crumbled Gorgonzola cheese

PREPARATION

1. Cut radicchio in wedges. Place in salad bowl with spinach, plums, nuts, and bacon.
2. In small bowl whisk together vinegar, mustard, salt, and pepper. Whisk in olive oil; drizzle on salad. Toss gently to combine. Sprinkle cheese. **MAKES 6 TO 8 SERVINGS.**

EACH SERVING *265 cal, 24 g fat (4 g sat. fat), 13 mg chol, 531 mg sodium, 9 g carbo, 2 g fiber, 6 g pro. Daily Values: 31% vit. A, 16% vit. C, 6% calcium, 6% iron.*

A mix of molasses, red wine vinegar, and soy sauce glazes **Pork Loin with Apples and Pears.** The glaze flavors pan juices too, creating a delicious drizzle-on sauce.

A BOWL OF SOUP, A QUICK ROAST PORK, AND DINNER FOR COMPANY OR FAMILY IS COMPLETE.

PORK LOIN WITH APPLES AND PEARS

PORK LOIN WITH APPLES AND PEARS

PREP 25 min. **ROAST** 65 min. **STAND** 10 min. **OVEN** 425°F

INGREDIENTS

2	tsp. ground black pepper
1	tsp. salt
1	tsp. garlic powder
1	3-lb. boneless pork top loin roast (single loin)
⅓	cup molasses
2	Tbsp. red wine vinegar
1	Tbsp. reduced-sodium soy sauce
3	apples, cut in halves, wedges, or slices
2	pears, cut in halves, wedges, or slices
2	Tbsp. sugar

PREPARATION

1. Preheat oven to 425°F. Line shallow roasting pan with heavy foil; lightly oil foil. Place meat rack in pan; set aside.
2. In bowl combine pepper, salt, and garlic powder. Brush pork with 1 tablespoon *olive oil;* rub with pepper mixture. Place pork on rack in roasting pan. Roast 35 minutes.
3. For glaze, in skillet combine molasses, vinegar, and soy sauce. Bring to boiling. Reduce heat; simmer 1 minute. Remove to bowl. Set glaze and skillet aside.
4. Brush pork with some glaze (reserve *2 tablespoons* glaze for fruit). Continue roasting 20 minutes, brushing with more glaze halfway through.
5. Roast pork 10 minutes more or until thermometer inserted in center registers 150°F. Remove from oven; cover with foil. Let stand 10 minutes before slicing.
6. Meanwhile, in skillet used for glaze heat 1 tablespoon *olive oil.* Toss fruit with sugar. Add fruit to skillet; cover and cook 2 minutes. Uncover and cook 3 minutes more or until crisp-tender. Serve with pork. Drizzle with pan juices. **MAKES 8 SERVINGS.**

EACH SERVING *361 cal, 10 g fat (3 g sat. fat), 107 mg chol, 444 mg sodium, 28 g carbo, 3 g fiber, 39 g pro. Daily Values: 1% vit. A, 7% vit. C, 5% calcium, 10% iron.*

GRAPE AND ROSEMARY FOCACCIA

As this bread bakes, the grapes become lightly roasted, turning soft and juicy. Recipe pictured on page 211.

PREP 20 min. **RISE** 30 min. **BAKE** 20 min. **OVEN** 450°F

INGREDIENTS

1	lb. refrigerated or thawed frozen pizza dough
2	Tbsp. extra virgin olive oil
½	tsp. coarse salt (kosher or sea salt)
½	tsp. dried basil, crushed
2	cups seedless red grapes, whole and/or halved
1	Tbsp. snipped fresh rosemary
1	Tbsp. grated Romano cheese

PREPARATION

1. Let pizza dough stand at room temperature 15 minutes. On lightly floured surface, roll dough to 12×8-inch rectangle. If dough begins to pull back while rolling, let rest 5 minutes. Transfer dough to lightly oiled baking sheet. Prick with fork. Cover; let rise in warm place 30 minutes.
2. Preheat oven to 450°F. Brush dough with *1 tablespoon* of the olive oil; sprinkle salt and basil. Arrange grapes on dough; sprinkle rosemary and cheese. Bake 20 to 22 minutes or until puffed and lightly browned. Drizzle remaining oil. Cut in strips with a pizza cutter or large knife. **MAKES 12 SERVINGS.**

EACH SERVING *111 cal, 4 g fat (1 g sat. fat), 0 mg chol, 208 mg sodium, 17 g carbo, 1 g fiber, 2 g pro. Daily Values: 1% vit. C, 1% calcium, 5% iron.*

BUTTERNUT SQUASH BAKE

Mascarpone is a mild, soft, butterlike cheese that adds a rich creaminess to this bake. Softened cream cheese can be substituted. Recipe pictured on page 211.

PREP 30 min. **ROAST** 30 min. **BAKE** 10 min. **OVEN** 425°F

1½	lb. butternut squash, peeled, seeded, cut in 1-inch cubes (3 cups)
2	Tbsp. olive oil
8	oz. dried extra-wide noodles
4	Tbsp. butter
6	shallots, chopped
1	Tbsp. lemon juice
1	8-oz. carton mascarpone cheese
¾	cup grated Parmesan cheese
½	cup fresh Italian (flat-leaf) parsley, snipped
1	cup panko (Japanese-style bread crumbs) or soft bread crumbs

PREPARATION

1. Preheat oven to 425°F. In bowl toss squash in oil; place in oiled 15×10×1-inch baking pan. Roast, uncovered, 30 minutes until lightly browned and tender, stirring twice.
2. Meanwhile, in Dutch oven cook noodles according to package directions. Drain; set aside. In same Dutch oven melt *2 tablespoons* of the butter. Add shallot; cook and stir over medium heat 3 to 5 minutes until shallots are tender and butter just begins to brown. Stir in lemon juice.
3. Add noodles to shallot mixture. Stir in mascarpone, *½ cup* of the Parmesan, *¼ cup* parsley, and *¼ teaspoon* each *salt* and *ground black pepper.* Transfer to greased 2-quart oval gratin dish or baking dish.
4. In small saucepan melt remaining butter; stir in panko, remaining Parmesan, and parsley. Sprinkle on noodle mixture. Bake, uncovered, 10 minutes until crumbs are golden. **MAKES 8 SERVINGS.**

EACH SERVING *413 cal, 26 g fat (13 g sat. fat), 82 mg chol, 278 mg sodium, 37 g carbo, 2 g fiber, 15 g pro. Daily Values: 127% vit. A, 31% vit. C, 14% calcium, 12% iron.*

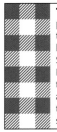

LOW FAT

CHERRY-POMEGRANATE CHUTNEY

Serve this ruby red chutney with your favorite blue or sharp cheddar cheese and crisp crackers. Or use it as a spread on sandwiches made with leftover Spice-Rubbed Chicken (page 213). Recipe pictured on page 211.

PREP 15 min. **COOK** 30 min.

INGREDIENTS

1   Tbsp. olive oil
2   medium onions, chopped (1 cup)
1   Tbsp. grated fresh ginger
2   cloves garlic, minced (1 tsp.)
¼   tsp. ground cinnamon
⅛   tsp. ground allspice
1   12-oz. pkg. frozen dark sweet cherries
½   cup unsweetened pomegranate juice
3   Tbsp. sugar
      Seeds from 1 small pomegranate (¾ cup)
¼   tsp. salt

PREPARATION

1. In large nonstick skillet heat oil over medium heat. Add onion, ginger, and garlic. Cook about 5 to 6 minutes, stirring occasionally, until tender and translucent. Stir in cinnamon and allspice; cook about 15 to 20 seconds until fragrant. Add cherries, pomegranate juice, and sugar.
2. Increase heat to medium-high. Bring onion-cherry mixture to boiling. Reduce heat to medium-low. Simmer, uncovered, about 30 minutes, stirring occasionally, until onion-cherry mixture is thickened. Remove from heat. Stir in pomegranate seeds and salt. Refrigerate chutney, covered, up to 1 week. **MAKES 1¾ CUPS.**

EACH SERVING (2 Tbsp.) *54 cal, 1 g fat (0 g sat. fat), 0 mg chol, 43 mg sodium, 11 g carbo, 1 g fiber, 1 g pro. Daily Values: 1% vit. A, 2% vit. C, 1% iron.*

TEST KITCHEN TIP To open a pomegranate, cut a thin slice from top and bottom. Score sides with a knife so it can be easily pulled apart. Submerge in a large bowl of water. Pull apart and use your fingers to free the seeds (they will sink to the bottom and the white membrane will float to the top). Discard membrane and strain seeds. Refrigerate up to a week.

WINTER WINNERS

Colorful winter squashes—acorn, buttercup, hubbard, spaghetti, and turban—have meaty, lightly sweet flesh that is high in iron and vitamins A and C. Select squashes that are firm, have a dull sheen, and feel heavy for their size. Avoid those with soft spots or cracks. Store these hard-shell vegetables in a cool, dry place up to 2 months. To peel uncooked winter squash, halve lengthwise and remove seeds. Cutting away from you, use a sturdy Y-shape carrot peeler to remove long strips of peel.

CABBAGE CUES

Supernutritious, the humble cabbage has more to offer than just coleslaw. Lightly sautéed, this vegetable becomes tender and sweet. Select a cabbage that is heavy for its size with firmly packed crisp leaves. Store in the refrigerator, tightly wrapped, for about 2 weeks.

ONION APPEAL

A pantry staple, aromatic onions are a cornerstone vegetable for developing depth and flavor. When cooked low and slow they become sweet and golden, or caramelized. Select firm onions with short necks and papery outer skins. Avoid those with soft spots or sprouts. Store dry, thick-skinned winter onions (available September through March) in a cool, dry, well-ventilated place for several weeks.

ONION MATH

1 small onion = ⅓ cup chopped
1 medium onion = ½ cup chopped
1 large onion = 1 cup chopped
1 large red onion = 2 cups chopped

MEET DAVID

Recipe whiz and *Better Homes and Gardens* contributor **David Bonom** created our cool-weather recipes. "When I see the first fall fruits and vegetables, I think roasts, casseroles, and thick, creamy soups. I love the satisfying, warming atmosphere these dishes create as they cook." As a chef and cooking teacher, David stays busy developing and testing recipes in his New Jersey kitchen.

DAVID SAYS BUILD FLAVOR

1. SPICE IT RIGHT "One of my favorite ways to build flavor with very little effort is to use a spice rub. I simply stir together some spices, then rub them over whatever I'm cooking—whether it's meat, poultry, or fish."

2. GO FOR GOLDEN "Another way to add depth is through caramelization. The browning of natural sugars in meat and vegetables adds a sweet nuttiness to the final dish."

3. BALANCING ACT "Adding fruit to savory dishes creates balance and complexity. The hint of sweetness in the fruit helps temper heartier, more intensely flavored fall ingredients."

Dinner Dash

Beat the back-to-routine blues with these quick and hearty weeknight dishes.

READY IN 20 MINUTES!

BY **ERIN SIMPSON** PHOTOS **ANDY LYONS** RECIPES AND FOOD STYLING **JILL LUST**

BROCCOLI-POTATO SOUP WITH GREENS

BROCCOLI-POTATO SOUP WITH GREENS

START TO FINISH 20 min.

INGREDIENTS

2   medium red potatoes, chopped
1   14-oz. can reduced-sodium chicken broth
3   cups small broccoli florets
2   cups milk
3   Tbsp. all-purpose flour
2   cups smoked Gouda cheese, shredded (8 oz.)
2   cups winter greens (such as curly endive, chicory, romaine, escarole, or spinach)
    Additional Gouda cheese, shredded (optional)

PREPARATION

1. In large saucepan combine potatoes and broth. Bring to boiling; reduce heat. Simmer, covered, 8 minutes. Mash slightly. Add broccoli and milk; bring just to simmering.
2. In medium bowl toss flour with cheese; gradually add to soup, stirring cheese until melted. Season to taste with *ground black pepper*. Divide among shallow serving bowls. Top with greens and additional cheese. **MAKES 4 SERVINGS.**

EACH SERVING *365 cal, 18 g fat (11 g sat. fat), 74 mg chol, 782 mg sodium, 28 g carbo, 4 g fiber, 23 g pro. Daily Values: 30% vit. A, 125% vit. C, 59% calcium, 9% iron.*

BALSAMIC PORK AND DUMPLINGS

START TO FINISH 20 min.

INGREDIENTS

1   16.9-oz. pkg. frozen potato-and-onion-filled pierogi (potato dumplings)
12   oz. fresh green and/or wax beans, trimmed (3 cups)
1   lb. pork tenderloin
2   Tbsp. olive oil
½   cup balsamic vinegar
2   tsp. chopped fresh rosemary (optional)

PREPARATION

1. Cook pierogi and beans in boiling water according to pierogi package directions. Drain pierogi and beans; divide among serving plates.
2. Meanwhile, slice pork in ½-inch medallions. Gently flatten pork slices by hand to ¼-inch thickness; lightly sprinkle with *salt* and *ground black pepper*. Heat oil in large skillet over medium heat. Add pork. Cook 2 to 3 minutes on each side or until no pink remains. Transfer to serving plates with pierogi and beans.
3. Drain fat from skillet. Add balsamic vinegar to hot skillet. Cook, uncovered, 1 minute or until reduced by half. Drizzle over pork, pierogi, and beans. Sprinkle chopped rosemary.
MAKES 4 SERVINGS.

EACH SERVING *419 cal, 11 g fat (2 g sat. fat), 79 mg chol, 636 mg sodium, 47 g carbo, 4 g fiber, 30 g pro. Daily Values: 14% vit. A, 38% vit. C, 6% calcium, 20% iron.*

BALSAMIC PORK AND DUMPLINGS

CRUNCHY CHICKEN AND FRUIT SALAD

START TO FINISH 20 min.

INGREDIENTS

1	2½-lb. deli-roasted whole chicken
3	oranges
⅓	cup light mayonnaise
1	5-oz. bag sweet baby lettuces
2	small red and/or green apples, cored and coarsely chopped
¼	cup pecan halves

PREPARATION

1. Remove chicken from bones. Tear chicken into bite-size chunks. Set aside.

2. Squeeze juice from *one* orange. Stir enough juice into mayonnaise to make dressing consistency. Season with *ground black pepper*. Peel and section remaining oranges.

3. On salad plates arrange greens, chicken, apples, and oranges. Sprinkle pecan halves. Pass dressing. **MAKES 4 SERVINGS.**

EACH SERVING *455 cal, 30 g fat (7 g sat. fat), 132 mg chol, 956 mg sodium, 23 g carbo, 5 g fiber, 29 g pro. Daily Values: 15% vit. A, 96% vit. C, 7% calcium, 14% iron.*

CRUNCHY CHICKEN AND FRUIT SALAD

PEANUT-SAUCED SHRIMP AND PASTA

PEANUT-SAUCED SHRIMP AND PASTA

START TO FINISH 20 min.

INGREDIENTS

½	a 14-oz. pkg. dried medium rice noodles
1	Tbsp. cooking oil
12	oz. peeled, deveined medium uncooked shrimp
12	oz. fresh asparagus spears, trimmed, cut in 2-inch pieces (3 cups)
1	large red and/or yellow sweet pepper, cut in ¾-inch pieces (1 cup)
½	cup bottled peanut sauce

PREPARATION

1. Place noodles in large bowl. Bring 4 cups water to boiling; pour boiling water over noodles in bowl. Let stand 10 minutes.

2. Meanwhile, heat oil in large skillet over medium-high heat. Add shrimp, asparagus, and sweet peppers. Cook and stir 3 to 5 minutes until shrimp are opaque. Add peanut sauce; heat through.

3. Drain noodles. Divide noodles among shallow serving bowls, using a fork to twist noodles into nests. Top with shrimp, asparagus, and sweet pepper mixture. **MAKES 4 SERVINGS.**

EACH SERVING *396 cal, 9 g fat (2 g sat. fat), 129 mg chol, 642 mg sodium, 55 g carbo, 5 g fiber, 21 g pro. Daily Values: 34% vit. A, 88% vit. C, 7% calcium, 22% iron.*

FAST!

BEEF AND BLUE CHEESE WRAPS

START TO FINISH 20 min.

INGREDIENTS

3 Tbsp. mayonnaise
1 tsp. dried thyme, crushed
2 Tbsp. yellow mustard
4 8-inch flour tortillas
12 oz. thinly sliced cooked roast beef
1 12-oz. jar roasted red sweet peppers, drained
⅓ cup crumbled blue cheese
4 cups mixed greens
Additional crumbled blue cheese (optional)

PREPARATION

1. In bowl combine mayonnaise and dried thyme. Remove and set aside *1 tablespoon* of the mayonnaise mixture. Stir mustard into remaining mayonnaise mixture.

2. Spread one side of each tortilla with mayonnaise-mustard mixture. Evenly divide roast beef, sweet peppers, and blue cheese among each tortilla. Roll; brush with reserved mayonnaise-dried thyme mixture.

3. In extra-large skillet over medium heat lightly brown tortilla wraps about 2 minutes per side. Cut wraps in half. Divide greens among salad dishes. Drizzle *olive oil* and sprinkle additional blue cheese; top with halved wraps. **MAKES 4 SERVINGS.**

EACH SERVING *395 cal, 23 g fat (7 g sat. fat), 50 mg chol, 1,145 mg sodium, 22 g carbo, 3 g fiber, 21 g pro. Daily Values: 12% vit. A, 261% vit. C, 12% calcium, 20% iron.*

BEEF AND BLUE CHEESE WRAPS

Rock the Crock

Fresh ingredients, fast prep, and three easy techniques bring your slow cooker up to speed.

BY **NANCY BYAL** AND **RICHARD SWEARINGER**
PHOTOS **ANDY LYONS**
FOOD STYLING **JILL LUST**

**VEGETABLE
CASSEROLE**

TECHNIQUE 1: ADD FRESH FLAVOR

Give this meatless dinner bright color and a little crunch by adding spinach and radicchio to the cooker just before serving. It's a trick that works with chopped herbs too.

VEGETABLE CASSEROLE

PREP 20 min. **COOK** 4 hr. on low; 2 hr. on high **STAND** 5 min.

INGREDIENTS

2	19-oz. cans cannellini beans
1	19-oz. can garbanzo or fava beans
¼	cup purchased basil pesto
1	medium onion, chopped
4	cloves garlic, minced
1½	tsp. dried Italian seasoning, crushed
1	16-oz. pkg. refrigerated cooked plain polenta cut in ½-inch-thick slices
1	8-oz. pkg. finely shredded Italian cheese blend (2 cups)
1	large tomato, thinly sliced
2	cups fresh spinach
1	cup torn radicchio

PREPARATION

1. Rinse and drain beans. In large bowl combine beans, *2 tablespoons* of the pesto, onion, garlic, and Italian seasoning.

2. In 4- to 5-quart slow cooker layer *half* of bean mixture, *half* of the polenta, and *half* of the cheese. Add remaining beans and polenta. Cover; cook on low heat setting 4 to 6 hours or on high heat setting 2 to 2½ hours. Add tomato, remaining cheese, spinach, and radicchio. Combine remaining pesto and 1 tablespoon *water*. Drizzle pesto mixture on casserole. Let stand, uncovered, 5 minutes.

MAKES 8 SERVINGS.

EACH SERVING *360 cal, 12 g fat (6 g sat. fat), 26 mg chol, 926 mg sodium, 46 g carbo, 10 g fiber, 21 g pro. Daily Values: 25% vit. A, 16% vit. C, 36% calcium, 19% iron.*

BIG-BATCH PUTTANESCA SAUCE

This sauce will keep up to 3 days in the refrigerator or 3 months in the freezer.

PREP 30 min. **COOK** 8 hr. on low; 4 hr. on high

INGREDIENTS

3	28-oz. cans diced tomatoes
½	of a 6-oz. can (⅓ cup) tomato paste
1	large onion, chopped
4	cloves garlic, minced
¼	cup pitted kalamata olives, chopped
¼	cup snipped fresh Italian (flat-leaf) parsley
2	Tbsp. capers, drained
1	Tbsp. anchovy paste
2	tsp. dried basil, crushed
¼	tsp. cayenne pepper
1	lb. fresh or frozen cooked shrimp, thawed, peeled, and deveined
¼	cup pitted kalamata olives, halved
	Hot cooked pasta or rice
	Shaved Parmesan cheese

PREPARATION

1. In 4- to 6-quart slow cooker stir together undrained tomatoes, tomato paste, onion, garlic, chopped olives, ¼ cup snipped parsley, capers, anchovy paste, basil, cayenne pepper, ¼ teaspoon *salt*, and ¼ teaspoon *ground black pepper*.

2. Cover and cook on low-heat setting 8 to 10 hours or high-heat setting 4 to 5 hours.

3. Remove *half* of sauce (about 5½ cups). Set aside for additional meals.

4. If using low-heat setting, turn to high-heat setting. Add shrimp and halved olives to sauce in cooker. Cover and cook 5 minutes more or until heated through. Serve over hot cooked pasta or rice. Sprinkle shaved Parmesan cheese. **MAKES 6 SERVINGS PLUS 5½ CUPS LEFTOVER SAUCE (4 TO 6 SERVINGS).**

EACH SERVING (WITH SHRIMP) *257 cal, 4 g fat (1 g sat. fat), 94 mg chol, 874 mg sodium, 36 g carbo, 5 g fiber, 20 g pro. Daily Values: 23% vit. A, 33% vit. C, 13% calcium, 18% iron.*

EACH SERVING (SAUCE ONLY) *33 cal, 0 g fat, 2 mg chol, 355 mg sodium, 7 g carbo, 2 g fiber, 1 g pro. Daily Values: 11% vit. A, 17% vit. C, 2% calcium, 3% iron.*

TECHNIQUE 2: BIG-BATCH IT

Making two meals at once—one for now, one for later—saves time. Use half the sauce now for the shrimp and freeze the other half to use as a sauce in which to simmer chicken, Italian sausage, or mushrooms.

TECHNIQUE 3: MARINATE

Marinating before slow cooking allows seasonings to both enhance the meat and flavor the cooking broth. Even if you only have an hour or two to let the marinade work, it's still worthwhile.

ALE-SAUCED PORK RIBS AND VEGETABLES

PREP 25 min. **COOK** 8 hr. on low;
4 hr. on high

INGREDIENTS

2½	to 3 lb. bone-in pork country-style ribs
1	12-oz. bottle dark ale or stout or nonalcoholic beer
3	cloves garlic, minced
1	Tbsp. finely shredded lemon peel
1	Tbsp. dried rosemary, crushed
¼	tsp. salt
¼	tsp. freshly ground black pepper
8	small gold or red potatoes (8 oz. total)
12	oz. peeled fresh baby carrots
¼	cup cold water
2	Tbsp. cornstarch
	Radishes (optional)
	Fresh rosemary sprigs (optional)
	Shredded lemon peel (optional)

PREPARATION

1. Place pork in a large self-sealing plastic bag set in a shallow dish. Add ale, garlic, lemon peel, dried rosemary, salt, and pepper. Seal bag. Turn to coat. Refrigerate 4 hours or overnight, turning bag occasionally.

2. Place potatoes and carrots in bottom of 5- to 6-quart slow cooker. Transfer pork ribs to bed of carrots and potatoes. Pour ale mixture over all. Cover and cook on low-heat setting 8 to 9 hours or on high-heat setting 4 to 4½ hours.

3. Remove pork and vegetables from cooker. Cover; keep warm. Pour cooking juices through fine-mesh sieve set over a heatproof bowl to strain. Measure *2 cups* of cooking juices, adding *water* to make 2 cups, if necessary. Stir together ¼ cup water and cornstarch in medium saucepan. Add 2 cups strained juices. Cook and stir until thickened and bubbly. Cook and stir 2 minutes more. Serve sauce with meat, vegetables, and radishes. Garnish with fresh rosemary and lemon peel. **MAKES 4 TO 6 SERVINGS.**

EACH SERVING *497 cal, 23 g fat (8 g sat. fat), 143 mg chol, 342 mg sodium, 25 g carbo, 4 g fiber, 40 g pro. Daily Values: 235% vit. A, 28% vit. C, 10% calcium, 18% iron.*

Cupcakes

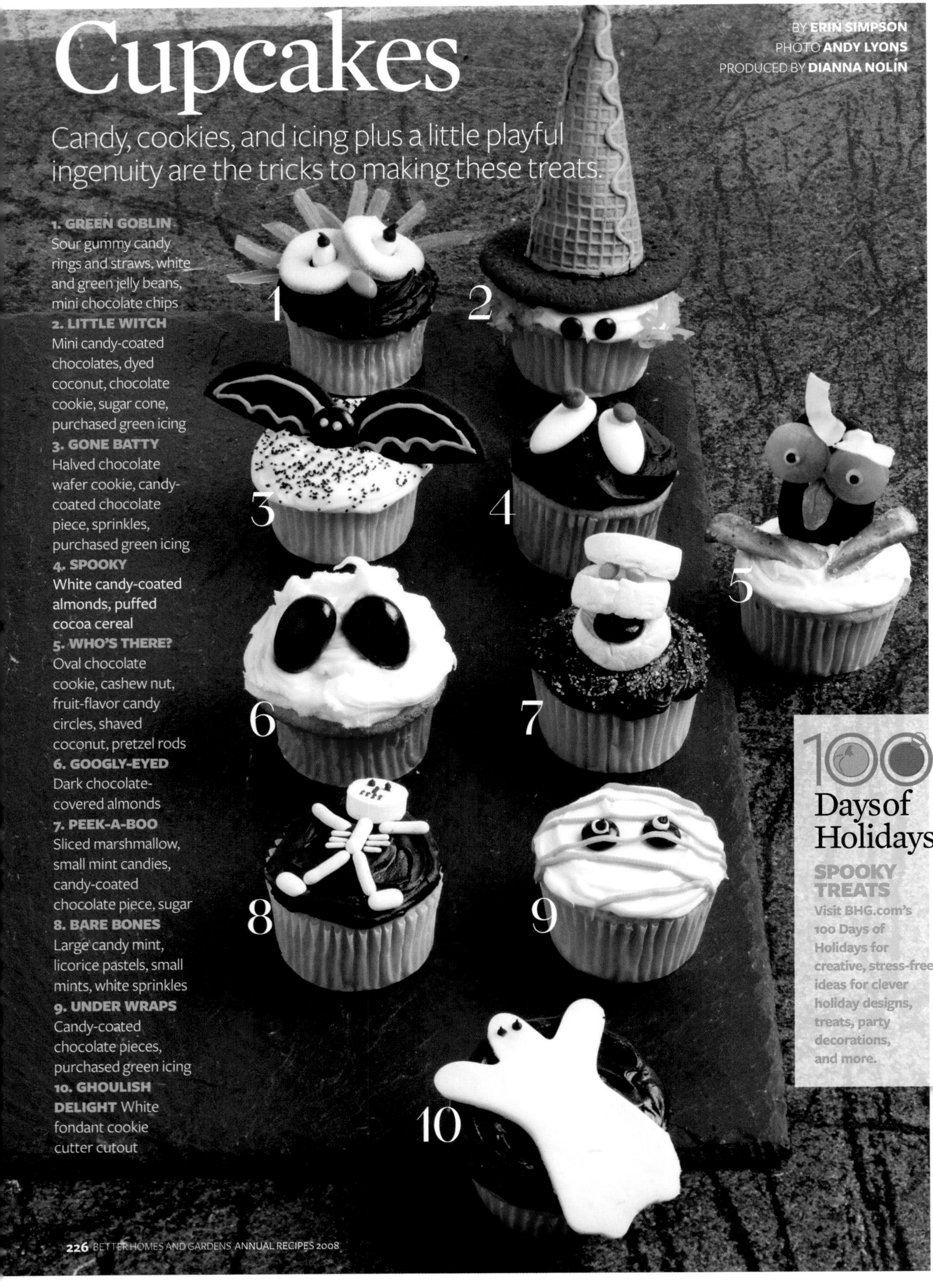

BY ERIN SIMPSON
PHOTO ANDY LYONS
PRODUCED BY DIANNA NOLIN

Candy, cookies, and icing plus a little playful ingenuity are the tricks to making these treats.

1. GREEN GOBLIN Sour gummy candy rings and straws, white and green jelly beans, mini chocolate chips

2. LITTLE WITCH Mini candy-coated chocolates, dyed coconut, chocolate cookie, sugar cone, purchased green icing

3. GONE BATTY Halved chocolate wafer cookie, candy-coated chocolate piece, sprinkles, purchased green icing

4. SPOOKY White candy-coated almonds, puffed cocoa cereal

5. WHO'S THERE? Oval chocolate cookie, cashew nut, fruit-flavor candy circles, shaved coconut, pretzel rods

6. GOOGLY-EYED Dark chocolate-covered almonds

7. PEEK-A-BOO Sliced marshmallow, small mint candies, candy-coated chocolate piece, sugar

8. BARE BONES Large candy mint, licorice pastels, small mints, white sprinkles

9. UNDER WRAPS Candy-coated chocolate pieces, purchased green icing

10. GHOULISH DELIGHT White fondant cookie cutter cutout

100 Days of Holidays

SPOOKY TREATS

Visit BHG.com's 100 Days of Holidays for creative, stress-free ideas for clever holiday designs, treats, party decorations, and more.

Fall's Here!

Savor the first evening of fall with a dish of warm, irresistibly smooth bread pudding.

PHOTO **ANDY LYONS** FOOD STYLING **JILL LUST**

BREAD PUDDING WITH CHOCOLATE AND CHERRIES

PREP 30 min **STAND** 15 min. **BAKE** 30 min.
OVEN 350°F

INGREDIENTS

	Nonstick cooking spray
1	cup dried cherries
¼	cup brandy or apple juice
3	cups half-and-half or light cream
½	cup sugar
2	eggs
2	egg yolks
1	tsp. vanilla
5	cups soft white bread cubes (6 to 7 slices of bread)
4	oz. bittersweet chocolate, coarsely chopped

PREPARATION

1. Preheat oven to 350°F. Lightly coat eight 6-ounce custard cups with nonstick cooking spray. Place cups in large roasting pan; set aside. In small bowl combine dried cherries and brandy or juice; set aside.
2. In medium saucepan combine half-and-half and sugar. Cook and stir over medium heat until sugar is dissolved.
3. In mixing bowl whisk together eggs and egg yolks. Slowly add half-and-half mixture to beaten egg mixture, whisking constantly. Whisk in vanilla. Stir in bread cubes. Let stand at room temperature for 15 minutes. Stir in dried cherry-brandy mixture and divide among custard cups. Evenly distribute chopped chocolate.
4. Place roasting pan on oven rack. Pour boiling water into pan to halfway up sides of custard cups. Bake 30 minutes until knife inserted near pudding centers comes out clean. Remove cups from water. Serve warm.
MAKES 8 SERVINGS.

EACH SERVING *391 cal, 19 g fat (11 g sat. fat), 139 mg chol, 188 mg sodium, 47 g carbo, 2 g fiber, 7 g pro. Daily Values: 18% vit. A, 1% vit. C, 15% calcium, 13% iron.*

CELEBRATE EVERY DAY *with*
Pam Anderson

NOVEMBER

TAKE A FRESH LOOK AT TURKEY AND ALL THE TRIMMINGS, TEN WAYS TO INDIVIDUALIZE STUFFING, AND HOLIDAY BAKING THAT GOES BEYOND PIES. HERE ARE NEW IDEAS FOR SEASONAL WEEKNIGHT DINNERS, AND THE CLASSIC PARTY SNACK—THE CHEESE BALL—GETS AN UPDATE.

Try (a Little) Something New

CHICKEN AND GNOCCHI WITH SQUASH
page 246

CARROT CAKE WITH SKILLET FRUIT page 251

CHEESE BALL
page 253

This Thanksgiving,

try
(a little)
something new

HOLIDAY TRADITIONS ARE PURE PLEASURE—BUT TRADITION ALSO BENEFITS FROM A BIT OF SHAKING UP. HERE ARE A BAKERS' DOZEN RECIPES THAT UPDATE THE CLASSICS, LIGHTEN RICH FARE, OR ADD A SENSE OF ADVENTURE TO YOUR MEAL.

BY **RICHARD SWEARINGER** PHOTOS **ANDY LYONS**
RECIPES **LISA KINGSLEY** FOOD STYLING **JILL LUST** PROP STYLING **SUE MITCHELL**

THINK OF
NEW DISHES AS
COMPANIONS,
NOT COMPETITION,
FOR HOLIDAY
FAVORITES SUCH AS
GREEN-BEAN BAKE
AND HOMEMADE
CRANBERRY RELISH.

VELVET MASHED POTATOES
page 240

Try (*dazzling*) potatoes

UPDATE A CLASSIC Tiny marshmallows are irresistible, but this year smother sweet potatoes with a mix of thyme-roasted apples and onions, *below center*. **BE ADVENTUROUS** Just before dinner saute a mix of button, shiitake, and oyster mushrooms and add them to smooth mashed potatoes, *bottom left*. **GO LIGHT** Even a rich dish like potato gratin can be lightened by using nonfat milk and goat cheese; we've kept it robust with caramelized leeks and garlic, *bottom right*.

CURRANT- GLAZED TURKEY
page 241

MASHED WHITE CHEDDAR SWEET POTATOES
page 240

POTATO-GOAT CHEESE GRATIN page 240

Try a (*fresher*) green salad

BE ADVENTUROUS Slices of Brie cheese-topped toast and creamy cranberry dressing, *right*, give bold flavor to a spinach salad. **UPDATE A CLASSIC** Ever had homemade ranch dressing? Drizzle it over a mix of lettuce and pear tomatoes, *below*, and discover why it's been a favorite for 50 years. A dash of smoked paprika is the subtle update. **GO LIGHT** We've added a refreshing kick of mint and ginger to an arugula salad and topped it with chopped fresh cranberries, *below right*.

SPINACH SALAD WITH BRIE TOAST

BUTTERHEAD SALAD WITH SMOKY RANCH

FRESH CITRUS AND CRANBERRY SALAD

SPINACH SALAD WITH BRIE TOAST

For easy slicing, freeze wrapped Brie for 30 minutes before cutting.

PREP 30 min. **COOK** 7 min. **BROIL** 1 min.

INGREDIENTS

2/3	cup fresh or frozen cranberries
1/4	cup sugar
1/4	cup white wine vinegar
1/4	cup orange juice
2	tsp. Dijon-style mustard
3/4	cup canola or olive oil
2	tsp. finely snipped fresh sage
1/2	tsp. kosher salt or salt
1/4	tsp. freshly ground black pepper
16	1/4-inch slices baguette, toasted
8	oz. Brie cheese, cut in 16 wedges
10	cups prewashed baby spinach
1/2	cup dried cranberries
1/4	cup shelled pumpkin seeds (pepitas), toasted (optional)

PREPARATION

1. For Creamy Cranberry Dressing, in saucepan combine cranberries, sugar, and vinegar. Cook over medium heat, stirring often, 5 minutes or until cranberries soften and begin to pop. Remove from heat; cool.
2. Transfer cranberry mixture to blender. Blend on high until nearly smooth. Add juice and mustard; process to blend. With blender running, slowly pour in oil until slightly thickened and creamy. Transfer to bowl. Whisk in sage, salt, and pepper.
3. For Brie toast, preheat broiler. Place wedge of cheese on each toasted bread slice. Broil 5 or 6 inches from heat 1 to 2 minutes, until cheese is melted.
4. Toss spinach, dried cranberries, and seeds with 3/4 cup cranberry dressing. Serve with toast. Pass additional dressing.
MAKES 8 SERVINGS.

EACH SERVING (WITH 2 BRIE TOASTS) *264 cal, 18 g fat (6 g sat. fat), 28 mg chol, 357 mg sodium, 19 g carbo, 2 g fiber, 8 g pro. Daily Values: 74% vit. A, 8% vit. C, 10% calcium, 10% iron.*

BUTTERHEAD SALAD WITH SMOKY RANCH

START TO FINISH 20 min.

INGREDIENTS

1	clove garlic, peeled (about 1/2 tsp.)
1	cup buttermilk
1/3	cup mayonnaise
1/3	cup dairy sour cream
2	Tbsp. *each* snipped fresh Italian (flat-leaf) parsley and snipped fresh chives
1	green onion, thinly sliced (2 Tbsp.)
1	tsp. white wine vinegar
1/2	tsp. smoked paprika
4	heads butterhead (Boston or Bibb) lettuce, torn
1	cup yellow pear tomatoes, halved

PREPARATION

1. For Smoky Ranch Dressing, place garlic clove on cutting board and use side of wide knife to smash. Sprinkle 1/2 teaspoon *salt* on garlic. Use side of knife to mash garlic and rub into paste. Transfer to bowl. Whisk in buttermilk, mayonnaise, sour cream, parsley, chives, green onion, vinegar, paprika, and 1/4 teaspoon *ground black pepper* into garlic paste until combined.
2. Toss lettuce with tomatoes. Serve with dressing. **MAKES 8 SERVINGS.**

EACH SERVING *70 cal, 5 g fat (1 g sat. fat), 5 mg chol, 158 mg sodium, 4 g carbo, 1 g fiber, 2 g pro. Daily Values: 61% vit. A, 12% vit. C, 6% calcium, 7% iron.*

FRESH CITRUS AND CRANBERRY SALAD

The cranberry topper is also a crunchy, good-for-you accompaniment to sliced turkey.

PREP 25 min. **CHILL** 1 to 48 hr.

INGREDIENTS

2	cups fresh or frozen cranberries, thawed
4	oranges
2	stalks celery, thinly sliced (1 cup)
1/3	cup finely chopped red onion
1/4	cup sugar
2	Tbsp. fresh lemon juice
1	tsp. grated fresh ginger
1	5-oz. pkg. baby arugula
1/4	cup fresh mint leaves, chopped
2	Tbsp. walnut oil or olive oil

PREPARATION

1. For cranberry topper, place cranberries in food processor. Cover; pulse cranberries 5 times to coarsely chop (or coarsely chop by hand). Transfer to bowl.
2. Cut peel from oranges. Section oranges over bowl to catch juice. Add sections and juice to cranberries. Stir in celery, onion, sugar, lemon juice, and ginger. Cover; refrigerate at least 1 hour or up to 2 days.
3. Toss arugula with mint and oil. Top with cranberry mixture. **MAKES 8 SERVINGS.**

EACH SERVING *92 cal, 4 g fat (0 g sat. fat), 0 mg chol, 16 mg sodium, 15 g carbo, 3 g fiber, 1 g pro. Daily Values: 11% vit. A, 44% vit. C, 5% calcium, 5% iron.*

GREEN BEANS WITH LIME

ROASTED KALE
AND RED ONIONS

Try (lively) green veggies

GO LIGHT Crisp green beans, *above*, get the lean treatment with parsley, rosemary, and a splash of olive oil. Chopped hazelnuts add crunch.

BE ADVENTUROUS If you've never cooked kale before, roasting is an easy way to ensure it cooks evenly and becomes tender. The balsamic-glazed onions go in just before serving.

UPDATE A CLASSIC Cream and green vegetables are a delicious pair—think creamed spinach. Brussels sprouts, *right,* take equally well to the treatment, especially with a little bacon and cracked black pepper.

CREAMY
BRUSSELS SPROUTS

FAST!

GREEN BEANS WITH LIME

PREP 15 min. **COOK** 6 min.

INGREDIENTS

2	lb. fresh green beans, trimmed
1/3	cup fresh Italian (flat-leaf) parsley
1	Tbsp. snipped fresh rosemary
2	tsp. finely shredded lime peel
1	Tbsp. fresh lime juice
1	clove garlic, minced (1/2 tsp.)
2	Tbsp. extra virgin olive oil
1/3	cup hazelnuts, toasted and chopped*
	Lime wedges (optional)

PREPARATION

1. Bring large saucepan of water to boiling. Add 1 tablespoon *salt* and green beans. Cook beans until crisp-tender, 3 to 4 minutes. Drain; immediately plunge in ice water. Drain well and set aside.
2. In small bowl combine parsley, rosemary, lime peel and juice, and garlic. Set aside.
3. In 12-inch skillet heat olive oil over medium-high heat. Add beans. Cook, stirring occasionally, 3 to 4 minutes or until heated through. Season with 1/2 teaspoon each *salt* and *ground black pepper*. Remove from heat. Stir in lime mixture and hazelnuts. Serve with lime wedges.
MAKES 8 SERVINGS.

***TIP** To toast hazelnuts, spread in single layer on baking sheet. Bake at 350°F for 5 to 10 minutes, stirring once or twice, until lightly browned. Remove papery skins from hazelnuts by rubbing nuts with clean towel.

EACH SERVING *103 cal, 7 g fat (1 g sat. fat), 0 mg chol, 299 mg sodium, 10 g carbo, 5 g fiber, 3 g pro. Daily Values: 19% vit. A, 33% vit. C, 5% calcium, 9% iron.*

ROASTED KALE AND RED ONIONS

Look for dark green, frilly-leaved kale in the produce aisle among other winter greens.

PREP 30 min. **COOK** 20 min. **ROAST** 15 min. **OVEN** 375°F

INGREDIENTS

3	large red onions, cut in wedges
6	Tbsp. olive oil
3/4	tsp. salt
1/2	tsp. ground black pepper
1/2	cup chicken broth
3	Tbsp. balsamic vinegar
1	Tbsp. butter
2	bunches (about 1 1/4 lb. total) kale, stems removed coarsely chopped
2	cloves garlic, minced

PREPARATION

1. Preheat oven to 375°F. Line roasting pan with foil; set aside. In bowl toss onions with *1 tablespoon* of the oil, *1/4 teaspoon* of the salt, and *1/4 teaspoon* of the pepper; set aside.
2. Heat *1 tablespoon* oil in large skillet; add onion mixture. Cook over medium-high heat 5 minutes, stirring occasionally, until onions begin to brown. Reduce heat to medium-low. Add broth and vinegar. Cover; cook 15 minutes or until onions are tender. Add butter. Increase heat to high. Cook 2 to 3 minutes, shaking pan occasionally, until onions are lightly glazed.
3. Meanwhile, add kale to prepared roasting pan. Toss with remaining oil, garlic, salt, and pepper. Roast, uncovered, 15 minutes, tossing 3 times. To serve, gently toss with onions.
MAKES 8 SERVINGS.

EACH SERVING *150 cal, 12 g fat (2 g sat. fat), 4 mg chol, 310 mg sodium, 10 g carbo, 1 g fiber, 2 g pro. Daily Values: 134% vit. A, 91% vit. C, 7% calcium, 5% iron.*

CREAMY BRUSSELS SPROUTS

This side dish is a crowd-pleaser, proving everything is better with bacon.

PREP 20 min. **COOK** 15 min.

INGREDIENTS

4	slices peppered bacon
2	lb. Brussels sprouts, trimmed and halved through stem end
3/4	cup reduced-sodium chicken broth
1/2	tsp. kosher salt
1/4	tsp. ground black pepper
3/4	cup whipping cream
	Cracked black pepper

PREPARATION

1. In 12-inch skillet cook bacon over medium heat until browned and crisp. Remove to drain on paper towels, reserving 2 tablespoons drippings in skillet.
2. In skillet add Brussels sprouts to drippings; cook and stir over medium heat 4 minutes. Add broth, salt, and pepper. Heat to boiling. Reduce heat. Simmer, covered, 5 minutes. Uncover; cook 2 to 4 minutes or until liquid is nearly evaporated. Add cream. Cook 4 minutes more or until thickened.
3. Transfer sprouts to serving dish. Sprinkle crumbled bacon and cracked pepper.
MAKES 8 SERVINGS.

EACH SERVING *174 cal, 14 g fat (7 g sat. fat), 38 mg chol, 305 mg sodium, 10 g carbo, 4 g fiber, 6 g pro. Daily Values: 21% vit. A, 123% vit. C, 6% calcium, 8% iron.*

MEET LISA

As a food writer and editor of dozens of cookbooks, as well as being her family's designated Thanksgiving cook, **Lisa Kingsley** works to balance tradition and fresh twists on recipes. "The basic ingredients are always familiar, like sweet potatoes or green beans, but the flavors and method of preparation make them fun and interesting," Lisa says. "Since I'm not good at delegating tasks, I do as much ahead as possible." Even simple things, such as toasting nuts or washing and chopping veggies one or two days before, ease the cooking chores on Thanksgiving Day. Lisa also looks for new ways to cook for a crowd. "Roasting kale not only makes it tender and sweet, it's also an easy way to prepare a large batch." See the chart on *page 241* for more tips on making dishes ahead of time, using alternate cooking methods, and doubling or lightening recipes.

DOUBLE PUMPKIN PIE WITH OAT CRUST

GINGER-PUMPKIN MERINGUE PIE

PUMPKIN-CHOCOLATE CHEESECAKE PIE

Try (homemade) pie

GO LIGHT An oat crust, *top*, means this pie is low in fat, high in fiber. The filling also has less sugar and uses egg whites instead of whole eggs. **UPDATE A CLASSIC** Brown sugar meringue, *center*, covers pumpkin filling sweetened with maple syrup and a gingersnap crust. Chocolate chips separate classic pumpkin pie filling from a cheesecake layer below, *bottom*.

DOUBLE PUMPKIN PIE WITH OAT CRUST

Find pumpkin butter with jams and jellies in supermarkets and specialty food stores.

PREP 30 min. **BAKE** 64 min.
OVEN 450°F/350°F

INGREDIENTS

1	recipe Oat Pastry
1	15-oz. can pumpkin
1	9-oz. jar pumpkin butter
1/2	tsp. ground cinnamon
3	egg whites, lightly beaten
3/4	cup fat-free milk

PREPARATION

1. Preheat oven to 450°F. Prepare and roll out Oat Pastry. Line 9-inch pie plate with pastry. Trim crust to 1/2 inch beyond pie plate. Flute edges as desired. Line with double thickness of foil. Bake 8 minutes. Remove foil and bake 6 minutes. Cool on wire rack. Reduce oven temperature to 350°F.
2. For filling, in bowl combine pumpkin, pumpkin butter, and cinnamon. Add egg whites; beat lightly with fork to combine. Gradually add milk; stir just until combined.
3. Carefully pour filling into pastry shell, spreading to edges. To prevent over-browning, cover edge of pie with foil. Bake 25 minutes. Remove foil. Bake 25 minutes more or until knife inserted near center comes out clean. Cool on wire rack. Cover and refrigerate within 2 hours.
MAKES 8 SERVINGS.

Oat Pastry In mixing bowl combine 1 cup *all purpose flour*, 1/3 cup *quick-cooking rolled oats*, and 1/2 teaspoon *salt*. Using pastry blender or two knives, cut in 1/4 cup *shortening* until pieces are pea size. Sprinkle 1 tablespoon *water* over part of flour mixture; gently toss with fork. Push moistened dough to side of bowl. Repeat, using 1 tablespoon *water* at a time, until all flour is moistened (4 to 5 tablespoons total) Form into ball. On lightly floured surface, flatten dough. Roll from center to edge into 12-inch circle.

EACH SERVING *242 cal, 7 g fat (2 g sat. fat), 0 mg chol, 223 mg sodium, 41 g carbo, 3 g fiber, 5 g pro. Daily Values: 166% vit. A, 4% vit. C, 5% calcium, 10% iron.*

GINGER-PUMPKIN MERINGUE PIE

Here a fluffy springtime meringue comes to harvest season. Prepare the Brown Sugar Meringue as the pie bakes. Completely spread meringue to edges of the hot pie; seal by lightly pressing to the crust.

PREP 30 min. **BAKE** 69 min. **COOL** 2 hr.
OVEN 375°F/350°F

INGREDIENTS

1	recipe Gingersnap-Graham Crust
1	15-oz. can pumpkin
1/3	cup sugar
1	tsp. ground ginger
1/2	tsp. salt
1/2	tsp. ground cinnamon
3	eggs, lightly beaten
2/3	cup milk
1/2	cup maple syrup
1	recipe Brown Sugar Meringue

PREPARATION

1. Preheat oven to 375°F. Prepare Gingersnap-Graham Crust; bake 4 minutes. Cool on wire rack.
2. For filling, in bowl combine pumpkin, sugar, ginger, salt, and cinnamon. Add eggs; lightly beat with fork to combine. Gradually stir in milk and maple syrup.
3. Pour filling into pastry shell. To prevent overbrowning, cover edge of pie with foil. Bake 50 to 55 minutes or until knife inserted near center comes out clean. Uncover edges. Reduce oven to 350°F.
4. Carefully spread Brown Sugar Meringue over hot filling; seal to edge. Bake 15 minutes or until golden. Cool on wire rack 2 hours. Serve immediately or loosely cover and refrigerate. **MAKES 8 SERVINGS.**

Gingersnap-Graham Crust In large bowl combine 3/4 cup finely crushed *gingersnaps* (about 12), 1/2 cup finely crushed *graham crackers*, and 2 tablespoons *granulated sugar*. Stir in 1/4 cup melted *butter*. Spread evenly on bottom and up sides of 9-inch pie plate.

Brown Sugar Meringue In large mixing bowl let 3 *egg whites* stand at room temperature 30 minutes. Add 1/2 teaspoon *vanilla*, 1/4 teaspoon *cream of tartar*, and 1/8 teaspoon *salt*. Beat on medium until soft peaks form. Gradually add 1/3 cup packed *brown sugar*, 1 tablespoon at a time, beating on high speed until mixture forms stiff peaks (tips stand straight).

EACH SERVING *316 cal, 10 g fat (5 g sat. fat), 96 mg chol, 404 mg sodium, 52 g carbo, 2 g fiber, 6 g pro. Daily Values: 172% vit. A, 4% vit. C, 8% calcium, 12% iron.*

PUMPKIN-CHOCOLATE CHEESECAKE PIE

PREP 30 min. **BAKE** 74 min.
OVEN 450°F/375°F

INGREDIENTS

1	recipe Deep-Dish Pie Pastry
12	oz. cream cheese, softened (1 1/2 8-oz. pkgs.)
1/4	cup granulated sugar
1	egg, lightly beaten
3/4	cup miniature semisweet chocolate pieces
1	15-oz. can pumpkin
2/3	cup packed brown sugar
2	tsp. pumpkin pie spice
4	eggs, lightly beaten
3/4	cup half-and-half or light cream Chopped chocolate (optional)

PREPARATION

1. Preheat oven to 450°F. Prepare and roll out Deep Dish Pie Pastry. Transfer pastry to a 9 1/2- to 10-inch deep-dish pie plate. Trim crust edge 1/2 inch beyond pie plate. Flute edge high. Line pastry with double thickness of foil. Bake 8 minutes. Remove foil; bake 6 minutes more or until golden. Cool on wire rack. Reduce oven temperature to 375°F.
2. In medium mixing bowl combine cream cheese, 1/4 cup granulated sugar, and 1 egg; beat on low speed until smooth. Spread cream cheese mixture in cooled pastry shell. Sprinkle with chocolate pieces.
3. In bowl combine pumpkin, brown sugar, and pie spice. Stir in 4 eggs. Gradually stir in half-and-half. Slowly pour pumpkin mixture on chocolate layer. To prevent overbrowning, cover pie edge with foil.
4. Bake 60 to 65 minutes or until knife inserted near center comes out clean. Remove foil. Cool on wire rack. Cover and refrigerate within 2 hours. Top with chopped chocolate. **MAKES 8 SERVINGS.**

Deep-Dish Pie Pastry In medium bowl stir together 1 1/2 cups *all-purpose flour* and 1/4 teaspoon *salt*. Using pastry blender or two knives, cut in 6 tablespoons *shortening* until pieces are pea size. Sprinkle 1 tablespoon cold *water* over part of flour mixture; gently toss with fork. Push moistened dough to side of bowl. Repeat, using 1 tablespoon *water* at a time, until all flour is moistened (5 to 6 tablespoons total). Form into ball. On lightly floured surface, flatten dough. Roll pastry from center to edge to 13-inch circle.

EACH SERVING *583 cal, 35 g fat (17 g sat. fat), 187 mg chol, 262 mg sodium, 59 g carbo, 3 g fiber, 12 g pro. Daily Values: 182% vit. A, 4% vit. C, 12% calcium, 20% iron.*

MASHED WHITE CHEDDAR SWEET POTATOES

PREP 40 min. **BAKE** 1 hr. 10 min.
MICROCOOK 5 min. **OVEN** 425°F/325°F

INGREDIENTS
3	lb. yams or sweet potatoes
¼	cup butter
1	tsp. kosher salt or salt
3	oz. aged white cheddar cheese, shredded
¼	cup bourbon or orange juice
¼	cup whipping cream
¼	cup packed dark brown sugar
1	large red onion, cut in thin wedges
2	medium red apples, cored and cut in wedges
2	tsp. snipped fresh thyme
¼	tsp. ground black pepper

PREPARATION

1. Preheat oven to 425°F. Scrub potatoes and prick with fork; place on foil-lined baking sheet. Bake 40 minutes or until tender. Reduce oven temperature to 325°F.
2. When potatoes are cool enough to handle, scrape pulp from skin. Transfer to bowl. Mash with *2 tablespoons* of the butter and *¾ teaspoon* of the salt. Stir in cheese, bourbon, cream, and *2 tablespoons* of the brown sugar. Transfer to buttered 1½-quart casserole. Cover; bake 30 minutes or until heated through.
3. Meanwhile, in microwave-safe 2-quart casserole combine remaining butter, brown sugar, and salt. Add onion. Microcook on 100% power (high) 3 to 4 minutes or until onion is crisp-tender. Add apples. Cover and microcook 2 minutes more or until apples are tender. Stir in thyme and pepper. Serve with sweet potatoes. **MAKES 8 SERVINGS.**

EACH SERVING *293 cal., 12 g fat (8 g sat. fat), 37 mg chol., 421 mg sodium, 38 g carbo., 5 g fiber, 5 g pro. Daily Values: 321% vit. A, 9% vit. C, 132% calcium, 6% iron.*

VELVET MASHED POTATOES

PREP 15 min. **BAKE** 55 min. **OVEN** 400°F

INGREDIENTS
1	head garlic
2½	lb. russet potatoes (about 5), scrubbed
2	Tbsp. butter
⅓	cup dairy sour cream
2	oz. cream cheese
½	cup milk, heated
1	recipe Mushroom Sauce

PREPARATION

1. Preheat oven to 400°F. Cut ¼ inch off pointed end of garlic to expose cloves. Drizzle with *olive oil;* wrap in foil. Prick potatoes with fork; place in oven. Bake 20 minutes. Add garlic. Continue baking potatoes and garlic 35 to 40 minutes or until potatoes are tender and garlic is soft and browned.
2. Holding hot potatoes with towel, split potatoes and scrape flesh into saucepan over low heat. Squeeze roasted garlic into potatoes. Add butter, sour cream, and cream cheese. Mash with potato masher. Season with 1 teaspoon *salt* and ¼ teaspoon *ground black pepper*. Gradually stir in hot milk until potatoes are light and fluffy. Transfer to serving bowl. Top with Mushroom Sauce.
MAKES 8 SERVINGS.
Mushroom Sauce Melt 3 tablespoons *butter* in skillet over medium-high heat. Add 1 pound sliced *assorted fresh mushrooms*. Cook, stirring occasionally, 4 minutes or until browned. Add 1 *shallot*, finely chopped; cook 2 minutes. Add ¼ cup *oil-packed dried tomatoes*, drained and chopped; 1½ teaspoons chopped fresh *thyme*; ½ teaspoon *salt*; and ¼ teaspoon *ground black pepper*. Add ½ cup dry *white wine* or chicken broth. Cook and stir, scraping up browned bits from pan. Add ⅓ cup *whipping cream*; bring to boiling. Simmer, uncovered, 2 minutes or until slightly thickened. Serve with Velvet Mashed Potatoes.

EACH SERVING (with 3 Tbsp. sauce) *402 cal., 25 g fat (15 g sat. fat), 70 mg chol., 634 mg sodium, 35 g carbo., 3 g fiber, 8 g pro. Daily Values: 20% vit. A, 43% vit. C, 8% calcium, 8% iron.*

POTATO-GOAT CHEESE GRATIN

PREP 30 min. **COOK** 20 min.
BAKE 1 hr. 25 min. **STAND** 10 min.
OVEN 400°F

INGREDIENTS
3	large leeks (white part only), trimmed, halved lengthwise, and thinly sliced (1¼ cups)
1½	cups fat-free milk
1	Tbsp. all-purpose flour
½	tsp. salt
¼	tsp. ground black pepper
⅛	tsp. ground nutmeg
1	clove garlic, minced
2¼	lb. Yukon gold potatoes, peeled and cut in ⅛-inch slices
4	oz. goat cheese (1 cup)
¼	cup panko or soft bread crumbs
¼	cup finely shredded Parmesan cheese Fresh Italian (flat-leaf) parsley

PREPARATION

1. Preheat oven to 400°F. In nonstick skillet cook leek in 1 tablespoon *olive oil* over medium-low heat 20 minutes or until tender and beginning to brown, stirring occasionally. Remove from heat.
2. In bowl whisk *2 tablespoons* of the milk into the flour. Whisk in remaining milk, salt, pepper, nutmeg, and garlic.
3. Coat 2-quart casserole or au gratin dish with *nonstick cooking spray*. Arrange *half* the potato slices in dish. Sprinkle with leeks and goat cheese. Pour half the milk mixture over potato/leek layer. Layer remaining potatoes; pour remaining milk over all. Cover with foil.
4. Bake 45 minutes. Remove foil and bake 25 minutes more or until potatoes are tender. In small bowl stir together the bread crumbs and Parmesan cheese. Sprinkle on potatoes. Bake, uncovered, 15 minutes more or until topping is browned. Let stand 10 minutes before serving. Top with parsley.
MAKES 8 SERVINGS.

EACH SERVING *209 cal., 6 g fat (3 g sat. fat), 9 mg chol., 278 mg sodium, 32 g carbo., 2 g fiber, 8 g pro. Daily Values: 17% vit. A, 30% vit. C, 14% calcium, 9% iron.*

CURRANT-GLAZED TURKEY

PREP 20 min. **ROAST** 2 ¾ hr. **STAND** 15 min.
OVEN 325°F

INGREDIENTS

1   10- to 12-lb. turkey
1   Tbsp. butter, melted
1   recipe Currant Glaze
1   recipe Pan Gravy (optional)
1   recipe Herb Drizzle (optional)

PREPARATION

1. Preheat oven to 325°F. Rinse inside of turkey; pat dry with paper towels. If desired, season body cavity with *salt*. Pull neck skin to back; fasten with skewer.

2. Tuck ends of drumsticks under band of skin across tail. If there is no band of skin, tie the drumsticks securely to tail. Twist wing tips under back.

3. Place turkey, breast side up, on rack in shallow roasting pan. Brush with butter. If desired, insert meat thermometer into center of inside thigh muscle, not touching bone. Cover turkey loosely with foil.

4. Place turkey in 325°F oven. Roast 2¾ to 3 hours. Remove foil last 45 minutes of roasting. Cut band of skin between drumsticks so thighs cook evenly. During last 15 minutes of roasting, brush twice with Currant Glaze. Roast until thermometer registers 180°F. (Juices should run clear and drumsticks should move easily in sockets.)

5. Remove turkey from oven. Let stand 15 to 20 minutes before carving. Carve turkey. Serve with Pan Gravy and/or Herb Drizzle.

MAKES 8 TO 10 SERVINGS.

Currant Glaze In saucepan combine ½ cup *red currant* or *plum jelly*, 1 tablespoon *lemon juice*, 1 teaspoon *dry mustard*, 1 teaspoon *Worcestershire sauce*, and ¼ teaspoon *ground black pepper*. Heat; stir until jelly is melted.

Pan Gravy While turkey stands after roasting, pour pan drippings into large measuring cup. Scrape browned bits from pan into cup. Skim and reserve fat from drippings. Heat ¼ cup of the fat in saucepan (discard any remaining fat). Cook; stir ¼ cup minced *shallot* or finely chopped onion in fat until tender. Stir in ¼ cup *all-purpose flour*. Add enough *chicken broth* to remaining drippings in cup to equal 2 cups; add broth mixture all at once to flour mixture. Cook and stir over medium heat until thickened and bubbly. Cook and stir 1 minute more. Season to taste with *salt* and *ground black pepper*.

Herb Drizzle: In saucepan melt 2 tablespoons *butter*; stir in 1 tablespoon *cornstarch* and ¼ teaspoon cracked *black pepper*. Add 1¼ cups *reduced-sodium chicken broth*. Cook and stir until thickened and bubbly. Stir in 2 teaspoons snipped fresh *thyme* and 1 teaspoon snipped fresh *rosemary*. Cook and stir 1 to 2 minutes more.

EACH SERVING *280 cal, 8 g fat (3 g sat. fat), 154 mg chol, 93 mg sodium, 7 g carbo, 0 g fiber, 42 g pro. Daily Values 1% vit. A, 1% vit. C, 3% calcium, 14% iron.*

SOMETHING NEW | november

Use this chart for tips on making dishes ahead of time, using alternate cooking methods, and doubling or lightening recipes.

	WHAT TO MAKE AHEAD	HOW TO DOUBLE	ALTERNATE COOKING METHOD	HOW TO LIGHTEN
Fresh Citrus and Cranberry Salad	Relish can be prepared up to 2 days ahead. Store, covered, in refrigerator.	Double all ingredients. Follow instructions provided.		
Butter-head Salad with Smoky Ranch	Dressing can be prepared up to 2 days ahead. Store, covered, in refrigerator.	For 16 servings, double all **except** the dressing. Follow instructions provided.		Use reduced-fat sour cream and mayonnaise in dressing.
Spinach Salad with Brie Toast	Dressing can be prepared up to 2 days ahead. Store, covered, in refrigerator. Toast pumpkin seeds and bread up to 1 day ahead and store, covered.	Double all ingredients. Follow instructions provided.	If oven is in use, place toast topped with Brie in hot oven. Bake until Brie is melted.	Leave off Brie Toast; reduce sugar in dressing to 2 tablespoons.
Potato-Goat Cheese Gratin	Prepare through Step 3. Cover and refrigerate up to 24 hours. Let stand at room temperature 20 minutes before baking. Proceed with Step 4.	Prepare two recipes. Bake one on top rack, one on bottom, switching places halfway through cooking time.		
Mashed White Cheddar Sweet Potatoes	Prepare up to 2 days ahead. Bake 40 to 45 minutes. Reheat apple-onion mixture in microwave.	Double all ingredients. Follow instructions provided.	Boil potatoes 20 to 25 minutes. Heat through mashed potato mixture on stovetop for 15 minutes.	Use milk instead of whipping cream. Leave out cheese.
Velvet Mashed Potatoes	Prepare up to 3 days ahead and reheat. Stir in additional milk as needed.	Double all ingredients. Follow instructions provided.	Boil potatoes with 3 peeled garlic cloves on stovetop, 15 minutes or until tender. Drain and mash as directed.	Use reduced-fat sour cream and cream cheese.
Green Beans with Lime	Toast bread and nuts 1 day ahead. Cook green beans 1 day ahead; cover and refrigerate.	Double all ingredients. Follow instructions provided.	Steam green beans, loosely covered with plastic, in microwave for 7 minutes.	
Creamy Brussels Sprouts	Prepare up to 3 days ahead. Add crumbled bacon at the last. Reheat in microwave oven 8 minutes, stirring twice.	Double all ingredients. Cook sprouts in 2 batches. Return all back to skillet. Add broth; continue as directed, simmering 6 minutes.		Use 2 Tbsp. olive oil in place of bacon and drippings. Leave out the cream.
Roasted Kale with Red Onions	Wash and chop kale up to 2 days ahead. Store in resealable bags in refrigerator.	Double all ingredients. Follow instructions provided.	Cook kale in large Dutch oven (in batches, if needed). When slightly wilted add garlic. Toss with onions as instructed.	Leave out the butter. Toss kale with just 2 Tbsp. of oil before roasting.
Double Pumpkin Pie with Oat Crust	Prepare and freeze crust 1 month ahead. Prepare pie up to 2 days ahead; cover and refrigerate.	Prepare two separate recipes.		
Ginger-Pumpkin Meringue Pie	Bake crust up to 1 day ahead. Cool and wrap in plastic. Prepare pie the night before; loosely cover and refrigerate.	Prepare two separate recipes.		
Pumpkin-Chocolate Cheese-cake Pie	Prepare pie up to 2 days ahead; cover and refrigerate.	Prepare two separate recipes.		Use light evaporated milk and reduced-fat cream cheese.

Turkey Roasting Guide

Our step-by-step instructions give you the easy way to prep, cook, and present.

BY **JEANNE AMBROSE**
PHOTOS **ANDY LYONS**
FOOD STYLING **JILL LUST**

november

Prep and Roast

PLAN Allow 1 to 1½ pounds per person. That amount will leave enough for leftovers too. Be sure to allow plenty of time—and space—to thaw the turkey in the refrigerator, if frozen. See the box at right for thawing tips.

PREP Find the giblets—heart, liver, gizzard—tucked inside the neck and body cavities and remove. Discard, if not using, or cook and add to stuffing or gravy. If you are stuffing the bird, plan about ¾ cup stuffing per pound of poultry. Do not stuff until just before roasting. Loosely spoon stuffing into the neck and body cavities, allowing room for expansion. If stuffing is too tightly packed it will not reach a safe eating temperature by the time the bird is done. Pull neck skin over stuffing; use a long skewer to hold it in place. Tuck drumsticks under band of skin near tail, reset leg clamp, or tie legs together with kitchen string (photo, *right*). Twist wing tips up and under the bird's back. If not stuffing the bird, bake stuffing in a casserole dish.

ROAST Use the roasting chart, *below right,* to determine cooking times. While oven is preheating to 325°F, place turkey, breast side up, on a rack in a shallow roasting pan. Pans with sides higher than 1 or 2 inches will act as a heat shield and prevent turkey thighs from cooking evenly. Brush bird with cooking oil. Cover loosely with foil and roast. After two-thirds of cooking time, cut string between drumsticks. Remove foil during the last 30 to 45 minutes of cooking to create a crisp, golden skin. According to the USDA, all turkey meat and stuffing is safe to eat when a meat thermometer reaches 165°F. However, for best flavor and ease in carving, thigh meat should be cooked to 180°F. For an accurate reading, be sure thermometer does not touch bone when inserted in meat.

ANSWERS TO COMMON TURKEY DILEMMAS

■ Fresh or frozen? It all comes down to personal preference. Some people like the flavor of fresh turkey. Others don't notice a flavor difference. Fresh birds don't need to be thawed but may be pricier. Frozen birds can be purchased in advance but need up to 1 week to thaw in the refrigerator.

■ When should I start thawing the turkey? Thawing the bird in the refrigerator is our favorite method. Allow 24 hours' thawing time for every 4 pounds of bird. That means a 12-pound turkey takes 3 days to thaw, but we recommend allowing an extra day to make sure it thaws completely. It's safe to keep a thawed bird in the fridge a day or two before roasting. If you find your turkey is still frozen Thanksgiving morning, place it in a clean sink filled with cold water. Change the water every 30 minutes until the turkey is thawed. Do not thaw the bird at room temperature or in warm water.

■ Can I roast the turkey in advance? Yes. Roast and carve per directions in this guide, then cover and refrigerate up to 2 days. For moist, make-ahead turkey, pour turkey or chicken broth over slices, then cover and refrigerate. Before serving, reheat, covered, in the microwave.

■ How long can I keep leftovers? The first step is to cover and refrigerate meat within 2 hours of cooking. Then eat it within 2 days. Otherwise freeze it for up to 6 months.

■ What if I have more questions? Fear not. Trusted resources are just a mouse click or phone call away. For specific instructions for roasting a whole bird—or a turkey breast or drumsticks—visit our Interactive Roasting Guide at *BHG.com/roastingguide.* Or visit *eatturkey.com,* the National Turkey Federation's site, or *butterball.com.* Call the Butterball Turkey Talk-Line, 800/288-8372, or the USDA Meat and Poultry Hot Line, 888/674-6854.

ROASTING TIMES AT 325°F

READY-TO-COOK TURKEY WEIGHT	UNSTUFFED	STUFFED
8 to 12 lb.	2¾ to 3 hr.	3 to 3½ hr.
12 to 14 lb.	3 to 3¾ hr.	3½ to 4 hr.
14 to 18 lb.	3¾ to 4¼ hr.	4 to 4¼ hr.
18 to 20 lb.	4¼ to 4½ hr.	4¼ to 4¾ hr.
20 to 24 lb.	4½ to 5 hr.	4¾ to 5¼ hr.

SOURCE: National Turkey Federation.

Beat the Clock

Schedule packed full? Quickly satisfy end-of-the-day appetites with five deliciously fresh meals.

READY IN 20 MINUTES!

LAYERED TURKEY ENCHELADAS

BY **PEG SMITH**
PHOTOS **ANDY LYONS**
RECIPES **JULIANA HALE**
FOOD STYLING **JILL LUST**

FAST!

LAYERED TURKEY ENCHILADAS

START TO FINISH 20 min.

INGREDIENTS

1	lb. turkey breast tenderloin, cut in bite-size strips
1	16-oz. pkg. frozen sweet peppers and onions stir-fry vegetables
1	10-oz. can enchilada sauce
½	cup whole berry cranberry sauce
9	6-inch corn tortillas, halved
1	8-oz. pkg. Mexican-blend shredded cheese (2 cups)
	Lime wedges (optional)
	Cilantro sprigs (optional)

PREPARATION

1. Position oven rack toward top of oven. Preheat oven to 450°F. In extra-large skillet cook turkey in 1 tablespoon hot *cooking oil* over medium heat 4 minutes or until no longer pink. Add frozen vegetables, enchilada sauce, and cranberry sauce. Bring to boiling. Sprinkle *salt* and *ground black pepper*.
2. In 2-quart baking dish layer *one-third* of the tortillas, then *one-third* of the cheese. Use a slotted spoon to layer half the turkey-vegetable mixture. Layer one-third tortillas, one-third cheese, remaining turkey-vegetables (with slotted spoon), and remaining tortillas. Spoon on remaining sauce from skillet; sprinkle remaining cheese. Bake 5 minutes or until cheese is melted. Cut in squares. Serve with lime and cilantro. **MAKES 4 SERVINGS.**

EACH SERVING *615 cal, 25 g fat (11 g sat. fat), 120 mg chol, 1,171 mg sodium, 52 g carbo, 6 g fiber, 45 g pro. Daily Values: 46% vit. A, 72% vit. C, 39% calcium, 14% iron.*

FAST!

POACHED EGG SALAD

START TO FINISH 20 min.

INGREDIENTS

8	eggs
2	medium leeks, thinly sliced
2	cups seedless red grapes
2	Tbsp. cider vinegar
	Salt and ground black pepper
4	slices crusty bread, toasted
1	10-oz. pkg. Italian mixed salad greens (romaine and radicchio)
2	oz. blue cheese, crumbled (½ cup)

PREPARATION

1. In large skillet pour *water* to halfway up sides. Bring water to simmering (bubbles break surface). Break an egg, one at a time, into measuring cup. Hold lip of cup close to water; carefully slide in egg, allowing each equal space in pan. Simmer, uncovered, 3 to 5 minutes until whites are set and yolks begin to thicken but are not hard.
2. Meanwhile, in second skillet cook leeks and grapes over medium heat in 2 tablespoons hot *olive oil* for 4 minutes, just until leek slices are tender and grape skins burst. Remove from heat. Add vinegar. Sprinkle salt and pepper. With slotted spoon transfer eggs to toast. Serve with greens, leeks, grapes, and cheese. **MAKES 4 SERVINGS.**

EACH SERVING *428 cal, 22 g fat (7 g sat. fat), 433 mg chol, 681 mg sodium, 39 g carbo, 4 g fiber, 21 g pro. Daily Values: 45% vit. A, 32% vit. C, 22% calcium, 25% iron.*

POACHED EGG SALAD

SPEEDY PAELLA

START TO FINISH 20 min.

INGREDIENTS

1	10-oz. pkg. frozen long grain white rice with vegetables (peas, corn, and carrots)
1	Tbsp. cooking oil
½	lb. fresh sea scallops (halve large scallops)
½	lb. cooked, peeled, deveined shrimp
4	Roma or plum tomatoes, coarsely chopped
½	to 1 tsp. ground turmeric
	Salt and ground black pepper
	Chopped fresh parsley (optional)

PREPARATION

1. Prepare rice according to package directions.

2. Meanwhile, in large skillet heat cooking oil over medium heat. Add scallops to hot oil in skillet; cook 3 minutes or until scallops are opaque. Add shrimp and chopped tomatoes; heat through.

3. Transfer rice to bowl; stir in turmeric. Spoon seafood-tomato mixture over rice; lightly toss. Season to taste with salt and pepper. Sprinkle fresh parsley. **MAKES 4 SERVINGS.**

EACH SERVING *229 cal, 5 g fat (1 g sat. fat), 129 mg chol, 374 mg sodium, 22 g carbo, 2 g fiber, 24 g pro. Daily Values: 23% vit. A, 25% vit. C, 5% calcium, 13% iron.*

SPEEDY PAELLA

CHICKEN AND GNOCCHI WITH SQUASH

CHICKEN AND GNOCCHI WITH SQUASH

START TO FINISH 20 min.

INGREDIENTS

1	1-lb. pkg. shelf-stable potato gnocchi
1	small acorn squash, halved and seeded
14	to 16 oz. chicken breast tenderloins
¾	cup chicken broth
1	Tbsp. chopped fresh sage
2	Tbsp. milk
	Tiny whole sage leaves
	Grated nutmeg (optional)

PREPARATION

1. Prepare gnocchi according to package directions. Drain. Cover and keep warm.

2. Meanwhile, place squash, cut sides down, in a microwave-safe baking dish with 2 tablespoons *water*. Microcook, covered, on high (100% power) 7 to 10 minutes; rearrange once. Let stand, covered, 5 minutes.

3. Sprinkle chicken with *salt* and *ground black pepper*. In large skillet cook chicken in 1 tablespoon hot *oil* over medium heat 6 to 8 minutes until no longer pink. Remove; cover, keep warm.

4. Scrape flesh from squash; mash. Transfer to hot skillet; stir in broth and chopped sage. Bring to boiling; simmer 1 minute. Stir in milk. Spoon into bowls. Top with chicken and gnocchi; sprinkle sage and nutmeg. **MAKES 4 SERVINGS.**

EACH SERVING *366 cal, 6 g fat (1 g sat. fat), 59 mg chol, 796 mg sodium, 50 g carbo, 4 g fiber, 29 g pro. Daily Values: 11% vit. A, 22% vit. C, 7% calcium, 10% iron.*

FAST!

FLAT IRON STEAK WITH BBQ BEANS

START TO FINISH 20 min.

INGREDIENTS

2 boneless beef shoulder top blade (flat iron) steaks, halved (1 to 1¼ lb.)
2 tsp. fajita seasoning
1 15-oz. can black beans, rinsed and drained
⅓ cup bottled barbecue sauce
2 to 3 tomatoes, sliced
Corn bread (optional)
Pickled jalapeño peppers (optional)

PREPARATION

1. Preheat grill pan over medium-high heat. Sprinkle steaks with fajita seasoning. On greased grill pan, grill steaks 8 to 12 minutes for medium-rare (145°F) or 12 to 15 minutes for medium (160°F) doneness.
2. Meanwhile, in medium microwave-safe bowl stir together beans and barbecue sauce. Cover loosely with plastic wrap. Microcook on high (100% power) for 3 minutes, stirring once.
3. Serve steaks with sliced tomatoes, beans, and corn bread. Top with pickled jalapeño slices.
MAKES 4 SERVINGS.

EACH SERVING *272 cal, 8 g fat (2 g sat. fat), 67 mg chol, 667 mg sodium, 25 g carbo, 6 g fiber, 29 g pro. Daily Values: 11% vit. A, 13% vit. C, 5% calcium, 21% iron.*

FLAT IRON STEAK WITH BBQ BEANS

Easy
Holiday
Baking

Plainly beautiful,
these five desserts
combine homey
flavors and simple
preparation.

BY **RICHARD SWEARINGER**
PHOTOS **ANDY LYONS**
RECIPES **DAVID BONOM**
AND **ANGELA McCROVITZ**
FOOD STYLING **CHARLES WORTHINGTON**

APPLE-PEAR TART

Purchased cookies are the crust's main ingredient. For crumb-free prep, crush them in a resealable plastic bag.

PREP 35 min. **BAKE** 20 min. **CHILL** 2 hr.
COOK 10 min. **OVEN** 350°F

INGREDIENTS

10	pecan shortbread cookies, crushed (1⅓ cups)
½	cup all-purpose flour
¼	cup butter, melted
1	8-oz. pkg. cream cheese, softened
1	egg
¼	cup caramel ice cream topping
2	medium firm ripe pears, peeled, cored, and cut in 12 wedges each
2	medium apples, cored and cut in 12 wedges each (do not peel)
2	Tbsp. butter
1	Tbsp. lemon juice
2	Tbsp. caramel ice cream topping

PREPARATION

1. Preheat oven to 350°F. In bowl combine crushed shortbread cookies, flour, and the ¼ cup melted butter. Pat mixture into bottom and up sides of 14×5×1-inch rectangular or 10-inch round tart pan with removable bottom. Bake crust 10 minutes. Set aside.

2. In medium bowl beat cream cheese with electric mixer on medium to high speed for 30 seconds. Add egg and ¼ cup caramel ice cream topping; beat until smooth. Spread mixture in bottom of baked crust. Bake 10 minutes more or until center appears set when pan is shaken. Cool on wire rack. Cover and chill at least 2 hours or up to 24 hours.

3. In 12-inch skillet cook pears and apples in the 2 tablespoons butter over medium heat 10 minutes or until tender but still holding their shape, stirring occasionally. Add lemon juice and heat through. Spoon fruit mixture over tart. Drizzle with 2 tablespoons caramel topping. Pass any remaining fruit. **MAKES 8 SERVINGS.**

EACH SERVING *391 cal, 25 g total fat (13 g sat. fat), 82 mg chol, 249 mg sodium, 38 g carbo, 3 g fiber, 5 g pro. Daily Values: 14% vit. A, 7% vit. C, 4% calcium, 6% iron.*

KID FRIENDLY

PEANUT BUTTER SANDWICH COOKIES

Insulated cookie sheets slow down baking, preventing burning. Darker sheets produce darker cookies; lighter ones, lighter results.

PREP 1 hr. **BAKE** 7 min. per batch **OVEN** 350°F

INGREDIENTS

½	cup chunky peanut butter
½	cup shortening
1	cup packed brown sugar
1	egg
1	tsp. vanilla
1	tsp. baking soda
⅛	tsp. salt
1¼	cups all-purpose flour
	Granulated sugar
1	recipe Peanut Cream Filling

PREPARATION

1. Preheat oven to 350°F. In bowl beat peanut butter and shortening with electric mixer on medium speed for 30 seconds. Add brown sugar, egg, and vanilla. Beat until combined, scraping sides of bowl. Beat in baking soda, salt, and as much flour as you can. Stir in any remaining flour.

2. Form dough into balls, using a level teaspoon each. Place 1½ inches apart on ungreased or parchment-lined baking sheets. Flatten by making crisscross marks with tines of fork dipped in sugar.

3. Bake 7 to 8 minutes or until edges are lightly browned. Cool on baking sheet 1 minute. Transfer to wire rack; cool.

4. Spread *1 teaspoon* Peanut Cream Filling on flat side of half of cookies. Top with remaining cookies. Store in airtight container at room temperature up to 3 days. Freeze unfilled cookies up to 1 month. **MAKES 4 DOZEN SANDWICH COOKIES.**

Peanut Cream Filling In medium bowl whisk together ¾ cup *chunky peanut butter*, ¾ cup *marshmallow creme*, 3 tablespoons *milk*, ¾ teaspoon *ground cinnamon*, and ¼ teaspoon *ground cumin*. Gradually whisk in 3 tablespoons *powdered sugar*.

EACH COOKIE *98 cal, 6 g fat (1 g sat. fat), 4 mg chol, 69 mg sodium, 11 g carbo, 1 g fiber, 2 g pro. Daily Values: 1% calcium, 2% iron.*

PUMPKIN SANDWICH CAKE

The cream cheese filling also makes a great spread for French toast or waffles.

PREP 30 min. **BAKE** 16 min. **CHILL** 1 hr.
OVEN 375°F

INGREDIENTS

¾	cup all-purpose flour
1½	tsp. pumpkin pie spice
1	tsp. baking powder
¼	tsp. salt
3	eggs
1	cup granulated sugar
¾	cup canned pumpkin
½	cup whipping cream
½	of an 8-oz. pkg. cream cheese, softened
½	cup powdered sugar
1	recipe Chocolate Cream Icing
	Pumpkin pie spice

PREPARATION

1. Preheat oven to 375°F. Grease bottoms and sides of two 8×1½-inch round cake pans. Line bottoms with waxed paper; lightly flour pans. In bowl combine flour, pumpkin pie spice, baking powder, and salt; set aside.
2. In a second bowl beat eggs and granulated sugar with an electric mixer on medium to high speed until thick, about 5 minutes. Beat in pumpkin. Add flour mixture; beat just until combined. Spread cake batter in prepared pans. Bake 16 to 18 minutes or until wooden pick inserted near centers comes out clean. Cool in pans on wire rack 10 minutes; remove and cool thoroughly.
3. For cream cheese filling, in chilled mixing bowl beat whipping cream to soft peaks; set aside. In a second mixing bowl beat cream cheese until smooth; beat in powdered sugar. Fold in whipped cream. To assemble, place one cake layer on serving platter. Spread cream cheese mixture evenly over bottom cake layer. Top with second cake layer. Refrigerate while preparing Chocolate Cream Icing.
4. If Chocolate Cream Icing is too thin, cover and chill 30 minutes until of spreading consistency. If it's too thick, add a teaspoon of milk or cream. Spread over top and sides of cake. Sprinkle lightly with pumpkin pie spice. Chill cake at least 1 hour before serving.
5. Store cake, loosely covered, in refrigerator.
MAKES 8 SERVINGS.

EACH SERVING WITH ICING *466 cal, 26 g fat (16 g sat. fat), 137 mg chol, 184 mg sodium, 56 g carbo, 3 g fiber, 7 g pro. Daily Values: 86% vit. A, 2% vit. C, 7% calcium, 16% iron.*

MAKE THE SMOOTHEST ICING

The secret to glossy, crumb-free icing is to start by laying a good-sized dollop on top of the cake, then spreading it outward to the uniced part of the cake. *Never backtrack from dry to iced.* Best tool for the job: an offset spatula.

FAST!

CHOCOLATE CREAM ICING

Also known as ganache, this icing firms up nicely and protects cakes from drying out.

PREP 10 min. **STAND** 5 min. **COOL** 15 min.

INGREDIENTS

½	cup whipping cream
1	cup bittersweet or semisweet chocolate pieces

PREPARATION

1. In small saucepan bring whipping cream just to boiling over medium-high heat. Remove from heat. Pour over chocolate pieces in medium bowl (do not stir). Let stand 5 minutes. Stir until smooth. Cool 15 minutes.
MAKES 1¼ CUPS.

CARROTT CAKE WITH SKILLET FRUIT

PREP 45 min. **BAKE** 30 min. **COOL** 15 min.
OVEN 350°F

INGREDIENTS

1	cup all-purpose flour
1	tsp. baking powder
1	tsp. pumpkin pie spice
¼	tsp. baking soda
¼	tsp. salt
¾	cup granulated sugar
¼	cup packed brown sugar
¾	cup canned pumpkin or mashed sweet potato*
2	eggs
¼	cup cooking oil
½	cup finely shredded carrot
⅓	cup buttermilk
¾	cup walnuts, toasted and chopped
1	recipe Buttercream Frosting
1	recipe Skillet Fruit

PREPARATION

1. Preheat oven to 350°F. Grease 8×8×2-inch square or 9×1½-inch round baking pan; line bottom of pan with waxed paper. Grease paper. Lightly coat pan with flour; set aside. In medium bowl combine flour, baking powder, pumpkin pie spice, baking soda, and salt; set aside.

2. In large mixing bowl combine sugars, pumpkin, eggs, and oil. Stir in carrot and buttermilk. Gradually beat in flour mixture; stir in walnuts. Transfer to pan. Bake for 30 to 35 minutes or until wooden pick inserted in center comes out clean. Cool on wire rack for 15 minutes. Remove from pan, cool completely.

3. Place cake on serving platter and top with Buttercream Frosting. Just before serving spoon on warm Skillet Fruit.

MAKES 8 SERVINGS.

Buttercream Frosting In large mixing bowl beat ¼ cup softened *butter* with an electric mixer on medium speed until smooth. Gradually beat in 1 cup *powdered sugar*. Beat in 2 teaspoons *milk* and ½ teaspoon *vanilla*. Gradually beat in ¼ to ½ cup additional powdered sugar until frosting reaches spreading consistency.

Skillet Fruit In large skillet melt 3 tablespoons *butter;* stir in 2 tablespoons *granulated sugar.* Add 2 cored and sliced *red-skin pears*, 6 thinly sliced *kumquats*, and ½ cup fresh *cranberries.* Cook, gently stirring occasionally, until pears are just tender (2 to 4 minutes). Remove from heat and let stand for 10 minutes.

***Mashed Sweet Potato** Peel and cube 8 ounces orange-flesh *sweet potatoes*. Cook, covered, in lightly salted boiling water for 20 minutes or until tender. Drain; cool slightly and mash.

EACH SERVING *409 cal, 20 g fat (5 g sat. fat), 65 mg chol, 212 mg sodium, 55 g carbo, 5 g fiber, 6 g pro. Daily Values: 102% vit. A, 18% vit. C, 7% calcium, 11% iron.*

LINE PANS THE EASY WAY

Getting parchment or waxed paper to fit precisely in the pan is easy when you use the pan itself as a template. Place pan on parchment paper on cutting board. Trace around edge of pan using a sharp knife held at slight inward angle.

SWEET POTATO CUPCAKES

PREP 45 min. **BAKE** 20 min. **OVEN** 350°F

INGREDIENTS

2   cups all-purpose flour
2   tsp. baking powder
1   tsp. ground cinnamon
½   tsp. baking soda
¼   tsp. salt
1   cup butter, softened
1½ cups sugar
3   eggs
1   17.2-oz. can vacuum-pack sweet potatoes (unsweetened), mashed
½   tsp. vanilla
1   recipe Cream Cheese Frosting
    Finely shredded orange peel

PREPARATION

1. Preheat oven to 350°F. Line twenty-four 2½-inch muffin cups with paper bake cups; set cups aside.

2. In bowl stir together flour, baking powder, cinnamon, baking soda, and salt; set aside.

3. In mixing bowl beat butter with an electric mixer on medium to high speed 30 seconds. Add sugar and beat on high speed until light and fluffy, about 2 minutes. Add eggs, 1 at a time, beating on low speed after each addition until combined. Add sweet potatoes and vanilla, beating until combined. Add flour mixture; beat until combined (batter will be thick).

4. Divide batter evenly among prepared muffin cups. Bake about 20 minutes or until tops spring back when lightly touched. Cool in pan on wire rack 1 minute. Remove from pan and cool completely.

5. Place Cream Cheese Frosting in large resealable plastic bag. Cut a ¼-inch opening in one corner of bag. Pipe frosting on top of cupcakes. Sprinkle with orange peel.

MAKES 24 CUPCAKES.

Cream Cheese Frosting In large mixing bowl beat one 8-ounce package *cream cheese*, softened, and ⅔ cup *butter*, softened, with electric mixer on medium speed for 30 seconds.

Add 2 tablespoons *bourbon* or milk and beat until combined. Beat in 8 cups *powdered sugar*, about ½ cup at a time, until smooth and of good piping consistency Makes 4⅓ cups.

Mini fluted tube variation Coat 8 fluted individual tube pans with *nonstick baking spray*. Spoon batter into pans. Bake 30 minutes or until tops spring back when lightly touched. Cool in pan on wire rack 1 minute. Remove from pan and cool completely. Omit Cream Cheese Frosting and finely shredded orange peel. Dust cooled cakes with *powdered sugar*.

To make ahead Freeze unfrosted cupcakes in airtight containers up to 1 month. Store frosting in an airtight container in refrigerator up to 3 days.

EACH CUPCAKE *400 cal, 17 g fat (10 g sat. fat), 71 mg chol, 210 mg sodium, 60 g carbo, 1 g fiber, 3 g pro. Daily Values 43% vit. A, 9% vit. C, 3% calcium, 5% iron.*

GIVE CUPCAKES IMPACT

To ensure piled-high icing, place the tip of the icing-filled plastic bag on the top of the cupcake, squeeze a dollop, release pressure, then lift away the bag. As you lift, jog the bag up and down to produce the ripples on sides of icing.

Cheese Ball

To revamp this party classic, blend different cheeses, get fresh with herbs, and stir in flavor.

BY **PEG SMITH** PHOTO **ANDY LYONS** FOOD STYLING **JILL LUST** RECIPE **STEPHEN EXEL**

CHEESE
For a complex flavor, blend goat cheese and cream cheese. Or mix shredded cheddars —mild, sharp, and white—with cream cheese. So the cheese ball will firm up when chilled, add ½ cup butter for each 1½ to 2 pounds of shredded cheese.

HORSERADISH OR BROWN MUSTARD
Either one gives a touch of spice and texture. Stir in a more intense flavor with a bit of horseradish. For a milder bite and trace of sweetness, add brown mustard.

FRESH GARLIC
A hint of this much-loved ingredient goes a long way. Mince or crush 1 clove of garlic per pound of cheese and thoroughly stir into the blended mixture.

NUTS
Toast chopped pecans or walnuts for the best crunch and flavor. Then, for this up-to-date version, stir the nuts into the cheese mixture rather than just coating the outside with them.

FRESH HERBS
Pat on or roll the ball in a combination of chopped fresh parsley, oregano, basil, thyme, and/or chives.

LEMON PEEL
For color and zest, lightly press on strips of fresh lemon, lime, or orange peel.

HEARTY RYE BREAD
Spread cheese on thin slices of soft bread rather than breakable crackers.

TEST KITCHEN TIP
Let butter and cheese stand at room temperature 30 minutes. Whip together with an electric mixer. The mixture will cream easily and have a lighter texture.

Stuffing

Try these stir-ins for a crunchy, spicy, or fruit-filled variation on turkey's best sidekick.

1. TRAIL MIX
Assorted dried fruits and nuts

2. CORN BREAD
Cooked giblets, chopped onion and celery, thyme sprigs

3. WILD BERRY
Cooked wild rice, fresh cranberries, Italian (flat-leaf) parsley

4. MEDITERRANEAN
Roasted red sweet peppers, toasted pine nuts, herbed goat cheese (chèvre)

5. ANTIPASTI
Olives, salami, Parmesan cheese

6. GOLD RUSH
Baked sweet potatoes, cooked bacon, sauteed garlic

7. JUICY FRUIT
Roasted grapes, fresh rosemary sprigs

8. FOREST BLEND
Wild mushrooms, sliced green onions

9. SOUTHWEST
Cooked chorizo sausage, corn, sliced jalapeño pepper

10. HOLIDAY
Purchased peeled and cooked chestnuts, fresh sage leaves, pomegranate seeds

BHG BASICS

Add stir-ins after the stuffing comes out of the oven or bird. Plan for about 1 cup of stir-ins per 8 cups homemade stuffing or 14-oz. box of purchased stuffing (prepared according to package directions).

BY **ERIN SIMPSON** PHOTO **ANDY LYONS**
PRODUCED BY **JILL LUST**

Afternoon Potluck

There are 29 other days in November to share a meal with family and friends. These Asian-flavored ribs can be the centerpiece of a casual potluck.

CELEBRATE EVERY DAY *with Pam Anderson*

OVEN-BARBECUED RIBS

PREP 30 min. **BAKE** 1 hr. 40 min. **OVEN** 350°F

INGREDIENTS

2   racks pork loin back (baby back) ribs (5 to 5½ pounds)
¼   cup packed brown sugar
2   Tbsp. garlic powder
1   Tbsp. ground black pepper
1   Tbsp. Chinese five-spice powder
1   tsp. ground ginger
¼   tsp. salt
¼   cup Dijon-style mustard
½   cup hoisin sauce
2   Tbsp. molasses
1   Tbsp. reduced-sodium soy sauce
1   Tbsp. rice vinegar
1   recipe Asian Slaw (optional)

PREPARATION

1. Preheat oven to 350°F. Cut ribs into serving-size pieces. In a small bowl combine brown sugar, garlic powder, pepper, Chinese five-spice powder, ginger, and salt.

2. Brush meaty sides of ribs with mustard. Sprinkle generously with spice mixture. Place ribs, bone sides down, in a large shallow roasting pan. Bake, covered, 1 hour. Carefully drain off fat.

3. In a small bowl stir together hoisin sauce, molasses, soy sauce, and rice vinegar. Spoon mixture evenly over ribs. Bake, uncovered, for 40 to 60 minutes more or until ribs are tender. Serve with Asian Slaw.

MAKES 6 SERVINGS.

Asian Slaw In a large bowl combine 4 cups finely shredded *bok choy* and 1 cup *shredded carrot*. Drizzle with a mixture of ¼ cup *seasoned rice vinegar*, 1 tablespoon *cooking oil*, and 1 to 2 teaspoons *sugar*. Season to taste with *salt* and *ground black pepper*.

PER SERVING OF RIBS *779 cal., 53 g fat (20 g sat. fat), 188 mg chol., 953 mg sodium, 28 g carbo, 1 g fiber, 40 g protein. Daily Values: 2% vit. C, 12% calcium, 20% iron.*

DECEMBER

CELEBRATE TRADITION! THIS MONTH CHEF MICHEL NISCHAN AND HIS FAMILY SHARE THE HOLIDAY FEAST RECIPES THEY PRACTICALLY KNOW BY HEART. PLUS, FIVE UPDATES ON FAMILIAR FAMILY FARE GET DINNER ON THE TABLE FAST ON BUSY WEEKNIGHTS DEVOTED TO SHOPPING, DECORATING, FRIENDS, AND FUN.

PEAR AND GOAT CHEESE BREAD TART
page 266

Christmas by Heart

PUMPKIN BREAD PUDDING
page 263

PAN-FRIED ANGEL'S FOOD CAKE
page 265

SKILLET VEGETABLES ON CHEESE TOAST
page 269

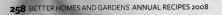

Christmas
by heart

**BAKED FRESH HAM
WITH CHERRY GLAZE** page 261

For chef Michel Nischan's family,
the holiday feast is an easy-going affair. Fresh,
seasonal, and locally grown ingredients take
only uncomplicated roasting, baking, and
pan-frying. "This is our tradition," Michel
says, "sustaining the family with good food
and honoring the farmers who grow it all."

BY **MELANIE BARNARD** RECIPES **MICHEL NISCHAN** PRODUCED BY **NANCY HOPKINS**
PHOTOS **REED DAVIS** FOOD STYLING **JILL LUST** PROP STYLING **SARAH CAVE**

"In December our farmstands and markets brim with the last of the winter vegetables. We cook them to holiday specialness by keeping the emphasis on simple and fresh."

—MICHEL NISCHAN

SKILLET-BROWNED BROCCOLI WITH PAN-TOASTED GARLIC

SPICY HONEY-ROASTED CAULIFLOWER

BAKED FRESH HAM WITH CHERRY GLAZE

Fresh ham is an uncured, unsmoked hind leg of pork similar to a roast. Since it's a large cut of meat, the level of tenderness throughout varies—the smaller end is fork-tender and easy to pull apart, while the larger end slices like a roast. You may need to special order the fresh ham from your butcher ahead of time. Recipe pictured on page 259.

PREP 45 min. **ROAST** 5³⁄₄ hr. **OVEN** 350°F

INGREDIENTS
¹⁄₄ cup coriander seeds
1 fresh pork leg (18 to 20 lb.), skinned and trimmed of top layer of fat
3 to 4 cups freshly pressed apple juice or good-quality apple cider
2 sticks cinnamon
6 green cardamom pods
1 red onion, cut in wedges
1 yellow onion, cut in wedges
2 cups dried tart red cherries or dried cranberries
¹⁄₄ cup loosely packed fresh thyme leaves
¹⁄₂ cup fresh parsley, snipped

PREPARATION
1. Preheat oven to 350°F. In skillet toast coriander seeds over medium-high heat about 1¹⁄₂ minutes or until fragrant, shaking pan often. Transfer to a dish to cool. Place seeds in coffee or spice grinder. Grind until seeds resemble coarse meal.
2. Rub pork with *salt, freshly ground black pepper,* and ground coriander seeds. Place on rack in large roasting pan. Add *3 cups* of the apple juice, the cinnamon, and cardamom to pan. Roast 5¹⁄₄ to 6 hours or until pork reaches an internal temperature of 140°F. Remove from oven. Transfer pork to a large platter; keep warm. Pour pan juices through a mesh strainer into large liquid measuring cup. Return pork to pan along with onions. Increase oven to 400°F.
3. Meanwhile, for Cherry Glaze, skim fat from strained pan juices (if necessary, add additional apple juice to make 2¹⁄₂ cups). Transfer to large saucepan. Add dried cherries. Place over medium-high heat. Simmer 10 to 15 minutes or until cherries rehydrate and liquid is consistency of syrup.
4. Brush pork with *¹⁄₄ cup* of the Cherry Glaze. Return to oven. Roast 30 to 60 minutes or until pork reaches internal temperature of 150°F and onions begin to brown (cover loosely with foil if pork becomes too brown). Remove from oven, cover with foil. Let stand 15 minutes.
5. To serve, place pork on a warm platter. Arrange roasted onions around pork. Stir *half* of the fresh thyme and parsley into the

Cherry Glaze. Carefully spoon some of the glaze over pork and top with remaining herbs. Serve with Cherry Glaze. **MAKES 8 (6-OZ. MEAT WITH ¹⁄₃-CUP SAUCE) SERVINGS.**
Test Kitchen Tip To check temperature, insert meat thermometer into thickest part of ham, close to bone but not touching bone. For accuracy, check multiple spots.

EACH SERVING *559 cal, 17 g fat (6 g sat. fat), 146 mg chol, 265 mg sodium, 42 g carbo, 5 g fiber, 51 g pro. Daily Values: 18% vit. A, 18% vit. C, 12% calcium, 20% iron.*

SPICY HONEY-ROASTED CAULIFLOWER

Look for smaller heads of cauliflower (1 to 1¹⁄₂ pounds). If the heads available in your local supermarket are larger, halve them through the stem end. Michel uses the herbs he has on hand for his cauliflower. The fresh herbs called for in this recipe can be whichever ones are lingering in the garden, what's on sale at the market, or simply parsley you have in the fridge.

PREP 20 min. **ROAST** 25 min. **OVEN** 350°F/400°F

INGREDIENTS
¹⁄₂ cup honey
¹⁄₄ cup whole grain mustard
¹⁄₄ cup butter, softened
¹⁄₂ cup fresh bread crumbs
¹⁄₃ cup chopped fresh herbs
2 whole heads cauliflower, trimmed and cleaned
  Coarsely chopped fresh herbs

PREPARATION
1. Preheat oven to 350°F. Combine the honey, mustard, butter, bread crumbs, and ¹⁄₃ cup herbs in a small bowl. Set aside.
2. Use a long slim paring knife to pierce the heart of each cauliflower stem. Place each head, stem side down, in a deep baking dish large enough to hold both heads. Add about ¹⁄₄ inch of *hot water* to the dish. Cover with foil. Bake 8 to 10 minutes or until the water begins to steam. Remove foil. Carefully pour off water. Return cauliflower to oven. Increase oven temperature to 400°F. Bake for 5 minutes to dry the heads. Remove from oven and coat well with the bread crumb mixture. Return to oven. Roast 12 to 15 minutes or until the cauliflower heads are well browned. To serve, top with additional chopped fresh herbs.
MAKES 8 SERVINGS.

EACH SERVING *158 cal, 6 g fat (4 g sat. fat), 15 mg chol, 275 mg sodium, 25 g carbo, 3 g fiber, 3 g pro. Daily Values: 6% vit. A, 75% vit. C, 4% calcium, 4% iron.*

FAST!
SKILLET-BROWNED BROCCOLI WITH PAN-TOASTED GARLIC

When buying garlic look for bulbs that are firm and plump with dry, papery skins. Garlic can be stored up to several months in a cool, dark, dry place, such as an open brown paper bag in the pantry. Keep the bulbs whole since individual cloves will dry out more quickly. Toasting sliced garlic makes it sharp and flavorful. Be sure to stir constantly so the slices do not burn.

PREP 15 min. **COOK** 15 min.

INGREDIENTS
3 large broccoli stems with stem ends attached
¹⁄₄ cup extra virgin olive oil
  Coarse sea salt
  Ground black pepper
3 Tbsp. thinly sliced garlic cloves

PREPARATION
1. Heat a 12-inch cast-iron skillet over medium heat. Slice broccoli heads lengthwise into 1-inch-thick slices, cutting from the bottom of the stem through the crown to preserve the shape of the broccoli (reserve any florets that fall away during slicing for another use). Brush both sides of each broccoli slice with some of the olive oil and sprinkle lightly with salt and pepper.
2. Place half the slices in heated skillet and set a heavy medium skillet on the slices to press them to cast-iron skillet. Cook over medium heat 3 to 4 minutes, or until well browned. Turn slices; cook second side for 3 to 4 minutes more or until browned (for more-tender broccoli, cook over medium-low heat for 5 to 6 minutes per side). Repeat with remaining broccoli slices. Transfer to a warm platter, cover, and keep warm.
3. Drizzle the remaining olive oil into the hot skillet and add the garlic slices (if skillet is too hot, reduce temperature to medium-low). Cook garlic, stirring gently and constantly for 2 minutes or until the slices are lightly browned. Transfer to a plate lined with paper towels and sprinkle lightly with salt and pepper.
4. Arrange broccoli on serving platter. Sprinkle the toasted garlic slices over broccoli. **MAKES 8 SERVINGS.**
Test Kitchen Tip Keep cooked broccoli slices warm in a 300°F oven or cover with foil while remaining broccoli cooks.

EACH SERVING *84 cal, 7 g fat (1 g sat. fat), 0 mg chol, 119 mg sodium, 5 g carbo, 2 g fiber, 2 g pro. Daily Values: 7% vit. A, 86% vit. C, 3% calcium, 3% iron.*

PUMPKIN BREAD PUDDING

PUMPKIN BREAD PUDDING

Look for fresh chestnuts in the produce section of the supermarket and roast them as instructed. Or buy them online at melissas.com. Pumpkins and other hard-shelled winter squashes stretch out the harvest since they can be stored in a cool, dark place for up to 2 months. For this dish have your pick of pumpkin or winter squashes such as butternut, delicata, golden nugget, acorn, sweet dumpling, or carnival squash.

PREP 30 min. **BAKE** 50 min. **OVEN** 350°F

INGREDIENTS

	Butter
1¼	cups whipping cream
1	cup milk
4	or 5 large croissants or 10 oz. egg bread, torn (about 6 cups)
1¼	cups roasted, shelled chestnuts, crumbled, or one 8- to 10-oz. can chestnuts, drained and crumbled
3	large eggs
1	egg yolk
1	cup granulated sugar
1	cup packed brown sugar
1	lb. roasted pumpkin flesh or hard squash flesh, mashed (2 cups), or one 15-oz. can pumpkin
1¼	cups dried currants or golden raisins
3	Tbsp. butter, melted
½	tsp. ground cardamom
½	tsp. ground ginger
	Seeds of one vanilla bean* or 2 tsp. vanilla extract
1	recipe Molasses Cream
	Fresh thyme (optional)

PREPARATION

1. Preheat oven to 350°F. _Butter_ a 2½- to 3-quart casserole; set aside. In large bowl combine whipping cream and milk. Add torn croissants and chestnuts. Gently press until everything is covered by the milk mixture. Let stand while preparing custard.

2. For custard, combine eggs, egg yolk, sugars, pumpkin, currants, melted butter, spices, and vanilla in the top insert of a large double boiler (or in a large heatproof bowl set over a saucepan of simmering water, making sure bowl does not touch water). Place double boiler over medium heat and stir constantly until mixture is warm and sugars have dissolved. Fold into croissant mixture. Pour all into prepared casserole. Bake, uncovered, 50 minutes or until set. Serve warm with Molasses Cream and thyme. Store any remaining bread pudding in refrigerator up to 2 days. **MAKES 12 SERVINGS.**

Molasses Cream In large bowl whisk 1 cup _whipping cream_ until it starts to thicken. Gradually whisk in 1 tablespoon _molasses,_ sorghum, or honey. Serve at once.

Roasting chestnuts Cut an X on flat side of each chestnut. Place in baking pan. Roast at 400°F for 15 minutes, tossing occasionally. Peel chestnuts while still warm.

Roasting pumpkin or squash Wash, halve lengthwise, and remove seeds of pie pumpkin or hard (winter) squash. Place halves, cut sides down, in baking dish. Bake at 350°F for 45 to 55 minutes or until tender; cool. Scrape flesh from shell with a spoon.

*Test Kitchen Tip To remove seeds from vanilla bean, use small knife to split bean in half lengthwise. Using tip of knife, scrape out the small black seeds from each half, discard pod or add to Vanilla Bean-Verbena Sugar, page 265.

EACH SERVING _520 cal, 26 g fat (15 g sat. fat), 154 mg chol, 213 mg sodium, 69 g carbo, 2 g fiber, 6 g pro. Daily Values: 76% vit. A, 8% vit. C, 11% calcium, 10% iron._

LEEK AND ROOT VEGETABLE GRATIN

Michel uses winter leeks from his garden, but any variety available in the supermarket is fine. Winter leeks are a variety that is hearty enough for harvesting through the winter months and stronger in flavor and texture than summer leeks.

PREP 35 min. **BAKE** 55 min. **STAND** 10 min. **OVEN** 350°F/400°F

INGREDIENTS

8	oz. mild cheddar or Muenster cheese, shredded (2 cups)
1	Tbsp. finely chopped fresh herbs, such as Italian (flat-leaf) parsley, thyme, chives, and/or chervil
1	Tbsp. extra virgin olive oil
3	large turnips or large rutabaga (about 1 pound), peeled and thinly sliced
1	lb. russet potatoes, thinly sliced*
2	cups thinly sliced winter leeks
1	lb. large parsnips, peeled and thinly sliced
1½	lb. sweet potatoes, peeled and thinly sliced
	Assorted fresh herbs (optional)

PREPARATION

1. Preheat oven to 350°F. In a small bowl toss together cheese and chopped herbs; set aside. Coat a 3-quart rectangular baking dish with olive oil. Layer sliced vegetables in the following order, sprinkling _salt, pepper,_ and 3 to 4 tablespoons of the cheese mixture between each layer: _half_ the turnip slices, _half_ the potato slices, _half_ the leek slices, _half_ the parsnip slices, and _half_ the sweet potato slices. Repeat, ending with sweet potato slices. Reserve remaining cheese mixture.

2. Cover with foil. Bake for 40 to 50 minutes. Remove foil. Sprinkle remaining cheese mixture over top. Increase oven temperature to 400°F. Continue baking, uncovered, 15 minutes or until cheese is melted and starting to brown.

3. Remove from oven. Sprinkle additional fresh herbs. Let stand 10 minutes. **MAKES 8 TO 10 SERVINGS.**

*Test Kitchen Tip Slice russet potatoes just before layering to prevent discoloring.

EACH SERVING _309 cal, 11 g fat (6 g sat. fat), 27 mg chol, 422 mg sodium, 44 g carbo, 8 g fiber, 11 g pro. Daily Values: 231% vit. A, 52% vit. C, 29% calcium, 12% iron._

LEEK AND ROOT VEGETABLE GRATIN

**PAN-FRIED
ANGEL'S FOOD CAKE**

ANGEL'S FOOD CAKE

It wouldn't be Michel's famous cake without the flavor and texture that comes from almond flour and Vanilla Bean-Verbena Sugar. Find almond flour in the baking aisle of large supermarkets and health stores or online at kingarthurflour.com. See Vanilla Bean-Verbena Sugar recipe, right.

PREP 1 hr. **BAKE** 40 min. **COOL** completely **OVEN** 200°F/325°F

INGREDIENTS

1½	cups egg whites
1¾	cup Vanilla Bean-Verbena Sugar or purchased vanilla sugar
1	cup cake flour
¼	cup almond flour
¼	tsp. salt
1	tsp. cream of tartar

PREPARATION

1. In a large wide bowl* let egg whites stand at room temperature 30 minutes. Meanwhile, sift the Vanilla Bean-Verbena Sugar once and set aside. Sift the flour and almond flour together four times, then add the salt and cream of tartar. Sift once more.

2. Preheat oven to 200°F. Beat egg whites with an electric mixer on medium-high speed until stiff peaks form (tips stand straight). Slowly and gently add Vanilla Bean-Verbena Sugar, followed immediately by the sifted flour mixture.

3. Pour batter into an ungreased 10-inch tube pan with removable bottom or 10-inch fluted tube pan (be sure pan is very clean with no residual oil).

4. Place in oven; close door. Increase oven temperature to 325°F. Do not open oven for at least the first 15 minutes of cooking. Bake 40 to 50 minutes or until a toothpick inserted near center comes out clean. Remove from oven. Immediately invert cake; cool thoroughly in inverted pan. Remove from pan, using a thin knife to loosen cake if necessary. **MAKES 1 CAKE OR 16 SLICES.**

*Test Kitchen Tip It is important to use a large wide bowl to whisk the egg whites. More surface area allows the sugar and flour to be gradually added without overbeating.

EACH SLICE *138 cal, 1 g fat (0 g sat. fat), 0 mg chol, 74 mg sodium, 29 g carbo, 0 g fiber, 4 g pro. Daily Values: 1% calcium, 4% iron.*

FAST! **KID FRIENDLY**

PAN-FRIED ANGEL'S FOOD CAKE

This is Michel's grandmother's recipe for using leftover cake. It has become the most popular dessert in his restaurant, The Dressing Room.

PREP 20 min. **COOK** 5 min. per batch

INGREDIENTS

1	Angel's Food Cake, above
8	Tbsp. butter, softened
	Homemade or purchased jam or honey

PREPARATION

1. Cut cake into 16 slices. Lightly spread cut sides of 8 cake slices with *half* of the butter. Add cake slices to a large nonstick skillet. Place skillet over medium-high heat. Cook 3 minutes or until golden brown. Turn slices. Cook 2 minutes more or until golden brown. Transfer slices to serving plate. Remove pan from heat and allow to cool while heating jam.

2. In small saucepan heat jam until it begins to melt. Transfer to serving bowl.

3. Lightly spread remaining cake slices with butter; add to cooled pan and toast as instructed above. Serve with heated jam. **MAKES 16 SLICES.**

Test Kitchen Tip A high-quality bakery angel food cake can be substituted in a pinch, but the flavor and texture will be different from Michel's cake.

EACH SLICE *244 cal, 7 g fat (4 g sat. fat), 15 mg chol, 122 mg sodium, 43 g carbo, 1 g fiber, 4 g pro. Daily Values: 4% vit. A, 3% vit. C, 1% calcium, 5% iron.*

VANILLA BEAN-VERBENA SUGAR

Flavored sugars have long been a way to stretch out the life of the herb garden, a technique passed to Michel from his grandmother. Verbena, also called lemon verbena, infuses the sugar (and the Angel's Food Cake) with a pleasantly herbaceous, lemonlike flavor.

PREP 10 min. **STAND** at least 1 week

INGREDIENTS

1	branch (about 12 inches) of lemon verbena with leaves*
4	cups white sugar
3	vanilla beans, split in half lengthwise

PREPARATION

1. Use a heavy-duty knife or sharp kitchen shears to cut verbena stem into pieces about 3 inches long. Layer verbena in bottom of a glass container large enough to hold all the sugar. Pour about *half* the sugar into the container. Stick split vanilla beans into sugar at even intervals. Add remaining sugar. Seal jar tightly and store at least 1 week before using. Once sugar is aromatic, remove verbena and vanilla. If sugar becomes hard or clumped, break pieces with a wooden spoon and sift before using. **MAKES 4 CUPS SUGAR.**

*Test Kitchen Tip If verbena is unavailable, substitute peel from one lemon and one 8-inch stalk of mint.

EACH SERVING (1 Tbsp.) *49 cal, 0 g fat, 0 mg chol, 0 mg sodium, 13 g carbo, 0 g fiber, 0 g pro.*

VANILLA BEAN-VERBENA SUGAR

PEAR AND GOAT CHEESE BREAD TART

Michel serves this dish between the main course and dessert in place of a traditional cheese course.

PREP 30 min. **COOK** 35 min. **COOL** 1 hr.
BAKE 10 min. **OVEN** 400°F

INGREDIENTS

1   recipe Candied Apples or Quince
1   10- to 12-inch diameter sourdough round loaf (boule) or focaccia
2   Tbsp. extra virgin olive oil
    Sea salt (preferably fleur de sel)
1   cup crumbled goat cheese (about 6 oz.)
2   Tbsp. fresh thyme leaves
2   Tbsp. finely shredded lemon peel
2   semiripe pears, cored and sliced
    Finely shredded lemon peel (optional)

1. Prepare Candied Apples or Quince recipe, reserving syrup for serving. Preheat oven to 400°F.
2. Remove the bottom crust of the round loaf by slicing a thin horizontal slice off the bottom with a long serrated knife. After removing bottom crust, create a 1-inch-thick horizontal slab of bread by cutting off the top of the loaf (set remaining bread aside to slice and serve later). Generously brush both sides of the slab of bread with olive oil until it is absorbed into the bread.
3. Preheat an extra-large, heavy-bottomed skillet over medium heat for 4 to 5 minutes. Place oiled bread slice in heated skillet. Cook 2 minutes or until lightly browned. Turn; cook the other side 2 minutes more or until lightly browned. Transfer toasted bread slice to baking sheet. Lightly sprinkle with sea salt. In small bowl gently toss together the crumbled cheese, thyme leaves, and the 2 tablespoons of lemon peel; set aside.
4. Arrange Candied Apples and pears over bread slice, sprinkling cheese and thyme mixture between layers.
5. Transfer to preheated oven. Bake 10 to 12 minutes or until cheese begins to lightly brown and the tart is heated through. Top with additional shredded lemon peel and serve with reserved Candied Apple syrup. **MAKES 8 SERVINGS.**

Candied Apples or Quince Peel 2 large *apples* or 1 large quince (about $3/4$ pound) and quarter lengthwise. Slice the core away from each quarter. Cut each wedge into thin slices. In medium saucepan combine the sliced apples or quince, 1 cup *water*, $1/2$ cup dry *Riesling wine* or apple juice, $1/2$ cup *granulated sugar*, $1/2$ cup packed *light brown sugar*, and 1 *cinnamon stick*. Bring to boiling over medium high heat. Reduce heat to a simmer. Simmer, uncovered, for 30 minutes for the apples or 1 to $1 1/4$ hours for the quince or until tender, stirring occasionally. Strain apples, reserving cooking syrup. The syrup should be the consistency of warm honey. If not, return the syrup to the pan to reduce more. Remove cinnamon stick; discard. Stir in 2 teaspoons *lemon juice*. Cool to room temperature before using, about 1 hour.

EACH SERVING *478 cal, 10 g fat (4 g sat. fat), 13 mg chol, 722 mg sodium, 84 g carbo, 4 g fiber, 15 g pro. Daily Values: 6% vit. A, 10% vit. C, 11% calcium, 21% iron.*

SUGAR COOKIES

KID FRIENDLY

SUGAR COOKIES

Every Christmas the family makes these soft, lightly lemony cookies together and serves them with hot cocoa for dipping. Be sure to chill the dough for at least 1 hour to make it easier to roll out and cut.

PREP 45 min. **CHILL** 1 hr. **BAKE** 8 min. per batch **OVEN** 375°F

INGREDIENTS

3¼   cups all-purpose flour
1½   tsp. baking powder
½   tsp. salt
1¼   cups unsalted butter, softened
1   cup sugar
1   egg
1   Tbsp. milk
2½   tsp. vanilla
¼   tsp. finely shredded lemon peel

PREPARATION

1. In medium mixing bowl combine flour, baking powder, and salt; set aside. In large mixing bowl beat butter on medium to high speed for 30 seconds. Add sugar. Beat until combined, scraping sides of bowl as necessary. Beat in egg, milk, vanilla, and lemon peel. Beat in as much flour as you can with the mixer. Stir in any remaining flour. Divide dough in half. Cover; chill 1 hour or until easy to handle.
2. Preheat oven to 375°F. Roll half the dough at a time, between sheets of waxed paper, sprinkling bottom sheet of waxed paper with flour if cookie dough sticks, to ¼-inch thickness. Cut with desired cutters (if dough become too soft, return to refrigerator). Place 1 inch apart on ungreased cookie sheets. Bake for 8 to 10 minutes or until edges are firm and bottoms are barely light brown. Transfer to wire rack to cool.
MAKES ABOUT 2½ DOZEN (2½- TO 3½-INCH) COOKIES.

EACH COOKIE *147 cal, 8 g fat (5 g sat. fat), 27 mg chol, 61 mg sodium, 17 g carbo, 0 g fiber, 2 g pro. Daily Values: 5% vit. A, 2% calcium, 4% iron.*

MEET MICHEL

Michel Nischan believes "the food we grow and cook, in the place we call home, defines who we are." He puts this belief into practice at The Dressing Room, his restaurant in Westport, Connecticut, and through his nonprofit Wholesome Wave Foundation. The Dressing Room was a collaboration with his friend and fellow food lover, the late Paul Newman. Adjacent to the Westport Country Playhouse, the restaurant serves American heirloom recipes prepared with homegrown and local ingredients.

The Wholesome Wave Foundation works to make locally grown, sustainable foods available to home cooks, communities, and college campuses through local farmers' markets, educational programs, and farm support initiatives. Helping Michel carry on traditions are his children: Lauren, 23; Courtney, 21; Chris, 18; Drew, 10; and Ethan, 7.

Michel is the author of two cookbooks: the James Beard award-winning *Taste Pure and Simple* (Chronicle; $35) and *Homegrown, Pure and Simple* (Chronicle; $35). For more information visit *dressingroom homegrown.com*. To learn more about sustainable foods and the Wholesome Wave Foundation, go to *wholesomewave.org*.

BY **PEG SMITH**

PHOTOS **ANDY LYONS**

RECIPES AND FOOD STYLING

JILL LUST

Simply Supper

Amid holiday happenings—work, family, shopping—these meals are ready in a jingle.

READY IN 20 MINUTES!

SKILLET VEGETABLES ON CHEESE TOAST

SKILLET VEGETABLES ON CHEESE TOAST

START TO FINISH 20 min.

INGREDIENTS

8	slices crusty wheat bread
½	an 8-oz. pkg. peeled fresh whole baby (not baby-cut) carrots, halved lengthwise
1	8-oz. pkg. button mushrooms, halved
4	cloves fresh garlic, peeled and coarsely chopped
1	small red onion, cut in thin wedges
2	Tbsp. olive oil
4	oz. soft goat cheese (chèvre)
	Fresh basil (optional)

PREPARATION

1. Preheat broiler. Place bread on baking sheet; set aside.

2. In large skillet cook carrots, mushrooms, garlic, and onion in hot olive oil over medium-high heat 2 to 3 minutes until vegetables just begin to brown. Add 2 tablespoons *water;* cover and cook over medium heat 5 minutes, until vegetables are crisp-tender, stirring once. Sprinkle *salt* and *ground black pepper.*

3. Meanwhile, for cheese toasts, lightly toast bread 3 inches from broiler heat for 1 to 2 minutes. Spread goat cheese on one side of each slice. Broil 3 inches from heat for 1 to 2 minutes until cheese is softened.

4. On plates, top cheese toasts with vegetables. Drizzle additional *olive oil;* sprinkle basil. **MAKES 4 SERVINGS.**

EACH SERVING *461 cal, 21 g fat (6 g sat. fat), 13 mg chol, 596 sodium, 56 g carbo, 8 g fiber, 15 g pro. Daily Values: 84% vit. A, 8% vit. C, 9% calcium, 23% iron.*

POTATO-TOPPED BEEF BOWL

START TO FINISH 20 min.

INGREDIENTS

1	lb. ground beef
1	16-oz. pkg. frozen mixed vegetables
1	8-oz. pkg. shredded cheddar cheese (2 cups)
¼	cup snipped fresh Italian (flat-leaf) parsley
	Salt and ground black pepper
2	cups instant mashed potato flakes
2	Tbsp. butter, melted

PREPARATION

1. Preheat broiler. In extra-large skillet brown beef over medium-high heat; drain off fat. Stir in frozen vegetables. Cook, stirring occasionally, until heated through. Stir in *half* the cheese, *half* the parsley, *¼ teaspoon* salt, and *⅛ teaspoon* pepper.

2. Meanwhile, in large bowl combine 2 cups boiling *water,* potato flakes, and *1 tablespoon* of the butter. Stir until smooth. Season with salt and pepper; set aside.

3. Divide beef mixture among four 16-ounce broiler-safe dishes. Top with potatoes; sprinkle remaining cheese. Broil 3 inches from heat for 2 to 3 minutes, until cheese is melted. Drizzle remaining melted butter; sprinkle parsley. **MAKES 4 SERVINGS.**

EACH SERVING *677 cal, 42 g fat (22 g sat. fat), 152 mg chol, 692 mg sodium, 35 g carbo, 5 g fiber, 41 g pro. Daily Values: 136% vit. A, 59% vit. C, 47% calcium, 24% iron.*

POTATO-TOPPED BEEF BOWL

CHUNKY BEAN AND CHICKEN CHILI

FAST!

START TO FINISH 20 min.

INGREDIENTS

3	cups tortilla chips
1	lb. skinless, boneless chicken breasts or thighs, cut in bite-size pieces
2	tsp. cooking oil
2	19-oz. cans cannellini beans, rinsed and drained
6	oz. shredded Monterey Jack cheese with jalapeño peppers (1½ cups)
1	4.5-oz. can diced green chiles
1	14-oz. can reduced sodium chicken broth
	Fresh cilantro (optional)

PREPARATION

1. Preheat broiler. Coarsely crush *2 cups* tortilla chips.

2. In 4- to 5-quart Dutch oven brown chicken in hot oil over medium-high heat. Add beans, *1 cup* of the cheese, the chiles, broth, ½ cup *water*, and crushed chips. Bring to boiling; reduce heat. Simmer, uncovered, 5 minutes, stirring occasionally.

3. Meanwhile, for tortilla crisps, place remaining 1 cup chips on baking sheet lined with nonstick foil. Sprinkle remaining ½ cup cheese. Broil 6 inches from heat for 1 to 2 minutes, until cheese is melted and begins to brown. Top chili with tortilla crisps. Sprinkle cilantro. **MAKES 4 SERVINGS.**

EACH SERVING *575 cal, 23 g fat (10 g sat. fat), 111 mg chol, 1,172 mg sodium, 52 g carbo, 14 g fiber, 55 g pro. Daily Values: 14% vit. A, 13% vit. C, 43% calcium, 23% iron.*

CHUNKY BEAN AND CHICKEN CHILI

CHICKEN AND PASTA IN PEANUT SAUCE

CHICKEN AND PASTA IN PEANUT SAUCE

FAST!

START TO FINISH 20 min.

INGREDIENTS

8	oz. thin spaghetti
1	bunch Broccolini, cut in 2-inch lengths
1	medium red sweet pepper, cut in bite-size strips
1	lb. skinless, boneless chicken breast halves
	Salt and ground black pepper
1	Tbsp. olive oil
½	cup bottled peanut sauce
	Crushed red pepper (optional)

PREPARATION

1. In Dutch oven cook pasta according to package directions, adding Broccolini and sweet pepper during last 2 minutes of cooking. Drain; return to Dutch oven.

2. Meanwhile, halve chicken breasts horizontally. Sprinkle chicken with salt and black pepper. In extra-large skillet cook chicken in hot oil over medium-high heat for 2 minutes each side until no longer pink (170°F). Transfer to cutting board. Slice chicken; add to pasta and vegetables. Add peanut sauce. Heat through. Pass crushed red pepper. **MAKES 4 SERVINGS.**

EACH SERVING *467 cal, 10 g fat (2 g sat. fat), 66 mg chol, 634 mg sodium, 55 g carbo, 5 g fiber, 37 g pro. Daily Values: 24% vit. A, 123% vit. C, 5% calcium, 15% iron.*

BREADED PORK WITH CABBAGE AND KALE

START TO FINISH 20 min.

INGREDIENTS

1¼   lb. center-cut pork loin, cut in 4 slices
2   cups corn bread stuffing mix, crushed
2   Tbsp. olive oil
2   cups sliced red cabbage
6   cups coarsely chopped kale
⅓   cup balsamic vinegar
     Salt and ground black pepper

PREPARATION

1. Preheat oven to 250°F. Place pork slices between plastic wrap. Use flat side of meat mallet to lightly pound slices to ¼-inch thickness. Place stuffing mix in shallow dish; coat pork with stuffing mix.

2. In extra-large skillet heat *1 tablespoon* of the oil over medium-high heat. Add 2 pork slices. Cook 2 to 3 minutes each side until crisp, golden, and cooked through. Transfer to baking sheet; keep warm in oven. Repeat with remaining oil and pork.

3. Wipe skillet. Add cabbage. Cook and stir until cabbage is crisp-tender. Add kale and vinegar; cook just until wilted. Lightly sprinkle with salt and pepper. Serve alongside pork.

MAKES 4 SERVINGS.

EACH SERVING *394 cal, 14 g fat (2 g sat. fat), 78 mg chol, 769 mg sodium, 35 g carbo, 4 g fiber, 32 g pro. Daily Values: 317% vit. A, 234% vit. C, 18% calcium, 20% iron.*

BREADED PORK WITH CABBAGE AND KALE

Prize Tested RECIPES®

EVERY YEAR READERS OFFER THEIR CREATIVE BEST WITH AWARD-WINNING RECIPES. THE 2008 COLLECTION KEEPS EASE AND SIMPLICITY TOP OF MIND.

MIXED BERRY TARTLETS page 282

Categories

SPINACH-CHICKEN BREAST ROLLS
page 276

CHEDDAR-APPLE BUNDLES
page 286

CHOCOLATE SYRUP CAKE
page 278

LAYERED GREEK DIP
page 300

PRIZE TESTED RECIPES

COMFORT FOOD THAT BEATS THE BLAHS

ANGELA MARTINEZ, HOWARD BEACH, N.Y.

BRENDA MELANCON, GONZALES, LA.

LOW FAT

HEARTY OKRA SKILLET

PREP 30 min. **COOK** 35 min.

INGREDIENTS

1	large onion, chopped
1	medium red sweet pepper, chopped
3	cloves garlic, minced
1	Tbsp. olive oil
½	tsp. dried oregano, crushed
½	tsp. ground coriander
½	tsp. ground cumin
½	tsp. ground turmeric
1	bay leaf
1	cinnamon stick
1	16-oz. pkg. frozen cut okra
1	28-oz. can diced tomatoes
1	15-oz. can garbanzo beans (chickpeas), rinsed and drained
3	oz. cooked smoked chorizo (sausage), sliced
¼	cup pitted Gaeta or black olives, halved
3	cups hot cooked rice

PREPARATION

1. In a large skillet cook onion, sweet pepper, and garlic in hot oil over medium heat 5 minutes or until tender. Stir in oregano, coriander, cumin, turmeric, bay leaf, cinnamon stick, and ⅛ teaspoon *salt*. Cook and stir 1 minute. Add okra, undrained tomatoes, beans, chorizo, and olives. Bring to boiling; reduce heat. Simmer, covered, 30 minutes; stir occasionally. Remove and discard bay leaf and cinnamon stick. Serve over rice. **Makes 6 servings.**

EACH SERVING *346 cal, 10 g fat (3 g. sat. fat), 120 mg chol, 748 mg sodium, 53 g carbo, 9 g fiber, 12 g pro. Daily Values: 29% vit. A, 82% vit. C, 15% calcium, 23% iron.*

CAJUN MAC AND CHEESE

PREP 30 min. **BAKE** 35 min. **STAND** 5 min. **OVEN** 350°F

INGREDIENTS

3	cups dried tricolor or plain elbow macaroni (12 oz.)
2	cups shredded cheddar cheese (8 oz.)
4	oz. American cheese, cubed
¾	cup chopped sweet onion
2	Tbsp. minced fresh garlic
2	Tbsp. butter
½	cup sliced green onion
1	cup chopped green and/or red sweet pepper
1	12-oz. can evaporated milk
2	eggs, lightly beaten
2	Tbsp. all-purpose flour
2	tsp. yellow mustard
2	tsp. bottled hot pepper sauce
½	tsp. salt
½	tsp. paprika

PREPARATION

1. Preheat oven to 350°F. Grease a 3-quart rectangular baking dish; set aside. In a large saucepan cook macaroni according to package directions; drain. Return to saucepan. Stir in cheddar and American cheeses; set aside.

2. In a medium skillet cook sweet onion and garlic in butter until tender. Stir in green onion and sweet pepper. Cook and stir 1 minute more; stir onion mixture into pasta-cheese mixture. Spoon into prepared baking dish; set aside.

3. In a medium bowl whisk together milk, eggs, flour, mustard, hot pepper sauce, salt, and paprika until smooth; pour evenly over pasta mixture in baking dish. Bake, covered, 20 minutes. Uncover; bake 15 to 20 minutes more or until bubbly and heated through. Let stand 5 minutes. **Makes 6 servings.**

EACH SERVING *600 cal, 29 g fat (17 g sat. fat), 154 mg chol, 846 mg sodium, 56 g carbo, 3 g fiber, 28 g pro. Daily Values: 37% vit. A, 62% vit. C, 57% calcium, 17% iron.*

CHILI AND GINGER TURKEY MEATBALLS IN GINGERED TOMATO SAUCE

PREP 20 min. **COOK** 20 min.

INGREDIENTS

1   medium onion, cut up
2   to 3 fresh serrano chile peppers, seeded, and cut up *
2   Tbsp. snipped fresh cilantro
1   Tbsp. grated fresh ginger
1   ½ cups fresh whole wheat bread crumbs
1   egg yolk, lightly beaten
1½   lb. ground raw turkey
2   Tbsp. canola oil
1   large onion, cut into thin wedges
2   cloves garlic, minced
1   15-oz. can tomato sauce
¼   cup water
1   tsp. sugar
     Hot cooked rice

PREPARATION

1. In food processor combine cut-up onion; *1 to 2* serrano chile peppers, cut up; cilantro; and ginger. Cover; process until finely chopped. Transfer to bowl; stir in bread crumbs, egg yolk, 1 teaspoon *salt*, and ¼ teaspoon *ground black pepper*. Stir in turkey. Shape into 1½-inch meatballs.
2. In very large skillet brown meatballs in hot oil. Remove meatballs; set aside. Reserve oil in skillet. Add onion wedges and garlic. Cook and stir 5 minutes. Stir in tomato sauce; water; remaining serrano pepper, finely chopped; sugar; and ¼ teaspoon each *salt* and *pepper*. Bring to boiling; reduce heat. Stir meatballs into tomato mixture. Cover; cook 10 to 15 minutes or until meatballs are no longer pink. Serve over hot cooked rice.
Makes 6 servings.
*Note: Because chile peppers contain volatile oils that can burn your skin and eyes, avoid direct contact with chiles as much as possible. When working with chile peppers, wear plastic or rubber gloves. If your bare hands do touch the chile peppers, wash hands well with soap and water.

EACH SERVING *385 cal, 16 g fat (3 g sat. fat), 125 mg chol, 1,024 mg sodium, 35 g carbo, 4 g fiber, 26 g pro. Daily Values: 8% vit. A, 19% vit. C, 7% calcium, 23% iron.*

FRANK'S MEXICAN RIBS

PREP 15 min. **COOK** 1½ hr.

INGREDIENTS

5   lb. boneless pork country-style ribs
2   Tbsp. cooking oil
1   14.5 oz. can diced tomatoes
1   8-oz. can tomato sauce
1   canned chipotle pepper in adobo sauce
1   Tbsp. snipped fresh cilantro

1   tsp. dried oregano, crushed
1   tsp. ground cumin
½   tsp. salt
2   15-oz. cans pinto beans or kidney beans, rinsed and drained
     Hot cooked rice or warm flour tortillas*

PREPARATION

1. In 6- to 8-quart Dutch oven brown ribs, one-fourth at a time, in hot oil over medium-high heat, turning to brown all sides. Drain any fat. Return all meat to pan.
2. Meanwhile, in food processor or blender combine *half* the undrained tomatoes, tomato sauce, chipotle pepper, cilantro, oregano, cumin, and salt. Cover; process or blend until nearly smooth. Stir in remaining tomatoes. Pour over ribs. Bring to boiling; reduce heat. Simmer, covered, 1¼ to 1½ hours or until meat is tender. Use tongs or slotted spoon to transfer ribs to a serving platter; keep warm.
3. In medium saucepan stir together beans and 1 cup of cooking liquid from ribs. Heat through. Serve ribs with beans, remaining sauce, and rice or warm tortillas.
Makes 10 servings.
*Note: To warm tortillas, wrap in foil. Heat in 350°F oven 10 minutes.

EACH SERVING *501 cal, 22 g fat (7 g sat. fat), 114 mg chol, 668 mg sodium, 37 g carbo, 6 g fiber, 37 g pro. Daily Values: 6% vit. A, 10% vit. C, 10% calcium, 25% iron.*

LOW FAT
PERUVIAN SHRIMP CHOWDER

PREP 15 min. **COOK** 30 min.

INGREDIENTS

8   oz. fresh or frozen flounder fillets (about 2 medium fillets)
8   oz. fresh or frozen peeled and deveined medium shrimp
1   large onion, chopped
2   cloves garlic, minced
1   Tbsp. canola oil
1   14.5-oz. can diced tomatoes
1   14-oz. can vegetable or chicken broth
12   oz. potatoes, scrubbed and cubed
1½   tsp. Creole seasoning
⅛   to ¼ tsp. crushed red pepper
     Dash bottled hot pepper sauce
1   3-oz. pkg. cream cheese, softened
1   cup milk
1½   cups frozen whole kernel corn

PREPARATION

1. Thaw flounder and shrimp, if frozen. Cut flounder into bite-size pieces. Set aside. In 4- to 5-quart Dutch oven cook onion and garlic in hot oil over medium heat 12 to 15 minutes or until onion is tender and lightly browned. Turn heat down as needed to prevent onion from overbrowning.
2. Stir in undrained tomatoes, broth, 1 cup *water*, potatoes, Creole seasoning, red

pepper, and hot pepper sauce. Bring to boiling; reduce heat. Simmer, covered, 15 to 20 minutes or until potatoes are just tender.
3. Meanwhile, in bowl beat cream cheese with an electric mixer on medium to high speed until smooth. Gradually beat in milk on low speed until mixture is very smooth.
4. Add cream cheese mixture, flounder, shrimp, and corn to soup. Return to boiling; reduce heat. Simmer, uncovered, 3 to 5 minutes or until shrimp are opaque.
Makes 6 servings.

EACH SERVING *276 cal, 10 g fat (4 g sat. fat), 94 mg chol, 593 mg sodium, 28 g carbo, 4 g fiber, 21 g pro. Daily Values: 17% vit. A, 37% vit. C, 12% calcium, 13% iron.*

KID FRIENDLY
PUFFED EGYPTIAN BREAD PUDDING

PREP 25 min. **BAKE** 15 min. plus 35 min.
OVEN 400°F/350°F

INGREDIENTS

1   17.3-oz. pkg. frozen puff pastry sheets (2 sheets), thawed
¾   cup packed brown sugar
1   tsp. ground cinnamon
1½   cups flaked coconut
¾   cup golden raisins
½   cup sliced almonds
2   eggs, beaten
2   12-ounce can evaporated milk
1   Tbsp. cornstarch
2   Tbsp. honey (optional)

PREPARATION

1. Preheat oven to 400°F. Cut puff pastry sheets along creases; cut each piece in half lengthwise. Cut pieces crosswise into about 1½-inch squares. Arrange squares about 1 inch apart on 2 large ungreased baking sheets. Bake on separate oven racks 15 minutes or until pastry squares are golden, rearranging baking sheets once during baking. Reduce oven temperature to 350°F.
2. Place hot baked squares in 3-quart rectangular baking dish. In bowl combine brown sugar and cinnamon; sprinkle about ⅔ of sugar mixture over pastry. Top with coconut, raisins, and almonds. In 4-cup glass measure whisk together eggs, evaporated milk, and cornstarch; pour evenly over mixture in dish. Sprinkle over remaining brown sugar mixture.
3. Bake, covered, 20 minutes. Uncover; bake 15 to 20 minutes more or until top is golden and mixture is set. Remove from oven. Cool in pan on wire rack 20 minutes. Serve warm. Drizzle with honey. **Makes 12 servings.**

EACH SERVING *450 cal, 25 g fat (7 g sat. fat), 52 mg chol, 274 mg sodium, 49 g carbo, 2.1 g fiber, 9 g pro. Daily Values: 3% vit. A, 2% vit. C, 18% calcium, 4% iron.*

DIET-FRIENDLY MAIN DISHES

COCONUT SALMON CURRY

START TO FINISH 40 min.

INGREDIENTS

1	lb. salmon fillet, skinned and cut in 1-inch cubes
1	Tbsp. cornstarch
1	tsp. salt
½	tsp. ground black pepper
	Nonstick cooking spray
1	large onion, cut in 1-inch pieces
1	medium red sweet pepper, cut in bite-size strips
1	cup packaged fresh julienned carrots
1	Tbsp. grated fresh ginger
1	clove garlic, minced
1	to 2 tsp. curry powder
¼	tsp. crushed red pepper (optional)
1	Tbsp. canola oil
1	8-oz. can pineapple chunks (juice pack)
⅓	cup unsweetened light coconut milk
2	cups hot cooked brown rice

PREPARATION

1. In bowl toss together salmon, cornstarch, salt, and black pepper; set aside.
2. Coat a large nonstick skillet with cooking spray. Heat skillet over medium-high heat. In hot skillet cook and stir onion, sweet pepper, carrots, ginger, garlic, curry powder, and crushed red pepper for 5 to 6 minutes or until vegetables are crisp-tender. Remove from skillet; set aside.
3. Add oil to skillet. Cook seasoned salmon in hot oil about 4 minutes or until fish flakes easily; occasionally stir gently. Stir in undrained pineapple and coconut milk. Reduce heat. Cook, uncovered, 1 minute or until thickened; stir gently. Stir vegetables into skillet; heat. Serve with rice. **Makes 4 servings.**

EACH SERVING *436 cal, 18 g fat (4 g sat. fat), 67 mg chol, 686 mg sodium, 42 g carbo, 5 g fiber, 26 g pro. Daily Values: 112% vit. A, 88% vit. C, 5% calcium, 9% iron.*

LOW FAT
SPINACH-CHICKEN BREAST ROLLS

PREP 30 min. **BAKE** 50 min. **STAND** 10 min. **OVEN** 375°F

INGREDIENTS

4	medium skinless, boneless chicken breast halves (about 1¼ lb. total)
1	egg white
½	a 10-oz. pkg. frozen chopped spinach, thawed and well drained
⅓	cup low-fat cottage cheese, drained
4	oz. part-skim mozzarella cheese, shredded (1 cup)
1¼	cups light spaghetti sauce with garlic and herbs (half a 26-oz. jar)
2	Tbsp. tomato paste
6	oz. dried multigrain or whole wheat spaghetti, cooked according to package directions and drained (optional)

PREPARATION

1. Preheat oven to 375°F. Place each chicken breast between plastic wrap; lightly pound with flat side of meat mallet to about ¼-inch thickness.
2. In bowl stir together egg white, spinach, cottage cheese, and ½ cup of the mozzarella; spoon on chicken, leaving ½-inch border. Roll up from narrow side. Place, seam sides down, in 2-quart rectangular baking dish. Combine spaghetti sauce and tomato paste; spoon over chicken. Bake, covered, for 25 minutes. Uncover; sprinkle with remaining mozzarella. Bake, uncovered, about 25 minutes more or until chicken is no longer pink (170°F) and cheese is light brown. Let stand 10 minutes. Serve with spaghetti. **Makes 4 servings.**

EACH SERVING *292 cal, 7 g fat (4 g sat. fat), 101 mg chol, 718 mg sodium, 10 g carbo, 3 g fiber, 46 g pro. Daily Values: 93% vit. A, 30% vit. C, 32% calcium, 17% iron.*

MEDITERRANEAN HALIBUT AND SQUASH

PREP 15 minutes **COOK** 20 minutes

INGREDIENTS

1   lb. fresh or frozen halibut steaks, cut 1 inch thick
    Salt and ground black pepper
1   3- to 3½-lb. spaghetti squash
¼   tsp. salt
¼   cup water
1   medium onion, chopped
2   cloves garlic, minced
1   Tbsp. olive oil
2   cups sliced fresh mushrooms
1   14.5-ounce can diced tomatoes with basil, garlic, and oregano
¼   cup pitted kalamata olives, chopped
¼   cup snipped Italian (flat-leaf) parsley

PREPARATION

1. Thaw fish steaks, if frozen. Rinse steaks; pat dry with paper towels. Cut into four serving-size pieces, if necessary. Season with salt and pepper.
2. Halve squash lengthwise; discard seeds. Wrap and refrigerate one squash portion for another use. Sprinkle remaining half with ¼ teaspoon salt. Place, cut side down, in 2-quart microwave-safe baking dish with the water. Cover dish with plastic wrap, turning back corner of wrap to allow steam to escape. Microcook on 100% power (high) 20 to 22 minutes or until tender, turning once. Cool slightly. Using fork, scrape stringy squash pulp from shell onto a serving platter; cover and keep warm.
3. Meanwhile, in large skillet cook onion and garlic in hot oil 2 minutes. Add mushrooms; cook until tender. Stir in undrained tomatoes, olives, and *half* the parsley. Bring to boiling. Place fish on top of sauce. Reduce heat; cook, covered, 4 to 6 minutes per ½-inch thickness of fish until fish flakes easily when tested with fork.
4. To serve, place fish on top of squash. Spoon tomato sauce around and on top of fish. Sprinkle with remaining parsley. **Makes 4 servings.**

EACH SERVING *250 cal, 8 g fat (10 g sat. fat), 36 mg chol, 991 mg sodium, 18 g carbo, 2 g fiber, 28 g pro. Daily Values: 23% vit. A, 28% vit. C, 15% calcium, 18% iron.*

MEDITERRANEAN STIR-FRY

START TO FINISH 25 min.

INGREDIENTS

1   5.8-oz. pkg. roasted garlic-flavor couscous mix
2   medium oranges
1   Tbsp. olive oil
2   cloves garlic, minced
1   lb. medium shrimp in shells, peeled, deveined
½   cup sliced green onion
4   tsp. snipped fresh oregano or 1 tsp. dried oregano, crushed
½   tsp. freshly ground black pepper
1½ cups chopped Roma tomato (4 tomatoes)
½   cup pitted kalamata olives, quartered

PREPARATION

1. Prepare couscous according to package directions. Meanwhile, cut peel from oranges. Section oranges over small bowl to catch juice; set sections aside.
2. In large skillet heat oil over medium heat. Add garlic; cook and stir 30 seconds. Add shrimp, green onion, oregano, and pepper. Cook and stir 2 to 3 minutes or until shrimp turn opaque. Add tomatoes and olives. Cook and stir 1 minute more. Stir in oranges and juice; heat through. Serve shrimp mixture with couscous. **Makes 4 servings.**

EACH SERVING *372 cal, 9 g fat (1 g sat. fat), 172 mg chol, 774 mg sodium, 44 g carbo, 5 g fiber, 31 g pro. Daily Values: 21% vit. A, 82% vit. C, 11% calcium, 21% iron.*

PAN-SEARED TILAPIA WITH BLACK BEAN AND PAPAYA SALSA

PREP 15 minutes **COOK** 6 minutes

INGREDIENTS

1   15-oz. can black beans, rinsed, drained
1   small papaya, halved, seeded, and cubed
¼   cup finely chopped red onion
1   small fresh jalapeño pepper, seeded and chopped (see Note, page 101)
1   tsp. finely shredded lime peel
1   Tbsp. lime juice
4   6-oz. fresh or frozen tilapia fillets, ½ to ¾ inch thick
2   tsp. lemon-pepper seasoning
2   Tbsp. olive oil

PREPARATION

1. For salsa, in medium bowl combine beans, papaya, onion, jalapeño, lime peel, and lime juice. Stir well to combine; cover and chill until serving time.
2. Thaw fish, if frozen. Rinse fish; pat dry with paper towels. Sprinkle both sides of fish with lemon-pepper seasoning.
3. In very large skillet heat oil over medium heat. Cook seasoned fish in hot oil about 6 minutes or until fish flakes easily when tested with fork, turning once. To serve, stir salsa and spoon over fish just before serving. **Makes 4 servings.**

EACH SERVING *330 cal, 10 g fat (2 g sat. fat), 85 mg chol, 1,241 mg sodium, 21 g carbo, 5.5 g fiber, 40 g pro. Daily Values: 14% vit. A, 57% vit. C, 8% calcium, 15% iron.*

SPICY WILD MUSHROOM AND CHICKEN STROGANOFF

PREP 20 minutes **COOK** 10 minutes

INGREDIENTS

1   8-ounce carton fat-free dairy sour cream
2   Tbsp. all-purpose flour
2   Tbsp. tomato paste
1   Tbsp. Worcestershire sauce
½   cup beef broth
2   tsp. finely chopped canned chipotle peppers in adobo sauce
2   Tbsp. olive oil
1   medium sweet onion, halved and thinly sliced (1 cup)
1   lb. assorted fresh mushrooms, sliced (cremini, oyster, stemmed shiitake, or button) (6 cups)
½   tsp. seasoned salt
¼   tsp. ground black pepper
⅛   tsp. paprika
1   lb. skinless, boneless chicken breast halves, cut into bite-size pieces
3   cups hot cooked egg noodles
    Chopped fresh parsley (optional)

PREPARATION

1. In small bowl combine ⅔ cup sour cream, flour, tomato paste, and Worcestershire sauce. Stir in broth and chipotle peppers. Set aside.
2. In very large skillet heat *1 tablespoon* oil over medium-high heat; add onion and mushrooms. Cook, stirring frequently, until onion is tender and most of the liquid has evaporated. Meanwhile, in medium bowl combine seasoned salt, black pepper, and paprika. Add chicken; toss to coat. Add to skillet with remaining 1 tablespoon oil. Cook and stir until chicken is browned.
3. Add sour cream mixture to skillet; cook and stir until thickened and bubbly. Reduce heat and cook 2 minutes more.
4. Serve over egg noodles topped with spoonfuls of the remaining sour cream and chopped parsley. **Makes 6 servings.**

EACH SERVING *314 cal, 7 g fat (1 g sat. fat), 70 mg chol, 394 mg sodium, 36 g carbo, 3 g fiber, 26 g pro. Daily Values: 5% vit. A, 11% vit. C, 8% calcium, 15% iron.*

CHOCOLATE SYRUP CREATIONS

PRIZE TESTED RECIPES® $400 WINNER

CLINT BOULDIN, KINGS MOUNTAIN, N.C.

PRIZE TESTED RECIPES® $200 WINNER

LAURIE BALCOM, LYNDEN, WASH.

KID FRIENDLY

CHOCOLATE SYRUP CAKE

PREP 30 min. **BAKE** 1¼ hr. **OVEN** 325°F

INGREDIENTS
3	cups all-purpose flour
¼	tsp. baking powder
¼	tsp. baking soda
2¾	cups sugar
½	cup cooking oil
5	eggs
1	cup buttermilk
⅔	cup chocolate syrup
1	tsp. vanilla
1	recipe Chocolate-Buttercream Drizzle
2	Tbsp. chocolate syrup

PREPARATION

1. Preheat oven to 325°F. Grease and flour a 10-inch fluted tube pan; set aside. In bowl stir together flour, baking powder, baking soda, and ¼ teaspoon *salt*; set aside.
2. In large mixing bowl beat sugar and oil with an electric mixer on medium to high speed 1 minute or until evenly moistened. Add eggs, 1 at a time, beating well after each addition; beat until smooth. Alternately beat in flour mixture and buttermilk. Add the ⅔ cup chocolate syrup and vanilla; beat well. Pour into pan. Bake 1¼ to 1½ hours or until toothpick inserted in center comes out clean. Cool on wire rack 15 minutes. Remove from pan; cool completely on rack. Transfer cake to platter; drizzle with Chocolate-Buttercream. Just before serving, drizzle 2 tablespoons syrup around top edge. **Makes 12 to 16 servings.**
Chocolate-Buttercream Drizzle In large bowl beat 3 tablespoons softened *butter* on medium speed 30 seconds. Add ½ cup *powdered sugar*; beat well. Beat in 2 tablespoons *chocolate syrup* and ½ teaspoon *vanilla*. Beat in ¾ cup *powdered sugar*. If necessary, stir in *milk* until mixture drapes.

EACH SERVING *550 cal, 15 g fat (4 g sat. fat), 97 mg chol, 168 mg sodium, 99 g carbo, 1 g fiber, 4 g pro. Daily Values: 4% vit. A, 5% calcium, 13% iron.*

KID FRIENDLY

RASPBERRY VELVET MÉLANGE

PREP 10 min. **CHILL** 1 hr.
FREEZE according to manufacturer's directions.

INGREDIENTS
1	6-oz. pkg. raspberry-flavor gelatin
2	cups boiling water
½	cup cold water
1	cup chocolate syrup
¾	cup whipping cream
	Fresh raspberries (optional)

PREPARATION

1. In a large bowl combine gelatin and boiling water. Stir until gelatin is dissolved. Stir in the cold water, ½ *cup* chocolate syrup, and whipping cream. Stir well to combine. Cover and chill about 1 hour or until cool but not set. Pour into a 1- to 2-quart electric ice cream maker; freeze gelatin mixture according to manufacturer's instructions. Ripen, if desired.
2. Top each serving with remaining chocolate syrup. Serve with raspberries. **Makes 8 servings.**

EACH SERVING *263 cal, 9 g fat (5 g sat. fat), 31 mg chol, 137 mg sodium, 44 g carbo, 1 g fiber, 3 g pro. Daily Values: 7% vit. A, 2% calcium, 5% iron.*

BROWNIE-RASPBERRY DESSERTS

PREP 40 min. **BAKE** 30 min.
OVEN 350°F

INGREDIENTS

½	cup butter, softened
¾	cup sugar
½	tsp. salt
3	eggs
1	tsp. vanilla
1	cup chocolate-flavored syrup
1	cup all-purpose flour
1	cup whipping cream
2	oz. white baking chocolate, chopped
5	large marshmallows
1½	cups fresh or frozen unsweetened red raspberries, thawed
2	tablespoons powdered sugar
1	tsp. vanilla
	Chocolate-flavored syrup
	Fresh raspberries
	Fresh mint sprigs (optional)

PREPARATION

1. Preheat oven to 350°F. Lightly grease 13×9×2-inch baking pan; set aside. In large mixing bowl beat butter with electric mixer on medium speed 30 seconds. Add sugar and salt; beat on medium speed until well combined. Add eggs and 1 teaspoon vanilla; beat until combined. Add 1 cup chocolate syrup; beat until combined. Beat in flour until combined. Pour into prepared pan. Bake 30 minutes. Cool completely in pan on wire rack.

2. Meanwhile, in saucepan heat and stir ¼ *cup* whipping cream, white chocolate, and marshmallows over low heat until melted and smooth, stirring frequently. Remove from heat; set aside to cool slightly.

3. Place 1½ cups raspberries in food processor or blender. Cover; process or blend until smooth. Press mixture through fine-mesh sieve; discard seeds. Stir raspberry puree into marshmallow mixture.

4. In chilled large mixing bowl beat remaining ¾ cup whipping cream, powdered sugar, and 1 teaspoon vanilla with electric mixer on medium speed until soft peaks form. Gradually fold raspberry mixture into whipped cream until well combined.

5. Cut brownies into twelve 3-inch squares. For each serving, place brownie square on dessert plate. Spoon raspberry mixture on top of brownie. Drizzle with chocolate syrup; top with additional berries and fresh mint sprigs. **Makes 12 servings.**

EACH SERVING *382 cal, 18 g fat (11 g sat. fat), 101 mg chol, 207 mg sodium, 50 g carbo, 204 g fiber, 4 g pro. Daily Values: 12% vit. A, 9% vit. C, 4% calcium, 8% iron.*

CHOCOLATE MOUSSE CAKE

PREP 30 min. **BAKE** 55 min. **CHILL** 4 hr.
OVEN 350°F

INGREDIENTS

	Nonstick cooking spray
12	chocolate-flavor graham cracker squares, crushed (about 1¼ cups)
¼	cup butter
2	oz. cream cheese (¼ cup)
½	cup chocolate fudge ice cream topping
½	cup sugar
1	4-serving-size pkg. chocolate instant pudding and pie filling mix
1	12-oz. can evaporated fat-free milk
⅓	cup all-purpose flour
2	egg yolks
1	tsp. vanilla
5	egg whites
½	of an 8-oz. container frozen light whipped dessert topping, thawed
¼	cup chocolate fudge ice cream topping

PREPARATION

1. Preheat oven to 350°F. Lightly coat 9-inch springform pan with cooking spray. Sprinkle crushed graham crackers in bottom of pan; set aside.

2. In medium saucepan melt butter and cream cheese together over medium-low heat, stirring occasionally (mixture will not come together). Stir in ½ cup ice cream topping and sugar until well combined; remove from heat and let cool.

3. In large bowl combine pudding mix and evaporated milk. Whisk until thoroughly combined. Whisk in chocolate mixture, flour, egg yolks, and vanilla until well combined and smooth. In medium bowl beat egg whites with electric mixer on medium speed until soft peaks form. Gradually fold into chocolate mixture.

4. Pour chocolate mixture into prepared pan. Bake 55 to 60 minutes or until edges are puffed and firm (center will not be fully set). Cool in pan on wire rack. Edges will fall as cake cools.

5. Loosen cake from sides of pan by running thin metal spatula around edge of cake. Remove sides of pan. Place cake on serving platter. In small bowl stir together dessert topping and ¼ cup ice cream topping. Spread over top of cake. Cover; chill 4 to 24 hours before serving. **Makes 12 servings.**

EACH SERVING *300 cal, 11 g fat (6 g sat. fat), 51 mg chol, 330 mg sodium, 44 g carbo, 1 g fiber, 6 g pro. Daily Values: 7% vit. A, 1% vit. C, 16% calcium, 6% iron.*

TACO SAUCE MOLE

START TO FINISH 10 minutes

INGREDIENTS

1	8-oz. bottle red chile flavored taco sauce
¼	cup chocolate-flavored syrup
1	Tbsp. sugar
1	Tbsp. ground cumin
1	tsp. chili powder
1	tsp. garlic powder
½	tsp. ground cinnamon

PREPARATION

1. In medium saucepan whisk together taco sauce, chocolate syrup, and sugar. Whisk in cumin, chili powder, garlic powder, and cinnamon. Heat through. Serve warm as a steak sauce or barbecue sauce.
Makes 1½ cups.

EACH SERVING *19 cal, 0 g fat (0 g sat. fat), 0 mg chol, 81 mg sodium, 5 g carbo, 0 g fiber, 0 g pro. Daily Values: 1% vit. A.*

ALMOND FUDGE CUPS

PREP 15 minutes **FREEZE** overnight

INGREDIENTS

½	cup chocolate ice cream topping
½	of an 8-oz. carton frozen whipped dessert topping, thawed
⅔	cup finely chopped almonds, toasted
6	3-oz. paper cups

PREPARATION

1. Place ice cream topping in large bowl. Gradually stir in whipped topping; fold in *half* of the almonds. Spoon into paper cups; sprinkle with remaining nuts. Cover cups with foil. Freeze overnight. **Makes 6 cups.**

EACH SERVING *245 cal, 8 g fat (4 g sat. fat), 0 mg chol, 20 mg sodium, 40 g carbo, 2 g fiber, 3 g pro. Daily Values: 3% calcium, 2% iron.*

SUPER BOWL SNACKS

PRIZE TESTED RECIPES® $400 WINNER

TERESA RALSTON, NEW ALBANY, OHIO

PRIZE TESTED RECIPES® $200 WINNER

L. D. MONTGOMERY, NASHVILLE, TENN.

SPICY SHRIMP NACHOS

PREP 30 min. **BROIL** 1 min.

INGREDIENTS

1   cup mango, seeded, peeled, and chopped
1   medium red sweet pepper, chopped
2   Tbsp. finely chopped red onion
1   fresh jalapeño chile pepper, seeded and finely chopped*
2   Tbsp. packed brown sugar
2   Tbsp. Jamaican jerk seasoning
1   lb. peeled, deveined uncooked shrimp
     Nonstick cooking spray
8   cups tortilla chips (8 oz.)
4   oz. Monterey Jack cheese with jalapeño peppers or Monterey Jack cheese, shredded

PREPARATION

1. Preheat broiler. For salsa, in bowl stir together mango, sweet pepper, onion, and chile pepper; set aside. In large bowl stir together brown sugar and jerk seasoning. Add shrimp and toss to coat. Coat grill pan or large skillet with cooking spray. Heat over medium-high heat. Add half the shrimp at a time to the pan. Cook 1 to 2 minutes each side or until shrimp are opaque. Remove and set aside. If desired, coarsely chop shrimp.
2. Spread tortilla chips on a broiler-safe platter or baking sheet. Top with shrimp and salsa. Sprinkle with cheese. Broil 4 inches from heat 1 to 2 minutes or until heated through and cheese is melted. **Makes 8 servings.**
*NOTE Because hot chile peppers contain volatile oils that can burn skin and eyes, avoid direct contact and wear plastic or rubber gloves. If your bare hands touch the chile peppers, wash your hands well with soap and water.

EACH SERVING *283 cal, 12 g fat (4 g sat. fat), 99 mg chol, 507 mg sodium, 27 g carbo, 2 g fiber, 17 g pro. Daily Values: 17% vit. A, 45% vit. C, 19% calcium, 13% iron.*

KID FRIENDLY

BURGER-POTATO BITES

PREP 15 min. **BAKE** 18 min. **COOK** 5 min. **OVEN** 400°F/Broil

INGREDIENTS

16   large frozen French-fried waffle-cut potatoes (⅓ of a 22-oz. pkg.)
1   lb. ground beef or turkey
2   to 3 tsp. grilling seasoning blend
4   slices cheddar cheese, cut in quarters (4 oz.)
4   cherry tomatoes, sliced
     Mustard, ketchup, dairy sour cream, and/or dill pickle slices

PREPARATION

1. Preheat oven to 400°F. Line baking sheet with foil. Evenly space potatoes on baking sheet. Bake potatoes 18 to 20 minutes or until crisp and lightly browned. Remove from oven. Adjust oven racks and preheat broiler.
2. Meanwhile, in medium bowl combine meat and seasoning. Form into sixteen 1-ounce mini burgers (about 2 tablespoons). In 12-inch skillet cook burgers, uncovered, over medium-high heat for 5 minutes or until temperature registers 160°F on an instant-read thermometer, turning burgers once halfway through cooking. Drain fat. Top each potato with a burger, cheese quarter, and tomato slice. Broil 4 to 5 inches from heat 1 to 2 minutes or until cheese is melted and tomato begins to brown. Serve with mustard, ketchup, sour cream, and/or pickles. **Makes 16 snacks.**

EACH SERVING (1 SNACK) *121 cal, 9 g fat (4 g sat. fat), 28 mg chol, 152 mg sodium, 3 g carbo, 0 g fiber, 7 g pro. Daily Values: 2% vit. A, 3% vit. C, 6% calcium, 4% iron.*

CHICKEN ARTICHOKE LOAF WITH BACON

START TO FINISH 30 min.

INGREDIENTS

1	1-lb. loaf French bread Romaine lettuce
2	medium Roma tomatoes, thinly sliced
¾	cup light mayonnaise or salad dressing
1	6-oz. jar marinated artichoke hearts, drained and chopped
2	tsp. finely shredded lemon peel
1	tsp. cracked black pepper
3	cups shredded cooked chicken
8	slices bacon, crisp cooked
12	pimiento-stuffed olives

PREPARATION

1. Preheat oven to 400°F. Cut thin slice from top of bread. Hollow out bottom of bread leaving ¼-to ½-inch-thick shell. Place bread, cut side up, on baking sheet. Bake, uncovered, 8 minutes or until lightly toasted. Let stand 5 minutes. Line bottom of loaf with lettuce leaves and tomato slices.
2. Meanwhile in bowl combine mayonnaise, artichoke hearts, lemon peel, and black pepper. Fold in chicken. Spoon chicken mixture atop tomatoes. Add bacon and bread top.
3. Insert hors d'oeuvre pick into each olive and space equally along loaf. Slice loaf into servings between picks. **Makes 12 servings.**

EACH SERVING *291 cal, 13 g fat (3 g sat. fat), 42 mg chol, 622 mg sodium, 25 g carbo, 1.5 g fiber, 17 g pro. Daily Values: 15% vit. A, 11% vit. C, 3% calcium, 12% iron.*

CHILI DIP

PREP 15 min. **BAKE** 8 min.
OVEN 400°F

INGREDIENTS

1	lb. lean ground beef
1	cup chopped onion
2	tsp. chili powder
1	15-oz. can pork and beans in tomato sauce
1	15-oz. can chili beans in chili gravy
2	to 4 Tbsp. chopped sliced pickled jalapeño peppers (see Note, page 280)
1	cup finely shredded cheddar cheese (4 oz.) Tortilla chips

PREPARATION

1. Preheat oven to 400° F. In large skillet cook beef and onion until beef is browned and onion is tender. Drain excess fat. Stir in chili powder; cook and stir 1 minute. Stir in undrained pork and beans, undrained chili beans, and jalapeños. Cook and stir until thickened and bubbly.*
2. Transfer to shallow 1½-quart baking dish. Sprinkle with cheese. Bake 8 to 10 minutes or until bubbly. Serve with tortilla chips. **Makes 20 servings.**

*NOTE If desired, transfer mixture to 2- to 3-quart slow cooker. Sprinkle with cheese. Cook on high-heat setting 45 to 60 minutes or on low-heat setting 1 to ½ to 2 hours until cheese is melted and mixture is bubbly on edges. Keep warm on low-heat setting up to 2 hours.

EACH SERVING (¼-cup) *178 cal, 8 g fat (3 g sat. fat), 21 mg chol, 251 mg sodium, 18 g carbo, 3.3 g fiber, 9 g pro. Daily Values: 3% vit. A, 2% vit. C, 8% calcium, 8% iron.*

SAUSAGE SPIRAL LOAF

PREP 30 min. **BAKE** 40 min.
STAND 10 min. **OVEN** 350°

INGREDIENTS

12	oz. bulk mild Italian sausage
2	cups sliced fresh mushrooms
1	cup chopped onion
2	cloves garlic, minced
1½	tsp. dried Italian seasoning, crushed
¼	tsp. ground black pepper
1	cup shredded mozzarella cheese (4 oz.)
¼	cup grated Parmesan cheese
1	13.8 oz. pkg. refrigerated pizza dough
½	of a 26-oz. jar pasta sauce (about 1½ cups)

PREPARATION

1. In large skillet cook sausage, mushrooms, onion, and garlic over medium heat until sausage is no longer pink and mushrooms are tender. Drain off fat. Stir in Italian seasoning and pepper. Cool mixture slightly (about 15 minutes). Stir in cheeses.
2. Preheat oven to 350° F. Roll out pizza dough on lightly floured surface to 15×10-inch rectangle. Spoon on meat mixture to within 1 inch of edge of dough. Roll up dough from long side in spiral. Pinch edges of dough to seal. Place diagonally in lightly greased 15×10×1-inch baking pan or shallow roasting pan. Bake 40 minutes. Let stand 10 minutes.
3. Meanwhile, in medium saucepan cook and stir pasta sauce over medium-low heat until heated through. To serve, slice roll into 1-inch-thick slices. Serve with warm pasta sauce for dipping. **Makes 15 slices.**

EACH SERVING (1 SLICE) *181 cal, 10 g fat (4 g sat. fat), 23 mg chol, 466 mg sodium, 14 g carbo, 1 g fiber, 8 g pro. Daily Values: 3% vit. A, 3% vit. C, 9% calcium, 7% iron.*

SHRIMP TACOS

PREP 20 min. **MARINATE** 30 min.
BROIL 4 min.

INGREDIENTS

1	lb. fresh or frozen medium shrimp in shells
¼	cup canola oil
1	tsp. finely shredded lime peel
2	Tbsp. fresh lime juice
¼	tsp. *each* salt, cayenne pepper, ground cumin, and freshly ground black pepper
1	clove garlic, minced
⅓	cup *each* mayonnaise or salad dressing, and dairy sour cream
⅛	tsp. *each* cayenne pepper and ground cumin
½	of a fresh medium jalapeño pepper, seeded and finely chopped (see Note, page 280)
2	Tbsp. snipped fresh Italian (flat-leaf) parsley
1½	cups shredded cabbage
1	medium tomato, chopped
8	white corn taco shells, warmed according to package directions
2	green onions, sliced Fresh lime wedges

PREPARATION

1. Thaw shrimp, if frozen. Peel and devein shrimp. Place shrimp in large resealable plastic bag set in shallow bowl.
2. In bowl combine oil; lime peel; lime juice; ¼ teaspoon *each* salt, cayenne pepper, ground cumin, and black pepper; and garlic. Pour over shrimp. Seal bag; turn bag to coat shrimp. Marinate in refrigerator 30 minutes.
3. Meanwhile, in small bowl stir together mayonnaise, sour cream, ⅛ teaspoon *each* cayenne pepper and ground cumin, jalapeño pepper, and parsley. Stir in cabbage and tomato until coated. Cover; refrigerate until serving time.
4. Preheat broiler. Drain shrimp; discard marinade. Arrange shrimp on unheated rack of broiler pan. Broil 4 to 5 inches from heat 2 minutes. Turn shrimp over; broil 2 to 4 minutes more or until shrimp turns opaque.
5. Divide cabbage mixture among taco shells; top with shrimp. Sprinkle with green onion. Serve with lime wedges.
Makes 8 servings.

EACH SERVING *278 cal, 20 g fat (3 g sat. fat), 93 mg chol, 270 mg sodium, 13 g carbo, 2 g fiber, 13 g pro. Daily Values: 10% vit. A, 24% vit. C, 7% calcium, 10% iron.*

FROZEN FRUIT TO THE RESCUE

SONALI RUDER, NEW YORK, N.Y.

LESLEY PEW, LYNN, MASS.

MIXED BERRY TARTLETS

PREP 25 min. **BAKE** 20 min. **COOL** 5 min. **OVEN** 400°F

INGREDIENTS
1   15-oz. pkg. rolled refrigerated unbaked piecrusts (2)
    Nonstick cooking spray
2   Tbsp. sugar
1   Tbsp. cornstarch
1   12-oz. pkg. frozen mixed berries
1   Tbsp. lemon juice
⅓   cup whipping cream
¼   cup purchased lemon curd
1   tsp. sugar
¼   tsp. vanilla
    Mint sprigs (optional)

PREPARATION
1. Let piecrusts stand at room temperature 15 minutes. Preheat oven to 400°F. Lightly coat twelve 2½-inch muffin cups with cooking spray. For pastry shells, unroll piecrusts. Use a 3½- to 4-inch round cutter to cut 6 rounds from each crust. Press rounds into prepared muffin cups, pleating to fit.
2. For tartlet filling, in medium bowl combine 2 tablespoons sugar and cornstarch; stir in berries and lemon juice. Spoon berry mixture into pastry shells. Bake 20 minutes or until pastry is golden. Cool in muffin cups on a wire rack for 5 minutes. Carefully remove tartlets from muffin cups; cool completely on wire rack.
3. In medium mixing bowl combine whipping cream, lemon curd, 1 teaspoon sugar, and vanilla; beat with wire whisk or with electric mixer on medium speed until cream mixture mounds and is fluffy. Spoon on tarts. Garnish each tartlet with a mint sprig.
Makes 12 servings.

EACH SERVING *229 cal, 12 g fat (5 g sat. fat), 17 mg chol, 152 mg sodium, 29 g carbo, 2 g fiber, 1 g pro. Daily Values: 2% vit. A, 13% vit. C, 1% calcium, 1% iron.*

CORNMEAL-BLUEBERRY SCONES

PREP 25 min. **BAKE** 12 min. **OVEN** 450°F

INGREDIENTS
    Nonstick cooking spray
1⅓ cups all-purpose flour
⅔   cup yellow cornmeal
2   Tbsp. *each* granulated sugar and packed brown sugar
1½ tsp. baking powder
¼   tsp. baking soda
⅓   cup cold butter, cut up
½   cup buttermilk
1   egg
1½ tsp. finely shredded lime peel
1   cup frozen blueberries*
1   tsp. cornstarch
3   to 4 tsp. lime juice
1   cup powdered sugar
3   Tbsp. chopped almonds, toasted

PREPARATION
1. Preheat oven to 450°F. Coat a baking sheet with cooking spray.
2. In large bowl combine flour, cornmeal, granulated sugar, brown sugar, baking powder, baking soda, and ½ teaspoon *salt*. Cut in butter until flour mixture resembles coarse crumbs. Make a well in center. Combine buttermilk, egg, and lime peel; add all at once to flour mixture. Stir with fork just until moistened.
3. Toss berries with cornstarch to coat; add to flour mixture. Stir gently 3 to 5 turns, just until berries are incorporated (do not overmix). Using large spoon, drop dough into 12 mounds on baking sheet, leaving 1 inch between mounds. Bake 12 to 15 minutes or until tops are golden. For icing, in small bowl whisk enough lime juice into powdered sugar until drizzling consistency. Drizzle over warm scones. Sprinkle with nuts. Serve warm. **Makes 12 scones.**
*NOTE Leave berries in the freezer until ready to toss with cornstarch.

EACH SERVING (1 SCONE) *203 cal, 7 g fat (4 g sat. fat), 32 mg chol, 225 mg sodium, 33 g carbo, 1 g fiber, 2 g pro. Daily Values: 4% vit. A, 3% vit. C, 7% calcium, 7% iron.*

ALOHA UPSIDE-DOWN CAKE

PREP 25 min. **BAKE** 25 min.
COOL 10 min. **OVEN** 350°F

INGREDIENTS

1	8-oz. can pineapple chunks (juice pack)
¼	cup butter
2	cups frozen chopped mango
⅓	cup flaked coconut, toasted
¼	cup macadamia nuts, coarsely chopped
¼	cup packed brown sugar
1	Tbsp. crystallized ginger, finely chopped
1	1-layer size yellow cake mix
2	eggs
	Fresh mint sprigs
	Mango sorbet

PREPARATION

1. Preheat oven to 350°F. Drain pineapple, reserving juice.
2. Melt butter in 10-inch oven-going skillet. Add pineapple chunks, frozen mango, coconut, macadamia nuts, brown sugar, and crystallized ginger. Stir to combine and dissolve sugar. Cook and stir until mixture is thickened and bubbly.
3. In large mixing bowl combine cake mix, eggs, and reserved pineapple juice. Beat with electric mixer on low speed until blended; beat 2 minutes on medium speed. Pour batter over fruit in skillet.
4. Bake 25 minutes or until wooden toothpick inserted near center comes out clean. Cool in skillet on wire rack 10 minutes. Carefully invert onto serving platter. Remove skillet. Serve warm with mint sprigs and mango sorbet.
Makes 8 servings.

EACH SERVING *426 cal, 15 g fat (6 g sat. fat), 87 mg chol, 79 g carbo, 2 g fiber, 4 g pro. Daily Values: 31% vit. A, 36% vit. C, 4% calcium, 10% iron.*

CHIPOTLE CHILE CHICKEN WITH BLUEBERRY PEPPER SALSA

START TO FINISH 25 min. **OVEN** 400°F

INGREDIENTS

	Nonstick cooking spray
2	Tbsp. honey
2	tsp. finely chopped chipotle chile pepper in adobo sauce
1	Tbsp. butter, melted
1	tsp. dried oregano, crushed
½	tsp. salt
4	skinless, boneless chicken breast halves
1½	cups frozen blueberries, thawed, drained
1	11-oz. can mandarin oranges, drained
3	Tbsp. finely chopped red onion
1	tsp. finely shredded lime peel
2	tsp. lime juice

PREPARATION

1. Preheat oven to 400°F. Coat 13×9×2-inch baking pan with cooking spray; set aside. In small bowl stir together *1 tablespoon* honey, *1 teaspoon* chipotle pepper, melted butter, oregano, and salt. Brush both sides of chicken with chipotle mixture. Arrange chicken in prepared pan. Bake 15 to 20 minutes or until done (170°F).
2. Meanwhile in bowl combine blueberries, oranges, red onion, remaining honey and chipotle, lime peel, and lime juice. Serve salsa with chicken. **Makes 4 servings.**

EACH SERVING *279 cal, 5 g fat (2 g sat. fat), 90 mg chol, 420 mg sodium, 25 g carbo, 2 g fiber, 34 g pro. Daily Values: 17% vit. A, 59% vit. C, 4% calcium, 9% iron.*

DOUBLE BERRY STREUSEL-TOPPED CAKE

PREP 25 min. **BAKE** 25 min.
COOL 30 min. **OVEN** 400°F

INGREDIENTS

2	cups all-purpose flour
¼	cup sugar
1	Tbsp. baking powder
½	tsp. salt
6	Tbsp. butter
¾	cup milk
1	egg, lightly beaten
1	tsp. vanilla
1	cup frozen blueberries, thawed, drained
1	16-oz. container frozen sweetened sliced strawberries, thawed
⅓	cup all-purpose flour
3	Tbsp. sugar
3	Tbsp. butter
	Sweetened whipped cream (optional)

PREPARATION

1. Preheat oven to 400°F. Grease bottom of 13×9×2-inch baking pan or coat with nonstick cooking spray; set aside.
2. In mixing bowl stir together 2 cups flour, ¼ cup sugar, baking powder, and salt. Cut in 6 tablespoons butter until mixture resembles coarse meal; set aside. In bowl stir together milk, egg, and vanilla; add to flour mixture, stirring until moistened. Fold in blueberries. Spread evenly in prepared pan (batter will be thin in pan). Spoon undrained strawberries over batter in pan.
3. In bowl stir together ⅓ cup flour and 3 tablespoons sugar. Cut in 3 tablespoons butter until mixture resembles fine crumbs. Sprinkle over berries. Bake 25 to 30 minutes or until set and top is evenly browned. Cool 30 minutes before serving. Serve with whipped cream.
Makes 12 servings.

EACH SERVING *256 cal, 10 g fat (6 g sat. fat), 42 mg chol, 231 mg sodium, 38 g carbo, 2 g fiber, 4 g pro. Daily Values: 7% vit. A, 15% vit. C, 5% calcium, 7% iron.*

LAYERED BLUEBERRY LEMON-GINGER PIE

PREP 30 min. **BAKE** 10 min.
CHILL up to 24 hr. **OVEN** 450°F

INGREDIENTS

½	of a 15-oz. pkg. rolled refrigerated unbaked piecrust (1 crust)
¾	cup sugar
3	Tbsp. cornstarch
3	cups frozen unsweetened blueberries
4	Tbsp. lemon juice
2	6-oz. containers lemon yogurt
2	to 3 tsp. finely chopped crystallized ginger
1	4-serving-size package vanilla instant pudding and pie filling mix
	Frozen whipped topping, thawed

PREPARATION

1. Prepare one 9-inch piecrust according to package directions. Cool.
2. In medium saucepan stir together sugar and cornstarch; stir in blueberries and *2 tablespoons* lemon juice. Cook and stir over low heat until berries are thawed and juicing out. Increase heat to medium; cook and stir until thickened and bubbly. Cook and stir 2 minutes more. Cool.
3. In large mixing bowl combine yogurt, remaining 2 tablespoons lemon juice, and crystallized ginger. Add pudding mix; beat with wire whisk or rotary beater until blended and slightly thickened. Spread blueberry mixture in baked pie shell; spread pudding mixture over blueberries. Cover surface; chill for up to 24 hours. To serve, top with whipped topping.
Makes 8 servings.

EACH SERVING *334 cal, 9 g fat (4 g sat. fat), 5 mg chol, 315 mg sodium, 62 g carbo, 1.6 g fiber, 2 g pro. Daily Values: 1% vit. A, 10% vit. C, 7% calcium, 2% iron.*

HOT DRINKS

CAROLYN BROWN, FLORENCE, AL.

ELAINE COLLINS-WYNTER, BRONX, N.Y.

LOW FAT

CITRUS TEA WITH TARRAGON

PREP 15 min. **STAND** 20 min.

INGREDIENTS
½ cup orange juice
½ cup sugar
¼ cup honey
¼ cup cold water
3 Tbsp. lemon juice
2 Tbsp. lime juice
½ cup packed fresh tarragon leaves
8 cups water
4 Earl Grey tea bags
 Orange slices (optional)
 Fresh tarragon sprigs (optional)

PREPARATION
1. In a small saucepan combine orange juice, sugar, honey, the ¼ cup cold water, lemon juice, and lime juice. Bring to boiling over medium-high heat, stirring constantly. Remove from heat; let stand 15 minutes.
2. Place citrus mixture in a blender. Add ½ cup tarragon leaves; cover and blend 30 seconds. Line a fine mesh strainer with a double thickness of cheesecloth. Strain citrus mixture through the sieve; discard any solids.
3. In a large saucepan bring the 8 cups water to boiling. Remove from heat. Add tea bags; steep for 5 minutes. Remove and discard tea bags. Stir strained citrus mixture into tea. Garnish each serving with orange slices and a tarragon sprig. **Makes 8 servings.**

EACH SERVING *91 cal, 0 g fat (0 g sat. fat), 0 mg chol, 10 mg sodium, 24 g carbo, 0 g fiber, 0 g pro. Daily Values: 7% vit. A, 28% vit. C, 2% calcium, 2% iron.*

FAST!

CHOCOLATE HONEY-BOURBON

PREP 10 min. **STAND** 10 min.

INGREDIENTS
4 cups milk
2 vanilla beans or 2 tsp. vanilla
4 oz. bittersweet chocolate, chopped
¼ cup honey-bourbon liqueur or bourbon
1 Tbsp. honey (optional)

PREPARATION
1. In a large saucepan heat milk just to simmering. Meanwhile, if using vanilla beans, split beans lengthwise. Scrape out seeds. Remove milk from heat; add beans and seeds. Let stand, covered, 10 minutes.
2. Add chocolate to milk mixture; return to low heat, stirring or whisking until chocolate is melted and milk mixture is hot. Whisk in liqueur and (if using) vanilla and honey. Serve immediately. **Makes 4 servings.**

EACH SERVING *303 cal, 16 g fat (10 g sat. fat), 20 mg chol, 101 mg sodium, 27 g carbo, 2 g fiber, 10 g pro. Daily Values: 9% vit. A, 1% vit. C, 30% calcium, 11% iron.*

APRICOT GREEN TEA

START TO FINISH 15 min.

INGREDIENTS

8	cups water
12	dried apricot halves
4	green tea bags
½	cup apricot nectar
¼	cup packed brown sugar or Demerara sugar
¼	tsp. ground ginger
8	cinnamon sticks

PREPARATION

1. In 4-quart Dutch oven combine water, apricot halves, green tea bags, nectar, brown sugar, and ginger. Bring to boiling. Reduce heat. Simmer, covered, 10 minutes. **2.** Place cinnamon stick in each mug. Strain tea mixture; pour into prepared mugs. **Makes 8 servings.**

EACH SERVING *64 cal, 0 g fat (0 g sat. fat), 0 mg chol, 10 mg sodium, 16 g carbo, 1 g fiber, 0 g pro. Daily Values: 8% vit. A, 3% calcium, 2% iron.*

DOUBLE CHOCOLATE HOT CHOCOLATE

START TO FINISH 25 min.

INGREDIENTS

3	cups milk
2	cups half-and-half or light cream
6	oz. dark chocolate baking pieces (1 cup)
2	Tbsp. unsweetened cocoa powder
2	Tbsp. sugar
1	tsp. vanilla

PREPARATION

1. In large saucepan whisk together milk, half-and-half, chocolate pieces, cocoa powder, and sugar. Stir over medium heat until chocolate is melted and mixture just comes to boiling. Remove from heat. Stir in vanilla. **Makes 6 servings.**

EACH SERVING *338 cal, 21 g fat (7 g sat. fat), 41 mg chol, 85 mg sodium, 31 g carbo, 2.4 g fiber, 8 g pro. Daily Values: 10% vit. A, 2% vit. C, 24% calcium, 5% iron.*

MINTY WARM TEA

PREP 15 min.

INGREDIENTS

3	cups apple juice
1	cup water
2	Tbsp. honey
1	Tbsp. lime juice
¼	cup lightly packed fresh mint leaves
3	green tea bags

PREPARATION

1. In large saucepan combine apple juice, water, honey, and lime juice. Bring to boiling. Remove from heat. Add mint leaves and tea bags. Cover; let steep 4 minutes. Remove tea bags and mint leaves before serving. **Makes 4 servings.**

EACH SERVING *143 cal, 0 g fat (0 g sat. fat), 0 mg chol, 10 mg sodium, 36 g carbo, .6 g fiber, 0 g pro. Daily Values: 6% vit. C, 3% calcium, 8% iron.*

RASPBERRY-SCENTED CHOCOLATE CHAI TEA

PREP 15 min. **STAND** 3 min.

INGREDIENTS

1	cup water
2	raspberry-flavor tea bags
2	Tbsp. sugar
3	Tbsp. unsweetened cocoa powder
2½	cups milk
½	tsp. ground cinnamon
¼	tsp. almond extract
	Whipped cream, fresh raspberries, and/or chocolate shavings

PREPARATION

1. In small saucepan bring water to boiling. Remove from heat. Add tea bags. Cover; let stand 3 minutes. Discard tea bags. Stir in sugar and cocoa powder. Bring to boiling. Stir in milk, cinnamon, and almond extract. Cook and stir over medium heat until heated through (do not boil). Ladle into coffee mugs. Garnish with whipped cream, fresh raspberries, and/or chocolate shavings. **Makes 4 servings.**

EACH SERVING *120 cal, 4 g fat (2 g sat. fat), 12 mg chol, 63 mg sodium, 16 g carbo, .2 g fiber, 6 g pro. Daily Values: 6% vit. A, 1% vit. C, 23% calcium, 4% iron.*

WHITE CHOCOLATE RASPBERRY COMFORT

START TO FINISH 15 min.

INGREDIENTS

3	cups whole milk
⅓	cup seedless raspberry preserves
3	oz. white chocolate, cut up, or white baking pieces
1	tsp. vanilla
⅛	tsp. *each* ground cloves and ground allspice
20	plain or flavored tiny marshmallows

PREPARATION

1. In a medium saucepan combine milk, preserves, white chocolate, vanilla, and spices. Cook and stir over medium heat until white chocolate is melted. Serve in mugs topped with marshmallows. **Makes 4 servings.**

EACH SERVING *333 cal, 13 g fat (8 g sat. fat), 22 mg chol, 113 mg sodium, 45 g carbo, .3 g fiber, 7 g pro. Daily Values: 4% vit. A, 4% vit. C, 24% calcium, 1% iron.*

CREATE WITH CHEESE

KID FRIENDLY
CHEDDAR-APPLE BUNDLES

PREP 25 min. **BAKE** 20 min. **COOL** 20 min. **OVEN** 400°F

INGREDIENTS

- ½ cup packed brown sugar
- ½ cup chopped pecans
- 2 cups all-purpose flour
- 8 oz. white cheddar cheese, shredded (2 cups)
- 1 Tbsp. granulated sugar
- ½ cup butter, cut up
- 6 to 8 Tbsp. cold water
- 2 medium Granny Smith or Jonathan apples, peeled, cored, and chopped (about 2 cups)
- 3 Tbsp. fig jam or apricot preserves

PREPARATION

1. Combine brown sugar and pecans; set aside. In food processor combine flour, ½ cup cheese, granulated sugar, and ¼ teaspoon *salt*; cover and process with one on/off turn. Add butter. Cover; process with several on/off turns until size of small peas. With processor running, slowly add water to make dough come together in a ball. Gently knead until smooth.

2. Preheat oven to 400°F. Divide dough in 8 pieces. For each bundle, on floured surface roll dough in 8-inch circle. Place 3 tablespoons cheese and ¼ cup apple in center. Sprinkle with 1 tablespoon nut mixture. Brush dough edges with water. Bring up dough edges and press together to seal. Sealed sides up, place on parchment-lined baking sheet. Bake 20 to 25 minutes or until pastry is golden. Spoon preserves on each bundle. Cool 20 minutes on baking sheet. Serve warm. **Makes 8 servings.**

EACH SERVING *474 cal, 26 g fat (14 g sat. fat), 60 mg chol, 340 mg sodium, 50 g carbo, 2 g fiber, 9 g pro. Daily Values: 13% vit. A, 4% vit. C, 23% calcium, 12% iron.*

BERRY BLUE CHEESE SPREAD

PREP 25 min. **CHILL** up to 4 hr.

INGREDIENTS

- ½ cup dried blueberries
- 1 cup boiling water
- 1 8-oz. pkg. cream cheese, softened
- 6 oz. blue cheese, coarsely crumbled
- 2 green onions, chopped
- 1 clove garlic, minced
- ½ cup coarsely chopped pecans
  Assorted whole grain crackers or cracker bread, broken

PREPARATION

1. Place dried berries in small bowl. Pour boiling water over berries. Let stand 1 minute. Drain; set aside.

2. In large mixing bowl beat cream cheese and blue cheese with an electric mixer on medium speed until nearly smooth. Stir in drained berries, green onion, and garlic just until combined. Transfer spread to serving bowl. Cover; refrigerate up to 4 hours before serving. To serve, sprinkle with pecans and serve with crackers. **Makes 16 (2-Tbsp.) servings.**

EACH SERVING *130 cal, 10 g fat (5 g sat. fat), 24 mg chol, 193 mg sodium, 6 g carbo, 1 g fiber, 4 g pro. Daily Values: 6% vit. A, 1% vit. C, 8% calcium, 3% iron.*

BLUE CHEESE APRICOT BITES

START TO FINISH 25 min.

INGREDIENTS

2	tsp.	butter
2	Tbsp.	finely chopped walnuts
2	tsp.	sugar
½	tsp.	finely snipped fresh rosemary or ¼ tsp. finely crushed dried rosemary
1	oz.	blue cheese, such as Gorgonzola cheese or Roquefort cheese
1	oz.	cream cheese (2 Tbsp.)
16		dried apricots

PREPARATION

1. In small skillet melt butter. Add walnuts and sugar; cook and stir 2 to 3 minutes or until walnuts are lightly toasted. Stir in rosemary; cook 30 seconds more. Transfer nuts to foil-lined baking sheet and cool.
2. Meanwhile, in small bowl beat blue cheese and cream cheese with electric mixer on medium speed until smooth.
3. Spoon small amount of cheese mixture on top of each apricot. Sprinkle each with nut mixture. **Makes 16 servings.**

EACH SERVING *33 cal, 2 g fat (1 g sat. fat), 5 mg chol, 24 mg sodium, 3 g carbo, 0 g fiber, 1 g pro. Daily Values: 4% vit. A, 1% calcium, 1% iron.*

BRIE BITES WITH GINGERED FIG

PREP 20 min. **BAKE** 5 min. **OVEN** 350°F

INGREDIENTS

½		of an 8-oz. round Brie cheese, chilled
2	Tbsp.	fig jam or preserves
2	tsp.	crystallized ginger, finely chopped
1	tsp.	finely shredded lemon peel
1		2.1-oz. box baked miniature phyllo dough shells
¼	cup	panko (Japanese-style bread crumbs)
2	tsp.	olive oil

PREPARATION

1. Preheat oven 350°F. Cut chilled Brie into 15 pieces; set aside. In small bowl combine fig jam, ginger, and lemon peel. Divide evenly among phyllo shells. Add cube of Brie. Combine panko and oil; sprinkle over Brie cups. Place in shallow baking pan. Bake 5 to 8 minutes or until crumbs are lightly browned. Serve warm.
Makes 15 appetizers.

EACH SERVING *70 cal, 4 g fat (1.4 g sat. fat), 8 mg chol, 62 mg sodium, 6 g carbo, 0 g fiber, 2 g pro. Daily Values: 1% vit. A, 2% vit. C, 2% calcium, 3% iron.*

BRIE QUESADILLA WEDGES

PREP 15 min. **COOK** 4 min.

INGREDIENTS

		Nonstick cooking spray
2		10-inch flour tortillas
4	tsp.	hot jalapeño jelly (red)
¼	cup	pecans, toasted and finely chopped
4	oz.	Brie cheese, diced
2	Tbsp.	slivered fresh basil

PREPARATION

1. Coat one side of each tortilla with cooking spray. Place tortillas, sprayed sides down, on a cutting board or waxed paper. Spread tortillas with pepper jelly; sprinkle with nuts. Place *half* of cheese on one half of each tortilla. Top cheese with basil. Fold tortillas over, pressing gently.
2. Heat very large nonstick skillet or griddle over medium heat until a drop of water sizzles. Cook quesadillas over medium heat 4 to 6 minutes or until light brown, turning once. Remove from pan; cut each into 3 wedges. **Makes 6 wedges.**

EACH SERVING *152 cal, 10 g fat (4 g sat. fat), 19 mg chol, 180 mg sodium, 11 g carbo, 0 g fiber, 5 g pro. Daily Values: 3% vit. A, 6% calcium, 4% iron.*

CHEESY BAKED PENNE AND SAUSAGE

PREP 25 min. **BAKE** 25 min. **OVEN** 350°F

INGREDIENTS

8	oz.	dried penne
8	oz.	bulk mild Italian sausage
⅓	cup	sliced green onion
2	Tbsp.	all-purpose flour
2	Tbsp.	whole-grain mustard
1¼	cups	milk
¼	tsp.	ground black pepper
½		of an 8-oz. carton mascarpone cheese
4	oz.	fontina cheese, shredded (1 cup)
4	oz.	provolone cheese, shredded (1 cup)

PREPARATION

1. Preheat oven to 350°F. Cook penne according to package directions; drain. Meanwhile, in very large skillet cook sausage until browned; drain fat well. Stir in green onion; cook 1 minute. Add flour and mustard; gradually stir in milk and pepper. Cook and stir until slightly thickened and bubbly. Reduce heat; stir in mascarpone until blended. Add remaining cheeses and pasta. Transfer to 2-quart rectangular baking dish. Bake, uncovered, 25 to 30 minutes or until heated through. **Makes 6 servings.**

EACH SERVING *461 cal, 24 g fat (14 g sat. fat), 74 mg chol, 687 mg sodium, 36 g carbo, 1.4 g fiber, 26 g pro. Daily Values: 10% vit. A, 2% vit. C, 33% calcium, 12% iron.*

CHEESY-SWEET CORN BREAD

PREP 20 min. **BAKE** 30 min. **OVEN** 400°F

INGREDIENTS

1	cup	all-purpose flour
1	cup	yellow cornmeal
¼	cup	sugar
2½	tsp.	baking powder
¼	tsp.	salt
¼	tsp.	baking soda
1		egg
1	cup	buttermilk
1	cup	shredded cheddar cheese (4 oz.)
½	cup	finely shredded Parmesan cheese (2 oz.)
3	Tbsp.	butter, melted
3	Tbsp.	cooking oil

PREPARATION

1. Preheat oven to 400°F. Grease and lightly flour 9×1½-inch round baking pan; set aside.
2. In large bowl stir together flour, cornmeal, sugar, baking powder, salt, and baking soda; set aside. In medium bowl stir together egg, buttermilk, ¾ cup cheddar cheese, ¼ cup Parmesan cheese, butter, and oil. Add buttermilk mixture to flour mixture and stir just until moistened. Spread evenly in prepared pan.
3. Bake 25 minutes. Sprinkle with remaining cheeses and bake 5 minutes more or until golden and wooden toothpick inserted in center comes out clean. Serve warm. **Makes 8 servings.**

EACH SERVING *318 cal, 17 g fat (8 g sat. fat), 57 mg chol, 436 mg sodium, 32 g carbo, 2 g fiber, 10 g pro. Daily Values: 8% vit. A, 1% vit. C, 23% calcium, 8% iron.*

SWEET LOAVES, BREADS, AND ROLLS

ZUCCHINI-OAT BREAD

PREP 35 min. **BAKE** 1 hr. 20 min. **COOL** 10 min. **OVEN** 350°F

INGREDIENTS

	Nonstick cooking spray
1½	cups sugar
2¼	tsp. ground cinnamon
2½	cups all-purpose flour
1	cup rolled oats
1	tsp. baking powder
¾	tsp. salt
½	tsp. baking soda
3	eggs
1	cup applesauce
¼	cup butter, melted
1	tsp. vanilla
2	cups shredded, unpeeled zucchini
1	cup chopped walnuts or pecans
¾	cup raisins

PREPARATION

1. Preheat oven to 350°F. Lightly coat 9×5×3-inch loaf pan with cooking spray; set aside. Combine *1 tablespoon* sugar and ¼ *teaspoon* cinnamon; set aside. Combine flour, oats, baking powder, salt, baking soda, and remaining cinnamon; set aside. In large mixing bowl beat eggs with electric mixer on medium speed 2 minutes or until foamy. Add remaining sugar, applesauce, butter, and vanilla. Gradually add flour mixture, beating on low speed just until combined. Stir in zucchini, nuts, and raisins. Spoon into prepared pan. Sprinkle with sugar-cinnamon mixture.

2. Bake 1 hour and 20 minutes or until toothpick inserted near center comes out clean. Cool in pan on wire rack 10 minutes. Remove from pan. Cool completely on rack. Wrap and store several hours before slicing. **Makes 16 slices.**

EACH SERVING *286 cal, 9 g fat (3 g. sat. fat), 47 mg chol, 200 mg sodium, 48 g carbo, 2 g fiber, 4 g pro. Daily Values: 3% vit. A, 5% vit. C, 3% calcium, 10% iron.*

WALNUT-FILLED MUFFINS

PREP 35 min. **BAKE** 20 min. **COOL** 5 min. **OVEN** 350°F

INGREDIENTS

1⅔	cups walnuts (about 6 oz.), toasted
2	Tbsp. sugar
½	tsp. salt
½	tsp. ground cinnamon (optional)
1	Tbsp. orange juice
1¾	cups all-purpose flour
2	tsp. baking powder
⅓	cup butter, softened
⅔	cup sugar
1	egg
½	cup orange juice
¼	cup milk
1	recipe Frosting

PREPARATION

1. Preheat oven to 350°F. Line 12 muffin cups with bake cups or lightly coat with *nonstick cooking spray*. In food processor finely grind nuts with 2 tablespoons sugar, ¼ *teaspoon* salt, and cinnamon. Add 1 tablespoon orange juice; process until combined. Using rounded teaspoon, shape some nut mixture into 12 balls; set aside remaining.

2. Combine flour, baking powder, and remaining salt; set aside. Beat butter with mixer 30 seconds; beat in ⅔ cup sugar. Beat in egg, orange juice, and milk on low until combined. Gradually add flour mixture; beat just until combined. Spoon half of batter into cups; top with walnut balls, then remaining batter. Bake about 20 minutes or until tops spring back when touched. Cool in pans 5 minutes. Cool on rack. Spread Frosting; top with reserved nut mixture. **Makes 12 muffins.**

Frosting Beat ⅓ cup softened *butter*, 1 tablespoon *whipping cream*, and ½ teaspoon finely shredded *orange peel* until combined. Beat in 1½ cups *powdered sugar.*

EACH SERVING *517 cal, 34 g fat (13 g sat. fat), 83 mg chol, 457 mg sodium, 50 g carbo, 2 g fiber, 5 g pro. Daily Values: 12% vit. A, 8% vit. C, 10% calcium, 10% iron.*

BANANA CHOCOLATE HAZELNUT BREAD

PREP 25 min. **BAKE** 35 min.
COOL 10 min. **OVEN** 350°F

INGREDIENTS

2 cups all-purpose flour
1½ tsp. baking powder
½ tsp. baking soda
½ tsp. salt
2 eggs
1½ cups mashed ripe banana (5 medium)
½ cup chocolate-hazelnut spread
⅔ cup sugar
¼ cup dairy sour cream
¼ cup cooking oil
½ cup hazelnuts, toasted* and chopped

PREPARATION

1. Preheat oven to 350°F. Grease bottoms of three 5¾×3×2-inch individual loaf pans; set aside. In bowl stir together flour, baking powder, baking soda, and salt; set aside.
2. In mixing bowl whisk eggs until blended. Add bananas, chocolate-hazelnut spread, sugar, sour cream, and oil; whisk until thoroughly mixed. Add flour mixture; stir until just combined. Stir in nuts. Divide batter among prepared pans; spread evenly. Bake about 35 minutes or until toothpick inserted in centers comes out clean. Cool on wire rack 10 minutes; remove from pans. Cool completely. **Makes 3 small loaves (6 servings each).**
***NOTE** To toast hazelnuts, place nuts in shallow baking pan. Bake in 350°F oven 8 minutes. Transfer to clean towel. Fold towel over nuts to cover; rub gently to remove loose skin.

EACH SERVING *190 cal, 8 g fat (1 g sat. fat), 25 mg chol, 146 mg sodium, 26 g carbo, 1 g fiber, 3 g pro. Daily Values: 1% vit. A, 2% vit. C, 4% calcium, 6% iron.*

CHERRY CHOCOLATE COCONUT BREAD

PREP 30 min. **STAND** 15 min. **BAKE** 50 min.
COOL 10 min. **OVEN** 350°F

INGREDIENTS

½ cup dried tart red cherries
1 cup boiling water
1½ cups all-purpose flour
1 cup sugar
½ cup toasted coconut
⅓ cup unsweetened cocoa powder
1½ tsp. baking powder
¼ tsp. *each* baking soda, salt, and ground cinnamon
1 egg, beaten
⅔ cup milk
⅓ cup cooking oil
2 tsp. vanilla
½ cup chopped pecans

Powdered Sugar Icing
Chopped toasted pecans (optional)

PREPARATION

1. Preheat oven to 350°F. Grease bottom and ½ inch up sides of 9×5×3-inch loaf pan; set aside. Place cherries in bowl and add boiling water. Let stand 15 minutes; drain.
2. Meanwhile, in bowl stir together flour, sugar, coconut, cocoa powder, baking powder, baking soda, salt, and cinnamon; set aside.
3. In bowl combine egg, milk, oil, and vanilla. Add egg mixture all at once to dry mixture. Stir just until moistened. Fold in cherries and nuts. Spoon into prepared pan.
4. Bake 50 minutes or until toothpick inserted near center comes out clean. Cool in pan on wire rack 10 minutes. Remove from pan. Cool completely. Wrap; store overnight before slicing. Drizzle with Powdered Sugar Icing and sprinkle with toasted pecans before serving. **Makes 1 loaf (16 slices).**
Powdered Sugar Icing In small bowl stir together ½ cup *powdered sugar*, ½ teaspoon *vanilla*, and enough *milk* (1 to 2 teaspoons) to make drizzling consistency.

EACH SERVING *206 cal, 9 g fat (2 g sat. fat), 14 mg chol, 112 mg sodium, 30 g carbo, 2 g fiber, 3 g pro. Daily Values: 2% vit. A, 6% calcium, 6% iron.*

CHOCOLATE RIBBON PUMPKIN BREAD WITH VANILLA GLAZE

PREP 35 min. **BAKE** 65 min. **STAND** 30 min.
OVEN 350°F

INGREDIENTS

6 oz. semisweet chocolate, chopped
3¼ cup sugar
2 Tbsp. butter, softened
1 cup cooking oil
4 eggs
3½ cups all-purpose flour
2 tsp. baking soda
1 tsp. salt
1 tsp. ground cloves
⅔ cup orange juice
1 15-oz. can pumpkin
Vanilla Glaze

PREPARATION

1. Preheat oven to 350°F. Grease bottom and ½ inch up sides of two 9×5×3-inch or three 8×4×2-inch loaf pans; set aside. In food processor combine chocolate, ¼ cup sugar, and butter; process with several off/on turns until crumbly; set aside.
2. In extra-large mixing bowl beat remaining sugar and oil with an electric mixer on medium speed. Add eggs. Beat well; set aside. In large bowl combine flour, baking soda, salt, and cloves. Alternately add flour mixture and orange juice to sugar mixture, beating on low speed after each addition just until combined. Beat in pumpkin. Divide half of batter evenly among prepared pans. Sprinkle chocolate mixture over batter in pans. Spoon on remaining batter; smooth top evenly.
3. Bake 65 to 75 minutes or until toothpick inserted near centers comes out clean. Cool in pans on wire racks 10 minutes. Remove from pans. Cool completely on wire racks. Wrap; store overnight. Top with Vanilla Glaze. Let stand at least 30 minutes before slicing. **Makes 2 or 3 loaves (36 servings).**
Vanilla Glaze: In a medium bowl combine 1½ cups *powdered sugar*, 2 teaspoons *vanilla*, and enough *water* (1 to 2 tablespoons) to reach glazing consistency.

EACH SERVING *231 cal, 9 g fat (2 g sat. fat), 25 mg chol, 148 mg sodium, 37 g carbo, 1 g fiber, 2 g pro. Daily Values: 38% vit. A, 5% vit. C, 1% calcium, 6% iron.*

RHUBARB-BANANA MUFFINS

PREP 25 min. **BAKE** 18 min.
COOL 5 min. **OVEN** 400°F

INGREDIENTS

½ cup granulated sugar
2 Tbsp. butter, softened
2¾ cups all-purpose flour
2 tsp. baking powder
2 tsp. ground cinnamon
½ tsp. baking soda
½ tsp. salt
2 eggs, beaten
1 cup packed brown sugar
1 cup mashed banana (3 large)
½ cup cooking oil
1½ cups frozen chopped rhubarb, thawed and drained

PREPARATION

1. Preheat oven to 400°F. Lightly grease 24 (2½-inch) muffin cups or line with paper bake cups. In bowl combine granulated sugar and softened butter. Using your fingers, combine until crumbly; set aside.
2. In large mixing bowl combine flour, baking powder, cinnamon, baking soda, and salt. Make well in the center; set aside.
3. In medium mixing bowl combine eggs, brown sugar, mashed banana, and cooking oil. Add egg mixture all at once to dry mixture. Stir just until moistened (batter should be lumpy). Fold in rhubarb.
4. Spoon batter into prepared muffin cups, filling each two-thirds full. Sprinkle with granulated sugar mixture. Bake about 18 minutes or until toothpick inserted in centers comes out clean. Cool in muffin cups on a wire rack 5 minutes. Remove from muffin cups; serve warm.
Makes 24 muffins.

EACH SERVING *166 cal, 6 g fat (1 g sat. fat), 20 mg chol, 110 mg sodium, 26 g carbo, 1 g fiber, 2 g pro. Daily Values: 1% vit. A, 2% vit. C, 2% calcium, 5% iron.*

ALL-VEGETABLE DINNER

PORTIA MILLER, ALPINE, ALA.

MARY GUDENKAUF, HOLLISTER, MO.

PORTOBELLO CURRY WITH GREEN RICE

PREP 30 min. **COOK** 15 min.

INGREDIENTS

1	cup basmati rice
1	cup unsweetened coconut milk
½	cup snipped fresh cilantro
4	tsp. finely minced fresh ginger
2	cloves garlic, minced
1	Tbsp. lime juice
1	lb. portobello mushrooms, cut in ½-inch slices
2	Tbsp. canola oil
½	cup sliced green onion
2	tsp. Madras (spicy) curry powder or curry powder
⅛	tsp. crushed red pepper
1	cup cherry tomatoes, halved or quartered
2	Tbsp. coarsely chopped cashews or peanuts

PREPARATION

1. In medium saucepan combine rice, 2 cups *water*, and ½ teaspoon *salt*. Bring to boiling; reduce heat. Simmer, covered, 15 to 20 minutes or until rice is tender and liquid is absorbed.
2. Meanwhile, in blender or food processor combine *½ cup* coconut milk, cilantro, *1 teaspoon* ginger, *1 clove* garlic, and lime juice. Cover; blend or process until nearly smooth. Stir into rice. Cover; keep warm.
3. In 12-inch skillet cook mushrooms in hot oil over medium heat 5 minutes; turn occasionally. Add green onion, curry powder, red pepper, and remaining ginger and garlic. Cook and stir 1 minute. Stir in tomatoes and remaining coconut milk. Heat through. Season to taste with *salt* and *ground black pepper*.
4. To serve, divide rice among plates. Top with mushroom mixture and sprinkle with nuts. **Makes 4 servings.**

EACH SERVING *438 cal, 24 g fat (14 g sat. fat), 0 mg chol, 465 mg sodium, 51 g carbo, 6 g fiber, 9 g pro. Daily Values: 23% vit. A, 36% vit. C, 6% calcium, 18% iron.*

ZUCCHINI AND EGGPLANT BAKE

PREP 35 min. **BAKE** 20 min. **STAND** 10 min. **OVEN** 350°F

INGREDIENTS

3	medium zucchini, thinly sliced (4 cups)
2	large red sweet peppers, coarsely chopped (2 cups)
2	medium onions, coarsely chopped (1 cup)
1	medium eggplant, peeled and coarsely chopped (5 cups)
2	cloves garlic, minced
3	Tbsp. olive oil
4	eggs
½	cup light mayonnaise
4	oz. Pecorino-Romano cheese, grated (1 cup)
8	oz. shredded mozzarella cheese (2 cups)
12	rich round crackers, crushed (⅔ cup)

PREPARATION

1. Preheat oven to 350°F. Grease 3-quart rectangular baking dish; set aside. In 12-inch skillet cook zucchini, sweet pepper, onion, eggplant, garlic, ½ teaspoon *salt*, and ¼ teaspoon *ground black pepper* in hot oil over medium-high heat 10 to 15 minutes or until vegetables are tender, stirring occasionally.
2. Meanwhile, in extra-large bowl whisk together eggs and mayonnaise until combined. Stir in Pecorino-Romano cheese and *1 cup* mozzarella cheese. Add cooked vegetables; toss to combine. Evenly spread vegetable mixture in prepared baking dish. Top with remaining mozzarella and cracker crumbs.
3. Bake, uncovered, 20 to 25 minutes or until top is lightly browned and knife inserted near center comes out clean. Let stand 10 minutes before serving. **Makes 6 to 8 servings.**

EACH SERVING *440 cal, 32 g fat (11 g sat. fat), 188 mg chol, 942 mg sodium, 21 g carbo, 5 g fiber, 23 g pro. Daily Values: 42% vit. A, 112% vit. C, 52% calcium, 10% iron.*

INDIAN-STYLE VEGETABLE AND LENTIL STEW

PREP 30 min. **COOK** 45 min.

INGREDIENTS

1	Tbsp. *each* mustard seed, cumin seed
1½	Tbsp. olive oil
3	medium carrots, chopped
1	medium green sweet pepper, chopped
1	medium onion, chopped
½	tsp. salt
¼	tsp. ground black pepper
4	cups water
1	6-oz. can tomato paste
1	15- to 16-oz. can garbanzo beans (chickpeas), rinsed and drained
1	14.5-oz. can diced tomatoes, drained
1	Tbsp. lemon juice
3	cloves garlic, minced
1	tsp. *each* curry powder, ground cumin
½	tsp. crushed red pepper
1	large sweet potato, peeled and cut in ½-inch pieces
1	cup dry red lentils
½	cup coarsely chopped fresh cilantro

PREPARATION

1. In Dutch oven toast mustard and cumin seeds in hot oil over medium heat until fragrant and beginning to pop.

2. Add carrots, sweet pepper, onion, salt, and black pepper. Cook; stir 8 minutes or until vegetables begin to soften.

3. Stir in water, tomato paste, garbanzo beans, drained tomatoes, lemon juice, garlic, curry powder, ground cumin, and crushed red pepper. Bring to boiling. Add sweet potato and lentils. Reduce heat. Cover, simmer 30 minutes or until lentils and sweet potato are tender, stirring occasionally. Stir in cilantro before serving. Season to taste. **Makes 6 servings.**

EACH SERVING *378 cal, 5 g fat (1 g sat. fat), 0 mg chol, 975 mg sodium, 68 g carbo, 22 g fiber, 19 g pro. Daily Values: 228% vit. A, 87% vit. C, 15% calcium, 41% iron.*

MEDITERRANEAN SANDWICHES

PREP 25 min. **ROAST** 10 min. **OVEN** 450°F

INGREDIENTS

½	of medium eggplant, peeled, cut in ¾-inch cubes (about 2½ cups)
4	oz. fresh button mushrooms, quartered
1	small red onion, coarsely chopped
2	Tbsp. olive oil
1½	tsp. lemon pepper seasoning
⅓	cup mayonnaise
4	pita bread rounds, halved
1	medium tomato, halved, thinly sliced
4	oz. feta cheese, crumbled

PREPARATION

1. Preheat oven to 450°F. In large bowl combine eggplant, mushrooms, red onion, olive oil, and 1 teaspoon lemon pepper. Spread in 15×10×1-inch baking pan. Roast, uncovered, 10 to 15 minutes or until vegetables are just tender, stirring once.

2. Meanwhile, in small bowl combine remaining lemon pepper and mayonnaise. Spread inside of each pita half with mayonnaise mixture. Divide tomato slices among pita halves; spoon in roasted vegetables. Sprinkle with feta cheese. **Makes 4 servings.**

EACH SERVING *470 cal, 28 g fat (7 g sat. fat), 33 mg chol, 1,154 mg sodium, 43 g carbo, 5 g fiber, 12 g pro. Daily Values: 9% vit. A, 12% vit. C, 21% calcium, 13% iron.*

PEPPERS STUFFED WITH QUINOA AND SPINACH

PREP 25 min. **BAKE** 45 min. **OVEN** 400°F

INGREDIENTS

1	14-oz. can vegetable broth
¼	cup quick-cooking barley
¼	cup quinoa
2	Tbsp. olive oil
1	medium onion, chopped
2	cloves garlic, minced
2	cups sliced fresh mushrooms
¼	tsp. *each* salt and ground black pepper
1	14.5-oz. can diced tomatoes
½	of a 10-oz. pkg. frozen chopped spinach, thawed and well drained
4	oz. Monterey Jack cheese with jalapeño peppers or Monterey Jack cheese, shredded (1 cup)
4	large red sweet peppers
	Salt and ground black pepper

PREPARATION

1. Preheat oven to 400°F. In medium saucepan bring broth to boiling. Add barley and quinoa. Return to boiling; reduce heat. Cook, covered, 12 minutes or until tender. Drain, reserving cooking liquid; set aside.

2. In large skillet heat oil over medium-high heat. Add onion and garlic. Cook and stir 2 minutes. Add mushrooms. Cook and stir 4 to 5 minutes more or until mushrooms and onion are tender. Stir in ¼ teaspoon each salt and black pepper, undrained tomatoes, and spinach. Add quinoa mixture and ½ cup cheese; stir to combine. Remove from heat.

3. Remove pepper tops. Remove and discard seeds and membranes from the peppers. Cut small slice from bottom of each pepper so that each stands straight. Sprinkle insides of peppers lightly with salt and black pepper. Fill peppers with quinoa mixture. Place peppers, filled sides up, in a 2-quart square baking dish. Pour reserved cooking liquid into dish around peppers.

4. Bake, covered, 35 minutes. Uncover. Top each with remaining cheese.

Bake, uncovered, 10 minutes more or until peppers are crisp-tender and cheese is browned. **Makes 4 servings.**

EACH SERVING *351 cal, 17 g fat (7 g sat. fat), 30 mg chol, 1,110 mg sodium, 36 g carbo, 9 g fiber, 15 g pro. Daily Values: 203% vit. A, 359% vit. C, 290% calcium, 3% iron.*

VEGETABLE LASAGNA WITH GRUYÈRE AND WALNUTS

PREP: 35 minutes **BAKE:** 55 minutes
STAND: 10 minutes **OVEN:** 350°F

INGREDIENTS

2	cups thinly sliced onion
1	cup shredded carrot
1	cup chopped celery
½	cup chopped green sweet pepper
2	cloves garlic, minced
2	Tbsp. extra-virgin olive oil
2	10-oz. pkg. frozen chopped spinach, thawed and well drained
1	15-oz. can tomato puree
2	tsp. Italian seasoning, crushed
½	tsp. salt
12	dried lasagna noodles
1	15-oz. carton ricotta cheese or 1¾ cups cottage cheese
2	eggs, beaten
1	cup chopped walnuts, toasted
1	lb. Gruyère or Swiss cheese, shredded (4 cups)

PREPARATION

1. Preheat oven to 350°F. In 12-inch skillet cook onion, carrot, celery, sweet pepper, and garlic in olive oil 5 minutes or until tender. Stir in spinach. Cook and stir 1 minute. Stir in tomato puree, Italian seasoning and salt.

2. Meanwhile, cook lasagna noodles according to package directions. Drain noodles; rinse with cold water. Drain well; set aside.

3. For filing, in bowl combine ricotta cheese, eggs, and walnuts; set aside.

4. Spread about ½ cup tomato sauce over bottom of 3-quart rectangle baking dish. Layer *one-third* of cooked noodles in dish, overlapping as needed. Spread with *half* the filling, 1⅓ cups vegetable mixture, and 1⅓ cups Gruyère cheese. Repeat layers. Top with remaining noodles. Spoon any remaining vegetable mixture over the noodles. Sprinkle any remaining cheese.

5. Bake, covered, 45 minutes. Uncover; bake 10 minutes more or until heated through. Let stand 10 minutes before serving. **Makes 12 servings.**

EACH SERVING *439 cal, 27 g fat (11 g sat. fat), 95 mg chol, 356 mg sodium, 27 g carbo, 4 g fiber, 23 g pro. Daily Values: 115% vit. A, 28% vit. C, 53% calcium, 11% iron.*

POTLUCK SALADS

PIZZA PIZZAZZ SALAD

PREP 30 min. **CHILL** up to 6 hr.

INGREDIENTS

1	8-oz. pkg. field greens
1	5-oz. pkg. baby lettuce
4	cups grape tomatoes
1/2	red onion, thinly sliced, separated in rings
1/2	red sweet pepper, cut in bite-size strips
1	15-oz. can cannellini beans, rinsed and drained
1	6-oz. link pepperoni, casing removed and thinly sliced
4	oz. crumbled blue cheese
1	recipe Herb Dressing
1	5.5 oz. box Italian-seasoned croutons

PREPARATION

1. In extra-large salad bowl combine greens and lettuce. Top with tomatoes, red onion, sweet pepper, beans, pepperoni, and cheese. Cover and chill up to 6 hours. Before serving, shake Herb Dressing well; pour over salad and toss to coat. Sprinkle with croutons.
Makes 20 servings.

Herb Dressing In screw-top jar combine 1/2 cup *extra virgin olive oil*; 1/3 cup *white balsamic vinegar*; 1/4 cup snipped *Italian (flat-leaf) parsley*; 1/4 cup snipped fresh *basil*; 4 cloves *garlic*, minced; 1 teaspoon *sea salt* or 3/4 teaspoon salt; and 1/2 teaspoon *ground black pepper*. Cover and shake. Chill until needed.

EACH SERVING *175 cal, 12 g fat (3 g sat. fat), 13 mg chol, 429 mg sodium, 12 g carbo, 2 g fiber, 6 g pro. Daily Values: 25% vit. A, 20% vit. C, 5% calcium, 4% iron.*

ZESTY THREE-BEAN SALAD

PREP 25 min. **CHILL** up to 24 hr.

INGREDIENTS

2	cups frozen sweet soybeans (edamame)
1	15-oz. can kidney beans, rinsed and drained
1	15-oz. can garbanzo beans (chickpeas), rinsed and drained
1/2	cup thinly sliced red onion
1/2	cup chopped fresh cilantro
1/4	cup olive oil
1	tsp. finely shredded lime peel
1/4	cup lime juice

PREPARATION

1. Prepare soybeans according to package directions. Drain in colander and rinse with cold water.
2. In large bowl combine cooked soybeans, kidney beans, garbanzo beans, onion, and cilantro.
3. In small bowl whisk together oil, lime peel, lime juice, and 1/2 teaspoon *salt*. Pour over bean mixture and toss to coat. Cover; refrigerate up to 24 hours. Stir well before serving.
Makes 10 servings.

EACH SERVING *174 cal, 8 g fat (1 g sat. fat), 0 mg chol, 317 mg sodium, 21 g carbo, 6 g fiber, 9 g pro. Daily Values: 5% vit. A, 17% vit. C, 5% calcium, 11% iron.*

ASIAN MUSHROOM TOSS

PREP 15 min. **COOK** 8 min.

INGREDIENTS

1	Tbsp. peanut oil
1	Tbsp. toasted sesame oil
1	lb. fresh button mushrooms, quartered
1	large clove garlic, minced
2	Tbsp. soy sauce
1	Tbsp. rice vinegar
¼	tsp. crushed red pepper
2	cups hot cooked rice
2	Tbsp. snipped fresh cilantro
2	to 3 Tbsp. honey-roasted peanuts, coarsely chopped

PREPARATION

1. In a large skillet combine peanut oil and sesame oil; heat over medium heat. Add mushrooms and garlic. Cook about 5 minutes or until tender, stirring occasionally. If necessary, cook for 2 to 3 minutes more or until most of the liquid has evaporated.

2. Add soy sauce, vinegar, and crushed red pepper to skillet; cook 1 minute. Spoon mushroom mixture over hot cooked rice. Sprinkle with cilantro and peanuts. **Makes 6 side-dish servings.**

EACH SERVING *144 cal, 6 g total fat (1 g sat. fat), 0 mg chol, 319 mg sodium, 18 g carbo, 1 g fiber, 5 g pro. Daily Values: 2% vit. A, 4% vit. C, 1% calcium, 6% iron.*

THAI PASTA SALAD

PREP 35 min. **COOK** 10 min. **CHILL** 2 ½ hr.

INGREDIENTS

8	oz. dried rotini pasta
8	oz. peeled and deveined shrimp, halved lengthwise
1	16-oz. pkg. shredded cabbage with carrot (coleslaw mix)
1	medium red sweet pepper, seeded and cut into thin strips
1	cup packaged coarsely shredded fresh carrot
½	cup coarsely chopped fresh cilantro
¼	cup teriyaki sauce
¼	cup lemon juice
2	Tbsp. salad oil
2	Tbsp. grated fresh ginger
1	Tbsp. sugar
2	tsp. toasted sesame seeds
2	tsp. toasted sesame oil
¼	tsp. bottled hot pepper sauce
⅓	cup honey-roasted peanuts, coarsely chopped

PREPARATION

1. Cook rotini according to package directions, adding shrimp last 2 minutes of cooking time (be sure shrimp is opaque after cooking); drain. Rinse under cold water and drain well.

2. Meanwhile, in very large bowl combine cabbage, red sweet pepper, shredded carrot, and cilantro; set aside. For dressing, in small bowl whisk together teriyaki sauce, lemon juice, salad oil, ginger, sugar, sesame seeds, sesame oil, and hot pepper sauce.

3. Add pasta and shrimp to cabbage mixture. Pour dressing over all; toss to coat. Cover; chill 2 to 24 hours, tossing occasionally. Sprinkle with peanuts before serving. **Makes 12 to 14 servings.**

EACH SERVING *169 cal, 5 g fat (1 g sat. fat), 29 mg chol, 267 mg sodium, 22 g carbo, 2 g fiber, 8 g pro. Daily Values: 63% vit. A, 65% vit. C, 5% calcium, 8% iron.*

GRILLED CHICKEN AND PASTA SALAD WITH CILANTRO PESTO

PREP 30 min. **GRILL** 12 min.

INGREDIENTS

12	oz. dried bow tie pasta (4 cups)
12	oz. skinless, boneless chicken breast halves
1	red sweet pepper, quartered lengthwise and seeded
1	green sweet pepper, quartered lengthwise and seeded
1	red onion, cut into ½-inch-thick slices
2	Tbsp. olive oil
1	15-oz. can black beans, rinsed and drained
2	large tomatoes, chopped
4	green onions, thinly sliced
1	recipe Cilantro Pesto
	Lime wedges (optional)
	Fresh cilantro sprigs (optional)

PREPARATION

1. Cook pasta according to package directions; drain. Rinse with cold water; drain again. Place drained pasta in a very large bowl; set aside.

2. Brush chicken, pepper quarters, and onion slices with the olive oil and sprinkle lightly with *salt* and *ground black pepper*. For charcoal grill, place chicken and vegetables on rack of uncovered grill directly over medium coals. Grill until chicken is no longer pink (170°F) and vegetables are crisp-tender, turning once halfway through grilling. Allow 12 to 15 minutes for chicken and 8 to 10 minutes for vegetables. (For gas grill, preheat grill. Reduce heat to medium. Place chicken and vegetables on grill rack over heat. Cover and grill as above.)

3. Remove chicken and vegetables from grill. Chop chicken, sweet peppers, and onion. Add all to bowl with pasta. Stir in beans, tomato, and green onion. Add Cilantro Pesto to pasta mixture; toss gently to coat. Season to taste with *salt* and *pepper*. Serve immediately or cover and chill up to 24 hours. Serve with fresh lime wedges and cilantro sprigs. **Makes 8 servings.**

Cilantro Pesto In food processor combine 2 cups fresh *cilantro leaves*; ⅓ cup *olive oil*; ½ cup grated *Parmesan cheese*; ¼ cup *pumpkin seeds*, shelled sunflower seeds, or toasted pine nuts; 2 cloves *garlic*; 3 tablespoons *lime juice*; ¼ teaspoon *salt*; and several dashes of bottled *hot pepper sauce*. Cover and process until well combined and nearly smooth, stopping and scraping down sides of bowl as necessary. Makes about 1 cup.

EACH SERVING *421 cal, 17 g fat (3 g sat. fat), 29 mg chol, 317 mg sodium, 46 g carbo, 6 g fiber, 23 g pro. Daily Values: 44% vit. A, 100% vit. C, 13% calcium, 22% iron.*

MILDRED'S RED SALAD

PREP 40 min.

INGREDIENTS

⅓	of a medium head red cabbage, shredded (about 4 cups)
1	14½-oz. can sliced beets, drained
1	large red sweet pepper, cut into thin strips
4	oz. radishes, thinly sliced (about ¾ cup)
2	large carrots, thinly sliced
½	of a large red onion, thinly sliced
2	large tomatoes, halved and sliced
4	oz. thinly sliced salami, quartered
1	recipe Red Russian Salad Dressing

PREPARATION

1. In very large bowl combine cabbage, beets, red sweet pepper, radishes, carrot, onion, tomatoes, and salami. Cover; chill until needed. Before serving, drizzle with Red Russian Salad Dressing; toss to coat. **Makes 20 servings.**

Red Russian Salad Dressing In blender or food processor combine ½ cup *dairy sour cream*; ⅓ cup *mayonnaise*; 1 teaspoon each *sugar, paprika, dried Italian seasoning, dried rosemary,* and *chili powder*; ¼ teaspoon *cayenne pepper*; and 1 teaspoon *lemon juice*. Cover; blend or process until combined. Transfer to airtight container; cover and chill until ready to serve.

EACH SERVING *90 cal, 6 g fat (2 g sat. fat), 8 mg chol, 175 mg sodium, 7 g carbo, 1.4 g fiber, 2 g pro. Daily Values: 32% vit. A, 32% vit. C, 2% calcium, 3% iron.*

CHICKEN LEGS, THIGHS, AND WINGS

LOW FAT

FRENCH CHICKEN STEW

PREP: 20 min. **COOK:** 3 hr. (high), 6 hr. (low)

INGREDIENTS

4	cups sliced button and/or shiitake mushrooms
1	14.5-oz. can diced tomatoes, undrained
2	medium carrots, thinly diagonally sliced
1	medium onion, chopped
1	medium red potato, cut in 1-inch pieces
½	cup fresh green beans, cut in 1-inch pieces
½	cup pitted ripe olives, halved
1	cup reduced-sodium chicken broth
½	cup dry white wine or chicken broth
2	Tbsp. quick-cooking tapioca
1	tsp. herbes de Provence or Italian seasoning, crushed
¾	tsp. dried thyme, crushed
¼	tsp. coarsely ground black pepper
8	skinless, boneless chicken thighs (1¾ to 2 lb. total)
½	tsp. seasoned salt
1	14-oz. jar tomato pasta sauce or one 16-oz. jar Alfredo pasta sauce
	French bread (optional)

PREPARATION

1. In 5- to 6-quart slow cooker combine mushrooms, undrained tomatoes, carrot, onion, potato, green beans, olives, broth, wine, tapioca, herbes de Provence, thyme, and pepper. Place chicken on top; sprinkle with seasoned salt. Cover; cook on low-heat setting 6 to 7 hours or on high-heat setting 3 to 4 hours.
2. Stir in pasta sauce. Serve with French bread. **Makes 8 servings.**

EACH SERVING *219 cal, 5 g fat (1 g sat. fat), 83 mg chol, 629 mg sodium, 17 g carbo, 3 g fiber, 23 g pro. Daily Values: 57% vit. A, 26% vit. C, 9% calcium, 14% iron.*

KID FRIENDLY

CHICKEN WITH SPICED TOMATO JAM

START TO FINISH: 30 min.

INGREDIENTS

1	recipe Spiced Tomato Jam
¾	cup fine dry bread crumbs
⅓	cup grated Romano cheese
1	Tbsp. snipped fresh chives
2	tsp. chili powder
⅛	tsp. ground black pepper
¼	cup olive oil
2	Tbsp. Dijon-style mustard
1	Tbsp. lemon juice
12	chicken drumsticks, skinned

PREPARATION

1. Start preparing jam. Preheat oven to 350°F. Line baking sheet with parchment paper.
2. In low, flat bowl combine crumbs, cheese, chives, chili powder, pepper, and ¼ teaspoon *salt.* In second bowl combine oil, mustard, lemon juice, and ½ teaspoon *salt;* brush on chicken. Roll in crumb mixture to coat. Place on prepared baking sheet. Bake 45 to 55 minutes or until no longer pink (180°F). Serve with jam. Makes 6 servings.

Spiced Tomato Jam In saucepan combine one 14.5-oz. can undrained *diced tomatoes,* ¼ cup *brown sugar,* 2 tablespoons *balsamic vinegar,* 2 teaspoons *frozen orange juice concentrate,* ¼ teaspoon *ground cinnamon,* ⅛ teaspoon *ground ginger,* ⅛ teaspoon *crushed red pepper,* and dash *ground allspice.* Bring to boiling; reduce heat to medium. Simmer, uncovered, 30 minutes; stir occasionally until most of liquid has evaporated and jam is thickened. Stir in 1 tablespoon cold *butter* until melted.
Makes about 1 cup.

EACH SERVING *476 cal, 20 g fat (5 g sat. fat), 167 mg chol, 905 mg sodium, 25 g carbo, 2 g fiber, 46 g pro. Daily Values: 15% vit. A, 27% vit. C, 12% calcium, 18% iron.*

CHICKEN WITH SALTIMBOCCA MUSHROOM SAUCE

START TO FINISH 40 min.

INGREDIENTS

2	cups sliced fresh mushrooms
4	oz. prosciutto, coarsely chopped
½	cup chopped shallot
2	cloves garlic, minced
2	Tbsp. olive oil
¾	cup dry white wine
8	skinless, boneless chicken thighs (about 1½ pounds)
	Ground black pepper
1	cup reduced-sodium chicken broth
½	cup half-and-half or light cream
1	Tbsp. snipped fresh sage or 1 tsp. dried sage, crushed
	Hot cooked pasta or rice (optional)

PREPARATION

1. In very large skillet cook mushrooms, prosciutto, shallots, and garlic in *1 tablespoon* oil over medium-high heat 5 minutes or until mushrooms are tender, stirring occasionally. Carefully add *¼ cup* wine. Bring to boiling; reduce heat. Boil, gently, uncovered, 5 minutes or until liquid is evaporated, stirring occasionally. Remove mushroom mixture from skillet. Set aside.
2. Meanwhile, place a chicken thigh between two pieces of plastic wrap. Using flat side of a metal mallet, lightly pound chicken to ¼- to ½-inch thickness. Repeat with remaining chicken thighs. Sprinkle thighs lightly with pepper.
3. In same skillet heat remaining oil over medium-high heat. Add chicken to hot skillet. Cook 6 to 8 minutes or until chicken is no longer pink (180°F), turning once halfway through cooking. Transfer chicken to serving platter; cover to keep warm.
4. Add remaining ½ cup wine to hot skillet, stirring to lift up any browned bits. Add mushroom mixture and broth to skillet. Bring to boiling; reduce heat. Boil gently, uncovered, 6 to 8 minutes or until liquid is reduced by about half. Add half-and-half and sage. Boil gently, uncovered, 3 to 5 minutes or until sauce is thickened slightly. Add chicken and heat through. Serve with pasta or rice. **Makes 4 servings.**

EACH SERVING *455 cal, 24 g fat (5 g sat. fat), 152 mg chol, 779 mg sodium, 9 g carbo, 1 g fiber, 44 g pro. Daily Values: 9% vit. A, 7% vit. C, 6% calcium, 12% iron.*

CRISPY CHICKEN WITH FIG SAUCE

PREP 20 min. **BAKE** 45 min. **OVEN** 375°F

INGREDIENTS

8	chicken drumsticks (2¼ lb.) and/or chicken thighs (3 lb.)
⅓	cup creamy Dijon-style mustard blend
1½	tsp. curry powder
1	cup panko (Japanese-style bread crumbs)
2	Tbsp. olive oil
⅓	cup fig or apricot jam
1	Tbsp. balsamic vinegar

PREPARATION

1. Preheat oven to 375°F. Line 15×10×1-inch baking pan with foil. Lightly grease foil; set aside. Skin chicken if desired. In small bowl combine mustard blend and curry powder; spread on chicken. Roll chicken in panko. Arrange in prepared baking pan. Drizzle with olive oil.
2. Bake, uncovered, 45 to 50 minutes or until no pink remains in chicken (180°F).
3. Meanwhile, in a small saucepan combine fig jam and vinegar; heat through. Pass with chicken. **Makes 4 servings.**

EACH SERVING *514 cal, 26 g fat (5 g sat. fat), 138 mg chol, 443 mg sodium, 33 g carbo, 1 g fiber, 35 g pro. Daily Values: 3% vit. A, 10% vit. C, 3% calcium, 11% iron.*

LOW FAT

ESPRESSO-GLAZED CHICKEN

PREP 20 min. **MARINATE** 2 to 4 hr.
COOK 15 min. **BAKE** 45 min. **OVEN** 375°F

INGREDIENTS

8	chicken thighs (3 lb.) and/or drumsticks (2¼ lb.), skinned
½	cup apple cider or juice
½	cup espresso or strong coffee
1	Tbsp. soy sauce
2	tsp. paprika
2	tsp. prepared mustard
½	tsp. salt
½	tsp. ground black pepper
1	recipe Espresso Syrup

PREPARATION

1. Place chicken in a resealable plastic bag set in a bowl; set aside. In medium bowl whisk together apple cider, espresso, soy sauce, paprika, mustard, salt, and pepper. Pour mixture over chicken. Seal bag. Chill in refrigerator 2 to 4 hours. Remove chicken from bag. Discard marinade.
2. Preheat oven to 375°F. Arrange chicken pieces, bone sides down and pieces not touching, in greased 15×10×1-inch baking pan. Bake, uncovered, 45 to 55 minutes or until chicken is no longer pink (180°F), brushing with Espresso Syrup last 10 minutes of baking. **Makes 4 servings.**

Espresso Syrup In large skillet combine 1 cup *apple cider*, ½ cup *espresso* or strong coffee, ¼ cup *maple syrup*, 2 tablespoons packed *brown sugar*, and 1 teaspoon *chili powder*. Bring mixture to boiling; reduce heat. Simmer, uncovered, about 15 minutes or until mixture is reduced to ⅔ cup.

EACH SERVING *346 cal, 7 g fat (2 g sat. fat), 161 mg chol, 317 mg sodium, 30 g carbo, 0 g fiber, 38 g pro. Daily Values: 9% vit. A, 1% vit. C, 4% calcium, 13% iron.*

TWICE-COOKED COCONUT CHICKEN WINGS

PREP 25 min. **BAKE** 35 min.
OVEN 375°F/425°F

INGREDIENTS

12	chicken wings (about 3 lb.)
2	tsp. Jamaican jerk seasoning
½	tsp. salt
½	tsp. cayenne pepper
3	Tbsp. peanut oil
1	tsp. finely shredded lime peel
1	Tbsp. lime juice
¾	cup flaked coconut
⅓	cup peanuts
	Lime wedges

PREPARATION

1. Preheat oven to 375°F. Line 15×10×1-inch baking pan with foil. Set aside.
2. Cut off and discard tips of wings. Cut wings at joint to form 24 pieces. In small bowl combine Jamaican jerk seasoning, salt, and cayenne pepper. Sprinkle over wing pieces and rub in with fingers; arrange in prepared pan.
3. Bake, uncovered, 25 minutes. Remove from pan. Cool slightly. Meanwhile, replace foil in pan with clean foil.
4. Increase oven temperature to 425°F. In small bowl whisk together peanut oil, lime peel, and juice. In food processor combine coconut and peanuts; process with several on/off turns until finely chopped; transfer to shallow dish. Brush chicken with lime-oil mixture and roll in coconut mixture, pressing to coat. Arrange in foil-lined baking pan. Bake 10 minutes more or until coating is crunchy and wings are heated through. Serve with lime wedges.
Makes 24 appetizers.

EACH SERVING *169 cal, 13 g fat (4 g sat. fat), 43 mg chol, 141 mg sodium, 1 g carbo, 0 g fiber, 11 g pro. Daily Values: 2% vit. A, 2% vit. C, 1% calcium, 3% iron.*

TREATS FOR FRIENDS AND FAMILY

KID FRIENDLY

OAT 'N' TOFFEE GRAHAMS

PREP 15 min. **BAKE** 21 min. **OVEN** 350°F

INGREDIENTS

12	whole graham crackers (rectangles)
1½	cups rolled oats
¾	cup granulated sugar
¾	cup packed brown sugar
3	Tbsp. all-purpose flour
⅔	cup butter, melted
1	egg, lightly beaten
1	tsp. vanilla
1	12-oz. pkg. semisweet chocolate pieces
½	cup smoke-flavor whole almonds, coarsely chopped

PREPARATION

1. Preheat oven to 350°F. Line 15×10×1-inch baking pan with foil, extending foil beyond edges of pan. Arrange whole graham crackers in single layer in prepared pan. In large bowl combine oats, sugars, and flour. Stir in melted butter, egg, and vanilla until well combined. Spoon over graham crackers; spread evenly to edges of pan to cover graham crackers.

2. Bake for 20 to 25 minutes or until oat mixture bubbles and is lightly browned on top. Remove from oven; sprinkle with chocolate pieces. Return to oven 1 minute. Spread melted chocolate over top to cover. Evenly sprinkle with almonds. Cool in pan on wire rack. Use foil to lift from pan. Remove foil. Cut or break into bars. **Makes 32 bars.**

EACH SERVING *193 cal, 9 g fat (5 g sat. fat), 17 mg chol, 77 mg sodium, 26 g carbo, 2 g fiber, 3 g pro. Daily Values: 3% vit. A, 2% calcium, 6% iron.*

KID FRIENDLY

LEMONY SCONES WITH DRIED FRUIT

PREP 25 min. **BAKE** 18 min. **OVEN** 375°F

INGREDIENTS

2	cups all-purpose flour
2	tsp. baking powder
½	tsp. baking soda
½	cup butter
1	8-oz. carton sour cream
1	egg
¼	cup granulated sugar
1½	tsp. finely shredded lemon peel
⅔	cup snipped dried apricots
⅔	cup snipped pitted dried plums (prunes)
½	cup powdered sugar
2	to 3 tsp. lemon juice
¼	cup chopped toasted walnuts (optional)

PREPARATION

1. Preheat oven to 375°F. Lightly grease large baking sheet; set aside. In bowl stir together flour, baking powder, soda, and ¼ teaspoon *salt*. Cut in butter to resemble coarse crumbs; set aside. In bowl stir together sour cream, egg, granulated sugar, and *1 teaspoon* peel; add to flour mixture. Combine just until moistened. Stir in apricots and dried plums. Drop dough onto baking sheet. Bake 18 to 20 minutes or until golden and toothpick inserted in center comes out clean. Cool slightly on rack.

2. For glaze, stir together powdered sugar and remaining lemon peel. Stir in enough lemon juice to make drizzling consistency; drizzle over scones. Sprinkle with walnuts. **Makes 16 to 18 scones.**

EACH SERVING *200 cal, 9 g fat (6 g sat. fat), 35 mg chol, 175 mg sodium, 28 g carbo, 1 g fiber, 3 g pro. Daily Values: 11% vit. A, 1% vit. C, 7% calcium, 6% iron.*

PINEAPPLE-MACADAMIA NUT BISCOTTI

PREP 25 min. **BAKE** 45 min. **COOL** 10 min.
OVEN 325°F

INGREDIENTS

¾	cup	chopped dried pineapple
⅓	cup	chopped macadamia nuts
⅓	cup	white baking pieces
⅓	cup	butter, softened
⅔	cup	granulated sugar
1½	tsp.	baking powder
¼	tsp.	salt
2		eggs
2	tsp.	finely shredded lemon peel
½	tsp.	vanilla
2	cups	all-purpose flour
		Coarse sugar (optional)

PREPARATION

1. Preheat oven to 325°F. Lightly grease cookie sheet; set aside. In food processor combine dried pineapple, macadamia nuts, and white baking pieces; process with several on/off turns until finely chopped. Set aside.

2. In large mixing bowl beat butter with electric mixer on medium to high speed 30 seconds. Add sugar, baking powder, and salt; beat until combined. Add eggs, lemon peel, and vanilla; beat until combined. Beat in as much flour as you can with mixer. Stir in any remaining flour and pineapple mixture. Divide dough in half.

3. On cookie sheet, shape each half of dough into 9-inch-long log, placing logs about 3 inches apart. Flatten to 2 inches wide. Sprinkle tops with coarse sugar. Bake 25 to 30 minutes or until golden.

4. Cool on cookie sheet 10 minutes. Remove each log to cutting board. Slice diagonally into 1-inch slices. Place slices, cut sides down, on cookie sheet. Bake 10 minutes. Turn slices. Bake 10 minutes more or until golden and crisp. Remove to wire racks. Cool completely. **Makes about 20 cookies.**
NOTE To store, pack cookies between waxed paper in an airtight container. Seal. Store at room temperature up to 3 days or freeze up to 3 months.

EACH SERVING *158 cal, 6 g fat (3 g sat. fat), 29 mg chol, 93 mg sodium, 23 g carbo, 1 g fiber, 2 g pro. Daily Values: 2% vit. A, 4% calcium, 4% iron.*

ALMOND BARS

PREP 25 min. **BAKE** 35 min.
COOL 20 min. **OVEN** 350°F

INGREDIENTS

½	cup	butter, softened
1	cup	packed brown sugar
2		egg yolks
½	tsp.	salt
½	tsp.	almond extract
¼	tsp.	baking soda

1½	cups	all-purpose flour
3		1.61-oz. chocolate-coated almond and sweetened coconut bars, chopped (Almond Joy) (1 cup)
2		egg whites
½	cup	granulated sugar
½	cup	flaked coconut

PREPARATION

1. Preheat oven to 350°F. Line 9×9×2-inch baking pan with foil, extending foil beyond edges; set aside. In bowl beat butter with electric mixer on medium to high speed 30 seconds. Add brown sugar. Beat until well combined. Beat in egg yolks, salt, almond extract, and soda. Beat in flour until crumbly. Pat into prepared pan. Sprinkle with chopped candy; press into base. Bake 15 minutes.

2. Thoroughly wash beaters. In bowl beat egg whites with electric mixer on high speed until soft peaks form. Gradually add granulated sugar, 1 tablespoon at a time, beating on high speed until mixture forms stiff peaks. Using back of spoon, carefully spread over cookie layer. Sprinkle with coconut. Bake 20 minutes more. Cool on wire rack 20 minutes. Use foil to lift from pan. Cut into bars while still warm. **Makes 24 bars.**
NOTE To store, layer cookies between waxed paper in an airtight container; cover. Store at room temperature up to 3 days or freeze up to 3 months.

EACH SERVING *159 cal, 7 g fat (4 g sat. fat), 28 mg chol, 111 mg sodium, 24 g carbo, 1 g fiber, 2 g pro. Daily Values: 3% vit. A, 2% calcium, 3% iron.*

BANANA-PEANUT FUDGE

PREP 15 min. **CHILL** 2 hr.

INGREDIENTS

		Butter
3	cups	white baking pieces
1		14-oz. can sweetened condensed milk
¼	cup	peanut butter
1	cup	chopped peanuts
¾	cup	banana chips, chopped or broken

PREPARATION

1. Line 9×9×2-inch baking pan with foil, extending foil over edges of pan. Butter foil; set pan aside.

2. In 2-quart saucepan cook and stir baking pieces, condensed milk, and peanut butter over low heat until pieces melt and mixture is smooth. Remove saucepan from heat. Stir in ¾ cup of the nuts and banana chips. Spread fudge in prepared pan. Sprinkle with remaining nuts; press lightly into fudge. Cover; chill 2 hours or until firm.

3. Use foil to lift fudge out of pan. Cut fudge into 1-inch squares. Store, tightly covered, up to 1 week. **Makes 2½ pounds (72 pieces).**

EACH SERVING *159 cal, 7 g fat (4 g sat. fat), 28 mg chol, 111 mg sodium, 24 g carbo, .6 g fiber, 2 g pro. Daily Values: 3% vit. A, 2% calcium, 3% iron.*

GROWN-UP CEREAL BALLS

PREP 15 min. **COOK** 5 min. **STAND** 30 min.

INGREDIENTS

¼	cup	butter, cut up
4	cups	tiny marshmallows
1	tsp.	instant espresso coffee powder*
½	tsp.	ground cinnamon
5	cups	crisp rice cereal
4	oz.	chocolate-flavored candy coating

PREPARATION

1. In large saucepan combine butter and marshmallows; cook and stir until just melted. Stir in espresso powder and cinnamon. Add cereal. Remove from heat. Let stand until just cool enough to handle. With buttered hands, shape into 1½- to 2-inch balls. Place on waxed paper-lined baking sheet.

2. In small saucepan stir candy coating over low heat until just melted; drizzle atop cereal balls. Let stand at room temperature about 30 minutes or until chocolate is set. **Makes 2½ dozen.**
*NOTE Do not substitute instant coffee crystals because they will not dissolve properly.

EACH SERVING *72 cal, 3 g fat (2 g sat. fat), 4 mg chol, 59 mg sodium, 12 g carbo, 0 g fiber, 0 g pro. Daily Values: 2% vit. A, 1% vit. C, 1% iron.*

ITALIAN CHEESE TWISTS

PREP 30 min. **BAKE** 12 min. **OVEN** 400°F

INGREDIENTS

1	cup	shredded Italian blend cheeses
⅓	cup	pine nuts, toasted and finely chopped
1	tsp.	dried Italian seasoning, crushed
1		17.3-oz. pkg. frozen puff pastry sheets (2 sheets), thawed
2	Tbsp.	butter, melted

PREPARATION

1. Preheat oven to 400°F. In medium bowl combine cheese, pine nuts, and Italian seasoning. Unfold one pastry sheet on lightly floured surface. Brush with butter. Sprinkle evenly with cheese mixture. Unfold remaining pastry sheet and place atop cheese mixture. Press edges lightly to seal. Roll to a 14-inch square.

2. Cut in half crosswise to make two 14×7-inch rectangles. Cut each rectangle crosswise, into 7×½-inch strips. Press down on each strip gently; twist each strip two to three times. Place on parchment lined baking sheets.

3. Bake 10 to 12 minutes or until lightly browned and crisp. Serve warm, or cool and serve at room temperature. Serve same day as prepared. **Makes about 50.**

EACH SERVING *71 cal, 5 g fat (2 g sat. fat), 3 mg chol, 42 mg sodium, 5 g carbo, .1 g fiber, 2 g pro. Daily Values: 1% calcium, 2% iron.*

LOW-CALORIE DESSERTS

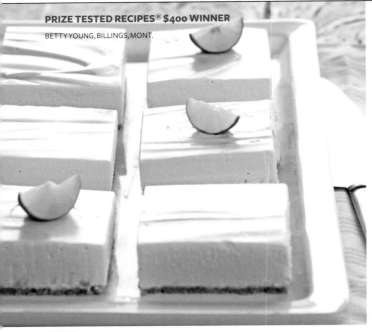

KID FRIENDLY

KEY LIME CHEESECAKE BARS

PREP 30 min. **CHILL** 8 hr.

INGREDIENTS

6   squares low-fat honey graham crackers, finely crushed (½ cup)
2   Tbsp. margarine, melted
1   tsp. sugar
1   4-serving-size pkg. sugar-free low-calorie lime-flavor gelatin
¾   cup boiling water
1   16-oz. container fat-free cottage cheese (1¾ cups)
1   8-oz. pkg. fat-free cream cheese, softened
1   8-oz. container frozen fat-free whipped dessert topping, thawed
      Key limes or limes, cut in wedges (optional)

PREPARATION

1. In small bowl combine graham crackers, margarine, and sugar. Press crumb mixture in bottom of 2-quart square baking dish. Refrigerate while preparing filling.

2. In large bowl combine gelatin and water. Stir until gelatin is dissolved. Set aside.

3. In blender or food processor combine cottage cheese and cream cheese. Cover; blend or process until smooth, stopping several times to scrape down sides. Whisk ½ cup cottage cheese mixture into gelatin mixture. Whisk in remaining cottage cheese mixture until smooth. Fold in whipped dessert topping. Spoon filling over chilled crumb mixture.

4. Cover and refrigerate 8 to 24 hours or until filling is firm. To serve, cut in squares. Top with lime wedges. **Makes 9 servings.**

EACH SERVING 147 cal, 3 g fat (1 g sat. fat), 4 mg chol, 410 mg sodium, 17 g carbo, 0 g fiber, 10 g pro. Daily Values: 9% vit. A, 7% calcium, 1% iron.

LOW FAT **FAST!**

RASPBERRY ANGEL FOOD BRUSCHETTA

START TO FINISH 25 min.

INGREDIENTS

½   small 7-inch angel food cake, cut in 8 wedges (about 4 oz. total)
3   cups raspberries
¼   cup fat-free caramel ice cream topping
1   Tbsp. mint or apricot jelly
1   cup frozen fruit sorbet
      Fresh mint sprigs

PREPARATION

1. In large nonstick skillet toast cake slices over medium-high heat 3 to 5 minutes, turning to brown evenly. Set aside.

2. Meanwhile, in blender container or food processor bowl combine 2 cups raspberries, caramel topping, and mint jelly. Cover; blend or process with several on/off turns to combine and puree berries. Strain through fine-mesh sieve. Stir remaining 1 cup berries into strained berry mixture.

3. To serve, place toasted cake slices on plates. Top with berry mixture, a small scoop of sorbet, and mint sprigs. **Makes 4 servings.**

EACH SERVING 273 cal, 1 g fat (0 g sat. fat), 0 mg chol, 250 mg sodium, 66 g carbo, 7 g fiber, 3 g pro. Daily Values: 1% vit. A, 45% vit. C, 7% calcium, 5% iron.

LEMON YOGURT POUND CAKE

PREP 30 min. **BAKE** 35 min. **OVEN** 350°F

INGREDIENTS

	Nonstick cooking spray
3	cups all-purpose flour
1	tsp. baking powder
½	tsp. baking soda
½	tsp. salt
1	cup granulated sugar
1	4-serving size pkg. sugar-free low-calorie lemon-flavor gelatin
½	of an 8-oz. pkg. reduced-fat cream cheese (Neufchâtel)
⅓	cup cooking oil
2	eggs
2	egg whites
⅓	cup fat-free milk
1	6-oz. carton fat-free lemon-flavor yogurt
2	tsp. finely shredded lemon peel
1	cup powdered sugar
3	to 4 tsp. lemon juice

PREPARATION

1. Preheat oven to 350°F. Lightly coat bottom and halfway up sides of two 8×4×2-inch loaf pans with nonstick spray. Set aside.

2. In medium bowl stir together flour, baking powder, baking soda, and salt; set aside. In large bowl stir together granulated sugar and gelatin; add cream cheese and oil. Beat with electric mixer on medium speed until combined. Beat in eggs and egg whites. Add flour mixture alternately with milk and yogurt, beating just until combined after each addition. Stir in *1 teaspoon* lemon peel. Spoon into prepared pans, spreading evenly.

3. Bake 30 to 35 minutes or until wooden toothpick inserted in centers comes out clean. Cool 10 minutes in pans on wire rack. Remove from pans. Cool completely.

4. In bowl stir together powdered sugar, remaining lemon peel, and enough juice to make drizzling consistency. Drizzle over loaves. **Makes 2 loaves (14 slices per loaf).**

EACH SERVING *137 cal, 4 g fat (1 g sat. fat), 18 mg chol, 110 mg sodium, 22 g carbo, .4 g fiber, 3 g pro. Daily Values: 2% vit. A, 1% vit. C, 2% calcium, 4% iron.*

`LOW FAT` `FAST!`

PEACHES AND BLUEBERRIES WITH LEMON CUSTARD SAUCE

PREP 20 min. **CHILL** 2 hr.

INGREDIENTS

¼	cup sugar
4	tsp. cornstarch
⅛	tsp. salt
1¾	cups fat-free milk
3	egg yolks
2	tsp. vanilla
1	tsp. finely shredded lemon peel
2	cups fresh peeled peach slices
2	cup fresh blueberries
	Ground cinnamon

PREPARATION

1. In heavy medium saucepan combine sugar, cornstarch, and salt. Whisk in milk and egg yolks. Cook and stir over medium heat until thickened and bubbly. Reduce heat; cook and stir 2 minutes more. Remove from heat.

2. Quickly cool custard by placing saucepan into bowl half-filled with ice water 3 minutes, stirring constantly. Strain mixture through fine-mesh sieve into medium bowl. Stir in vanilla and lemon peel. Cover surface with plastic wrap. Chill 2 to 24 hours.

3. Divide peaches and berries among six dessert dishes. Spoon on custard sauce; sprinkle cinnamon. **Makes 6 servings.**

EACH SERVING *147 cal, 2 g fat (1 g sat. fat), 106 mg chol, 83 mg sodium, 27 g carbo, 3 g fiber, 4 g pro. Daily Values: 12% vit. A, 15% vit. C, 10% calcium, 2% iron.*

`LOW FAT`

SWEET POTATO CUSTARD

PREP 15 min. **BAKE** 40 min. **OVEN** 325°F

INGREDIENTS

	Nonstick cooking spray
1	cup mashed cooked sweet potato
½	cup mashed banana
1	cup evaporated low-fat milk
2	egg whites or ⅓ cup refrigerated or frozen egg product
2	Tbsp. packed brown sugar
1	tsp. granulated sugar
1	tsp. ground cinnamon
½	tsp. salt
½	cup raisins
	Frozen fat-free whipped dessert topping, thawed (optional)

PREPARATION

1. Preheat oven to 325°F. Lightly coat 1-quart casserole with nonstick spray; set aside.

2. In medium bowl combine sweet potato and banana. Whisk in evaporated milk, egg whites, brown sugar, granulated sugar, cinnamon, and salt until well mixed. Stir in raisins. Pour into prepared dish.

---

3. Bake 40 to 45 minutes or until knife inserted near center comes out clean. Serve warm topped with whipped dessert topping. **Makes 6 to 8 servings.**

EACH SERVING *146 cal, 1 g fat (0 g sat. fat), 7 mg chol, 251 mg sodium, 30 g carbo, 2 g fiber, 5 g pro. Daily Values: 172% vit. A, 14% vit. C, 11% calcium, 4% iron.*

`KID FRIENDLY`

THREE-FRUIT CRISP

PREP 15 min. **BAKE** 45 min. **OVEN** 350°F

INGREDIENTS

4	cups fresh blueberries
2	cups fresh raspberries
1	cup peeled, sliced peaches
¼	cup granulated sugar
¼	cup whole wheat flour
3	Tbsp. granulated sugar
2	Tbsp. toasted wheat germ
¾	tsp. ground cinnamon
1	Tbsp. butter, melted
	Low-fat vanilla frozen yogurt (optional)

PREPARATION

1. Preheat oven to 350°F. In 2-quart casserole combine blueberries, raspberries, and peaches. Sprinkle ¼ cup granulated sugar over fruit; set aside.

2. In small bowl combine whole wheat flour, 3 tablespoons sugar, wheat germ, and cinnamon; stir in butter. Sprinkle over fruit mixture.

3. Bake, uncovered, 45 minutes or until fruit mixture bubbles around edge of dish and topping is lightly browned. Serve warm with frozen yogurt. **Makes 6 servings.**

EACH SERVING *187 cal, 3 g fat (1 g sat. fat), 5 mg chol, 15 mg sodium, 41 g carbo, 6 g fiber, 3 g pro. Daily Values: 4% vit. A, 37% vit. C, 2% calcium, 6% iron.*

YOUR BEST DIPS

LAYERED GREEK DIP

PREP 20 min. **CHILL** 2 to 24 hr.

INGREDIENTS

1   8-oz. pkg. cream cheese, softened
1   Tbsp. lemon juice
1   tsp. dried Italian seasoning
3   cloves garlic, minced
1½   cups prepared hummus
1   cup chopped cucumber
1   cup chopped tomato
½   cup chopped pitted kalamata olives
½   cup crumbled feta cheese
⅓   cup sliced green onion
    Pita chips and/or multigrain tortilla chips

PREPARATION

1. In medium mixing bowl beat cream cheese, lemon juice, Italian seasoning, and garlic with electric mixer on medium speed until smooth and combined.

2. Spread cream cheese mixture into deep 9-inch pie plate or shallow serving dish. Evenly spread hummus on cream cheese layer. Top with cucumber, tomato, olives, feta cheese, and green onion. Cover and refrigerate 2 to 24 hours. Serve with pita chips and/or multigrain tortilla chips. **Makes about 2 ½ cups.**

EACH SERVING (ABOUT 2 1/2 TBSP. WITHOUT DIPPERS) *114 cal, 9 g fat (4 g sat. fat), 20 mg chol, 198 mg sodium, 7 g carbo, 1 g fiber, 3 g pro. Daily Values: 7% vit. A, 7% vit. C, 5% calcium, 4% iron.*

SPICY CURRY-GINGER DIP

PREP 15 min. **CHILL** 4 hr.

INGREDIENTS

1   8-oz. carton sour cream
¾   cup mayonnaise
2   Tbsp. honey
3   to 4 tsp. curry powder
2   to 3 tsp. grated fresh gingerroot
¼   to ½ tsp. cayenne pepper
¼   to ½ tsp. ground black pepper
    Curry powder and grated fresh gingerroot (optional)
    Vegetable dippers

PREPARATION

1. In medium bowl whisk together sour cream, mayonnaise, honey, curry powder, gingerroot, cayenne pepper, and black pepper. Cover and refrigerate 4 to 24 hours.

2. Sprinkle dip with additional curry powder and fresh gingerroot. Serve with vegetable dippers. **Makes about 2 cups.**

EACH SERVING (1/4 CUP) *230 cal, 23 g fat (7 g sat. fat), 20 mg chol, 128 mg sodium, 6 g carbo, 0 g fiber, 1 g pro. Daily Values: 4% vit. A, 1% vit. C, 4% calcium, 2% iron.*

ZESTY SALSA

PREP 25 min. **CHILL** up to 24 hr.

INGREDIENTS

1	medium Granny Smith apple, cored and chopped
2	medium Roma tomatoes, seeded and chopped
1	cup chopped fresh pineapple
2	fresh jalapeño chile peppers, seeded and finely chopped*
¼	cup chopped sweet onion
¼	cup chopped orange sweet pepper
¼	cup pineapple juice
½	tsp. ground white pepper
½	tsp. ground cumin
¼	tsp. salt
	Toasted baguette slices or pita chips

PREPARATION

1. In bowl combine apple, tomatoes, pineapple, jalapeño, sweet onion, sweet pepper, pineapple juice, white pepper, cumin, and salt. Transfer *half* the mixture to food processor or blender; process with several on/off turns until finely chopped. Stir into remaining mixture.

2. Serve at once or cover and chill up to 24 hours. Serve with baguette slices or pita chips. **Makes 3 cups salsa.**

*NOTE Because hot chile peppers, such as jalapeños, contain volatile oils that can burn your skin and eyes, avoid direct contact with chiles as much as possible. When working with chile peppers, wear plastic or rubber gloves. If your bare hands do touch the chile peppers, wash your hands well with soap and water.

EACH SERVING (¼ CUP) *23 cal, 0 g fat (0 g sat. fat), 0 mg chol, 50 mg sodium, 5 g carbo, 1 g fiber, 0 g pro. Daily Values: 6% vit. A, 25% vit. C, 1% calcium, 1% iron.*

ARTICHOKE LEMON PESTO WITH PARMESAN PITA CRISPS

PREP 25 min. **BAKE** 10 min. **OVEN** 350°F

INGREDIENTS

½	cup lightly packed fresh Italian (flat-leaf) parsley
2	Tbsp. extra virgin olive oil
1	clove garlic, cut up
¼	tsp. salt
¼	tsp. crushed red pepper
1	13.75- to 14-oz. can artichoke hearts, drained and quartered
1	Tbsp. lemon juice
2	Tbsp. pine nuts, toasted (optional)
2	pita bread rounds
	Olive oil nonstick cooking spray
	Salt and ground black pepper
¼	cup grated Parmesan cheese

PREPARATION

1. For pesto, in food processor* combine parsley, olive oil, garlic, ¼ teaspoon salt, and crushed red pepper. Cover; process until finely chopped. Add artichoke hearts and lemon juice; pulse with several on/off turns until artichokes are finely chopped but not mushy. Spoon into serving bowl. (Or, cover and chill up to 4 hours.) Top with pine nuts before serving.

2. To make pita crisps, preheat oven to 350°F. Cut pita bread rounds into sixths and divide each wedge in half horizontally. Spread in single layer on large baking sheet, placing rough sides up. Lightly coat with nonstick cooking spray. Sprinkle with salt, pepper, and Parmesan cheese. Bake 10 to 12 minutes or until golden brown and crisp. Serve with pesto. **Makes 8 servings.**

*NOTE To prepare by hand, finely snip parsley and finely chop artichoke hearts. Combine in medium bowl with olive oil; 1 tablespoon lemon juice; 1 clove garlic, minced; ¼ teaspoon salt; and ¼ teaspoon crushed red pepper. Serve as above.

EACH SERVING *98 cal, 4 g fat (1 g sat. fat), 2 mg chol, 427 mg sodium, 11 g carbo, 2 g fiber, 3 g pro. Daily Values: 9% vit. A, 12% vit. C, 6% calcium, 10% iron.*

CRISP APPLE SALSA

START TO FINISH 25 min.

INGREDIENTS

1	medium Granny Smith apple, cored and quartered
1	medium red cooking apple, cored and quartered
1	medium onion, quartered
2	fresh jalapeño chile peppers, seeded and quartered*
6	cloves garlic, minced
1	14.5-oz. can petite diced tomatoes, drained
2	Tbsp. lime juice
1	tsp. ground cumin
½	tsp. salt
	Scoop-shape tortilla or corn chips

PREPARATION

1. In food processor place apple, onion, jalapeño, and garlic. Cover; process with several off/on turns until chopped. (Or finely chop apples, onion, and jalapeño.) Transfer mixture to bowl. Stir in drained tomatoes, lime juice, cumin, and salt. Serve immediately or cover and chill up to 4 hours. Serve with chips. **Makes 3 cups.**

*NOTE Because hot chile peppers, such as jalapeños, contain volatile oils that can burn your skin and eyes, avoid direct contact with chiles as much as possible. When working with chile peppers, wear plastic or rubber gloves. If your bare hands do touch the chile peppers, wash your hands well with soap and water.

EACH SERVING (2 TBSP.) *13 cal, 0 g fat (0 g sat. fat), 0 mg chol, 83 mg sodium, 3 g carbo, 1 g fiber, 0 g pro. Daily Values: 2% vit. A, 5% vit. C, 1% calcium, 1% iron.*

CURRIED CARROT DIP

PREP 15 min. **COOK** 15 min.

INGREDIENTS

1	lb. carrots, peeled and cut into 1-inch pieces
1	Tbsp. curry powder
½	tsp. salt
1	cup mayonnaise
1	tsp. snipped fresh chives
	Dippers, such as pita chips, sweet pepper strips, celery sticks, and/or crackers

PREPARATION

1. In large saucepan cook carrot pieces in small amount of water 15 to 20 minutes or until carrots are very tender; drain.

2. In food processor combine drained carrots, curry powder, and salt. Cover; process until mixture is smooth. Add mayonnaise. Cover; process until just combined. Transfer mixture to serving bowl. Sprinkle with chives. Serve dip at room temperature with desired dippers. **Makes about 2½ cups.**

EACH SERVING (2 TBSP.) *159 cal, 11 g fat (2 g sat. fat), 4 mg chol, 290 mg sodium, 12 g carbo, 10 g fiber, 1 g pro. Daily Values: 76% vit. A, 29% vit. C, 3% calcium, 1% iron.*

PEANUT BUTTER CUP DIP

START TO FINISH 10 min.

INGREDIENTS

2	8-oz. cartons mascarpone cheese, softened
1	cup chocolate-hazelnut spread
½	cup chunky peanut butter
½	to ¾ cup half-and-half or light cream
	Apple slices, pretzel rods, and/or biscotti

PREPARATION

1. In large bowl beat mascarpone cheese with electric mixer until fluffy. Beat in chocolate-hazelnut spread, peanut butter, and ½ cup half-and-half. Add additional half-and-half to desired consistency. Serve with apple slices, pretzel rods, and/or biscotti. **Makes 4 cups (sixteen ¼-cup servings).**

EACH SERVING *303 cal, 22 g fat (8 g sat. fat), 39 mg chol, 73 mg sodium, 25 g carbo, 3 g fiber, 9 g pro. Daily Values: 1% vit. A, 6% vit. C, 2% calcium, 1% iron.*

FEATURING FRESH HERBS

FAST!

HERBED GARDEN COUSCOUS

START TO FINISH 30 min.

INGREDIENTS

- 1 cup whole wheat or plain couscous
- 2 cups cherry tomatoes, halved
- 1 medium cucumber, coarsely chopped
- 1 medium green sweet pepper, coarsely chopped
- ½ cup snipped fresh chives
- ¼ cup snipped fresh Italian (flat-leaf) parsley
- ¼ cup snipped fresh mint
- ¼ cup snipped fresh oregano
- ⅓ cup balsamic vinegar
- ⅓ cup olive oil
- 2 tsp. sugar
- ½ cup crumbled feta cheese
- ½ cup coarsely chopped walnuts, toasted

PREPARATION

1. Cook couscous according to package directions. Fluff with a fork.
2. Meanwhile, in large bowl combine tomatoes, cucumber, sweet pepper, chives, parsley, mint, and oregano. Fold in couscous.
3. In small bowl whisk together balsamic vinegar, olive oil, sugar, ½ teaspoon *salt*, and ¼ teaspoon *freshly ground black pepper*. Pour over couscous mixture; toss to combine. Spoon into serving bowl or cover and chill up to 24 hours. To serve, top with feta cheese and walnuts. **Makes 12 side-dish servings.**

EACH SERVING *196 cal, 11 g fat (2 g sat. fat), 6 mg chol, 172 mg sodium, 21 g carbo, 3 g fiber, 5 g pro. Daily Values: 11% vit. A, 29% vit. C, 6% calcium, 8% iron.*

FAST! **LOW FAT**

GREEN BEANS WITH BASIL AND MINT

PREP 10 min. **COOK** 7 min.

INGREDIENTS

- 6 cups water
- 2 lb. fresh green beans, trimmed if desired
- 2 cloves garlic, chopped
- ½ cup shredded fresh basil
- ⅓ cup shredded fresh mint
- 1 small red sweet pepper, chopped
- 2 Tbsp. olive oil
- ½ tsp. salt

PREPARATION

1. In 4-quart Dutch oven bring water to boiling. Add green beans and return to boiling; reduce heat. Simmer, uncovered, 7 to 8 minutes or until beans are crisp-tender, adding garlic the last minute of cooking. Drain.
2. Meanwhile, in large bowl combine basil, mint, sweet pepper, olive oil, and salt. Add drained green beans and garlic. Toss gently to combine. **Makes 8 servings.**

EACH SERVING *71 cal, 4 g fat (1 g sat. fat), 0 mg chol, 154 mg sodium, 9 g carbo, 4 g fiber, 2 g pro. Daily Values: 25% vit. A, 54% vit. C, 6% calcium, 10% iron.*

GARLIC HERB SMASHED POTATOES

START TO FINISH 30 min.

INGREDIENTS

1½ lb. tiny new potatoes, quartered
4 cloves garlic, peeled
½ of an 8-oz. pkg. cream cheese, cubed and softened
½ of an 8-oz. carton dairy sour cream
2 Tbsp. butter, softened
¼ tsp. *each* salt and ground black pepper
1 Tbsp. *each* snipped fresh dill, rosemary, and basil
2 Tbsp. crumbled, crisp-cooked bacon (optional)
1 Tbsp. sliced green onion (optional)

PREPARATION

1. In 3-quart saucepan cook potatoes and garlic in lightly salted boiling water 12 to 15 minutes or until tender. Drain; return to pan.
2. Add cream cheese, sour cream, butter, salt, and pepper to potatoes. Using a potato masher or electric mixer, mash potatoes lightly to combine. Stir in fresh herbs. Spoon into serving bowl. Top with bacon and onion. **Makes 6 to 8 side-dish servings.**

EACH SERVING *231 cal, 14 g fat (9 g sat. fat), 39 mg chol, 221 mg sodium, 22 g carbo, 3 g fiber, 5 g pro. Daily Values: 11% vit. A, 39% vit. C, 6% calcium, 7% iron.*

SPLIT PEA SOUP WITH HERBED CROSTINI

PREP 20 min. **BAKE** 6 min. **COOK** 50 min.
OVEN 425°F

INGREDIENTS

1 lb. dry split peas
4 cups water
1 14-oz. can vegetable broth
2 large carrots, peeled and chopped
1 large onion, chopped
2 Tbsp. *each* snipped fresh basil and oregano
1 Tbsp. snipped fresh sage
1 recipe Herbed Crostini

PREPARATION

1. Rinse and drain split peas. In 4- to 5-quart Dutch oven combine split peas, water, and broth. Bring to boiling; reduce heat. Simmer, covered, 30 minutes. Add carrot and onion. Cover; cook 20 to 30 minutes more or until peas and vegetables are tender.
2. Stir in basil, oregano, and sage. Cook and stir 1 minute. Season to taste with *salt* and *ground black pepper*.
3. Divide soup among 6 soup plates; place 1 crostini on each. **Makes 6 servings.**

Herbed Crostini Preheat oven to 425°F. Brush six ½-inch-thick slices of *French bread* with mixture of 3 tablespoons *olive oil*, and 1 tablespoon each finely snipped *basil* and *oregano*. Place on greased baking sheet. Bake 6 to 8 minutes or until lightly toasted, turning once. Sprinkle hot crostini with 2 tablespoons finely shredded *Parmesan cheese*.

EACH SERVING *442 cal, 9 g fat (2 g sat. fat), 1 mg chol, 623 mg sodium, 69 g carbo, 21 g fiber, 23 g pro. Daily Values: 75% vit. A, 10% vit. C, 11% calcium, 27% iron.*

VEGETABLE AND HERB CABBAGE SALAD

START TO FINISH 25 min.

INGREDIENTS

⅓ cup cider vinegar
⅓ cup salad oil
¼ cup finely chopped shallot
3 Tbsp. sugar
1 Tbsp. water
2 cloves garlic, minced
1 tsp. snipped fresh rosemary
1 tsp. finely shredded lemon peel
2 Tbsp. lemon juice
1 tsp. *each* salt and ground black pepper
1 16-oz. pkg. shredded cabbage with carrot (coleslaw mix)
2 cups small broccoli florets
1 green sweet pepper, chopped
1 large tomato, chopped
¼ cup *each* snipped fresh cilantro and basil

PREPARATION

1. In large screw-top jar combine vinegar, oil, shallots, sugar, water, garlic, rosemary, lemon peel, lemon juice, salt, and pepper. Cover jar; shake until sugar is dissolved.
2. In very large bowl toss together coleslaw mix, broccoli, sweet pepper, tomato, cilantro, and basil. Shake dressing; add to vegetable mixture. Toss to coat. Serve immediately or cover and chill up to 4 hours. Stir before serving.
Makes 10 to 12 servings.

EACH SERVING *109 cal, 7 g fat (1 g sat. fat), 0 mg chol, 255 mg sodium, 10 g carbo, 2 g fiber, 2 g pro. Daily Values: 26% vit. A, 85% vit. C, 4% calcium, 3% iron.*

WHOLE WHEAT SPAGHETTI WITH FRESH HERBS

START TO FINISH 30 min.

INGREDIENTS

8 oz. whole wheat spaghetti
1 medium zucchini and/or yellow summer squash, halved lengthwise and sliced ¼ inch thick
2 Tbsp. extra virgin olive oil
1 large shallot, finely chopped
1 tsp. finely shredded lemon peel
2 tsp. lemon juice
1 Tbsp. *each* snipped fresh chives, basil, oregano, and dill
1 clove garlic, minced
½ tsp. salt
¼ tsp. ground black pepper
½ cup cherry tomatoes, halved
⅓ cup finely shredded fresh Parmesan cheese, plus additional cheese for sprinkling

PREPARATION

1. Prepare pasta according to package directions, adding squash last 2 minutes of cooking. Drain.
2. Meanwhile, in large bowl combine olive oil, shallot, lemon peel, lemon juice, fresh herbs, garlic, salt, and pepper. Add hot cooked pasta. Toss to combine. Add tomatoes and ⅓ cup Parmesan cheese; toss to combine.
3. Transfer spaghetti mixture to serving bowl. Sprinkle with additional Parmesan cheese. **Makes 6 side-dish servings (5 cups).**

EACH SERVING *215 cal, 7 g fat (2 g sat. fat), 5 mg chol, 319 mg sodium, 32 g carbo, 1 g fiber, 9 g pro. Daily Values: 7% vit. A, 17% vit. C, 12% calcium, 10% iron.*

TOMATO PALOOZA

GINA LANDAU, IOWA CITY, IOWA

LISA BOTTIGLIO, BURLINGTON, MASS.

TRICOLOR TOMATO RAVIOLI

START TO FINISH 35 min.

INGREDIENTS

1	24- to 25-oz. pkg. frozen cheese-filled ravioli
4	large tomatoes, such as green zebra, yellow, and/or red, cut in thin wedges and seeded (about 4 cups)
¾	cup small fresh basil leaves
¼	cup drained capers
½	tsp. ground black pepper
¼	tsp. salt
2	Tbsp. butter
6	cloves garlic, minced
2	cups fresh baby spinach
½	cup shredded Parmesan cheese

PREPARATION

1. Cook frozen ravioli according to package directions; drain. Meanwhile, in large bowl combine tomatoes, basil, capers, pepper, and salt; set aside.

2. In large skillet melt butter over medium heat. Add garlic and cook 30 seconds. Add tomato mixture; cook just until heated through. Remove from heat; gently stir in spinach.

3. To serve, place cooked ravioli on serving platter. Spoon tomato mixture over ravioli. Sprinkle Parmesan. **Makes 4 servings.**

EACH SERVING *480 cal, 18 g fat (11 g sat. fat), 93 mg chol, 914 mg sodium, 57 g carbo, 5 g fiber, 22 g pro. Daily Values: 79% vit. A, 53% vit. C, 42% calcium, 20% iron.*

FAST!

TOMATO AND GRILLED VEGGIE STACK

PREP 20 min. **GRILL** 8 min.

INGREDIENTS

1	medium eggplant (diameter similar to tomatoes), cut crosswise in 6 slices
2	medium yellow sweet peppers, seeded and cut lengthwise in thirds
3	Tbsp. extra virgin olive oil
2	large tomatoes, each cut in 6 slices
1	lb. fresh mozzarella, cut in 12 slices
6	slices prosciutto
	Small fresh basil leaves
1	Tbsp. balsamic vinegar

PREPARATION

1. Brush eggplant slices and sweet pepper pieces with *2 tablespoons* of the olive oil. Sprinkle *salt* and *ground black pepper.*

2. For a charcoal grill, grill eggplant and sweet pepper on rack of uncovered grill directly over medium coals for 8 minutes or until tender, turning once. (For a gas grill, preheat grill. Reduce heat to medium. Place eggplant and sweet peppers on rack over heat. Cover; grill as above.) Cool to room temperature.

3. On individual plates layer tomato slices, mozzarella slices, prosciutto, eggplant, and sweet pepper with several basil leaves. Drizzle on remaining olive oil and vinegar. **Makes 6 servings.**

EACH SERVING *396 cal, 29 g fat (11 g sat. fat), 60 mg chol, 911 mg sodium, 13 g carbo, 4 g fiber, 23 g pro. Daily Values: 21% vit. A, 202% vit. C, 40% calcium, 6% iron.*

PARMESAN CRUSTED SHRIMP WITH NAPOLI SAUCE

START TO FINISH 50 min.

INGREDIENTS
2	Tbsp. butter
1	Tbsp. olive oil
3	cloves garlic, minced
5	Roma tomatoes, chopped (2⅓ cups)
1	medium fresh poblano chile pepper, halved, seeded, and chopped* (⅔ cup)
1	Tbsp. honey
1	tsp. paprika
2	Tbsp. finely shredded Parmesan cheese
2	green onions, thinly sliced
1	Tbsp. snipped fresh oregano
1	lb. large shrimp, peeled and deveined
2	Tbsp. cooking oil
½	cup fine dry bread crumbs
½	cup finely shredded Parmesan cheese
2	egg whites, beaten

PREPARATION

1. Preheat oven to 400°F. In large skillet heat butter and olive oil. Add garlic; cook 1 minute. Add tomatoes, poblano pepper, honey, and paprika. Bring to boiling; reduce heat and simmer, uncovered, about 10 minutes or until most of liquid is evaporated. Stir in the 2 tablespoons Parmesan, green onion, and oregano. Season to taste with *salt* and *ground black pepper*.

2. Meanwhile, rinse shrimp; pat dry with paper towels. Spread cooking oil on bottom of 15×10×1-inch baking pan; set pan aside. In shallow dish combine bread crumbs and the ½ cup Parmesan. Place egg whites in another shallow dish. Dip shrimp in egg whites; coat shrimp with bread crumb mixture. Arrange in prepared pan. Bake 10 minutes or until shrimp is opaque.

3. Divide tomato sauce among four plates; top with shrimp. **Makes 4 servings.**

*NOTE Because hot chile peppers contain volatile oils that can burn your skin and eyes, avoid direct contact with chiles as much as possible. When working with chile peppers, wear plastic or rubber gloves. If your bare hands do touch the chile peppers, wash your hands well with soap and water.

EACH SERVING *400 cal, 22 g fat (8 g sat. fat), 154 mg chol, 670 mg sodium, 24 g carbo, 2 g fiber, 27 g pro. Daily Values: 35% vit. A, 151% vit. C, 26% calcium, 23% iron.*

ROASTED CHICKEN-VEGGIE PASTA SALAD WITH ROASTED TOMATO VINAIGRETTE

PREP 30 min. **ROAST** 40 min. **OVEN** 400°F

INGREDIENTS
4	cups grape tomatoes, halved
1½	cups sliced baby portabello mushrooms
1	medium red sweet pepper, chopped
⅓	cup chopped red onion
5	Tbsp. extra virgin olive oil
1	cup dried multigrain elbow macaroni (about 4 oz.)
½	of purchased roasted chicken
2	Tbsp. light mayonnaise
2	Tbsp. red wine vinegar
2	tsp. sugar
¾	tsp. salt
½	tsp. ground black pepper
1	6- to 7-oz. pkg. fresh baby spinach

PREPARATION

1. Preheat oven to 400°F. Line a 15×10×1-inch baking pan with foil. Place tomatoes on one half of prepared pan. Combine mushrooms, sweet pepper, and red onion; spoon on other half of pan. Drizzle *2 tablespoons* of the olive oil over tomatoes and mushroom mixture. Roast, uncovered, for 40 minutes.

2. Meanwhile, cook pasta according to package directions. Drain. Chop chicken, discarding skin and bones. In bowl combine pasta and chicken. Stir in mushroom mixture and *half* of the tomatoes; set aside. In blender or food processor combine remaining tomatoes, remaining olive oil, mayonnaise, vinegar, sugar, salt, and black pepper. Cover; blend or process until mixture is smooth. Pour over pasta mixture; toss to combine.

3. To serve, arrange spinach on serving platter. Spoon pasta mixture over spinach. Serve immediately.
Makes 4 to 6 servings.

EACH SERVING *480 cal, 30 g fat (6 g sat. fat), 65 mg chol, 954 mg sodium, 35 g carbo, 6 g fiber, 23 g pro. Daily Values: 129% vit. A, 124% vit. C, 8% calcium, 22% iron.*

ROASTED TOMATO VINAIGRETTE

PREP 15 min. **BAKE** 20 min. **COOL** 10 min.
OVEN 400°F

INGREDIENTS
4	Roma tomatoes
¼	cup extra virgin olive oil
2	cloves garlic, minced
2	Tbsp. white wine vinegar
1	tsp. Dijon-style mustard
1	tsp. snipped fresh thyme

PREPARATION

1. Preheat oven to 400°F. Line shallow baking pan with parchment paper; set aside. Cut off stem ends of tomatoes. Cut tomatoes in half lengthwise.

2. In bowl toss tomatoes, *2 tablespoons* of the olive oil, and garlic. Place tomatoes in prepared pan, cut sides down. Drizzle tomatoes with any oil mixture left in bowl.

3. Bake 20 minutes. Remove pan from oven; cool tomatoes slightly.

4. In blender combine tomatoes and any pan juices, vinegar, remaining olive oil, mustard, and thyme; cover and blend until smooth. Season to taste with *salt* and

ground black pepper. Serve immediately or cover and chill up to 3 days. **Makes 1⅓ cups.**

EACH SERVING (1 TBSP.) *28 cal, 3 g fat (0 g sat. fat), 0 mg chol, 35 mg sodium, 1 g carbo, 0 g fiber, 0 g pro. Daily Values: 4% vit. A, 5% vit. C, 1% iron.*

LOW FAT

SWEET AND SPICY GREEN TOMATO RELISH

PREP 45 min. **COOK** 25 min.
PROCESS 15 min.

INGREDIENTS
12	green tomatoes (5½ to 6 lb.), cored
2	large sweet onions
2	large red sweet peppers, seeded
10	cayenne chile peppers*
5	fresh jalapeño chile peppers*
1½	cups sugar
1	Tbsp. salt
2	cups white vinegar

PREPARATION

1. Cut up tomatoes, onions, and peppers (remove seeds from cayenne and jalapeño peppers, if desired). In food processor place some of the vegetables; cover and process until finely chopped. Transfer to large kettle or stock pot. Repeat until all vegetables are chopped (8 to 10 portions).

2. Add sugar and salt; mix well. Stir in vinegar. Heat to boiling. Reduce heat and simmer, uncovered, 25 minutes, stirring occasionally. Remove from heat.

3. Ladle hot mixture into hot, clean pint canning jars, leaving ½ inch headspace. Wipe jar rims; adjust lids. Process in boiling-water canner 15 minutes (start timing when water returns to boil). Remove jars; cool on racks. **Makes 6 pints (about 12 cups).**

*NOTE Because hot chile peppers contain volatile oils that can burn your skin and eyes, avoid direct contact with chiles as much as possible. When working with chile peppers, wear plastic or rubber gloves. If your bare hands do touch the chile peppers, wash your hands well with soap and water.

EACH SERVING (1 TBSP.) *10 cal, 0 g fat, 0 mg chol, 37 mg sodium, 2 g carbo, 0 g fiber, 0 g pro. Daily Values: 3% vit. A, 6% vit. C.*

OLIVE DISHES

DONNA RICCI, SCOTTSDALE, ARIZ.

CHICKEN WITH OLIVES

PREP 15 min. **COOK** 25 min.

INGREDIENTS

4   skinless, boneless chicken breast halves (1¼ to 1½ lb. total)
2   Tbsp. olive oil
1   medium onion, sliced
2   cloves garlic, minced
1   15-oz. can crushed tomatoes
1   5.75-oz. jar sliced pitted green olives, drained
1   2.25-oz. can sliced pitted ripe olives, drained
2   Tbsp. capers, drained
2   Tbsp. finely shredded lemon peel
1   tsp. dried oregano, crushed
3   Tbsp. snipped fresh Italian (flat-leaf) parsley

PREPARATION

1. In large skillet brown chicken in hot oil over medium-high heat for 5 minutes, turning once. Remove chicken from skillet; set aside. Add onion to skillet. Cook over medium heat 8 to 10 minutes or until tender and lightly browned, stirring occasionally; add garlic last 1 minute of cooking.

2. Stir tomatoes, olives, capers, lemon peel, and oregano into onion mixture. Place chicken on tomato mixture. Bring to boiling; reduce heat. Simmer, covered, 13 to 15 minutes or until chicken is no longer pink (170°F).

3. To serve, place chicken on platter. Season tomato mixture to taste with *salt* and *ground black pepper*. Spoon tomato mixture over chicken. Sprinkle parsley. **Makes 4 servings.**

EACH SERVING *340 cal, 16 g fat (2 g sat. fat), 82 mg chol, 1,311 mg sodium, 13 g carbo, 5 g fiber, 35 g pro. Daily Values: 10% vit. A, 36% vit. C, 10% calcium, 14% iron.*

CRISTINA MATHERS, SAN MIGUEL, CALIF.

OLIVE MEDLEY PINWHEELS

PREP 25 min. **CHILL** 2 to 4 hr.

INGREDIENTS

1   8-oz. pkg. cream cheese, softened
½   cup pitted green olives, chopped
½   cup pitted ripe olives, chopped
½   cup pitted kalamata olives, chopped
1   tsp. finely shredded lemon peel
¼   tsp. garlic powder
4   10-inch flour tortillas
8   large basil leaves
½   cup bottled roasted red sweet peppers, well drained and cut in strips

PREPARATION

1. In medium mixing bowl beat cream cheese with electric mixer on medium speed until smooth. Stir in olives, lemon peel, garlic powder, and ¼ teaspoon *ground black pepper;* set aside.

2. Warm tortillas according to package directions. Spread olive mixture on each tortilla; arrange basil leaves and sweet pepper strips along center. Roll tortillas parallel with sweet pepper strips. Wrap in plastic; refrigerate 2 to 4 hours. To serve, trim off ends of each roll; cut rolls in ½-inch slices. **Makes 10 servings (about 40 slices).**

EACH SERVING *161 cal, 12 g fat (6 g sat. fat), 25 mg chol, 435 mg sodium, 11 g carbo, 1 g fiber, 3 g pro. Daily Values: 8% vit. A, 35% vit. C, 5% calcium, 7% iron.*

BLACK OLIVE-TOMATO PESTO SCONES

PREP 25 min. **BAKE** 12 min. **OVEN** 425°F

INGREDIENTS
1	cup (2½ oz.) dried tomatoes (not oil-packed)
2	2.25-oz. cans sliced black olives
¾	cup milk
2	cups all-purpose flour
1	0.5-oz. envelope pesto sauce mix
2	tsp. baking powder
½	tsp. baking soda
2	Tbsp. cold butter

PREPARATION
1. Preheat oven to 425°F. Grease large baking sheet; set aside. Place tomatoes in small bowl; add *boiling water* to cover. Let stand 10 minutes. Drain and chop (should have about ¾ cup); set aside. Drain olives, reserving ¼ cup liquid (should have about 1 cup olives). In small bowl combine reserved liquid and milk; set aside.

2. In bowl combine flour, pesto sauce mix, baking powder, and baking soda. Using pastry blender cut in butter until mixture resembles coarse crumbs. Make a well in center of flour mixture. Add milk mixture, olives, and tomatoes; stir to combine. Turn out on floured surface; knead 10 strokes (dough will be slightly sticky). Transfer to prepared baking sheet. With floured hands, pat to 10-inch circle. Cut into 8 wedges (do not separate). Brush with 1 tablespoon *olive oil*.

3. Bake 12 to 14 minutes or until lightly browned. Cut into wedges. Remove and cool slightly on wire rack. Serve warm. **Makes 8 scones.**

EACH SCONE 206 cal, 7 g fat (3 g sat. fat), 9 mg chol, 693 mg sodium, 30 g carbo, 2 g fiber, 5 g pro. Daily Values: 5% vit. A, 5% vit. C, 8% calcium, 14% iron.

FAST!

EXTRA OLIVE MUFFULETTAS

START TO FINISH 25 min.

INGREDIENTS
¼	cup *each* pitted green olives; pitted kalamata olives; oil-cured black olives, pitted
¼	cup purchased dried tomato pesto
1	tsp. snipped fresh thyme
2	cloves garlic, minced
4	hoagie buns, split
8	oz. thinly sliced ham
4	oz. thinly sliced salami
4	oz. thinly sliced provolone cheese
1	cup bottled roasted red sweet peppers, well drained
¼	cup mayonnaise

PREPARATION
1. In small food processor combine olives, pesto, thyme, and garlic; process until olives are finely chopped.*

2. Halve hoagie buns. Hollow out bottom halves of buns, leaving ¼-inch shells. Spoon olive mixture into buns. Layer ham, salami, and provolone over olives. Cut peppers into strips; pat dry with paper toweling; lay over cheese. Spread cut sides of bun tops with mayonnaise; place on tops of sandwiches and serve.
Makes 4 sandwiches.
*NOTE Olives may be finely chopped by hand and mixture stirred together.

EACH SANDWICH 730 cal, 40 g fat (13 g sat. fat), 79 mg chol, 2,413 mg sodium, 59 g carbo, 4 g fiber, 34 g pro. Daily Values: 9% vit. A, 183% vit. C, 35% calcium, 27% iron.

GREEK OLIVE NACHOS

START TO FINISH 35 min.

INGREDIENTS
6	whole wheat pita bread rounds
2	Tbsp. olive oil
8	oz. bulk mild Italian sausage
⅔	cup beer
1	8-oz. pkg. cream cheese, cubed
1½	cups feta cheese with herbs, crumbled
¼	cup grated Parmesan cheese
1	clove garlic, minced
1½	cups pitted ripe and/or kalamata olives, coarsely chopped
¼	cup finely chopped red sweet pepper
1	Tbsp. snipped fresh dill (optional)

PREPARATION
1. Preheat oven to 400°F. Cut each pita bread round into 6 wedges. Separate each wedge at fold. Spread in even layers on two baking sheets, cut sides up. Brush with olive oil. Bake 8 to 10 minutes or until golden.

2. In skillet brown sausage; drain fat. Stir in beer; bring to simmer. Stir in cream cheese, *1 cup* of the feta, Parmesan, and garlic. Cook and stir over medium heat until cheese is melted. Stir in olives and red sweet pepper.

3. To assemble, place warm chips on serving platter. Spoon on sauce; sprinkle with remaining cheese and dill. **Makes 10 to 12 appetizer servings.**

EACH SERVING 377 cal, 26 g fat (11 g sat. fat), 59 mg chol, 872 mg sodium, 25 g carbo, 4 g fiber, 14 g pro. Daily Values: 14% vit. A, 9% vit. C, 13% calcium, 14% iron.

LEMON-OLIVE-CHEESE TOASTS

PREP 20 min. **CHILL** 1 to 24 hr. **BAKE** 5 min.
STAND 30 min. **OVEN** 450°F

INGREDIENTS
6	oz. pitted kalamata olives (1 cup)
4	oz. pitted green olives (¾ cup)
3	Tbsp. drained capers
2	cloves garlic, quartered
2	Tbsp. lemon juice
⅓	cup extra virgin olive oil

2	tsp. finely shredded lemon peel
¼	tsp. crushed red pepper
6	oz. goat cheese (chèvre)
1	8-oz. baguette-style French bread, sliced into ¼-inch-thick slices

PREPARATION
1. Place olives, capers, garlic, and lemon juice in food processor. Cover; pulse while adding *3 tablespoons* of the olive oil, scraping down sides occasionally. Mixture should be finely chopped, not smooth. Transfer mixture to medium bowl. Stir in lemon peel and crushed red pepper. Cover and chill 1 to 24 hours to blend flavors.

2. Let olive mixture and cheese stand at room temperature 30 minutes before serving. Meanwhile, preheat oven to 450°F. Brush both sides of bread slices with remaining olive oil. Arrange in single layer on baking sheets. Bake 5 to 7 minutes or until browned.

3. To serve, spread bread slices with cheese; top with olive mixture. **Makes 26 toasts.**

EACH TOAST 90 cal, 6 g fat (1 g sat. fat), 3 mg chol, 287 mg sodium, 6 g carbo, 1 g fiber, 2 g pro. Daily Values: 1% vit. C, 2% calcium, 3% iron.

FAST!

PASTA TAPENADE

START TO FINISH 30 min.

INGREDIENTS
1½	cups mixed olives (such as cerignola, picholine, kalamata, and/or catalan)
8	oz. dried radiatore or rotini
1	large clove garlic
2	canned anchovy fillets, drained
1	tsp. finely shredded lemon peel
1	cup lightly packed fresh Italian (flat-leaf) parsley leaves
¼	cup olive oil
2	Tbsp. lemon juice
½	cup finely shredded Parmesan cheese Lemon wedges

PREPARATION
1. Pit olives, if necessary; set aside. Cook pasta according to package directions; drain, reserving ¼ cup cooking liquid. Return pasta to pan.

2. Meanwhile, in food processor combine garlic, anchovy fillets, and lemon peel. Cover; process until finely chopped. Add olives, parsley, olive oil, and lemon juice; process with several on-off turns until coarsely chopped. Add to cooked pasta; toss to coat. If desired, add reserved cooking liquid and toss (pasta will absorb liquid). Toss with Parmesan; sprinkle with *cracked black pepper* to taste. Pass lemon wedges.
Makes 6 side-dish servings.

EACH SERVING 309 cal, 16 g fat (3 g sat. fat), 6 mg chol, 545 mg sodium, 33 g carbo, 3 g fiber, 8 g pro. Daily Values: 18% vit. A, 29% vit. C, 11% calcium, 12% iron.

TUBE PAN CAKES

AMARETTO CAKE WITH CINNAMON SWIRL

PREP 45 min. **BAKE** 55 min. **COOL** 10 min. **OVEN** 350°F

INGREDIENTS
1   cup sliced almonds
1   Tbsp. ground cinnamon
3   Tbsp. almond paste
1   pkg. 2-layer-size white cake mix
1   4-serving-size pkg. white chocolate instant pudding
     and pie filling mix
1   8-oz. carton light sour cream
4   eggs, lightly beaten
½   cup cooking oil
½   cup amaretto or ½ cup water plus 1 tsp. almond extract
1   recipe Glaze

PREPARATION
1. Preheat oven to 350°F. Generously grease 10-inch (12-cup) fluted tube pan. In food processor combine almonds and cinnamon. Cover; process until nuts are finely chopped. Coat bottom and sides of pan with half the mixture. Add almond paste to remaining mixture in processor. Process until combined.
2. In large mixing bowl combine cake and pudding mixes, sour cream, eggs, ½ cup *water*, oil, and amaretto. Beat with mixer on low speed to combine. Beat on medium speed 2 minutes, scraping bowl as needed. Spoon half the batter into pan. Evenly sprinkle cinnamon-almond paste mixture over batter. Spoon remaining batter on cinnamon mixture.
3. Bake about 55 minutes or until wooden pick inserted near center comes out clean. Cool in pan 10 minutes. Remove from pan. Place on rack over waxed paper. Using wooden skewer, poke several holes in cake. Prepare Glaze; spoon over cake. **Makes 12 to 16 servings.**
Glaze In small saucepan combine ⅓ cup *water*, ¼ cup *sugar*, and 2 tablespoons *butter*. Stir over medium heat until sugar is dissolved. Reduce heat; simmer, uncovered, 5 minutes.

EACH SERVING *456 cal, 23 g fat (6 g sat. fat), 82 mg chol, 458 mg sodium, 51 g carbo, 1 g fiber, 7 g pro. Daily Values: 4% vit. A, 13% calcium, 8% iron.*

KID FRIENDLY

ORANGE-CRANBERRY CAKE

PREP 30 min. **BAKE** 50 min. **COOL** 10 min. **OVEN** 350°F

INGREDIENTS
2¼   cups all-purpose flour
1½   cups rolled oats
1   Tbsp. baking powder
½   tsp. baking soda
½   tsp. salt
¾   cup butter, softened
1   cup sugar
3   eggs
1   cup milk
2   cups fresh cranberries, chopped
2   Tbsp. sugar
2   tsp. finely shredded orange peel
1   recipe Orange Glaze

PREPARATION
1. Preheat oven to 350°F. Grease and flour 10-inch tube pan; set aside. In bowl stir together flour, oats, baking powder, soda, and salt.
2. In large mixing bowl beat butter with electric mixer on medium speed 30 seconds. Add the 1 cup sugar; beat until combined. Add eggs; beat until well combined. Alternately add flour mixture and milk, beating on low speed after each addition until combined.
3. Toss cranberries with the 2 tablespoons sugar; fold into batter with orange peel. Spoon batter into prepared pan; spread evenly.
4. Bake 50 to 60 minutes or until wooden pick inserted near center comes out clean. Cool in pan 10 minutes. Remove from pan. Cool on rack. Prepare Orange Glaze; spoon over cooled cake. Let stand until glaze is set. **Makes 12 servings.**
Orange Glaze In small bowl combine 1 cup *powdered sugar* and ½ teaspoon finely shredded *orange peel*. Add 2 to 3 teaspoons *orange juice* to make drizzling consistency.

EACH SERVING *374 cal, 14 g fat (8 g sat. fat), 85 mg chol, 318 mg sodium, 57 g carbo, 3 g fiber, 6 g pro. Daily Values: 9% vit. A, 6% vit. C, 6% calcium, 10% iron.*

ALMOND POLENTA CAKE WITH ALMOND GLAZE

PREP 25 min. **BAKE** 40 min. **OVEN** 350°F

INGREDIENTS

1 cup butter
4 eggs
1½ cups all-purpose flour
½ cup yellow cornmeal
2 tsp. baking powder
½ tsp. salt
1 cup granulated sugar
1 tsp. almond extract
1 tsp. vanilla
1 cup milk
1½ cups powdered sugar
½ tsp. almond extract
2 to 3 Tbsp. milk
  Sliced almonds, toasted (optional)

PREPARATION

1. Allow butter and eggs to stand at room temperature 30 minutes. Grease and flour an 8-inch fluted tube pan; set aside. In medium bowl stir together flour, cornmeal, baking powder, and salt; set aside.
2. Preheat oven to 350°F. In mixing bowl beat butter with electric mixer on medium to high speed 30 seconds. Add the granulated sugar and beat on medium speed until well combined. Add eggs, 1 at a time, beating well after each addition. Beat in 1 teaspoon almond extract and vanilla until just combined. Alternately add flour mixture and milk, beating on low speed after each addition just until combined. Spread batter evenly into prepared pan.
3. Bake 40 to 45 minutes or until wooden toothpick inserted near center of cake comes out clean. Cool cake in pan on wire rack 10 minutes. Remove cake from pan. Cool cake completely on rack.
4. Meanwhile, for glaze, in medium bowl combine powdered sugar, ½ teaspoon almond extract, and *1 tablespoon* of milk. Stir in additional milk, 1 teaspoon at a time, until glaze reaches drizzling consistency. Drizzle over cooled cake. Sprinkle with sliced almonds. **Makes 12 servings.**

EACH SERVING *372 cal, 18 g fat (10 g sat. fat), 113 mg chol, 281 mg sodium, 49 g carbo, 1 g fiber, 5 g pro. Daily Values: 12% vit. A, 6% calcium, 7% iron.*

APPLE BUTTER-PECAN CAKE

PREP 25 min. **BAKE** 60 min. **COOL** 25 min. **OVEN** 325°F

INGREDIENTS

  Nonstick cooking spray for baking
2 cups all-purpose flour
1 tsp. baking powder
1 tsp. baking soda
1 tsp. ground cinnamon
½ tsp. salt
½ tsp. ground nutmeg
½ cup butter, softened

1 cup granulated sugar
1 cup packed brown sugar
3 eggs
1⅓ cups apple butter
2 Tbsp. milk
1 cup chopped pecans
1 cup powdered sugar
1 Tbsp. butter, melted
1 tsp. vanilla
2 to 3 tsp. warm water

PREPARATION

1. Preheat oven to 325°F. Coat 10-inch fluted tube pan with cooking spray; set aside. In medium bowl stir together flour, baking powder, baking soda, cinnamon, salt, and nutmeg; set aside.
2. In mixing bowl beat ½ cup butter with electric mixer on medium speed 30 seconds. Beat in granulated and brown sugars until combined. Add eggs and beat well. Beat in flour mixture until combined. Beat in apple butter and milk. Stir in pecans. Spoon into prepared pan, spreading evenly.
3. Bake 60 to 70 minutes or until top springs back when lightly touched and wooden toothpick inserted in center of cake comes out clean. Cool cake in pan on wire rack 10 minutes. Loosen edges of cake; invert cake onto wire rack and cool 15 minutes more.
4. Meanwhile, in small bowl combine powdered sugar, melted butter, vanilla, and enough warm water until icing reaches drizzling consistency. Drizzle over cake; cool completely. **Makes 12 to 16 servings.**

EACH SERVING *576 cal, 17 g fat (6 g sat. fat), 76 mg chol, 322 mg sodium, 103 g carbo, 3 g fiber, 5 g pro. Daily Values: 7% vit. A, 1% vit. C, 6% calcium, 10% iron.*

KID FRIENDLY

FRESH FRUIT CAKE

PREP 30 min. **BAKE** 70 min. **COOL** 15 min. **OVEN** 325°F

INGREDIENTS

3 cups all-purpose flour
2 cups sugar
2 Tbsp. unsweetened cocoa powder
1 tsp. baking soda
½ tsp. salt
1 cup shredded coconut
1 cup chopped fresh pineapple
1 small apple or pear, cored
  and chopped
1 small banana, chopped (½ cup)
⅔ cup cooking oil
3 eggs, lightly beaten
½ cup coarsely chopped pecans, toasted
2 Tbsp. brandy
1 tsp. vanilla
½ tsp. almond extract
  Powdered sugar

PREPARATION

1. Preheat oven to 325°F. Grease and flour 10-inch fluted tube pan; set aside.

2. In mixing bowl stir together flour, sugar, cocoa powder, baking soda, and salt. Add coconut, pineapple, apple, banana, oil, eggs, pecans, brandy, vanilla, and almond extract. Stir just until blended (do not overmix).
3. Spoon mixture into prepared pan. Bake about 70 minutes or until wooden toothpick inserted near center comes out clean. Cool in pan on wire rack 15 minutes. Invert cake onto wire rack and remove cake from pan; cool completely. Sprinkle with powdered sugar before serving. **Makes 16 servings.**

EACH SERVING *291 cal, 7 g fat (3 g sat. fat), 40 mg chol, 193 mg sodium, 52 g carbo, 2 g fiber, 5 g pro. Daily Values: 1% vit. A, 9% vit. C, 1% calcium, 8% iron.*

TANGY MARGARITA COFFEE CAKE

PREP 30 min. **BAKE** 50 min. **COOL** 20 min. **OVEN** 350°F

INGREDIENTS

3 cups all-purpose flour
1½ tsp. baking powder
1 tsp. baking soda
1 tsp. ground ginger
¾ cup butter, softened
1½ cups packed brown sugar
3 eggs
4 teaspoons finely shredded lime peel
3 Tbsp. fresh lime juice
2 Tbsp. golden tequila or orange juice
1 cup lime-flavored yogurt
1 recipe Lime Icing

PREPARATION

1. Preheat oven to 350°F. Grease and flour 10-inch fluted tube pan; set aside. In bowl stir together flour, baking powder, baking soda, ginger, and ½ teaspoon *salt*; set aside.
2. In mixing bowl beat butter with electric mixer on medium speed 30 seconds. Add brown sugar; beat until combined. Add eggs, 1 at a time, beating well after each addition. In bowl combine lime peel, lime juice, tequila, and yogurt; add alternately with flour mixture, beating on low to medium speed after each addition just until combined. Pour into prepared pan.
3. Bake 50 to 55 minutes or until wooden toothpick inserted near center of cake comes out clean. Cool in pan on wire rack 10 minutes. Remove from pan. Cool 10 minutes. Drizzle with Lime Icing. Cool completely on wire rack.
Makes 12 servings.

LIME ICING In small mixing bowl stir together 1 cup *powdered sugar* and 1 tablespoon *lime juice*. Stir in additional lime juice, if necessary, until icing is of drizzling consistency.

EACH SERVING *405 cal, 13 g fat (8 g sat. fat), 84 mg chol, 367 mg sodium, 66 g carbo, 1 g fiber, 6 g pro. Daily Values: 9% vit. A, 4% vit. C, 11% calcium, 11% iron.*

MACARONI AND CHEESE

MACARONI AND BRIE WITH CRAB

PREP 40 min. **BAKE** 20 min. **OVEN** 350°F

INGREDIENTS

	Nonstick cooking spray
1	medium sweet onion, halved and thinly sliced
5	Tbsp. butter
1	lb. dried medium shell pasta
1/3	cup all-purpose flour
3/4	tsp. salt
1/2	tsp. ground black pepper
3	cups milk
1	lb. Brie cheese, trimmed and chopped (reserve 8 small wedges for topping, if desired)
2	6- to 6.5-oz. cans lump crabmeat, drained, flaked, and cartilage removed
3	slices firm white bread, torn into large pieces

PREPARATION

1. Preheat oven to 350°F. Lightly coat eight 14- to 16-ounce individual baking dishes with cooking spray; set aside. In large skillet cook onion in butter over medium-low heat about 15 minutes or until tender and golden brown, stirring occasionally. Meanwhile, cook pasta in 4-quart Dutch oven according to package directions; drain and return to pan.

2. Add flour, salt, and pepper to onion in skillet; stir until combined, about 1 minute. Add milk all at once. Cook and stir until slightly thickened and bubbly. Gradually add chopped cheese; cook over medium-low heat until cheese melts. Stir into pasta. Fold in crab. Transfer to baking dishes.

3. Place bread pieces in food processor; cover and process to coarse crumbs. Sprinkle crumbs over pasta mixture. Bake, uncovered, 20 to 25 minutes or until heated through and crumbs are golden brown. If desired, add a wedge of Brie to each dish the last 5 minutes of baking time. **Makes 8 servings.**

EACH SERVING *595 cal, 217 g fat (16 g sat. fat), 137 mg chol, 905 mg sodium, 57 g carbo, 2 g fiber, 31 g pro. Daily Values: 15% vit. A, 2% vit. C, 28% calcium, 16% iron.*

SOUTH INDIAN-STYLE MACARONI AND CHEESE

PREP 25 min. **BAKE** 25 min. **OVEN** 350°F

INGREDIENTS

8	oz. dried macaroni
2	cups frozen peas
1/2	cup soft bread crumbs
1/4	cup freshly grated Asiago cheese (1 oz.)
1/2	tsp. paprika
1/2	tsp. *each* salt and garam masala
1/4	tsp. *each* cayenne pepper, ground turmeric, and ground black pepper
3	Tbsp. butter
1	tsp. garlic paste
1/2	tsp. finely shredded fresh ginger
2	Tbsp. all-purpose flour
3	cups milk
2	cups shredded sharp cheddar cheese (8 oz.)

PREPARATION

1. Preheat oven to 350°F. Cook macaroni according to package directions; drain over peas in colander.

2. Meanwhile, in small bowl combine bread crumbs, Asiago, and paprika; set aside. In another bowl stir together salt, garam masala, cayenne, turmeric, and black pepper; set aside.

3. In large saucepan melt butter. Add garlic paste and ginger; cook and stir 1 minute. Add salt-spice mixture; cook 2 minutes. Stir in flour. Add milk all at once, stirring until smooth. Cook and stir until slightly thickened and bubbly. Stir in cheddar cheese until melted. Stir in cooked macaroni. Transfer to 2-quart rectangular baking dish; sprinkle with bread crumb mixture. Bake, uncovered, 25 to 30 minutes or until bubbly and crumbs are golden.
Makes 6 servings.

EACH SERVING *481 cal, 23 g fat (14 g sat. fat), 70 mg chol, 652 mg sodium, 46 g carbo, 4 g fiber, 23 g pro. Daily Values: 40% vit. A, 15% vit. C, 49% calcium, 15% iron.*

BAKED MEXICAN MACARONI AND CHEESE

PREP 30 min. **BAKE** 30 min. **STAND** 5 min.
OVEN 350°F

INGREDIENTS

6	oz. dried whole wheat elbow macaroni (1½ cups)
2	Tbsp. butter
2	Tbsp. all-purpose flour
1¼	cups half-and-half or light cream
2	cups shredded cheddar and Monterey Jack cheese (8 oz.)
1	1.25-oz. envelope reduced-sodium taco seasoning mix
1	15-oz. can black beans, rinsed and drained
1	14.5-oz. can diced tomatoes, drained
1	medium green sweet pepper, chopped
1	medium red sweet pepper, chopped
½	cup chopped red onion
½	cup bottled chunky salsa
4	green onions, sliced
1	medium avocado, peeled, pitted, and chopped
1	lime, cut into wedges

PREPARATION

1. Preheat oven to 350°F. Cook macaroni according to package directions. Drain and transfer to very large bowl; set aside.
2. In medium saucepan melt butter over low heat. Whisk in flour until smooth. Add half-and-half. Increase heat to medium; whisk constantly until mixture is boiling. Boil gently 2 minutes, whisking frequently. Remove from heat. Stir in *1½ cups* of the cheese and taco seasoning mix. Pour over macaroni in bowl.
3. Add beans, tomatoes, green pepper, red pepper, red onion, and salsa to macaroni mixture in bowl. Stir to combine well. Transfer mixture to greased 3-quart rectangular baking dish. Sprinkle with green onion and remaining ½ cup cheese.
4. Bake about 30 minutes or until heated through. Let stand 5 minutes before serving. Sprinkle with avocado. Serve with lime wedges. **Makes 8 servings.**

EACH SERVING *371 cal, 20 g fat (11 g sat. fat), 51 mg chol, 790 mg sodium, 98 g carbo, 7 g fiber, 16 g pro. Daily Values: 29% vit. A, 67% vit. C, 30% calcium, 14% iron.*

PENNE WITH HAM, SPINACH, AND ARTICHOKES

PREP 20 min. **BAKE** 30 min. **STAND** 10 min.
OVEN 350°F

INGREDIENTS

6	oz. dried miniature penne pasta
1	8-oz. frozen spinach artichoke dip, thawed
6	oz. Swiss cheese, shredded (1½ cups)
⅔	cup milk
2	tsp. Dijon-style mustard
	Dash bottled hot pepper sauce
6	oz. chopped cooked ham

PREPARATION

1. Preheat oven to 350°F. Butter 1½-quart casserole dish. Cook pasta according to package directions. Drain; return to pan. Stir in thawed dip, *1 cup* of the Swiss cheese, milk, mustard, hot pepper sauce, and ham. Transfer to prepared casserole.
2. Bake, covered, 25 minutes. Uncover; sprinkle with remaining ½ cup cheese. Bake, uncovered, 5 minutes more or until cheese on top is melted and mixture is heated through. Let stand 10 minutes before serving. **Makes 4 servings.**

EACH SERVING *454 cal, 18 g fat (10 g sat. fat), 70 mg chol, 1,092 mg sodium, 39 g carbo, 1 g fiber, 30 g pro. Daily Values: 22% vit. A, 4% vit. C, 50% calcium, 8% iron.*

SALMON-DILL PENNE AND CHEESE

PREP 30 min. **BAKE** 25 min. **OVEN** 350°F

INGREDIENTS

2	cups dried multigrain penne pasta (about 7 oz.) or dried penne pasta
2	Tbsp. butter
1	Tbsp. all-purpose flour
1	cup milk
12	oz. Havarti cheese with dill, shredded (3 cups)
½	of an 8-oz. tub light cream cheese with chive and onion
2	tsp. finely shredded lemon peel
8	oz. smoked salmon, flaked, with skin and bones removed
¾	cup soft rye bread crumbs
1	Tbsp. butter, melted

PREPARATION

1. Preheat oven to 350°F. Cook pasta minimum cooking time according to package directions. Drain; return to pan.
2. Meanwhile, in medium saucepan melt 2 tablespoons butter; stir in flour. Add milk; cook and stir until bubbly. Add cheeses; cook and stir until melted. Stir in lemon peel. Pour over pasta; fold in flaked salmon.
3. Transfer to 2-quart rectangular baking dish. In small bowl combine bread crumbs and 1 tablespoon melted butter. Sprinkle over pasta. Bake, uncovered, 25 minutes or until heated through. **Makes 4 servings.**

EACH SERVING *791 cal, 51 g fat (10 g sat. fat), 160 mg chol, 1,181 mg sodium, 43 g carbo, 4 g fiber, 43 g pro. Daily Values: 12% vit. A, 2% vit. C, 68% calcium, 13% iron.*

SMOKIN' MACARONI AND BLUE CHEESE

START TO FINISH 40 min.

INGREDIENTS

8	oz. dried campanelle or rotini pasta (3 cups)
1	small portobello mushroom
1	Tbsp. olive oil
8	oz. smoked turkey, chopped
2	oz. Gruyère cheese, shredded (½ cup)
1	Tbsp. all-purpose flour
1	cup milk
4	oz. blue cheese or Gorgonzola, crumbled
¼	tsp. ground black pepper
1	Tbsp. snipped fresh sage
¼	cup pine nuts, toasted (optional)
	Snipped fresh sage

PREPARATION

1. In 4-quart Dutch oven cook pasta according to package directions; drain and return to pan. Set aside.
2. Meanwhile, cut off mushroom stem even with cap; discard stem. Coarsely chop mushroom. In large skillet cook mushroom in hot oil over medium heat 5 minutes or until mushroom is tender. Remove from skillet. Add turkey and cook 3 to 5 minutes or until heated through. Return mushroom to skillet.
3. In small bowl toss together Gruyère cheese and flour. Add milk, blue cheese, Gruyère mixture, and pepper to skillet. Cook and stir until thickened and bubbly. Stir sauce mixture and the 1 tablespoon sage into cooked pasta, stirring just until combined.
4. Spoon mixture into serving bowl. Garnish with toasted pine nuts and additional snipped fresh sage.
Makes 4 servings.

EACH SERVING *498 cal, 18 g fat (10 g sat. fat), 66 mg chol, 1,155 mg sodium, 50 g carbo, 2 g fiber, 31 g pro. Daily Values: 13% vit. A, 4% vit. C, 39% calcium, 18% iron.*

PURCHASED COOKIE FIX-UPS

KID FRIENDLY

GRAHAM CRACKER BARS

PREP 30 min. **COOL** 30 min. **CHILL** 4 hr.

INGREDIENTS

¾	cup butter
¾	cup granulated sugar
¼	cup milk
1	egg, lightly beaten
1	cup chopped pecans, toasted
1	cup graham cracker crumbs
12	graham cracker rectangles
1	Tbsp. butter, softened
½	cup powdered sugar
2	to 3 tsp. milk

PREPARATION

1. For filling, in medium saucepan combine ¾ cup butter, granulated sugar, ¼ cup milk, and egg. Stirring constantly, cook over medium heat until mixture comes to full boil. Remove from heat. Stir in pecans and crumbs. Cool 30 minutes.

2. Meanwhile, place *six* of the graham cracker rectangles, side by side, on foil-lined baking sheet to make rectangle about 10×7 inches in size. Spoon filling in small mounds onto graham cracker rectangles. Carefully spread to an even layer, being careful not to move crackers. Place remaining cracker rectangles on top to match up with bottom rectangles. Lightly cover bars with plastic wrap. Chill in the refrigerator at least 4 hours or until filling is firm. Cut into bars.

3. In small bowl beat 1 tablespoon butter with whisk or electric mixer until smooth. Gradually whisk in powdered sugar and enough milk to make a thick drizzling consistency. Drizzle over bars. Let stand until set. **Makes 24 bars.**

EACH BAR *171 cal, 11 g fat (4 g sat. fat), 26 mg chol, 110 mg sodium, 18 g carbo, 1 g fiber, 2 g pro. Daily Values: 4% vit. A, 1% calcium, 3% iron.*

PUMPKIN-SPICED GINGERSNAP TRUFFLES

PREP 30 min. **STAND** 5 min. **CHILL** 2 ½ hr.

INGREDIENTS

1¼	cups semisweet chocolate pieces
¼	tsp. pumpkin pie spice
¼	tsp. vanilla
½	cup whipping cream
¾	cup chopped gingersnaps (about 10 cookies)
⅓	cup finely crushed gingersnaps (about 7 cookies) and/or ¼ cup unsweetened cocoa powder

PREPARATION

1. In medium bowl combine chocolate pieces, pumpkin pie spice, and vanilla.

2. In medium microwave-safe bowl place whipping cream. Microwave on 100% power (high) for 70 seconds or until boiling (or place cream in saucepan and bring just to boiling). Pour cream over chocolate mixture. Let stand 5 minutes. Whisk until smooth. Stir in chopped gingersnaps. Cover; refrigerate 1½ to 2 hours or until firm but soft enough to form into balls.

3. Place crushed gingersnaps and/or cocoa powder in small bowl(s). Using small spoon, scoop 1-tablespoon portions of truffle mixture and shape into balls. Roll in crushed gingersnaps and/or cocoa powder to coat. Refrigerate 1 hour or until firm. Store, covered, in refrigerator up to 3 days. **Makes 20 to 25 truffles.**

EACH TRUFFLE *97 cal, 6 g fat (3 g sat. fat), 8 mg chol, 42 mg sodium, 12 g carbo, 1 g fiber, 1 g pro. Daily Values: 2% vit. A, 1% calcium, 4% iron.*

ALMOND-APRICOT SUGAR COOKIE TARTLETS

PREP 30 min. **BAKE** 12 min. **COOL** 20 min. **OVEN** 350°F

INGREDIENTS

Nonstick cooking spray
1   16.5-oz. pkg. refrigerated sugar cookie dough
¾   cup slivered almonds, toasted and ground
⅔   cup tub-style reduced-fat cream cheese (Neufchâtel)
½   cup apricot preserves
4   oz. white chocolate, melted and cooled
36 sliced almonds
    Powdered sugar

PREPARATION

1. Preheat oven to 350°F. Lightly coat 1¾-inch muffin cups with cooking spray. Cut sugar cookie dough into 36 equal pieces. Roll pieces in ground almonds. Press each piece into bottom and up sides of muffin cups.

2. In medium bowl combine cream cheese, preserves, and *2 ounces* melted white chocolate; spoon heaping teaspoon in each cup. Top each with almond slice.

3. Bake 10 to 12 minutes or until golden brown. Cool completely in pans. (Centers will sink slightly.) Remove from cups. Drizzle with remaining white chocolate. Dust with powdered sugar.
Makes 36 tartlets.

EACH TARTLET *111 cal, 6 g fat (2 g sat. fat), 32 mg chol, 82 mg sodium, 14 g carbo, 0 g fiber, 2 g pro. Daily Values: 1% vit. A, 1% vit. C, 3% calcium, 2% iron.*

AUTUMN TRIFLE

PREP 25 min. **CHILL** 1 hr.

INGREDIENTS

2   cups milk
1   4-serving-size pkg. French vanilla instant pudding and pie filling mix
1   cup canned pumpkin
2   Tbsp. sugar
½   tsp. pumpkin pie spice
4   cups coarsely crushed gingersnaps (48 cookies)
1   21-oz. can apple pie filling
1   recipe Spiced Whipped Cream
½   cup chopped pecans or pecan halves, toasted
    Gingersnap cookie (optional)

PREPARATION

1. Place milk in large mixing bowl; add pudding mix. Whisk 2 minutes. Cover; chill 5 minutes. In medium mixing bowl combine pumpkin, sugar, and pumpkin pie spice. Fold in half of pudding mixture.

2. In 2 to 3-quart trifle dish, clear soufflé dish, or 3-quart casserole place *half* of the crushed cookies. Top with remaining plain pudding mixture, spreading evenly. Spread apple pie filling over pudding layer. Top with remaining cookies. Spread pumpkin pudding mixture over cookie layer.

3. Chill at least 1 hour before serving. To serve, top with Spiced Whipped Cream and pecans. Garnish with gingersnap cookie.
Makes 8 to 10 servings.

Spiced Whipped Cream In a chilled medium mixing bowl combine ⅔ cup *whipping cream*, 1 tablespoon *sugar*, 1 teaspoon *vanilla bean paste* or vanilla extract, and ¼ teaspoon *pumpkin pie spice*. Beat with an electric mixer on medium-high speed until soft peaks form.

Individual Autumn Trifles Prepare filling mixtures as directed. Divide mixtures evenly among eight to ten 12-ounce wine glasses, layering in order as directed in recipe. Chill and serve as directed.

EACH SERVING *472 cal, 18 g fat (7 g sat. fat), 32 mg chol, 519 mg sodium, 75 g carbo, 3 g fiber, 6 g pro. Daily Values: 104% vit. A, 5% vit. C, 13% calcium, 20% iron.*

DIRT BARS

PREP 30 min. **CHILL** 2 hr.

INGREDIENTS

2   cups chopped chocolate creme-filled cookies (about 20 cookies)
1   cup chopped peanuts
1⅔ cups semisweet chocolate pieces
1   cup creamy peanut butter
¼   cup milk
¼   cup butter

PREPARATION

1. Line 9×9×2-inch baking pan with foil extending over edges; set aside. In large bowl combine chopped cookies and peanuts; set aside.

2. In medium saucepan combine chocolate pieces, peanut butter, milk, and butter. Cook and stir over medium-low heat until melted and smooth. Pour over cookies and peanuts; stir to combine. Transfer to prepared baking pan. Spread mixture evenly in baking pan, using spatula to smooth surface. Cover; chill 2 hours or until firm.

3. Remove pan from refrigerator. Remove bars from pan by lifting foil edges. Cut into small bars. **Makes 64 pieces.**

EACH PIECE *82 cal, 6 g fat (2 g sat. fat), 2 mg chol, 63 mg sodium, 7 g carbo, 1 g fiber, 2 g pro. Daily Values: 1% calcium, 3% iron.*

DOUBLE PEANUT BUTTER CHOCOLATE BARS

PREP 20 min. **BAKE** 24 min. **OVEN** 375°F

INGREDIENTS

2   16.5-oz. rolls refrigerated peanut butter cookie dough
1   9.5-oz. pkg. (18 cookies) fudge-covered round cookies with peanut butter filling, chopped
⅓   cup chocolate-flavored ice cream topping*
½   cup peanut butter-flavored pieces
½   cup semisweet chocolate pieces
⅓   cup chopped dry honey-roasted peanuts

PREPARATION

1. Preheat oven to 375°F. Press *two-thirds* (about 3 cups) of cookie dough into bottom of ungreased 13×9×2-inch baking pan. Bake 12 minutes. Remove from oven.

2. Sprinkle crust with chopped cookies; drizzle ice cream topping. Sprinkle evenly with peanut butter pieces, chocolate pieces, and peanuts. Dot top with small pieces remaining cookie dough. Bake about 12 minutes more or until top is lightly browned. Cool completely on wire rack. Cut into bars. **Makes 24 bars.**

*NOTE Warm ice cream topping according to package directions, if needed to make drizzling consistency.

EACH BAR *308 cal, 17 g fat (6 g sat. fat), 10 mg chol, 217 mg sodium, 35 g carbo, 1 g fiber, 5 g pro. Daily Values: 4% calcium, 6% iron.*

BIG SANDWICHES

KATIE ROBINSON, PORTLAND, ORE.

PORK WITH CHUTNEY SANDWICHES

PREP 25 min. **MARINATE** 1 hr. **COOK** 4 min.

INGREDIENTS

12	oz. boneless pork loin
2	Tbsp. honey
2	Tbsp. ketchup
2	Tbsp. soy sauce
1	tsp. garlic powder
2	tsp. cooking oil
2	kaiser rolls, split and toasted
¼	cup mayonnaise or tub-style cream cheese
2	Tbsp. bottled peach or mango chutney
2	romaine lettuce leaves
2	thin slices red onion

PREPARATION

1. Cut pork into 4 slices. Place each slice between plastic wrap; pound to ¼-inch thickness. Place meat in resealable plastic bag. In small bowl combine honey, ketchup, soy sauce, and garlic powder; add to bag. Seal bag; turn to coat meat. Chill 1 hour.
2. Remove meat slices from bag; discard marinade. Heat oil in very large nonstick skillet over medium heat. Add pork; cook 2 to 3 minutes per side or until no pink remains.
3. Spread cut sides of roll tops with mayonnaise and cut sides of roll bottoms with chutney. Layer meat on chutney; top with romaine, onion, and roll tops. **Makes 2 sandwiches.**

EACH SANDWICH *906 cal, 53 g fat (12 g sat. fat), 113 mg chol, 1,858 mg sodium, 65 g carbo, 2 g fiber, 42 g pro. Daily Values: 42% vit. A, 18% vit. C, 8% calcium, 22% iron.*

DONNA PINTO, NEWTON, MASS.

FAST!

COBB SALAD CLUB SANDWICHES

START TO FINISH 30 min.

INGREDIENTS

4	hard-cooked eggs
¾	cup bottled chunky blue cheese salad dressing
	Salt and gound black pepper
12	slices home-style whole grain white bread, toasted
½	medium red onion, thinly sliced
4	romaine lettuce leaves
12	slices bacon, crisp cooked and well drained
2	medium tomatoes, thinly sliced
	Cherry tomatoes, cut into wedges (optional)

PREPARATION

1. In small bowl mash eggs with ¼ *cup* of blue cheese dressing; season to taste with salt and pepper. Set aside.
2. Spread 8 of the toast slices with salad dressing. Spread egg mixture on 4 remaining slices; top with onion and lettuce. Arrange bacon on the 4 slices spread with salad dressing; top with sliced tomato. Place one egg-topped toast on top of each bacon-topped toast. Top with remaining toast slices, spread sides down. Secure with wooden picks; garnish with cherry tomato wedges. Cut each sandwich in half diagonally. **Makes 4 sandwiches.**
To make ahead Cook eggs the day ahead; peel, cover, and chill until needed. Cook bacon the day ahead; wrap and chill until needed.

EACH SANDWICH *674 cal, 42 g fat (11 g sat. fat), 250 mg chol, 1,647 mg sodium, 51 g carbo, 4 g fiber, 27 g pro. Daily Values: 53% vit. A, 23% vit. C, 46% calcium, 25% iron.*

BBQ RANCH SANDWICHES

PREP 15 min. **BAKE** 7 min. **OVEN** 450° F

INGREDIENTS

1	10-oz. (12-inch) Italian bread shell (such as thin crust Boboli) Nonstick cooking spray
1½	cups shredded Colby and Monterey Jack cheese (6 oz.)
1	cup cooked shredded chicken
2	Tbsp. barbecue sauce
6	slices packaged ready-to-serve cooked bacon
1½	cups shredded lettuce
2	Tbsp. finely chopped sweet onion
1	Tbsp. bottled ranch salad dressing
1	medium tomato, sliced

PREPARATION

1. Preheat oven to 450°F. Place bread shell on baking sheet, bottom side up. Spray bread shell with nonstick cooking spray. With pizza cutter, cut bread in half. Sprinkle cheese over both halves of bread. Combine chicken and barbeque sauce. Top one bread half with chicken mixture and bacon slices.

2. Bake 7 to 9 minutes or until cheese is melted and bacon is crisp. Cool on baking sheet 2 minutes. Meanwhile, in bowl combine lettuce, onion, and ranch salad dressing.

3. To serve, cut each half into quarters to make 8 wedges. Spoon lettuce mixture on top of each chicken-topped wedge. Top with tomato slice. Invert remaining wedges over toppings. **Makes 4 sandwiches.**

EACH SANDWICH 597 cal, 27 g fat (11 g sat. fat), 84 mg chol, 1,190 mg sodium, 55 g carbo, 1 g fiber, 37 g pro. Daily Values: 16% vit. A, 8% vit. C, 47% calcium, 6% iron.

GULF COAST "RICH BOYS"

START TO FINISH 45 min.

INGREDIENTS

4	hoagie rolls
½	cup reduced-calorie Thousand Island salad dressing
2	cloves garlic, minced
¼	tsp. bottled hot pepper sauce
½	cup buttermilk
1	cup panko (Japanese-style bread crumbs)
1	tsp. dried dill
½	tsp. salt
¼	tsp. ground black pepper
1	lb. large shrimp, peeled and deveined
2	cups shredded cabbage with carrot (coleslaw mix)
2	Roma tomatoes, thinly sliced

PREPARATION

1. Preheat oven to 400°F. Cut ¼-inch-thick slice off top of each hoagie roll. Hollow out roll, leaving ¼- to ½-inch-thick shell. Set aside (save bread crumbs for another use).

In small bowl combine salad dressing, garlic, and hot pepper sauce. Set aside.

2. Grease shallow baking pan. Place buttermilk in shallow dish. In another dish combine panko, dill, salt, and black pepper.

3. Coat shrimp in buttermilk, then in panko mixture. Place in prepared pan; bake 8 to 10 minutes or until shrimp are opaque.

4. Combine cabbage and half of dressing mixture; spoon into hollowed rolls. Top with tomato slices and shrimp. Add bun tops. Pass remaining dressing. **Makes 4 sandwiches.**

EACH SANDWICH 639 cal, 14 g fat (2 g sat. fat), 130 mg chol, 1,439 mg sodium, 97 g carbo, 6 g fiber, 32 g pro. Daily Values: 38% vit. A, 33% vit. C, 21% calcium, 36% iron.

PORTOBELLO FONTINA PESTO BIG SANDWICH

START TO FINISH 50 min.

INGREDIENTS

1	12-inch round garlic Italian flatbread (focaccia)
4	large portobello mushroom caps, stems and gills removed
2	Tbsp. olive oil
2	Tbsp. balsamic vinegar
¼	cup purchased basil pesto
2	to 4 Tbsp. mayonnaise
⅛	tsp. ground black pepper
1	cup roasted red pepper strips, drained (optional)
3	oz. fontina cheese, thinly sliced
2	cups arugula or fresh spinach

PREPARATION

1. Preheat broiler. Split focaccia in half horizontally. Place bread halves, cut sides up, on large baking sheet. Broil 4 to 5 inches from the heat 3 to 4 minutes or until lightly toasted. Cool slightly.

2. Arrange mushroom caps on unheated rack of broiler pan. In small bowl whisk together oil and vinegar. Brush over both sides of mushroom caps. Broil 8 to 10 minutes or until tender, turning once halfway through broiling time; cool slightly.

3. Meanwhile, spread cut side of bottom bread slice with pesto. Spread cut side of top bread slice with mayonnaise. Sprinkle mayonnaise with black pepper.

4. Transfer mushrooms to cutting board. Cut each mushroom into quarters; arrange quarters on top of pesto. Top with roasted red pepper strips. Top with cheese. If desired, return to broiler; broil 1 minute to melt cheese. Add arugula and bread top. Cut into quarters to serve. **Makes 4 servings.**

EACH SERVING 565 cal, 31 g fat (10 g sat. fat), 31 mg chol, 307 mg sodium, 55 g carbo, 5 g fiber, 22 g pro. Daily Values: 9% vit. A, 6% vit. C, 31% calcium, 10% iron.

SALMON-MANGO SANDWICHES

PREP 45 min. **BAKE** 20 min. **OVEN** 400°F

INGREDIENTS

4	¼-inch-thick slices sweet onion
2	tsp. olive oil
1	lb. salmon fillet, skinned and finely chopped
1	cup finely chopped mango
¼	cup thinly sliced green onion
2	Tbsp. snipped fresh Italian (flat-leaf) parsley
2	Tbsp. light mayonnaise or salad dressing
½	tsp. salt
¼	tsp. ground black pepper
1½	cups panko (Japanese-style bread crumbs) Honey mustard
4	kaiser rolls, split and toasted
½	cup deli coleslaw

PREPARATION

1. Preheat oven to 400°F. Brush onion slices with oil; place on greased foil-lined 15×10×1-inch baking pan. Set aside.

2. In large bowl combine salmon, ½ cup mango, green onion, parsley, mayonnaise, salt, and pepper. Stir in ½ cup of bread crumbs. Shape into four ½-inch-thick patties (patties will be soft; handle carefully); coat with remaining crumbs. Place on baking pan next to onions.

3. Bake, uncovered, 20 minutes or until just golden and instant-read thermometer inserted into centers of patties registers at least 160°F.

4. Spread honey mustard on bottom halves of rolls; add cooked onion and salmon patties. Stir remaining mango into prepared coleslaw; spoon on top of patties. Add roll tops. **Makes 4 sandwiches.**

EACH SANDWICH 555 cal, 20 g fat (4 g sat. fat), 70 mg chol, 828 mg sodium, 58 g carbo, 4 g fiber, 32 g pro. Daily Values: 13% vit. A, 42% vit. C, 10% calcium, 15% iron.

CREAMY CASSEROLES

CHICKEN FLORENTINE ARTICHOKE BAKE

PREP 30 min. **BAKE** 30 min. **OVEN** 350°F

INGREDIENTS

8	oz. dried bow tie or rotini pasta (3½ cups)
1	small onion, chopped
2	eggs
1¼	cups milk
1	tsp. dried Italian seasoning, crushed
¼	to ½ tsp. crushed red pepper (optional)
2	cups chopped cooked chicken
2	cups shredded Monterey Jack cheese (8 oz.)
1	14-oz. can artichoke hearts, drained and quartered
1	10-oz. pkg. frozen chopped spinach, thawed and well drained
½	cup oil-packed dried tomatoes, drained and chopped
¼	cup grated Parmesan cheese
½	cup soft bread crumbs
½	tsp. paprika

PREPARATION

1. Preheat oven to 350°F. Cook pasta according to package directions; drain. Meanwhile, in medium skillet cook onion in 1 tablespoon *butter* over medium heat about 5 minutes or until tender, stirring occasionally. Remove from heat; set aside.

2. In very large bowl whisk together eggs, milk, Italian seasoning, ½ teaspoon *salt*, ¼ teaspoon *ground black pepper*, and crushed red pepper. Stir in chicken, Monterey Jack cheese, artichoke hearts, spinach, tomatoes, *half* of the Parmesan cheese, cooked pasta, and cooked onion mixture. Transfer mixture to 3-quart rectangular baking dish.

3. Bake, covered, 20 minutes. Meanwhile, in small bowl combine remaining Parmesan cheese, bread crumbs, and paprika. Stir in 1 tablespoon *melted butter*. Sprinkle crumb mixture over pasta. Bake, uncovered, 10 minutes more or until heated through.
Makes 6 to 8 servings.

EACH SERVING *531 cal, 24 g fat (13 g sat. fat), 163 mg chol, 897 mg sodium, 41 g carbo, 5 g fiber, 36 g pro. Daily Values: 87% vit. A, 25% vit. C, 47% calcium, 26% iron.*

HOT 'N' CHEESY CHICKEN CASSEROLE

PREP 30 min. **BAKE** 40 min. **OVEN** 350°F

INGREDIENTS

3	cups chopped cooked chicken
1	14-oz. pkg. frozen broccoli florets
2	cups cooked rice*
1½	cups frozen peas
1	10.75-oz. can condensed cream of chicken soup
1	10.75-oz. can condensed fiesta nacho cheese soup
1	10- to 10.5-oz. can diced tomatoes and green chiles or diced tomatoes and habaneros
½	cup milk
½	tsp. crushed red pepper (optional)
½	cup shredded cheddar cheese (2 oz.)
½	cup shredded mozzarella cheese (2 oz.)
1	cup crushed rich round crackers

PREPARATION

1. Preheat oven to 350°F. Place chicken in bottom of 3-quart rectangular baking dish. In large bowl combine broccoli, rice, and peas. Spread mixture over chicken. In medium bowl combine cream of chicken soup, nacho cheese soup, diced tomatoes and chiles, milk, and crushed red pepper. Stir in ¼ cup of the cheddar cheese and ¼ cup of the mozzarella cheese. Pour mixture over broccoli mixture in baking dish. Sprinkle crushed crackers evenly over all. Sprinkle with remaining cheeses.

2. Bake, uncovered, 40 to 50 minutes or until topping is golden.
Makes 8 to 10 servings.

*NOTE If you don't have leftover rice, cook ⅔ cup *long grain white rice* and ¼ teaspoon *salt* in 1⅓ cups *boiling water* 15 minutes or until water is absorbed. (To use brown rice, cook ⅔ cup brown rice and ¼ teaspoon salt in 1⅓ cups water for 40 minutes.)

EACH SERVING *354 cal, 15 g fat (6 g sat. fat), 65 mg chol, 886 mg sodium, 29 g carbo, 4 g fiber, 26 g pro. Daily Values: 27% vit. A, 43% vit. C, 20% calcium, 13% iron.*

KID FRIENDLY

CHEESE FONDUE CASSEROLE

Do not substitute preshredded cheese because it will not melt as well.

PREP 30 min. **BAKE** 35 min. **OVEN** 350°F

INGREDIENTS
	Nonstick cooking spray
2	cups dried elbow macaroni (8 oz.)
8	oz. Swiss cheese, shredded
6	oz. Gruyère cheese, shredded
3	Tbsp. all-purpose flour
2	cloves garlic, minced
1¼	cups chicken broth
½	cup dry white wine
6	oz. Swiss cheese, cubed
1½	cups crushed saltine crackers (24)
2	Tbsp. butter, cut up
	Salt and ground black pepper

PREPARATION
1. Preheat oven to 350°F. Spray 2-quart casserole with nonstick cooking spray; set aside. In 4-quart Dutch oven cook macaroni according to package directions. Drain; return to pan. Set aside.

2. Meanwhile, in large bowl combine shredded Swiss cheese, Gruyère cheese, flour, and garlic. Toss to combine. In large saucepan heat broth and wine over medium heat just until bubbles form around edge of pan. Whisk in cheese mixture 1 cup at a time, whisking constantly until cheese is melted and making sure mixture does not boil. Remove from heat.

3. Gently stir cheese mixture into cooked pasta. Fold in cubed Swiss cheese. Spoon mixture into prepared casserole. Sprinkle crushed crackers over all. Dot with butter. Bake, uncovered, about 35 minutes or until topping is golden. Season to taste with salt and pepper. **Makes 6 servings.**

EACH SERVING *629 cal, 33 g fat (20 g sat. fat), 103 mg chol, 679 mg sodium, 44 g carbo, 2 g fiber, 33 g pro. Daily Values: 19% vit. A, 1% vit. C, 83% calcium, 13% iron.*

CHICKEN ALFREDO CASSEROLE

PREP 30 min. **BAKE** 25 min. **OVEN** 350°F

INGREDIENTS
1	19-oz. pkg. frozen cheese-filled tortellini
3	cloves garlic, minced
1	Tbsp. olive oil
1	lb. skinless, boneless chicken breast halves, cubed
1	cup pepperoni, chopped
¾	cup oil-packed dried tomatoes, drained and chopped
1	15- to 16-oz. jar Alfredo pasta sauce
½	cup shredded Italian-blend cheeses (2 oz.)
	Chopped fresh parsley (optional)

PREPARATION
1. Preheat oven to 350°F. Cook tortellini according to package directions; drain.

2. Meanwhile, in large skillet cook garlic in hot oil 15 seconds; add chicken. Cook, stirring occasionally, 3 to 4 minutes or until no pink remains. Stir in pepperoni and tomatoes; cook 2 minutes. Add Alfredo sauce; heat through.

3. In large bowl combine tortellini and chicken mixture; transfer to 2-quart casserole. Sprinkle with cheese.

4. Bake, covered, 25 to 30 minutes or until heated through. Sprinkle parsley. **Makes 6 servings.**

EACH SERVING *588 cal, 32 g fat (15 g sat. fat), 130 mg chol, 1,059 mg sodium, 42 g carbo, 2 g fiber, 36 g pro. Daily Values: 14% vit. A, 25% vit. C, 19% calcium, 13% iron.*

CHICKEN, SPINACH, AND RICE CASSEROLE

PREP 15 min. **BAKE** 1¼ hr. **OVEN** 375°F

INGREDIENTS
1	10-oz. pkg. frozen chopped spinach, thawed and well drained
½	of an 8-oz. tub cream cheese spread with chives and onion
1	10.75-oz. can condensed cream of chicken soup
1	cup milk
¼	cup snipped fresh oregano
¼	cup grated Parmesan cheese
2	cloves garlic, minced
¼	tsp. crushed red pepper
1	cup long grain rice
6	small bone-in chicken breast halves, skinned
	Salt and ground black pepper

PREPARATION
1. Preheat oven to 375°F. Lightly coat 3-quart rectangular baking dish with *nonstick cooking spray*. In medium bowl combine spinach and cream cheese; spread in bottom of prepared dish. In medium mixing bowl combine soup, milk, *3 tablespoons* of the oregano, *3 tablespoons* of the cheese, garlic, and crushed red pepper; reserve ½ cup of mixture. Stir rice into remaining soup mixture and spoon on top of spinach. Place chicken, bone sides down, in dish. Sprinkle chicken with salt and pepper. Spoon reserved soup mixture over chicken.

2. Cover tightly with foil and bake 1¼ hours or until rice is tender and chicken is no longer pink. Sprinkle with remaining oregano and Parmesan before serving. **Makes 6 servings.**

EACH SERVING *470 cal, 13 g fat (6 g sat. fat), 137 mg chol, 743 mg sodium, 33 g carbo, 2 g fiber, 51 g pro. Daily Values: 73% vit. A, 12% vit. C, 18% calcium, 19% iron.*

ITALIAN PASTA CASSEROLE

PREP 25 min. **BAKE** 30 min. **OVEN** 350°F

INGREDIENTS
1	1.29-lb. pkg. mild or hot Italian sausage links, sliced ½ inch thick
1	Tbsp. olive oil
1	12-oz. pkg. dried medium shell macaroni
½	cup bottled Italian salad dressing
1	10.75-oz. can condensed cream of chicken soup
1	8-oz. carton dairy sour cream
1	8-oz. pkg. shredded Italian-blend cheeses
2	Tbsp. all-purpose flour
3	garlic cloves, minced
2	medium zucchini and/or yellow summer squash, halved lengthwise and sliced ½ inch thick

PREPARATION
1. Preheat oven to 350°F. In large skillet cook sausage in hot oil until no longer pink, stirring frequently. Drain in colander. Meanwhile, cook pasta according to package directions; drain over sausage in colander.

2. In large bowl combine salad dressing, soup, sour cream, *1 cup* of the cheese, flour, and garlic. Stir in squash and pasta/sausage mixture. Pour into 3-quart rectangular baking dish. Cover with foil and bake 25 minutes. Uncover; sprinkle with remaining 1 cup cheese. Bake 5 minutes more or until hot and bubbly. **Makes 8 servings.**

EACH SERVING *658 cal, 43 g fat (17 g sat. fat), 91 mg chol, 1,281 mg sodium, 41 g carbo, 2 g fiber, 26 g pro. Daily Values: 6% vit. A, 17% vit. C, 23% calcium, 15% iron.*

30-MINUTE SOUPS

JULIE BAGNULL, JEFFERSON CITY, MO.

[LOW FAT]

TORTELLINI FLORENTINE SOUP

START TO FINISH 30 min.

INGREDIENTS

1   9-oz. pkg. refrigerated 3-cheese tortellini
2   14-oz. cans reduced-sodium chicken broth
1   10-oz. container refrigerated light Alfredo pasta sauce
2   cups shredded deli-roasted chicken
½   cup oil-packed dried tomato strips, drained
3   cups lightly packed packaged fresh baby spinach
1   oz. Parmesan cheese, shaved or shredded (optional)

PREPARATION

1. In 4-quart Dutch oven cook tortellini according to package directions. Drain; set aside. In same pan combine broth and Alfredo sauce. Stir in chicken and tomato strips. Heat just to boiling; reduce heat. Simmer, uncovered, 5 minutes. Add tortellini and spinach. Cook 1 to 2 minutes to heat through and wilt spinach. To serve, sprinkle with cheese. **Makes 6 servings.**

EACH SERVING *286 cal, 15 g fat (6 g sat. fat), 77 mg chol, 1,094 mg sodium, 21 g carbo, 1 g fiber, 20 g pro. Daily Values: 34% vit. A, 23% vit. C, 17% calcium, 10% iron.*

MOLLY NEELY, FRESNO, CALIF.

[FAST!] [LOW FAT]

MEXI-CHICKEN SOUP

START TO FINISH 30 min.

INGREDIENTS

1   32-oz. box reduced-sodium chicken broth
1   15-oz. can black beans, rinsed and drained
1   15-oz. can golden hominy, rinsed and drained
1   cup bottled salsa
1   cup bottled nopalitos (cactus leaves), drained, or bite-size green sweet pepper strips
1   4-oz. can diced green chiles
1   Tbsp. chili powder
1   tsp. ground cumin
2½   cups chopped cooked chicken
      Snipped fresh herbs (optional)

PREPARATION

1. In 4-quart Dutch oven combine chicken broth, black beans, hominy, salsa, nopalitos, undrained green chiles, chili powder, and cumin. Bring to boiling; reduce heat. Simmer, covered, 20 minutes. Add chicken; heat through. To serve, sprinkle with fresh herbs. **Makes 6 servings.**

EACH SERVING *240 cal, 6 g fat (1 g sat. fat), 52 mg chol, 1,060 mg sodium, 25 g carbo, 7 g fiber, 25 g pro. Daily Values: 15% vit. A, 12% vit. C, 10% calcium, 14% iron.*

CHICKEN SOUP DIJONAISE

START TO FINISH 30 min.

INGREDIENTS

1	Tbsp. butter
1	Tbsp. extra virgin olive oil
1	large onion, chopped (1 cup)
2	leeks, trimmed and sliced
1	Tbsp. Dijon-style mustard
2	14-oz. cans reduced-sodium chicken broth
1	medium Yukon gold potato, cut into ½-inch pieces (about 1 cup)
¾	cup half-and-half or light cream
2	Tbsp. all-purpose flour
2	cup chopped cooked chicken
1	tsp. snipped fresh thyme
⅛	tsp. ground white pepper
2	Tbsp. snipped fresh parsley

PREPARATION

1. In large saucepan heat butter and olive oil over medium heat. Add onion and leek. Cook 5 minutes or until tender, stirring occasionally. Stir in mustard. Stir in chicken broth and potato. Bring to boiling; reduce heat. Simmer, covered, 10 minutes or until potato is tender.

2. In small bowl whisk together half-and-half and flour until smooth. Stir into broth mixture. Add chicken, thyme, and pepper. Cook and stir until thickened and bubbly. Cook and stir 2 minutes more. Sprinkle parsley. **Makes 4 servings.**

EACH SERVING *344 cal, 17 g fat (7 g sat. fat), 86 mg chol, 674 mg sodium, 21 g carbo, 2 g fiber, 26 g pro. Daily Values: 24% vit. A, 29% vit. C, 10% calcium, 14% iron.*

CURRIED TOMATO-RED PEPPER SOUP

START TO FINISH 25 min.

INGREDIENTS

1	cup orzo
2	10.75-oz. cans condensed tomato soup
2½	cups milk
2	cups chopped cooked chicken
1	cup bottled roasted red sweet peppers, drained and chopped
1	tsp. curry powder
	Dash ground black pepper
2	Tbsp. refrigerated basil pesto

PREPARATION

1. Cook pasta according to package directions. Drain; set aside.

2. Meanwhile, in large saucepan stir together soup and milk. Heat over medium heat until soup comes to simmer. Stir in cooked pasta, chicken, sweet peppers, curry powder, and black pepper; heat through. Swirl spoonful of basil pesto into each serving. **Makes 6 servings.**

EACH SERVING *362 cal, 9 g fat (2 g sat. fat), 50 mg chol, 705 mg sodium, 45 g carbo, 2 g fiber, 23 g pro. Daily Values: 13% vit. A, 122% vit. C, 13% calcium, 14% iron.*

ITALIAN PUMPKIN SOUP

PREP 10 min. **COOK** 15 min.

INGREDIENTS

1	lb. bulk mild Italian sausage
2	14-oz. cans reduced sodium chicken broth
2	medium potatoes, peeled and chopped
1	cup canned pumpkin
1	cup milk
1	tsp. dried thyme, crushed
2	cups shredded fresh spinach

PREPARATION

1. In Dutch oven brown sausage over medium-high heat, stirring to break into smaller pieces. Drain fat. Add chicken broth and potatoes; bring to boiling. Reduce heat; simmer, covered, 10 minutes.

2. Stir in pumpkin, milk, and thyme; bring just to boiling. Remove from heat; stir in spinach. **Makes 6 servings.**

EACH SERVING *354 cal, 25 g fat (9 g sat. fat), 60 mg chol, 896 mg sodium, 18 g carbo, 2 g fiber, 15 g pro. Daily Values: 147% vit. A, 17% vit. C, 9% calcium, 11% iron.*

PEANUT CORN CHOWDER

START TO FINISH 25 min.

INGREDIENTS

2	Tbsp. butter
½	cup chopped celery
¼	cup chopped onion
½	cup chunky peanut butter
1	14-oz. can reduced sodium chicken broth
1	16-oz. pkg. frozen whole kernel corn
1¼	cups half-and-half or light cream
¼	tsp. crushed red pepper
	Snipped fresh cilantro (optional)

PREPARATION

1. In 2-quart saucepan heat butter over medium heat. Add celery and onion. Cook and stir 4 minutes or until tender. Remove from heat. Stir in peanut butter. Return to heat; gradually whisk in broth. Bring to boiling. Add corn. Return to boiling; reduce heat. Simmer, covered, 5 minutes, stirring occasionally. Stir in cream and red pepper; heat through. Garnish with cilantro. **Makes 4 to 6 side-dish servings.**

EACH SERVING *450 cal, 31 g fat (12 g sat. fat), 43 mg chol, 477 mg sodium, 35 g carbo, 6 g fiber, 15 g pro. Daily Values: 14% vit. A, 15% vit. C, 11% calcium, 7% iron.*

TILAPIA CHOWDER WITH SAGE

START TO FINISH 30 min.

INGREDIENTS

2	small carrots, peeled
1	medium onion, quartered
1	stalk celery
1	medium zucchini, halved lengthwise
3	Tbsp. butter
3	14-oz. cans reduced-sodium chicken broth
1	14.5-oz. can diced tomatoes with basil, garlic, and oregano
¼	tsp. salt
⅛	tsp. ground black pepper
1½	lb. tilapia fillets, cut into 2-inch pieces
3	Tbsp. chopped fresh sage
1	Tbsp. lemon or lime juice
½	cup dairy sour cream
	Snipped fresh sage (optional)

PREPARATION

1. Fit food processor with slicing blade. Process carrots, onion, and celery to thinly slice. Remove vegetable mixture from food processor. Process zucchini to thinly slice; set aside. (Or thinly slice the vegetables.)

2. In Dutch oven cook carrot, onion, and celery in hot butter over medium heat 4 minutes or until crisp-tender. Add chicken broth, undrained tomatoes, salt, and pepper. Cover; bring to boiling. Add tilapia, zucchini, and sage. Return to boiling; reduce heat. Simmer, uncovered, 3 minutes or until fish flakes easily when tested with a fork, stirring occasionally. Stir in lemon juice. Top each serving with sour cream; sprinkle additional sage. **Makes 6 servings.**

EACH SERVING *254 cal, 11 g fat (7 g sat. fat), 78 mg chol, 1,054 mg sodium, 12 g carbo, 2 g fiber, 28 g pro. Daily Values: 87% vit. A, 28% vit. C, 10% calcium, 11% iron.*

FRUIT CAKES

ALLENE BARY-COOPER, WICHITA FALLS, TEXAS

CHUNKY NUT AND DRIED FRUIT CAKE

PREP 30 min. **BAKE** 1¼ hr. **COOL** 15 min. **OVEN** 325°F

INGREDIENTS

½   cup butter, softened
⅓   cup butter-flavor shortening
1   cup sugar
¾   tsp. baking powder
4   eggs
1½   tsp. almond extract
1½   cups all-purpose flour
⅓   cup orange juice
1¼   cups Brazil nuts, coarsely chopped (8 oz.)
¾   cup blanched whole almonds (4 oz.)
1   cup *each* dried apricots, halved (7 oz.), dried cherries (6 oz.), and pecan halves (4 oz.)
¾   cup *each* dried blueberries (4 oz.), dried cranberries (3 oz.), and pitted whole dates, halved (4 oz.)
      Brandy or orange juice

PREPARATION

1. Preheat oven to 325°F. Grease and flour 10-inch tube pan; set aside. In bowl beat butter and shortening with electric mixer on medium speed 30 seconds. Add sugar, baking powder, and ½ teaspoon *salt*. Beat until combined, scraping sides of bowl as needed. Add eggs, 1 at a time, beating well after each addition. Beat in extract. Alternately beat in flour and orange juice, beating on low speed after each addition just until combined. Stir in nuts and fruits until combined. Spoon batter into prepared pan, spreading top evenly.
2. Bake 1¼ hours or until wooden skewer inserted into cake comes out clean. If necessary, cover top of cake with foil last 15 to 20 minutes to prevent overbrowning. Cool cake in pan on wire rack 15 minutes. Remove cake from pan; cool completely on rack.
3. Wrap cake in cheesecloth that has been soaked in brandy. Wrap cake in foil; refrigerate up to 1 month. Moisten cheesecloth every week. **Makes 20 servings.**

EACH SERVING *396 cal, 21 g fat (6 g sat. fat), 55 mg chol, 124 mg sodium, 45 g carbo, 5 g fiber, 6 g pro. Daily Values: 10% vit. A, 4% vit. C, 7% calcium, 14% iron.*

MARY BETH MANDOLA, HOUSTON, TEXAS

HOLIDAY NUT CAKE

PREP 30 min. **BAKE** 1½ hr. **COOL** 10 min. **OVEN** 300°F

INGREDIENTS

      Nonstick cooking spray
1   cup candied red cherries, coarsely chopped
1   cup dried apricots, chopped
½   cup golden raisins
½   cup semisweet chocolate pieces
6   Tbsp. butter, softened
½   cup packed brown sugar
¼   cup granulated sugar
3   eggs
¼   cup orange juice
½   tsp. almond extract
1   cup all-purpose flour
½   tsp. baking powder
⅛   tsp. salt
1   cup walnuts, toasted and chopped
¾   cup pecans, toasted and chopped
¼   cup sliced almonds
      Powdered sugar (optional)

PREPARATION

1. Preheat oven to 300°F. Lightly coat 9×5×3-inch loaf pan with nonstick cooking spray. Line bottom of pan with parchment paper or waxed paper; set aside. In bowl combine cherries, apricots, raisins, and chocolate; set aside.
2. In mixing bowl beat butter and both sugars with electric mixer on medium speed until mixture is light and fluffy. Beat in eggs, 1 at a time, just until combined. Beat in orange juice and extract. Add flour, baking powder, and salt. Beat just until combined. Stir in fruit mixture, walnuts, and pecans. Spoon mixture into prepared pan. Sprinkle with almonds.
3. Bake 1½ hours or until wooden toothpick inserted near center comes out clean. Cool in pan on wire rack 10 minutes. Remove from pan; cool completely on rack. Wrap; store overnight before slicing. Before serving, sprinkle powdered sugar. **Makes 16 servings.**

EACH SERVING *311 cal, 16 g fat (5 g sat. fat), 51 mg chol, 78 mg sodium, 41 g carbo, 3 g fiber, 5 g pro. Daily Values: 10% vit. A, 6% vit. C, 5% calcium, 8% iron.*

CHOCOLATE SOUR CREAM FRUITCAKE

PREP 30 min. **BAKE** 1 hr. **COOL** 10 min.
OVEN 300°F

INGREDIENTS

2 eggs
¼ cup milk
1½ cups granulated sugar
1 8-oz. carton dairy sour cream
1 tsp. vanilla
⅓ cup butter, melted
2 cups all-purpose flour
½ cup unsweetened cocoa powder
1 tsp. baking soda
1 tsp. salt
¼ tsp. ground cloves
1½ cups chopped walnuts
1 cup *each* red or green candied cherries; candied pineapple; raisins; and dried figs, chopped
   Powdered sugar

PREPARATION

1. Preheat oven to 300°F. Grease 10-inch fluted tube pan; set aside. In large bowl stir together eggs, milk, granulated sugar, sour cream, vanilla, and butter; set aside.
2. In medium bowl stir together flour, cocoa powder, baking soda, salt, and cloves. Add to egg mixture; stir to combine. Stir in nuts and fruit. Spoon into prepared pan, spreading evenly.
3. Bake 1 hour or until wooden toothpick inserted near center comes out clean. Cool in pan on wire rack 10 minutes. Remove from pan; cool completely on rack. Wrap; refrigerate up to 1 week before serving. Let stand at room temperature 1 hour before serving. Sprinkle with powdered sugar before serving. **Makes 20 servings.**

EACH SERVING *336 cal, 12 g fat (4 g sat. fat), 34 mg chol, 227 mg sodium, 54 g carbo, 2 g fiber, 5 g pro. Daily Values: 4% vit. A, 14% vit. C, 8% calcium, 9% iron.*

FAST!

DRIED FRUIT FRUITCAKE

PREP 30 min. **BAKE** 1 hr. **COOL** 10 min.
OVEN 300°F.

INGREDIENTS

1 cup unsweetened applesauce
½ tsp. baking soda
1½ cups all-purpose flour
1 cup sugar
½ tsp. ground cinnamon
½ tsp. ground cloves
¼ tsp. vanilla
⅛ tsp. salt
1 8-oz. pkg. chopped, pitted dates
1½ cups dried cherries, dried cranberries, dried blueberries, and/or chopped dried pineapple
¾ cup dark and/or golden raisins

1 cup coarsely chopped walnuts, pecans, and/or almonds
¼ cup butter, melted

PREPARATION

1. Preheat oven to 300°F. Grease 9-inch springform pan or 9-inch round baking pan. Line bottom of pan with parchment paper. Grease paper; flour inside of pan. Set pan aside.
2. In large bowl stir together applesauce and baking soda until combined. Stir in flour, sugar, cinnamon, cloves, vanilla, and salt until combined. Stir in dried fruits. Stir in nuts. Stir in melted butter.
3. Spoon batter into prepared pan, spreading evenly. Bake 1 to 1¼ hours or until wooden toothpick inserted near center comes out clean. Cool in pan on wire rack 10 minutes. Remove from pan; remove parchment paper. Cool completely, top side up, on wire rack. When cool, wrap in plastic wrap and refrigerate up to 1 week.
Makes 16 to 20 servings.

EACH SERVING *272 cal, 8 g fat (2 g sat. fat), 8 mg chol, 83 mg sodium, 50 g carbo, 3 g fiber, 3 g pro. Daily Values: 9% vit. A, 1% vit. C, 3% calcium, 7% iron.*

HURRY UP FRUITCAKE

PREP 15 min. **BAKE** 1 hr. **COOL** 10 min.
OVEN 325°F

2½ cups all-purpose flour
1½ tsp. baking powder
½ tsp. *each* baking soda and salt
⅔ cup shortening
1 cup sugar
⅓ cup currant or plum jelly
3 eggs
¼ cup orange or apple juice
1 tsp. vanilla
1 27-oz. jar mincemeat
2 cups chopped pecans
1 cup raisins
1 cup chopped, pitted dates
¼ cup currant or plum jelly

PREPARATION

1. Preheat oven to 325°F. Grease and flour two 9×5×3-inch loaf pans; set aside. In medium bowl stir together flour, baking powder, baking soda, and salt; set aside.
2. In large bowl beat shortening with electric mixer on medium to high speed 30 seconds. Add sugar; beat until combined. Add ⅓ cup jelly, eggs, orange juice, and vanilla; beat until combined. Beat in flour mixture. Stir in mincemeat, pecans, raisins, and dates. Divide batter between prepared pans and spread evenly. Bake 1 to 1¼ hours or until a wooden toothpick inserted in center comes out clean. Cool in pans on wire rack 10 minutes; remove from pans. Heat the ¼ cup jelly in small saucepan; brush on top loaves. Cool completely.
Makes 16 servings.

EACH SERVING *497 cal, 20 g fat (3 g sat. fat), 40 mg chol, 293 mg sodium, 78 g carbo, 3 g fiber, 5 g pro. Daily Values: 1% vit. A, 4% vit. C, 5% calcium, 14% iron.*

PUMPKIN FRUIT CAKE

PREP 40 min. **BAKE** 1 hr. **COOL** 10 min.
OVEN 350°F

INGREDIENTS

3⅓ cups all-purpose flour
2½ tsp. baking powder
2 tsp. ground cinnamon
1 tsp. salt
¼ tsp. ground cloves
⅔ cup shortening
2¼ cups sugar
4 eggs
1 15-oz. can pumpkin
⅔ cup water
1 cup chopped nuts
½ cup *each* chopped, pitted dates; golden raisins; raisins; snipped dried apricots; and diced mixed candied fruit

PREPARATION

1. Preheat oven to 350°F. Grease two 9×5×3-or 8×4×2-inch loaf pans; set aside. In medium bowl stir together flour, baking powder, cinnamon, salt, and cloves; set aside.
2. In large mixing bowl beat shortening with electric mixer on medium speed 30 seconds. Add sugar; beat until combined. Add eggs, pumpkin, and water; beat well. Beat in flour mixture on low speed until moistened. Stir in nuts and fruits. Divide between prepared pans; spread evenly. Bake 1 to 1¼ hours or until toothpick inserted in center comes out clean. If necessary, cover with foil after 45 minutes of baking to prevent over browning. Cool in pans on wire racks 10 minutes. Remove from pans; cool completely on wire racks.
Makes 2 loaves (14 servings each).

EACH SERVING *246 cal, 8 g fat (2 g sat. fat), 30 mg chol, 121 mg sodium, 41 g carbo, 2 g fiber, 3 g pro. Daily Values: 50% vit. A, 1% vit. C, 3% calcium, 8% iron.*

ANNUAL Recipes 2008

Nutrition information.
With each recipe, we give important nutrition information you easily can apply to your own needs. You'll find the calorie count of each serving and the amount, in grams, of fat, saturated fat, cholesterol, sodium, carbohydrates, fiber, and protein to help you keep tabs on what you eat. You can check the levels of each recipe serving for vitamin A, vitamin C, calcium, and iron, if they are present. These are noted in percentages of the Daily Values. The Daily Values are dietary standards determined by the Food and Drug Administration (FDA). To stay in line with the nutrition breakdown of each recipe, follow the suggested number of servings.

How we analyze.
The Better Homes and Gardens₂ Test Kitchen computer analyzes each recipe for the nutritional value of a single serving.
- The analysis does not include optional ingredients.
- We use the first serving size listed when a range is given. For example: If we say a recipe "Makes 4 to 6 servings," the nutrition information is based on 4 servings.
- When ingredient choices (such as butter or margarine) appear in a recipe, we use the first one mentioned for analysis. The ingredient order does not mean we prefer one ingredient over another.
- When milk and eggs are recipe ingredients, the analysis is calculated using 2 percent (reduced-fat) milk and large eggs.

What you need.
The dietary guidelines below suggest nutrient levels that moderately active adults should strive to eat each day. There is no real harm in going over or under these guidelines in any single day, but it is a good idea to aim for a balanced diet over time.

Calories: About 2,000
Total fat: Less than 65 grams
Saturated fat: Less than 20 grams
Cholesterol: Less than 300 milligrams
Carbohydrates: About 300 grams
Sodium: Less than 2,400 milligrams
Dietary fiber: 20 to 30 grams

Low Fat icon.
Certain recipes throughout the book have an icon above the recipe title that indicates the recipe is low fat. For a recipe to earn this icon, it must meet certain nutritional requirements. For a main dish one serving should have 12 grams of fat per serving or less, one serving of a side dish should have 5 grams of fat or less, an appetizer serving should have 2 grams of fat or less, and cookies and desserts should have 2 grams of fat or less per serving. Occasionally the fat level will slightly exceed one of the recommended numbers, but typically they remain below the listed amounts.

Metric Information

The charts on this page provide a guide for converting measurements from the U.S. customary system, which is used throughout this book, to the metric system.

Product Differences

Most of the ingredients called for in the recipes in this book are available in most countries. However, some are known by different names. Here are some common American ingredients and their possible counterparts:

- Sugar (white) is granulated, fine granulated, or castor sugar.
- Powdered sugar is icing sugar.
- All-purpose flour is enriched, bleached or unbleached white household flour. When self-rising flour is used in place of all-purpose flour in a recipe that calls for leavening, omit the leavening agent (baking soda or baking powder) and salt.
- Light-colored corn syrup is golden syrup.
- Cornstarch is cornflour.
- Baking soda is bicarbonate of soda.
- Vanilla or vanilla extract is vanilla essence.
- Green, red, or yellow sweet peppers are capsicums or bell peppers.
- Golden raisins are sultanas.

Volume and Weight

The United States traditionally uses cup measures for liquid and solid ingredients. The chart below shows the approximate imperial and metric equivalents. If you are accustomed to weighing solid ingredients, the following approximate equivalents will be helpful.

- 1 cup butter, castor sugar, or rice = 8 ounces = ½ pound = 250 grams
- 1 cup flour = 4 ounces = ¼ pound = 125 grams
- 1 cup icing sugar = 5 ounces = 150 grams

Canadian and U.S. volume for a cup measure is 8 fluid ounces (237 ml), but the standard metric equivalent is 250 ml.

1 British imperial cup is 10 fluid ounces.

In Australia, 1 tablespoon equals 20 ml, and there are 4 teaspoons in the Australian tablespoon.

Spoon measures are used for smaller amounts of ingredients. Although the size of the tablespoon varies slightly in different countries, for practical purposes and for recipes in this book, a straight substitution is all that's necessary. Measurements made using cups or spoons always should be level unless stated otherwise.

Common Weight Range Replacements

Imperial / U.S.	Metric
½ ounce	15 g
1 ounce	25 g or 30 g
4 ounces (¼ pound)	115 g or 125 g
8 ounces (½ pound)	225 g or 250 g
16 ounces (1 pound)	450 g or 500 g
1¼ pounds	625 g
1½ pounds	750 g
2 pounds or 2¼ pounds	1,000 g or 1 Kg

Oven Temperature Equivalents

Fahrenheit Setting	Celsius Setting*	Gas Setting
300°F	150°C	Gas Mark 2 (very low)
325°F	160°C	Gas Mark 3 (low)
350°F	180°C	Gas Mark 4 (moderate)
375°F	190°C	Gas Mark 5 (moderate)
400°F	200°C	Gas Mark 6 (hot)
425°F	220°C	Gas Mark 7 (hot)
450°F	230°C	Gas Mark 8 (very hot)
475°F	240°C	Gas Mark 9 (very hot)
500°F	260°C	Gas Mark 10 (extremely hot)
Broil	Broil	Grill

*Electric and gas ovens may be calibrated using celsius. However, for an electric oven, increase celsius setting 10 to 20 degrees when cooking above 160°C. For convection or forced air ovens (gas or electric), lower the temperature setting 25°F/10°C when cooking at all heat levels.

Baking Pan Sizes

Imperial / U.S.	Metric
9×1½-inch round cake pan	22- or 23×4-cm (1.5 L)
9×1½-inch pie plate	22- or 23×4-cm (1 L)
8×8×2-inch square cake pan	20×5-cm (2 L)
9×9×2-inch square cake pan	22- or 23×4.5-cm (2.5 L)
11×7×1½-inch baking pan	28×17×4-cm (2 L)
2-quart rectangular baking pan	30×19×4.5-cm (3 L)
13×9×2-inch baking pan	34×22×4.5-cm (3.5 L)
15×10×1-inch jelly roll pan	40×25×2-cm
9×5×3-inch loaf pan	23×13×8-cm (2 L)
2-quart casserole	2 L

U.S. / Standard Metric Equivalents

⅛ teaspoon = 0.5 ml	
¼ teaspoon = 1 ml	
½ teaspoon = 2 ml	
1 teaspoon = 5 ml	
1 tablespoon = 15 ml	
2 tablespoons = 25 ml	
¼ cup = 2 fluid ounces = 50 ml	
⅓ cup = 3 fluid ounces = 75 ml	
½ cup = 4 fluid ounces = 125 ml	
⅔ cup = 5 fluid ounces = 150 ml	
¾ cup = 6 fluid ounces = 175 ml	
1 cup = 8 fluid ounces = 250 ml	
2 cups = 1 pint = 500 ml	
1 quart = 1 litre	